Black Women in American Bands and Orchestras

Second Edition

D. Antoinette Handy

The Scarecrow Press, Inc.
Lanham, Md., & London
1998

SCARECROW PRESS, INC.

Published in the United States of America
by Scarecrow Press, Inc.
4720 Boston Way
Lanham, Maryland 20706

4 Pleydell Gardens
Kent CT20 2DN, England

British Library Cataloguing in Publication Information Available

Library of Congress Cataloging-in-Publication Data

Handy, D. Antoinette, 1930–
    [Black women in American bands & orchestras]
    Black women in American bands and orchestras / D. Antoinette
Handy.—2nd ed.
        p.   cm.
    Includes bibliographical references and indexes.
    ISBN 0-8108-3419-7 (cloth : alk. paper)
    1. Afro-American women musicians.   I. Title.
ML82.H36   1998
784.2'092'396073—dc21
    [B]   98-14765
                                                                        CIP
                                                                        MN

ISBN 0-8108-3493-6 (cloth : alk. paper)

∞ ™ The paper used in this publication meets the minimum
requirements of American National Standard for Information
Sciences—Permanence of Paper for Printed Library Materials,
ANSI Z39.48—1984. Manufactured in the United States of America.

BEN

To
MOTHER AND DADDY
William Talbot and Darthney Pauline Handy

HUSBAND
Calvin Montgomery Miller

DAUGHTER
Michelle

SONS
Blaine and Obiora

Contents

Preface to Second Edition

I began encountering additional worthy subjects for inclusion in the publication *Black Women in American Bands and Orchestras* as soon as the first edition had been completed. To be sure, this scenario will replay itself as soon as this second edition has been completed. Many new names and additional performing organizations have been added to preliminary discussions in each chapter.

The second edition required indexing assistance. For that I am grateful to Loana Clayton (retired English Professor, Jackson State University) and Carrie Bernadine Daniels (counselor, Jackson Public Schools). The author, however, assumes total responsibility for the end product.

April 1997
Jackson, Mississippi

Preface

This publication originated in the mind of a fourteen-year-old black American female who decided that she wanted to be a symphonic orchestral flutist. That she would be a musician had already been decided. With this in mind (and parental consent to purchase an instrument) she went to a New Orleans Philharmonic concert, and shortly before the end proceeded backstage from the "reserved for colored" section to the orchestra's first flutist. Question: "Are you accepting any pupils?" Answer: "Do you mean that you, a Negro, want to study flute?"

After more than a quarter of a century of making orchestral statements, this "Negro" felt the urge to make some verbal statements. The Sixtieth Anniversary Meeting of the Association for the Study of Afro-American Life and History (ASALH), held in Atlanta, Georgia, October 1975, permitted this writer's reading of a paper entitled "Black Women in American Symphony Orchestras."

The decision to go beyond black female involvement in "symphony" orchestras in this book-length treatment was prompted by one questioner's curiosity as to why such persons as Lillian Hardin Armstrong and Mary Lou Williams were not included. The answer was obvious, but there was merit in the inquiry. With the writer's acceptance of all musics as music, it was conceivable to treat its makers collectively. Also, a review of the literature instantly revealed that the black female instrumentalist was slighted in areas outside of symphonic orchestral circles (though to a lesser extent) as well.

My data-collection methods included reading primary and secondary sources, personal interviews, surveys of orchestras, and compilation of "personal data." The only criterion for a black woman instrumentalist's inclusion was involvement with an instrumental ensemble wherein the performer functioned as a

ix

member of the ensemble, rather than as a soloist, in a leadership or "followship" capacity.

The omission of an individual from the Profile sections should not imply lesser significance. The case might be that her "moment in history" lacked sufficient written coverage or preservation, or that this writer was unsuccessful in locating same. The length of an entry does not relate to the quantity or quality of the instrumentalist's musical output. If a well-known "living" personality is omitted, it may be that my efforts at personal contact were unsuccessful. Finally, some living females preferred not to disclose their ages. This request was honored.

I was indeed fortunate to have Eileen Southern as commentator on my paper "Black Women in American Symphony Orchestras," presented at the 1975 ASALH meeting. She, too, envisioned an expanded work and to this end advised, encouraged, and guided me in bringing this publication to a successful conclusion. To Dr. Southern I owe the deepest gratitude.

Many others demand acknowledgment, preeminent being 1) the black women orchestral/band members and leaders whose exciting lives and careers gave me something to write about; 2) the many who responded to my requests for interviews and information; and 3) those who identified and aided in my search for others. Additionally, I must recognize those individuals who engaged in the research process on my behalf; chief among them were: Samuel Banks, Pauline Braddy, Consuella Carter, Marion Cumbo, L. Sharon Freeman, Carlotta Gary, William Talbot Handy, Jr., Robert L. Holmes, Jr., Jeanette Jennings, Wanda Jones, Josephine Harreld Love, Claude Phifer, Janice Robinson, William Singleton, Harry Smyles, Geneva Handy Southall, Nancy Jo Taylor, Yvonne Plummer Terrelongue, William E. Terry, and Oscar R. Williams, Jr.

I am greatly obliged to the following institutions and libraries: Schomburg Collection, New York Public Library; Moorland-Spingarn Research Center, Howard University; Special Collections, Fisk University; National Archives and Library of Congress, Washington, D.C.; Dillard University Library and Amistad Research Center at Dillard University (located now at Tulane University); Johnston Memorial Library; Virginia State Library; Archive and Manuscript Division, Thomas Jefferson Library, University of Missouri-St. Louis; Music Room, St. Louis Public

Library; Preservation Hall Archives; Louisiana Room, New Orleans Public Library; William Ranson Hogan, Jazz Archive, Tulane University; Indiana State Library; Illinois State Historical Library; Vivian G. Harsh Collection of Afro-American History and Literature, Chicago Public Library; Chicago Historical Society; E. Azalia Hackley Collection, Detroit Public Library; Eva Jessye Afro-American Collection, University of Michigan; and the American Symphony Orchestra League.

My greatest debt is to my husband, Calvin, and children, Michelle, Blaine, and Obiora. Without their understanding, tolerance, and support this project could neither have been launched nor completed.

D. Antoinette Handy
November 1979

Foreword

In 1973 I had the pleasure of working with D. Antoinette Handy for the first time. The event was the first of four Black Music Symposia I directed, being held that year in Baltimore. Among the works scheduled for performance was Ulysses Kay's "Aulos," for flute and chamber orchestra. Handy was the soloist with the Baltimore Symphony Orchestra. Since that time I have become increasingly aware of her talents not only as a performing musician but as an administrator and scholar.

Her flute studies were under such masters as Georges Laurent, Lois Schaefer, James Poppoutsakis, Emil Eck, and Gaston Crunelle. She received a bachelor's degree from the New England Conservatory, a master's degree from Northwestern University, and a diploma from the Conservatoire National de Musique in Paris.

She has been a member of the Chicago Civic Orchestra, Orchestre Internationale (Paris), Orchestre Ensemble de Paris, Orchestra Musica Viva (Geneva), Orchestra of America, the Symphony of the Air, Radio City Music Hall Orchestra, the Bach Festival Orchestra (Carmel), the Symphony of the New World, the Voice of Firestone Orchestra (ABC Television), and the Richmond Symphony in Virginia.

In addition to her solo work with the Baltimore Symphony Orchestra, she has appeared as guest soloist with the New Orleans Philharmonic, the Orchestre Internationale, the Orchestra Musica Viva, the Bach Festival Orchestra, and the Mostovoy Soloists of Philadelphia. Under the sponsorship of the United States Information Service she toured as soloist in nine major cities of Germany, and has also been heard at Cooper Union and the New York Flute Club.

While in Europe (1954–55) Handy organized the Trio Pro Viva, an ensemble that also includes piano and cello, dedicated to the performance of music by black composers. This group has since toured throughout the United States, including Washington's Kennedy Center. The repertoire of the Trio Pro Viva encompasses more than two centuries, reaching back to works by the eighteenth-century Saint-Georges and including premieres of works by contemporary Afro-American composers, many of which were written specifically for the ensemble.

The Trio Pro Viva has issued a recorded anthology of "Contemporary Black Images in Music for the Flute," on Eastern ERS-513. In the lengthy review that appeared in the Fall 1973 issue of *The Black Perspective in Music*—Dr. Dominique-Rene de Lerma wrote:

> There are several gems to be discovered in this two-disc album, and the most valuable of these might be the flutist. She has a wonderfully warm, rich and beautiful sound; her phrasing is totally musical. She has done music a great service by organizing the . . . Trio Pro Viva and in stimulating the creation of numerous works for that ensemble, but those acquiring this album will be most deeply impressed with her own substantial talents as a soloist.

Her earlier research has been published in *The Black Perspective in Music, The Western Journal of Black Studies,* and by the *Six Institutions Consortium* Publications. In 1974 she issued a significant gathering of her contributions to the *Richmond Afro-American* under the title *Black Music: Opinions and Reviews.*

Handy has appeared as speaker before the American Musicological Society and the Association for the Study of Afro-American Life and History, and on the campuses of Bennett, St. Augustine's, Kentucky State, and Robert Morris colleges; the University of South Carolina, University of D.C., and Jackson State University; and others.

She has served on the faculties of Florida A&M, Virginia State, Virginia Union, and Jackson State Universities; the New York College of Music; the Metropolitan Music School; and the Henry Street Settlement; and, as a music therapist, at the Alfred Adler Mental Hygiene Clinic in New York. In 1976 she began a period of artist residency in the Richmond Public Schools, through the Special Arts Project of the Emergency School Aid Act (OE).

In addition, she has shared her knowledge with the public on two radio series, broadcast by WRFK-FM in Richmond, on whose advisory council she also serves. The Virginia Alliance for Arts Education, the Virginia Bicentennial Committee, the Virginia Commission on the Arts, *The Black Perspective in Music*, Trio Student Special Services (OE), and the Virginia Committee for the National Black Colloquium and Competition are among the organizations that have called on Handy's expertise.

With her present contribution, based both on her extensive research and her rich experiences, Antoinette Handy is providing important documentation on the past and a clear challenge for the future. She is writing as a qualified scholar and an experienced performer.

PAUL FREEMAN

Music Director, Victoria Symphony Orchestra, British Columbia, Canada, and Artistic Director, The Black Composers Series, Columbia Records; since 1987, Music Director and Conductor, Chicago Sinfonietta

I.

The American Orchestra: A Historical Overview

The history of instrumental ensembles is not to be found in a single source. For a history of the orchestra we turn to one source; for a history of the band, to another. Since the acceptance of jazz as "art" is of only recent vintage, it of necessity created its own historians, who generally lacked a traditional grounding in musicology and who generally treated the development of their ensembles as something special and unique—again, under a separate cover. Though necessarily lines of demarcation have been drawn in the following coverage of instrumental ensemble development in America, it is hoped that unification under a single chapter heading reflects a composite significance and suggests that artistic standards of quality are neither absent in one development nor necessarily present in another.

The Orchestra

Seeds of the American orchestra were sown in Europe in the late Middle Ages. But according to orchestra historian Adam Carse,

> [W]e need not look for any instrumental organisation that foreshadows the modern orchestra much earlier than the seventeenth century. . . . During the fifteenth and sixteenth centuries, musicians were accustomed to play together in small groups of allied instruments rather than in large mixed tone-colours [Carse, *The Orchestra*, pp. 13–14].

1

By the end of the seventeenth century the strings had consolidated their position as the fundamental basis of the orchestra, and today that position remains unchallenged. Winds and percussions were added during the next two centuries, but bowed stringed instruments remained the nucleus.

The expansion of the orchestra from the European small instrumental ensemble of the seventeenth century to the current assemblage of a hundred or more players is considered by many to be one of the most significant developments in the history of Western music, if not the history of *all* music. The word "orchestra" of course implies the modifier "symphony"[1] and can be defined as an instrumental group capable of performing symphonies—in terms of size, technical capacity, and leadership/followship orientation. European models, in their organization (into four groups: strings, woodwinds, brass, and percussion) and repertory selection, were followed by those who developed the early American orchestras.

The year 1842 saw the establishment of America's first and oldest extant "professional" orchestra, the Philharmonic Society of New York, later renamed the New York Philharmonic. It began as a cooperative venture and maintained that status until 1901, when musicians began receiving guaranteed salaries. Said one commentator about the orchestra's early years:

> It was essentially a club, . . . organized on a cooperative basis, with only the conductor and librarian receiving salaries. The sixty-odd members . . . received equal shares of the income from their concerts. Fortunately, all relied on other occupations for their living. . . . In their nadir season, . . . each player netted eighteen dollars [Soblosky, *American Music*, pp. 87–88].

Said another, "[T]he New York Philharmonic [was] a band whose members played together more for the love of it than for any artistic results they achieved, or for any notable support they had from the public" (Howard, *Our American Music*, pp. 281–282).

The year 1862 is perhaps the next of historical significance after 1842, for this was the year that orchestral leadership in the U.S. was taken over by Theodore Thomas, one "who combined the strongest qualities of the Cultured musician with some of the badges of eccentric luminescence" (Musselman, *Music in the Cul-*

tured Generation, p. 68). The Thomas Orchestra completed its first tour in 1869, establishing what has been referred to as "The Thomas Highway," which extended from New England to the Pacific Coast. These tours were gradually reduced as major cities began establishing their own permanent orchestras.

By 1900 there were four "established" orchestras in America that closely approximated "permanency": Boston, Chicago, Cincinnati, and Pittsburgh. Other orchestras—New York Philharmonic, St. Louis, San Francisco, and Los Angeles—were also in existence, though lacking in stability. The Philadelphia Symphony, which revealed traits of permanency from its infancy, was established in 1900.

A report entitled *The Movement for Symphony Orchestras in American Cities*, compiled in 1938 by the Construction and Civic Development Department of the Chamber of Commerce of the United States of America, listed 179 symphony orchestras. Of this number, 162 were developing, semiprofessional, and semipermanent organizations and only seventeen were fully professional orchestras. Today there are close to 1,500 orchestras in the United States, of which forty-eight are fully professional and eighty-four have a majority of players who are professionally trained but not earning their main source of income from the orchestra.

So rapid was orchestral growth in America that in 1942 the American Symphony Orchestra League, Inc., was founded. As its name reveals, its concern was for symphony orchestras only. Though membership in the League was and continues to be open to "anyone who is interested in the current and future condition of the symphony orchestra," voting rights are held only by member symphony orchestras, which have one vote each.

The ASOL was granted a Federal Charter by the U.S. Congress in 1962. The League's purpose, as stated in the law, was

to serve as a coordinating, research, and educational agency and clearinghouse for symphony orchestras in order to help strengthen the work in their local communities; to assist in the formation of new symphony orchestras; through suitable means, encourage and recognize the work of America's musicians, conductors, and composers; and to aid the expansion of the musical and cultural life of the United States through suitable educational and service activities [Public Law 87-817, October 15, 1962].

The 1965 Rockefeller Panel on the future of theater, dance, and music in America reported:

> Of all existing professional organized activity in the performing arts, the longest established, most widely dispersed, and most stable is the symphony orchestra. . . . American orchestras today occupy an eminent position in our cultural life [*The Performing Arts: Problems and Prospects,* pp. 20–21].

American symphony orchestra historian Philip Hart wrote in 1973:

> The United States today enjoys an unrivaled quality and quantity of orchestral performance. Though our orchestras have borrowed important aspects of their functions from abroad, . . . their institutional structure, artistic and business direction, and the manner in which they both serve and represent the communities in which they perform are uniquely American [Hart, *Orpheus in the New World,* p. xv].

New York Times music critic Harold Schonberg, reporting on the status of symphony orchestras in America in 1978, indicated that they were now native, from podium to timpani; were, for the first time, out in the real world; had embraced business principles in marketing, publicity, budgets, etc.; and were providing an increased number of services to their community. He noted a greater responsiveness of legislators and the American public. In short, the symphony orchestra was thriving in America as it never had before ("The Symphony Has Refused to Die," *New York Times,* May 7, 1978, pp. D19, 27).

As reported by the American Symphony Orchestra League, "Symphony orchestra classifications are primarily based on an orchestra's annual income or expense budget for the most recently completed season." Shown below is the symphonic orchestral picture as of September 1977:

MAJOR ORCHESTRAS

Orchestras with audited annual income in excess of $1.5 million. No. of orchestras: 34 (31 in the United States; 3 in Canada). Budget range: $1.5 million to over $10 million (approximate). Musicians are engaged on a full-time basis for a contracted number of weeks per year, and the orchestra employment provides their major source of income.

REGIONAL ORCHESTRAS

Orchestras with annual income between $500,000 and $1.5 million. No. of orchestras: 19 (17 in the United States; 2 in Canada). Regional orchestras engage musicians for seasons ranging between 15 and 36 weeks per year.

METROPOLITAN ORCHESTRAS

Orchestras with annual income between $100,000 and $500,000. No. of orchestras: 92 (84 in the United States; 8 in Canada). Musicians do not earn their main source of income from the orchestra, although the great majority of these players are professionally trained.

URBAN ORCHESTRAS

Orchestras with budgets between $50,000 and $100,000 per year. No. of orchestras: The League is able to certify 58 orchestras in this category. It is likely that there are additional urban orchestras not listed because they have not filed statistics with the League. Generally speaking, the conductor and manager are engaged on a full-time basis. Many of the musicians are professionally trained, but do not depend on orchestra income as their main source of support.

COMMUNITY ORCHESTRAS

Orchestras with budgets less than $50,000 per year. No. of orchestras: Approximately 550. Conductors and managers may be full-time or may work with the orchestra on an avocational basis. Musicians include professional musicians, avocational musicians, and possibly others.

COLLEGE ORCHESTRAS

No. of orchestras: Approximately 500. Orchestras composed exclusively of faculty and students of a college or university.

YOUTH ORCHESTRAS

No. of orchestras: Approximately 200. Orchestras composed of young people of college, high school, and junior high school ages from a certain area but not from a single educational institution.

A more recent classification (1996) of professional orchestras by the American Symphony Orchestra League (ASOL) is as follows: (1) orchestras with annual budgets greater than $1 million, (2) orchestras with annual budgets between $250,000 and $1 million, and (3) orchestras with annual budgets less than $250,000. The two other classifications are (4) university, college, or conservatory orchestras and (5) youth orchestras.

A few unique symphonic orchestral developments should be mentioned. For example, Boston Pops maestro Arthur Fiedler assembled a World Symphony Orchestra in 1971, "to affirm the world-wide heritage of music and the international understanding which can be achieved through this form of artistic communication." The orchestra was composed of instrumentalists from more than 140 professional orchestras in sixty nations, twenty-seven American states, and the District of Columbia. Under the sponsorship of the Federation of People-to-People Programs, the group played three major invitational concerts. There was Third World and American black participation ("World Symphony Orchestra Displays Artistic Harmony Among Nations," *International Musician*, November 1971, p. 3). Making its debut in 1975 was New York City's Symphony of the United Nations (SUN).[2] The group, "designed to accommodate musicians from all countries," had a repertory that consisted of "folk, pop and western classical music" (Ericson, "Two Conductors Plan Offbeat Events," *New York Times*, January 8, 1978, p. D17).

Were it not for such black authors as James Monroe Trotter, Alain Locke, Maud Cuney-Hare, and Eileen Southern; an occasional "update on black musical activities" in white music journals; and the black press, one would assume that a black presence in symphonic orchestral circles was nonexistent. Though it is not the purpose of this writing to fill the void, attention to the completeness of black orchestral/band involvement is essential.

The black presence in the business of "elite art" instrumental ensemble music making dates back to the early 1800s. Four "colored" musicians were observed in an otherwise all-white orchestra playing in Philadelphia in 1826—their names, Joseph and William Appo and the Newton brothers. Flutist/violinist Peter

O'Fake played on one occasion with the celebrated Jullien Society in New York City (1850s).

Two blacks were members of the 1872 Peace Jubilee Orchestra in Boston under the direction of Patrick S. Gilmore: Henry F. Williams and F.E. Lewis, violinists. Both men were subjected to severe musical tests prior to their acceptance. The orchestra's organizer explained his action accordingly:

> What we wanted for the grand orchestra was "good musicians," and when anyone objected to our two colored performers, we triumphantly referred to the exacting and satisfactory test they had undergone as sufficient answer to the foolish clamors of all those afflicted with "colorphobia" [Trotter, *Music and Some Highly Musical People*, pp. 107–108].

A "quality" orchestra under the direction of Frank Johnson provided a concert at St. Philip's Church in Philadelphia in 1827. A Negro Philharmonic Society of more than one hundred blacks was organized in New Orleans during the 1830s, led by violinists Constantin Debarque and Richard Lambert. New York blacks organized a Philharmonic Society in 1876.

Several such groups came into existence in the late 1800s, for example, the Ida Club and Lyre Club symphony orchestras in New Orleans. During the same period master musician N. Clark Smith was leading his thirteen-piece Little Symphony Orchestra in Chicago.

At the turn of the century at least two such orchestras existed in Washington, D.C.; the Columbian, directed by Sylvester Thomas, and the Invincible, directed by Edward Ambler. In 1903 the twenty-two-piece Bloom Philharmonic Orchestra, organized by flutist Joseph Bloom and directed by clarinetist Luis Tio, gave four concerts in New Orleans. The Philadelphia Concert Orchestra, under the direction of E. Gilbert Anderson, was organized in 1905. Charles Sullivan founded the Victorian Concert Orchestra in Boston in 1906. The Orchestra Association of Philadelphia came into existence in 1907.

During the second decade of this century the Camden (New Jersey) Negro Symphony (1912) and the Anderson Orchestra of Philadelphia (1913) came into existence. Violinist John Robichaux, though remembered best for his dance and theater orchestra leadership, led a thirty-six-piece symphonic ensemble in New Orleans in 1913.

In Chicago the Ferrell Symphony Orchestra was founded by violinist/educator Harrison H. Ferrell in 1921 and existed for more than a decade. Concert violinist Clarence Cameron White wrote in 1924 that he personally knew two members of leading all-white symphony orchestras who were Negroes, but who for obvious reasons preferred to be known as Spanish ("The Musical Genius of the American Negro," *The Etude*, May 1924, p. 306). Composer/arranger/conductor/music educator William Dawson played first trombone with the Chicago Civic Orchestra for several seasons in the mid-1920s.[3]

An unknown donor, who was "moved by the commendable relations between the white and Negro races in Baltimore," provided funds for the formation of a Negro symphony orchestra in late 1929. Modeled after the Baltimore Symphony (whose conductor served as adviser to the new orchestra), the Baltimore City Colored Orchestra's first conductor was Charles Harris. Beginning in 1930 the "orchestra for colored citizens" was maintained by the city's Municipal Department of Music and was the only "race" orchestra included in the U.S. Chamber of Commerce's 1938 report on *The Movement for Symphony Orchestras in American Cities*. By this date the leadership had been taken over by W. Llewellyn Wilson.

Other black orchestras that came into existence during the 1930s were the Coleridge Taylor Concert Orchestra in Pittsburgh, directed by Howard Rogers, and a symphonic ensemble led by Carl Rossow in St. Louis. The Gilbert Anderson Memorial Symphony Orchestra came into being in Philadelphia, as a result of a merged Camden Negro Symphony and the Philadelphia Anderson Orchestra.

The Works Progress Administration's Federal Music Project, launched in 1935, afforded orchestral opportunities for the previously trained but unemployed black (as well as white) instrumentalists, assisted in training younger ones and began creating new listening audiences. Though ensembles remained essentially divided along racial lines, black musicians and black listeners benefited. For example, the Richmond (Virginia) Colored Concert Orchestra, composed of ten to fourteen players, performed 275 concerts for an aggregate audience of 71,280 between November 1935 and November 1937.

Despite the war years black symphonic activity by way of their own ensembles continued. Maestros Dean Dixon and Everett Lee founded the American Youth Orchestra (1944) and the Cosmopolitan Symphony Orchestra (1948), respectively, both in New York City. In Chicago no less than three all-black orchestras existed: the Community Concert Orchestra, led by Charles A. Elgar; the Criterion Concert Orchestra, led by Owen Lawson; and the Mid-Southside Concert Orchestra, led by E. J. Robinson.

To be sure, black institutions encouraged "elite art" instrumental music and its production in ensemble at schools as well known as Hampton Institute (Virginia) and as little known as Alcorn State College (Mississippi). In the first decades of this century the orchestra of Haines Normal and Industrial Institute in Augusta, Georgia, provided "good music" for black and white residents of the state. When composer/arranger/pianist/conductor R. Nathaniel Dett arrived at Lincoln Institute in Missouri in 1911 he found a thriving fourteen piece orchestra.

The Washington Concert Orchestra of Washington Conservatory of Music in the nation's capital gave its first concert at the Howard Theatre in 1912, under the direction of Harry A. Williams. In New York City's Harlem both the Music School Settlement for Colored People (founded in 1911) and the Martin-Smith School of Music (founded in 1916) had senior and children's orchestras, with David I. Martin, Sr., serving as conductor at both institutions. Upon his death violinists David I. Martin, Jr., and his sister Gertrude took over the leadership.

By the mid-1950s black "classically" trained instrumentalists were becoming impatient with the snail-paced progress being made in integration of American symphony orchestras. They also rejected the reasons offered by the Establishment explaining their absence in American symphonic circles. For example, 1) few have prepared themselves to be symphonic instrumentalists, 2) the cost of training is beyond the means of many, and 3) environmental deprivations—black children are not exposed at a young enough age to the satisfaction of playing a musical instrument.

In January 1956 *New York Times* music critic Howard Taubman, discussing a forthcoming tour of the Symphony of the Air (former NBC) to India and the Middle East in the interest of American goodwill, concluded his article with a noteworthy recommendation:

There is another point about the Symphony of the Air's tour that is worth mentioning . . . Some of the members of this cooperative orchestra have commitments here and may not be able to make the trip. One gathers that the committee of the orchestra has considered inviting women and Negroes to join the band. . . . Why not? In practically all our orchestras women have won their way on their merits as musicians. As for Negro instrumentalists, they have not reached the ranks of the major ensembles.[4] If there are capable Negro musicians, they have every right to consideration . . . [T]he addition of Negro players to the ensemble, assuming that they had stature as musicians, would be a benefit to our standing in countries like India ["Making Friends," January 22, 1956, p. X9].

Several capable black "musicians of stature" met with Taubman, and in April of the same year he wrote an article entitled "An Even Break," wherein he stated:

For the Negro instrumentalist who wishes to make a career in the so-called long-hair fields of symphony, opera and ballet, the struggle is in its early stages. Musical organizations in the North as well as the South act largely as if Negro string, wind, brass and percussion players did not exist [*New York Times*, April 22, 1956, p. X9].

Capable black instrumentalists called at the office of the Urban League of Greater New York. In 1958 the organization's Board of Directors recommended that

the Industrial Relations Department undertake a project designed to facilitate the inclusion of qualified Negro professional musicians in all areas of the music world, particularly with respect to the classical music field [Douglas G. Pugh, Job Status of the Negro Professional Musician in the New York Metropolitan Area, May 1958].

Douglas G. Pugh, Industrial Relations Secretary of the Urban League of Greater New York, undertook the study and released his report in May of 1958. The subject was explored nationwide, though emphasis was on New York City. There was evidence that "token hiring" had begun (Boston, Cleveland, and Buffalo); more was to follow.

Two New York City orchestras hailed for inclusion of blacks from their inception were the Orchestra of America, organized in 1959, and the American Symphony Orchestra, organized in 1962.

Both were "determined to afford opportunity to highly gifted musicians regardless of age, sex, or national origin."

Several "integration concerned" orchestras resulted from black initiatives. In the fall of 1957 a group of trained, talented, and enthusiastic (but rejected) persons in Los Angeles organized themselves into a body known as the Angel City Symphony Society. Membership was open to instrumentalists, composers, and conductors, without regard to race, creed, or color. The conductor was Leroy Harte, a black.

Eight years later, in 1965, a group of twelve professional black instrumentalists (and two whites) organized the Symphony of the New World in New York City. Its founding purpose was that of

> righting the wrongs in hiring practices in major symphony orchestras and establishing a highly artistic musical aggregation that would bring great music, not only to the regular concert audiences, but to the communities as well, while concurrently programming the works of outstanding black composers [SNW Formation Announcement, 1965].

Within a short period of time the Symphony of the New World began servicing other orchestras. Former members moved on to the Baltimore, Syracuse, Denver, Quebec, Minneapolis, Milwaukee, and North Carolina Symphony Orchestras.

Other such orchestras came into existence, for example, the Concerts in Black and White Orchestra (Boston), the New York Housing Authority Orchestra (New York City), and the Urban Philharmonic (New York City/Washington, D.C.). All three orchestras placed emphasis on opportunities for their black players, had black conductors, and included the music of black composers but were well integrated.

Black bassoonist Gail Hightower founded the Universal Symphony in 1978 and served as the group's artistic director. Based in Queens, New York, the orchestra was a multi-ethnic/cultural organization with a national and international scope and character. It was comprised of fifty-six of the nation's leading musicians, and the intent was to present innovative programs and service the general public, churches, colleges, schools, children's shelters, penal institutions, and senior-citizen facilities.

But intentionally all-black orchestras continued to emerge. The Harlem Youth Symphony Orchestra came into being in 1968, "when several young and unaffiliated musicians in Harlem wanted to offer a fitting memorial tribute to the recently assassinated Martin Luther King." The group soon broadened to include the Spanish-speaking community. In 1970 the name was changed to the Harlem Philharmonic Society.

In the spring of 1974 the Chatham Village Symphony Orchestra came into being in Chicago. The National Afro-American Philharmonic Orchestra, based in Philadelphia and receiving support from the "self-help for minorities" program of the Opportunities Industrialization Center, gave its first concert in 1978. Plans were immediately under way for a national tour.

Because of the prestige of the New York Philharmonic, a 1969 suit brought against it attracted unprecedented attention to the plight of professional black instrumentalists. Two black musicians (Arthur Davis, bassist, and Earl Madison, cellist) accused the New York Philharmonic of discrimination in auditioning and placed their case in the hands of the New York City Commission on Human Rights (Donal Henahan, "Philharmonic's Hiring Policy Defended," *New York Times,* July 31, 1969, p. L26).

Fifteen months later the slate was cleared of the charges, but the Commission found the orchestra guilty of a "pattern of bias in not hiring substitute and extra musicians from minority groups." Management soon hired a black conductor to serve as its Director of Educational Activities (Leon Thompson) and assist in the orchestra's minority-interest outreach. During the fall of 1971 it scheduled a one-week Orchestra Repertory Institute for black and other minority musicians. The Philharmonic had offered a similar program in 1965, open to all musicians of New York State orchestras.

In 1977 the New York Philharmonic did a preseason "Black Composers Week" of concerts under the leadership of black conductors Leon Thompson and Paul Freeman.[5] Such orchestras as the Baltimore, Houston, and Minneapolis had held similar events following initiatives taken by black conductor Paul Freeman and the Minneapolis-based Afro-American Music Opportunities Association.

The years of civil-rights legislation had indeed begun to have an impact on the "elite art" instrumental ensemble business.

Black visibility at the nation's leading university schools of music and conservatories was on the increase. Nationwide attention had been attracted by frequent articles, such as "Can the Negro Overcome the Classical Music Establishment?" *(High Fidelity)*, "The Strange Case of the Missing Musicians" *(The Reporter)*, "Why Are There So Few Blacks in Symphony Orchestras Today?" *(Boston Globe)*, "The Negro in Search of an Orchestra" *(New York Times)*, and "Richmond [Virginia] Negro Named to Board of Symphony" *(New York Times)*.

Several orchestras began participating in an Orchestral Fellowship Program, made available to orchestras with the assistance of the International Conference of Symphony and Opera Musicians by the Music Assistance Fund and supporting grants from the National Endowment for the Arts and the Exxon Corporation. With responsibilities to be met by both fellowship recipient and the involved orchestra, the program was designed "to give exceptionally talented and sufficiently advanced black musicians an opportunity to gain experience in orchestral playing, learn orchestral routine and orchestral discipline, and learn the orchestral repertoire." The Music Assistance Fund was established in 1965 for the purpose of providing financial assistance to black music students through major conservatories. The Orchestral Fellowship Program was the experience phase of a program previously confined to training. Previously administered by the New York Philharmonic, since 1992 the program has been administered by the American Symphony Orchestra League.

The Los Angeles Philharmonic launched its own affirmative-action program. This orchestra conceived, developed, and began executing an Orchestral Training Program for Minority Students in 1972. Participants received instruction from a member of the Philharmonic, "coaching for auditions, professional advice, teaching and performance opportunities, free tickets to concerts, admittance to rehearsals, and financial assistance for instruments, repairs, and upkeep . . ." (Myra Per-Lee, "Reaching Out to Minority Musicians," *Symphony News*, April 1979, pp. 16–17). Some predicted that the next wave of symphonic orchestral musicians would be blacks, and there were some indications that such might very well be the case, if not in the immediate, certainly sometime in the distant, future.

Worth noting is the American Symphony Orchestra League's

survey and study titled "The Participation of Blacks in Professional Orchestras (1990) and "The Participation of Black, Hispanic, Asian, and Native Americans in American Orchestras"
(1991–92 inclusive survey).

The Band: Military and Civilian

As early as 1630 four Dutch citizens, playing trumpet, flute, violin, and drum, began giving free concerts at New York City's
Bowling Green. A few years later a seven-piece group of similar
makeup began performing in Boston. Since there was a majority
of winds in these ensembles, we might accept this as evidence of
"band" beginnings in America. Band historians place the origin
of the modern "wind as nucleus" ensemble at 1789, with the formation of the forty-five-player National Guard in Paris. Though
recognition is given to late-sixteenth and seventeenth-century
Italian and German town fifers and tower musicians, it is believed
that their contribution was insignificant.

The organizer of France's National Guard was Bernard Sarrette. When economic problems compelled the band's dissolution
in 1792 the group (now augmented to seventy players) was kept
together by Sarrette to form a free music school, with band members as teachers. The band's membership included the virtuosi of
Europe; its leadership was provided by France's leading composers, including Gossec, Mehul, and Cherubini. In time the "Institut
National de Musique" provided bands for all the "corps d'ar-
mée" of France. In 1875 the school merged with the "Ecole du
Chant et du Declamation," forming the "Conservatoire de Musique." Though it may seem strange, "the world-renowned Paris
Conservatoire had its origin in the ranks of military music"
(Farmer, *The Rise and Development of Military Music*, p. 80).

The next significant personality in band history was Wilhelm
Wieprecht (1802–1872) of Prussia, who made significant changes
in instrumentation and band repertory. Most importantly, he
demonstrated the advantages of using valve horns and trumpets.
It was Wieprecht who gave birth to the massed-band festivals and
he who transcribed for band Beethoven and Mozart symphonies
and numerous overtures of Classic and Romantic composers.
Many deplored the performance by military bands of classical

masterpieces, but others argued that an assortment of wind instruments "giving an artistic and intelligible rendering of a good work is, to the discerning auditor, . . . much to be preferred to a poor rendering of the same or a similar work by a second-rate organization or inferior orchestra . . ." *(ibid.)*.

England is significant in band history not only for the high quality of her bandmasters but also because of her efforts at instrumental standardization and the mid-nineteenth-century beginnings of a regular publication of military-band arrangements by Carle Boose. In 1846 Boose began editing and issuing the *Boose Journal*. The result was uniform instrumentation and available well-arranged band music for bands within and outside of England (Goldman, *The Wind Band*, p. 34).

American bands in general followed English models. The reasons are understandable: in the early days small units accompanied British troops; American settlers brought to America their instrumental recollections; and outstanding early personalities in America's band history were either English (Thomas Dodworth) or Irish (Patrick Sarsfield Gilmore), or had come under British influence prior to their American arrival (Louis-Antoine Jullien).

The first notable American band—which is still extant—was The United States Marine Band, organized in 1798. Its composition was "drum major, fife major and thirty two drums and fifes." The oldest civilian concert band (municipal) still performing today was formed in Allentown, Pennsylvania, in 1828, making it second only to the Marine Band in terms of continuous existence. The Bangor (Maine) Band, organized in 1859, also performs during the summer months. The first important completely professional band was The Independence Band of New York, established in 1825. Associated with the Independence Band was Thomas Dodworth, who changed the band's instrumentation to brass exclusively. Most famous bands in the country became brass bands during the 1830s. The idea of mixing reeds and brasses originated in the mid-1800s.

The United States Navy carried three or more musicians aboard its various ships and by 1838 had a naval band consisting of five musicians and a bandmaster. Neither the United States Navy nor Army had bands of any great importance until World War I. The United States Air Force's Band was not formed until the late 1940s. The organizing idea was to form "a band that could give a performance of 'Scheherazade' or 'The Flying Dutch-man' comparable to that by any orchestra, and in the next breath could rival Benny Goodman" (Graham, *Great Bands of America*, p. 53).

At one time all bands in America were associated with the military: encouraging the troops, sounding the call to arms, arousing and instilling patriotism, conveying signals and orders, and playing the hymns of peace. But band interest extended beyond the military, as professional and amateur bands began to appear all over the country. Industrial bands became quite popular. Employers sought workers who could also play a band instrument. By the last decade of the nineteenth century it was not infrequent to see such notices as

WANTED: Piccolo, clarinet and saxophone players, who are coal miners, tailors or barbers.

Harness Maker who can play anything in brass.

Cornetist who is a glass blower.

Good Clarinetist who is a competent photographer

One of the oldest industrial sponsors was the Pennsylvania Railroad, which sponsored the Altoona Works Band, organized in 1853. The Missouri-Kansas and Texas Railroad sponsored a band in Parson, Kansas. It enjoyed a full-time music supervisor and in the 1920s boasted five bands of white workers, one Mexican band, and one Negro band. Most industrial bands however disappeared during the Depression.

At the turn of the century almost every American town of any size had a municipal (town) band. Many were supported by subscriptions and taxation plans. More than half the states in the nation followed the lead of Iowa in allowing towns and cities of less than 40,000 to levy a local tax "for maintenance or employment of a band for musical purposes." Newspapers, police and fire departments, service clubs, and fraternal orders sponsored juvenile bands.

As town bands gradually disappeared, institutions of secondary and higher learning took them over. Currently, most American schools have a band unit. The American Music Conference estimates that a least 1.5 million American students perform in 22,500 high school marching bands. High schools sponsor some 25,000 concert bands and about 12,000 stage bands. University bands are to be found on most college campuses. The concert bands carry such names as Wind Orchestra, Wind Ensemble, Symphonic Band, and Wind Symphony, distinguishing them from the marching units, associated primarily with football, the all-American sport.

In consideration of black band involvement, we note that the Revolutionary War permitted blacks to be employed as drummers and fifers. Black musicologist Eileen Southern recalled the names of drummers Jazeb Jolly, William Nickens, "Negro Tom," and "Negro Bob" and those of fifers Barzillai Lew and Richard Cozzens, known musical members of various military regiments. She identified a few as drummers in the War of 1812 (*The Music of Black Americans*, pp. 74–77).

During the Civil War the Confederate Army continued to use slaves as fifers and drummers. Various black regiments were established in the Union Army, wherein many blacks earned the position of principal musician or chief bugler. The experience gained in the military, coupled with natural gifts and a love for music, resulted in the formation of "wind as nucleus" instrumental ensembles throughout the country in the postwar years.

An all-Negro marching band led by Matt Black was noted in Philadelphia as early as 1818. One of its most famous members was Frank Johnson (1792–1844),[6] organizer and leader of a band that earned an enviable position in Philadelphia during the 1820s and 30s. Primarily a woodwind band, the group added strings when playing for dances. This is believed to be the first American band to go abroad (1837), and while there the ensemble did a command performance for Queen Victoria at Buckingham Palace. After Johnson's death the band continued under the leadership of Joseph G. Anderson.

In Newburgh, New York, Samuel Dixon organized The Dixon Brass Band in 1827. There existed in Philadelphia a band led by A.J.R. Connor in the 1850s and another led by Isaac Hazzard. At mid-nineteenth century several black bands were operating on the West Coast, including Groom's Brass Band, The Pacific Brass Band, and Allen's Quadrille Band, all in San Francisco.

The Sciota-Valley Brass Band was organized in Chillicothe,

Ohio, in 1855. The Roberts Band was organized in 1857, in the same city. The two organizations consolidated in 1859 to form The Union-Valley Brass Band. Black music historian James Monroe Trotter wrote:

> The Band contained several performers of such excellent natural and acquired abilities as would render them prominent among the best musicians of any section of the country [*Music and Some Highly Musical People*, p. 314].

A decade later The Great Western Ethiopian Brass and String Band was organized in Toledo, Ohio. Prior to the 1880s there existed in New York City Johnson's Brass Band and Becker's Brass Band. The 1960s and '70s interest in composer/pianist Scott Joplin revived the name of The Queen City Concert Band in Sedalia, Missouri, in which Joplin played second cornet during the late 1890s.

Turning to the South, we note that a group of blacks, operating under the name National Band, existed in Portsmouth, Virginia, as early as 1830. In the mid-nineteenth century fiddlers Sy Gilliat and George Walker led The Richmond Blues Band in Richmond, Virginia. After Emancipation there came into existence in rural Alabama The Lapsey Brass Band, The Old Oak Grove Band, and The Laneville Brass Band. And of course there was New Orleans, with an instrumental tradition that takes us back to eighteenth-century Congo Square. The tradition continued; formal study was available for many from members of the French Opera House and the city orchestras. Many improved their musical skills in Paris. But the New Orleans black-brass-band story by no means falls within the category of "historical neglect" and so will not be discussed here.

During World War I, several black bands and their leaders became known for their musical ability and distinguished service: the 349th, conducted by Norman Scott; the 367th ("Buffaloes"), conducted by Egbert Thompson; the 351st, conducted by Dorsey Rhodes; the 807th, conducted by Will Vodery; the 370th, conducted by George Duff; the 368th, conducted by A. Jack Thomas; the 369th, conducted by James Reese Europe; and the 350th, conducted by Tim Brymn—all affiliated with the U.S. Army. Many of the bands continued upon their return to the States.

Alton August Adams was the Navy's only black bandmaster. He was detailed to organize a band in the Virgin Islands in 1917, shortly after the island was purchased and placed under the administration of the Navy. Many considered Adams's band to be the best in the United States Navy. Prior to assuming the Navy assignment Adams served as editor of the Band Department of the popular *Jacobs Band Monthly*.[7]

Turning to World War II, we must consider that it was 1954 before the policy of all-Negro units in the armed forces was abolished. The Navy consistently offered the greatest amount of resistance to integration. Great Lakes, Illinois, served as headquarters of the Ninth Naval District, the largest in the United States. Camps Moffett, Lawrence, and Smalls, of the many Great Lakes camps, were designated for blacks. St. Louis arranger/conductor/composer Len Bowden assembled a Great Lakes Naval Training Station Band of seventeen pieces and served as leader for approximately 135 black musicians stationed at the Naval Center.

Acceptance into the band was by audition or professional referral. "Ship's Company" was the approximate forty-five-piece band that remained at Great Lakes, servicing camps Moffett, Lawrence, and Smalls, and training others "for further transfer" (FFT). The Great Lakes group was one of the most illustrious musical gatherings ever assembled. Included were many of the nation's finest instrumentalists: jazz performers Clark Terry, Jimmie Nottingham, Major Holly, and Al Grey, as well as subsequent "elite art" performers Donald White, Thomas Bridge, and Charles Burrell, members of the Cleveland, Richmond, and Denver symphony orchestras, respectively.

Walter Howard Loving was selected by then governor of the Philippines, William Howard Taft, to organize and develop the Philippine Constabulary Band, which he directed in 1902–16, 1919–23, and 1937–41. This was the first band in history to share honors with the U.S. Marine Band at a presidential inauguration (1909). The occasion was the inauguration of President Walter Howard Taft. (See Handy, *Black Conductors,* pp. 334–40.)

A few other black bands merit consideration. Following the organization of several Pullman Porter singing quartets in the early 1920s, composer/band-orchestra leader N. Clark Smith was called in as music supervisor. He immediately set out to organize the more than 9,000 black employees into Pullman Porter bands and orchestras. The all-black Memphis Letter Carriers Band began participating in competitions at the Letter Carriers Convention as early as 1925. For more than a decade the band competed annually and more frequently than not departed with top convention laurels. The Drum and Bugle Corps of Post 168 of Charlotte, North Carolina, made its first appearance at the National Convention of the American Legion at Louisville in 1929. The group received top honors in its category.

There were Sunday School bands and those affiliated with various fraternal orders. Black colleges sported marching and concert bands, best known of which was Florida Agricultural and Mechanical's Marching "100," under the direction of William P. Foster. With emphasis on pageantry, this was the first black band invited to participate in the Festival of States annual parade (the twenty-ninth, in 1950). The group made its television debut at the Orange Bowl in 1963.

The Theater Orchestra

Theatrical performances were considered frivolous activities that young America could ill afford. Nevertheless, a theater did exist in Williamsburg, Virginia, as early as 1722. A decade later theaters were operating in Charles Town (Charleston), South Carolina, and New York City. The "New York Company of Comedians" performed *The Beggar's Opera* with Instrumental Music to each air, given by a "Set of Private Gentlemen" in 1752 at a theater in Upper Marborough, Maryland. The first permanent theater in America was built in Philadelphia in 1766.

Soon most urban cities boasted at least one theater, be it legitimate or not so legitimate. Before 1830 New York City had four theaters, one of which was the black-operated African Grove Theater. Small instrumental ensembles, made up primarily of "private gentlemen" (amateurs), performed before, after, and/or during the evening's main feature, what may have been nothing more than "strung together" sentimental ballads and folk and comic songs. Exclusive New Orleans opera houses, though primarily devoted to the performance of French opera, did allow for the occasional performance of plays and ballets. Imported (English, French, and later Italian) theatrical productions constituted the program material.

Gradually public taste for native musical entertainment began to increase. By the mid-1800s blackface minstrelsy was becoming the most popular form of theatrical entertainment. The Virginia, Christy, and Bryant Minstrels; Ethiopian Serenaders; and Kentucky Rattlers all carried along a band, frequently composed only of fiddle, banjo, tambourine, and bones. Following the Civil War, minstrel, carnival, and showboat bands (white and black) traveled throughout the United States, with memberships composed of as few as two and as many as forty. The evening's performance was routinely preceded by an afternoon parade and a concert at the public square.

Black minstrel companies came into existence during the 1860s, the most popular of which were Lew Johnson's Plantation Minstrel Company, the Georgia Minstrels, and The W.A. Mahara Minstrels. Each company included a band, varying in size. Best known of the minstrel band leaders was of course William C. Handy, who joined The W.A. Mahara Minstrels as cornetist in 1896. Handy took over the leadership of a thirty-five-piece parade band that became forty-two pieces for concerts. He remained with the company for several successful seasons.

Cornetist P.G. Lowery, a contemporary of Handy, gained his experience from the lesser-known Lowery-Morgan and Harvey Greater minstrel companies and enjoyed a brief period with The Mahara Minstrels. But his most memorable association was as leader of a sideshow band for the Ringling-Barnum Circus.

In the first decades of the twenty-first century black carnival and tent-show bands were frequent, as were those touring with various vaudeville companies. As black theaters were the vogue of the day, so were black pit orchestras. On-stage happenings of the popular all-black shows that enjoyed successful Broadway runs at the turn of the century and during the 1920s and '30s were supported by all-black instrumental ensembles in the pit.

The black instrumentalist encountered "hard times" in terms of theatrical involvement on Broadway during the 1940s and '50s. As the Urban League Report of 1958 revealed:

Negro musicians are usually employed when the musical has a Negro theme or the star of the production is a Negro. Employment

for the Negro musician is most often secured at the insistence of
the Negro headliner, a liberal producer, theatre owner, or pressures
exerted by the Negro musician [Pugh, "Job Status of the Negro Professional Musician in the New York Metropolitan Area," p. 4].

Minimal productions meeting these requirements meant minimal
employment for the black instrumentalist.

The "Heart and Feet" Orchestra

American "popular art" instrumental ensemble development
consistently followed a nonelitist course. The trend toward an
"Art-for-Life's Sake" instrumental ensemble was clearly evident
by the turn into the twentieth century. A music of the heart and
feet (only later the brain), with roots in the tribal rhythms of Africa, the work songs of America's southern fieldhands, and the
spirituals and blues of a despised rural and urban slave and semi-
freed people, was emerging.

Blacks provided greater exposure to their "chalk-line walk"
with their performances at the 1876 celebration of the Centennial
of American Independence at Philadelphia. By 1900 the cakewalk
had become the dance craze of the nation. Syncopated rhythms
(a deliberate upsetting of the normal pulse of meter, accent, and
rhythm), once the private possession of black communities, were
now becoming the vogue of musical America. All of America
began to sing with the blues and express the ragged rhythms
formerly associated with the keyboard through instruments of
the orchestra. According to orchestra historian Paul Bekker:

[O]pened [was] a new field for instrumental activity no less or more
important and stimulating than the pavanne of the 17th, the gavotte
and the minuet of the 18th, the valse of the 19th centuries [*The Story
of the Orchestra*, pp. 307–309].

Then in 1905 a black group that called itself The Memphis Students (none were students and none were from Memphis) made
its debut at the Proctor Twenty-third Street Theatre in New York
City. The combination was unorthodox; the music played was
distinctly different. About twenty experienced entertainer-instru-
mentalists made up the playing-singing-dancing orchestra. Will

Dixon was the dancing conductor of an orchestra comprised of banjos, mandolins, guitars, saxophones, a violin, a double bass, a couple of brass instruments, and drums. This spring of 1905 event represented the first public concert of syncopated music in America. The Memphis Students moved to other sites in New York City and then to Europe, where they remained for about a year.

James Reese Europe, a member of the group, organized the Clef Club in 1910, essentially a black musician's union.[8] This was the source of contact for dance orchestras of from three to thirty men for any occasion. In May of 1912 Europe's Clef Club Orchestra of 145 black men gave a concert at Carnegie Hall. Several years later one white member of the audience recalled the event and favorably reported her and the audience's reaction in *The Musical Quarterly:*

> Music-loving Manhattan felt a thrill down its spine such as only the greatest performances can inspire. . . . There were many violins, violas, 'cellos and double basses; but it was a motley group of plectrum instruments of all sorts and sizes—mandolins, guitars, banjos, and a few ukeleles. . . . Then there was an indiscriminate assortment of reed and wind instruments . . . ; there were drums and tambourines, big and little, whose sharp accents danced across the jagged syncopations of the music, recalling the elaborate drum-orchestras of Africa; there was an inspired timpanist . . . ; there was a huge bass drum [Curtis-Burlin, "Black Singers and Players," October 1919, pp. 501-594].

Other unique features were the ten upright pianos in five pairs and the "singing as they played" string and percussion members. The man playing the bass drum and cymbals might well have been singing a high falsetto, while a first-violin player sang a second bass. Despite reminders of elaborate drum-orchestras of Africa, this group was distinctly American. Artistic credibility for a new-sounding instrumental organization—the jazz orchestra—was in its infancy. In time the group roster became most extensive, the personalities still more extensive. These groups and individuals discovered a suitable means for encouraging and recognizing the work of a broader segment of America's musicians, conductors, and composers. They too would "aid the expansion of the musical and cultural life of the United States."

Female Involvement

Women have always been associated with music, as serenaders of their cradle-bound little ones and as encouragers and molders of their male offspring's musical talents. These activities were centered in the home, where a woman's musical participation was to remain. Training in music was tolerated and often encouraged, but primarily for purposes of obtaining polish and refinement, again, in relation to her homebound status. If she was to engage in anything professional, her media was restricted to the voice and piano.

Understandably, early instrumental female group participation was confined to family ensembles. A musician father frequently made the best use of his talented wife and daughters. But female instrumental acceptance in other professional musical circles was not soon forthcoming.

An anonymous writer acknowledged female instrumental ability as early as 1895, but the writer summarized the prevailing attitude toward orchestral affiliation in an article that appeared in *Scientific American:*

> It is one thing to be able to perform a solo well and quite another to sustain a position in an orchestra. . . . The most capable and intelligent of women can never become factors in an orchestra of any serious aims. . . . [H]er physical incapacity to endure the strain of four or five hours a day rehearsal, followed by the prolonged tax of public performances, will bar her against possible competition with male performers. . . . There are dozens of young women who play well enough for an orchestral place. But even were a mixed orchestra of men and women together a condition probable enough to consider, about how many works of novelty and magnitude in a year would the ordinary woman find herself physically equipped to carry through rehearsal? Not more than a third, probably, of what men are able to do ["Orchestral Women," November 23, 1895, p. 327].

All-female orchestras seemed to be the only outlet. What is believed to be the first independent "Ladies' Orchestra" was established as early as 1884, in Chelsea, Massachusetts. The group of six players (soon increased to ten) accepted its first playing engagement during the same season. The Marion Osgood Ladies

Orchestra existed for about ten years, and according to its leader, Marion Osgood, the group "played at the best halls and parties in and around Boston and in various cities in Connecticut" (Osgood, "America's First 'Ladies Orchestra.' " *The Etude*, October 1940, p. 713).

The Boston Fadettes was organized in 1888, by Caroline B. Nicholas, first violinist in the Osgood Orchestra. During its thirty-two-year history the group played 6,063 concerts. Carl Lachmund's Women's String Orchestra was organized in New York City in 1896. It existed for at least a decade.

Producing orchestral music "on the lighter side" in and around Philadelphia in the late teens was a sixteen-member Mandolin Orchestra. At the same time (and for many years following) Anna C. Byrnes was in great demand as a conductor of all-male orchestras, covering the circuit of summer resorts in New York State. Thelma Terry ("the petite mistress of the string bass") and Her Playboys had a large following in the Midwest and recorded for Columbia in 1928.

Clay Smith, journalist for *Jacob's Band Monthly*, commented in 1930 on his enlightening experience as an adjudicator for high school state and district band contests throughout the country. He wrote:

> When I was a boy it was considered . . . out of place for a girl to take up a wind instrument. She was sort of classed with a "whistling girl," and everyone knows that a girl was considered coarse and rude, and very much a tomboy, if she whistled in public. But, Oh! how the world has changed ["The Girl in Bands," February 1930, p. 9].

Smith indicated that training and hard work were paying off financially, using as his example a popular all-girl group working out of Indianapolis known as The Brick Tops. With members recruited from New York to California, the group was organized in 1927. The fourteen-member band made its first transcontinental tour during the same year, heading the big-time vaudeville circuits. Twenty-one-year-old pianist, clarinetist, and drummer Bobby Grice served as leader. According to Smith, "Band King" John Philip Sousa pronounced the group's featured cornetist Orrel Johnson "the finest lady cornetist he had ever heard (*ibid.*, p. 38).[9]

There were several other successful "lady-fronted" all-female orchestras. Singer/dancer Ina Ray Hutton, better known as "the Blonde Bombshell of Rhythm," formed her Melodears in 1934. The group played theaters, made several movie shorts, recorded for Victor and Brunswick, and toured Europe in 1935. She formed a second all-girl band in 1937 and another in the early 1950s; however, Ina Ray was more respected in the industry for her leadership of male bands. Other women leaders of all-girl bands in the 1940s were Joan Lee, June Grant, Jean Wald, and Ada Leonard, to name a few.

Two very special female instrumental groups were the Kentucky-based four-piece Coon Creek Girls (late '30s) and the Chicago-based thirty-piece Grandma's Ragtime Band (late '40s), led by Kathryn Skeffington. The Coon Creek Girls had the pleasure of appearing before the King and Queen of England at the White House in 1939. Playing guitar, mandolin, violin, and string bass, the group entertained with a genuine rendition of traditional hillbilly music. The one requirement for membership in Skeffington's band was that you had to be at least a grandmother. The group of retired housewives, businesswomen, schoolteachers, and nurses were also former musicians. In 1949 the group gave seventy concerts. Finances were handled by the director, and profits were equally divided at year's end.

Several men achieved their fame based on leadership of all-female jazz ensembles. Phil Spitalny fronted a group of thirty competent musicians, organized in 1934 and still in existence in the mid-1950s. According to Spitalny, his musicians were selected on the basis of musicianship, indications of musical artistry, gifts of rhythm and melodic perception, reading ability, and experience. Believing that the "inherent personal chemistry" of women was well suited to musical sweetness and charm, he also sought musicians who could convey this feeling to listeners ("The Hour of Charm," *The Etude*, October 1938, p. 640).

In organizing the group, Spitalny publicized the fact that

> women were responsible for more than 80 per cent of the commodity purchases in the country and that the housewife got a great deal more pleasure and satisfaction listening to a feminine musical group. It gave them a feeling that sex was unshackling the conventional bonds and stepping out in the professional world ["Are Girl Musicians Superior?," *Up Beat*, January 1939, p. 27].

Spitalny boasted the fact that many of his group's members were conservatory graduates and veterans of symphony orchestras. Under the sponsorship of General Electric his female musical unit went on a weekly coast-to-coast NBC radio broadcast in 1936, under the program title "The Hour of Charm."

Another ladies' "big band" that enjoyed widespread recognition was The Hormel Girls' Caravan, better known as "The Darlings of the Airwaves." Again, leadership was in the hands of males (Ernest Villas and Al Woodbury). The group started in 1947 as an advertising gimmick for the Hormel Company, manufacturers of canned meat products. The original idea was to hire ex-servicewomen. It started out with six recent discharges from the military, was soon expanded to twenty-six, and by 1951 a sixty-piece orchestra was advertised, by which time the ex-GI restriction had been dropped.

The Hormel Orchestra worked throughout the year, making music and product-selling from coast to coast. It programmed standard popular tunes, top hits, and medleys from current Broadway and movie musicals. Smaller units specialized in dixieland or music with a Latin American flavor. A drum and bugle corps played for parades throughout the country. The "Darlings of the Airwaves" label stemmed from the group's regular broadcasts over a national network of 227 radio stations, beginning in 1948. Enjoying more local (New York and Massachusetts) than national recognition was male leader Ving Merlin's troupe of all-girl violinists. Originally four violinists, the group was expanded to thirteen for a forty-city tour in nine states in 1953.

Several female instrumentalists were affiliated with male "popular art" ensembles for brief periods in earlier years and gained for themselves a fair amount of recognition: accordionist Doris Peavey with husband Hollis Peavey's Band; pianist Norma Teagarden and Mildred Shirley with Jack Teagarden's Band; Marian McPartland with Jimmy McPartland and His Dixieland Band; pianist/harpist Corky Hale with bands led by Harry James, Jerry Gray, Freddy Martin, Dave Rose, and Liberace; harpist Adele Girard with Joe Marsala; guitarist Mary Osborne with Russ Morgan, Terry Shand, Joe Venuti, and Raymond Scott; bassist Bonnie Wetzel with Tommy Dorsey; trumpeters Billie Rogers with Woody Herman and Jerry Wald and Leona May Smith (Seuffert) with the Seuffert and Goldman bands and Radio City Music Hall and Fred

Waring orchestras; saxophonists L'Ana Webster with Mike Riley's Big Band and Kathy Stobart with The Humphrey Lytleton
Band; drummers Dottie Dodgion with Benny Goodman, Wild
Bill Davison, and Zoot Sims and Elaine Leighton with Jackie
Cain-Roy Kral; and, finally, vibraharpist Marjorie Hyams with
Woody Herman and George Shearing's all-star quintet. Many of
these women retired from the business, while others remained
active through the late 1970s, when they took their rightful places
beside their male counterparts.

British-born jazz pianist Marian McPartland gave recognition
to some of the "neglected ones" in her article "You've Come a
Long Way, Baby," written for *Esquire's World of Jazz, 1975*, the
year that the General Assembly of the United Nations proclaimed
International Women's Year. Jazz historian Frank Driggs recalled
countless other women instrumentalists (white and black) who
"rode buses on one-night stands and played theater, ballroom
and hotel engagements" in his book *Women in Jazz: A Survey*
(Stash Records, 1977).

Nationwide women's jazz festivals and salutes (most notably
in Kansas City and New York City) in the late 1970s provided an
added dimension to female jazz recognition. These events show-
cased the better-known as well as some of the lesser-known
women musicians, providing the instrumentalists with "equal
time." The woman's role in jazz between 1926 and 1961 was compiled and aurally documented on three disks released by Stash
Records (ST-111—"All Women Groups"; ST-112—"Pianists"; ST-
109—"Jazz Women: A Feminist Retrospective") in 1977–78. *New
York Times* critic John S. Wilson wrote,

> [T]here is nothing on any of these disks to indicate that the per-
> formers are women. Or men. They are just musicians and their
> playing is as good as—and often better than—the performances
> you hear on other records of the same periods and styles. And yet,
> at the time, few people were aware that there were this many ac-
> complished women in jazz. Today there are even more ["Women in
> Jazz, Past and Present," *New York Times*, June 11, 1978, p. 28].

And now let us turn to "elite art" instrumental ensembles, a
label more or less synonymous with the term "symphony orchestras." Here again, a female desire for participation warranted the
establishment of their own orchestras.

The Los Angeles Women's Orchestra was organized in 1893. The next all-female group to concentrate exclusively on the more "elite art" repertory was organized in Philadelphia, in 1921. Chicago followed in 1924; Long Beach, California, in 1925; and Boston in 1926. More than a dozen women's symphony orchestras came into existence during the 1930s in such cities as New York, Cleveland, Pittsburgh, Baltimore, St. Louis, and Minneapolis. Two women's symphony orchestras were established in the 1940s: a second New York Women's Symphony Orchestra and the Detroit Women's Symphony Orchestra.

This writer succeeded in identifying twenty-eight such orchestras that came into existence during the ladies' symphony orchestras' half-century reign. A few existed for one season only, but most enjoyed many successful years, such as The Cleveland Women's Orchestra, founded in 1935. The same can be said for the Detroit Women's Symphony, founded in 1947.

Leopold Stokowski, one of the world's most gifted (and liberal) conductors, referred to the exclusion of women symphony players as "an incomprehensible blunder" as early as 1916. Said Stokowski:

> The particular spirit that women put into music, their kind of enthusiasm, their devotion to anything they undertake, would be invaluable in the formation of symphony orchestras. . . . What poor economy it is to take it for granted that women are not ready to enter the world of art, are not capable of becoming fluent channels for the expression of genius. We are deliberately shutting away great forces for beauty and progress by leaving women out of our scheme of things in the art world ["Women in the Orchestra," *Literary Digest*, February 26, 1916, p. 504].

Though the practice of sex (and race) discrimination was firmly entrenched in American symphony orchestras from the very genesis of their operation, things began to change. The Cleveland Symphony Orchestra dared to hire four women in 1923; the Philadelphia hired a woman as principal harpist in 1930. World War II produced the necessity for hiring more women players, if not the realization that attitudes needed changing.

Music journalist Quaintance Eaton reported the following in 1955:

Women do not need to band together and aggressively announce themselves as "all-female" aggregations any more. . . . The ladies are infiltrating in depth into ensembles previously manned only by—let us merely say "manned"! In our major symphony orchestras, women constitute 18.4 percent of the personnel today ["Women Come into Their Own in Our Orchestras," *Musical America,* February 15, 1955, p. 30].

The American Symphony Orchestra League's report prepared for the National Commission on the Observance of International Women's Year (1975) indicated that during the 1964–65 season the number of women players in the majors showed an average of 18.3 percent. Ten years later the average was 24.9 percent. The percentage of women players in regional orchestras (then classified as metropolitan) averaged 36.5 percent for the 1964–65 season and 40.6 percent for the 1974–75 season. The figures were still higher in urban and community orchestras. It stood to reason that "orchestras with the highest budgets, longest seasons, and most generous salaries [had] the fewest women musicians" ["Women in American Symphony Orchestras," *Symphony News,* April 1976, pp. 13–14].

Well known in symphonic orchestral circles were the names of flutists Doriat Anthony (Boston) and Lois Schaefer (Chicago, New York City Center, Boston), oboist Lois Wann (St. Louis), trombonist Betty Semple Glover (Cincinnati), English hornist Natalie Hollern (National), violinist Vida Reynolds (Philadelphia), cellist Elsa Hilger (Philadelphia), and bassists Isabel Baughman (Baltimore) and Laurene Sarin (Pittsburgh), all assuming their positions before full acceptance of their sex. Their names are unknown, but the Kansas City, Houston, and Seattle symphony orchestras all included female percussionists, and Nashville carried on its roster a female tuba player, all in the early '50s.

In 1943, a fourteen-year-old girl directed a question to Karl Gehrkens, former Oberlin professor and director of *The Etude's* "Music Information Service":

Why is it that nobody has ever seen or heard of an orchestra leader that is a woman? Is it because no woman has courage enough or talent to lead an orchestra, or is it because an orchestra will not be led by a woman?

Dr. Gehrkens responded,

> [P]opular assumption has been that "woman's place is in the home". . . . [M]ost symphony orchestra players are men, and men don't like to play under a woman conductor—just as men in an office don't like to work under a woman executive. And in the second place, people generally don't have as much faith in a woman conductor as in a man. . . . I believe that a change is coming and that in another generation there will be more women players in orchestras and probably more women conductors. But I feel that there will always be more men in both fields because to a man his work is his permanent life; whereas to a woman, in ninety-nine cases out of a hundred her professional life is a temporary thing, and she is thinking in terms of eventually becoming a wife and a mother. Like alcohol and driving, home-making and leading an orchestra do not go together very well, and I myself am "old fashioned" enough to feel that this is all right ["Questions and Answers," *The Etude*, March 1943, p. 168].

Such was the prevailing point of view.

For those women conductors who did break through in the early years, their orchestral leadership role was confined to all-female ensembles, except for an occasional guest appearance. This list of women would include such pioneer conductors as Eva Anderson, Ethel Leginska, Ebba Sundstrom, Frederique Joanna Petrides, Ruth Sandra Rothstein, Elizabeth Kuyper, and Antonia Brico.

In the 1930s Antonia Brico conducted the National Symphony and a few other all-male orchestras. She formed the New York Women's Symphony Orchestra in 1934 and in the 1950s served as conductor of the Denver Businessmen's Orchestra, made up, curiously enough, of 50 percent women.

Several 1975 showings of the film *Antonia, Portrait of the Woman* assisted greatly in bringing the cause of women conductors to the public's attention. Other names to the fore were Sara Caldwell, Eve Queler, Judith Somogi, and Victoria Bond (Herbert Kupferberg, "Women of the Baton—The New Music Masters," *Parade*, May 14, 1978, pp. 4–5). The 1980 and '90s brought to the fore the names Judith Somogi, Catherine Comet, JoAnn Falleta, Rachel Worby, and Maria Alsop. A few black women were available, but somehow, consistently overlooked.

Notes

1. An instrumental sounding together; since the time of Haydn (1732–1809), an orchestral work of a serious nature and of substantial size.

2. United Nations Director of Press William C. Powell, in a "letter to editor," published in the *New York Times* (January 15, 1978, p. D20), cautioned the public to not see this group as a United Nations Symphony. He said, the United Nations had not singled out any performers or organization for official status.

3. An idea of Theodore Thomas, the Chicago Civic Orchestra was founded in 1920. Under auspices of its parent body, the Chicago Symphony, the orchestra (composed of 90 percent professionals) provided experience and routine in orchestral playing under skilled conductors. This orchestra still exists today.

4. Black bassist/conductor Henry Lewis joined the Los Angeles Philharmonic in 1948 (the orchestra's youngest) and black timpanist Elayne Jones joined the New York City Opera and New York City Ballet Orchestras in 1949.

5. The same week, violinist Sanford Allen, the New York Philharmonic's only black member (since 1962), resigned. Stating that he was "simply tired of being a symbol," Allen planned to pursue a career as a freelance violinist and soloist (Donal Henahan, "Only Black in Philharmonic Is Resigning After 15 Years," *New York Times*, August 29, 1977, p. C36).

6. For more on the formidable musician Frank Johnson see John W. Cromwell, "Frank Johnson's Military Band," *Southern Workman* 29 (1900): 532–535 (reprinted in *The Black Perspective in Music*, July 1976, pp. 208–212); and Eileen Southern, "Frank Johnson and His Promenade Concerts," *Black Perspective in Music*, Spring 1977, pp. 3–29.

7. For a detailed account of the life and musical times of Adams see Samuel A. Floyd, "Alton Augustus Adams: The First Black Bandmaster in the U.S. Navy," *Black Perspective in Music*, Fall 1977, pp. 173–187.

8. The New Amsterdam Musical Association, Inc., is the oldest black music organization in the United States. Formed in New York City in 1905, this association paralleled the segregated musicians union, Local 310. Though Europe's group was believed to be more progressive at the time, it is interesting to note that at this writing, the NAMA is still in operation.

9. Several female instrumentalists appeared as featured soloists with the Sousa Band both here and abroad: Nicoline Zedeler, Jeanette Powers, Bertha Bucklin, and Florence Hardeman, all violinists.

II.

Orchestras and Orchestra Leaders

Through the years black female instrumentalists and instrumental leaders have refused to let discriminatory practices and biased attitudes prevent them from making positive contributions to the history of band/orchestral performance in America. They have met the challenges of various musical organizations, often with honor and distinction.

Black female instrumentalists and instrumental leaders have dominated; they have shared the spotlight with members of the opposite sex. In recognition of their activities and accomplishments we project these individuals to center stage, in the hope that American band/orchestral history will continue to advance their names (as well as those yet to be discovered) into the roster of worthy contributors.

As was the case with white women, exclusion stimulated creativity. Both large and small "all double-minority" ensembles came into existence, providing "popular art" as well as "elite art" music. Leadership roles were assumed by males and females alike.

Male Leaders of Female Bands

Many of the male opponents to masculine instrumental exclusiveness were master teachers. Professor W. Thomas Adams, editor of the *Boston Advocate* and director of the Regent Music School of the same city, organized and directed the Female Symphony Orchestra in Cambridge, Massachusetts, around 1900. At the same time, Professor Henry Hart, "one of the best known colored violinists in the United States," led a "much in demand" orches-

33

tra in Indianapolis. When presidents arrived in the Hoosier State, when governors were inaugurated, when any social event of significance took place, the Hart Family Orchestra—composed of Professor Hart and his five daughters—provided the musical entertainment.

Master professor and nationally recognized bandsman N. Clark Smith of Chicago

> assembled twelve of the cities' prominent ladies and trained them. This organization became well-known as The Ladies' Mandolin Club. . . . Maj. Smith again distinguished himself by organizing The Young Ladies Orchestra in 1904 [*The Negro in Chicago, 1779 to 1929*, p. 47].

At the same time, Professor William J. Nickerson, Southern University's (then only a high school) music department chair and founder/director of the Nickerson School of Music, both in the city of New Orleans, organized and directed the Nickerson Ladies' Orchestra. And since the first edition of this publication musicologist Doris McGinty has made us aware of the turn-of-the-century, fifteen-piece Female Brass and Reed Band of Washington, D.C., under the direction of Professor James E. Miller (Doris Evans McGinty, "Black Women in the Music of Washington, D.C., 1900–1920," in *New Perspectives on Music: Essays in Honor of Eileen Southern* [Warren, Mich.: Harmonie Park Press, 1992], p. 429).

In Cleveland in 1921, Professor Walden's ladies' band was one of several assembled to greet and entertain bandsman P. G. Lowery of the Ringling Brothers/Barnum and Bailey Circus. (The Silver Seal Ladies' Band was another of the welcoming bands—leader unknown.) In the early 1920s Papa Waddles fronted a female brass band in Omaha, Nebraska. In the late 1920s Captain W. Carey Thomas, Florida Agricultural and Mechanical College's first official band director, organized and directed the Tallahassee (Florida) College's own fifteen-piece girls' orchestra and its own thirty-six-piece girls' drum and bugle corps. Professor H. O. Davis led a ladies brass band in Nashville, Tennessee, probably during the 1920s. The group consisted of ten brass players and two percussionists—all female. In the late 1930s Professor W. H. Wooten trained and directed the Outer South End Community Orchestra in Boston. The group's name avoided a female designation, but a surviving photograph suggests that the label Outer South End Ladies' Community Orchestra would have been most appropriate (*Boston Guardian*, August 19, 1939).

Frequently forgotten is the fact that the organizer of the world-famous International Sweethearts of Rhythm, in the late 1930s, was the Little Professor from Mississippi's Piney Woods Country Life School, Missouri-born and Iowa-educated Laurence C. Jones. Dr. Jones recruited black women master teachers and conductors for the group's leadership. More will be devoted to this group and Dr. Jones's other all-girl band sensation, The Swinging Rays of Rhythm, later in this chapter. Concert violinist Kemper Harreld, at Spelman College (Atlanta, Georgia) and concert clarinetist F. Nathaniel Gatlin, at Bennett College (Greensboro, North Carolina), organized and directed all-girl ensembles in the late '30s and early '40s. Prairie View College's band director William Henry Bennett organized the Prairie View College Co-Eds (a jazz ensemble) in the early 1940s and soon took to the road. Under management of a professional New York City agency, the group completed several years of successful touring.

Though it was not designated a ladies' ensemble, a review of the roster of composer/conductor/educator Robert Holmes's Cremona Strings, organized in 1958 at Nashville, Tennessee, discloses a female predominance (twenty females/four males). The exclusively-string group existed for more than a decade, was featured on a weekly radio program (WVOL), made several local television appearances, and in 1968 appeared at the National Association of Radio and Television Announcers' Convention in Miami.

Several male leaders lacked a pedagogic interest and affiliation but saw merit in the business of all-black female organizations. Joining the Uncle Tom's Cabin Company in 1896 was Levy Payne's Female Band. In 1910 Indianapolis's Pekin Theatre Orchestra trombonist/arranger George Bailey organized and directed the city's Female Brass Band. Composer/conductor/violinist Will Marion Cook fronted a ladies' orchestra that performed at Harlem's Lafayette Theatre in 1919.

Drummer Sylvester Rice organized and directed the Harlem Playgirls "hot band" in 1935. He also briefly directed the popular mid-'30s Dixie Sweethearts. Guitarist/arranger/composer Eddie Durham in the early '40s led The Eddie Durham All-Girl Band

and for a brief period directed The International Sweethearts of
Rhythm. Also serving as musical directors (and arrangers) with
the latter group were Maurice King and Jesse Stone. James Polite
was the male musical mainstay behind the Swinging Rays of
Rhythm. Booking agents worked out of Piney Woods, Mississippi; Minneapolis and St. Paul, Minnesota; Washington, D.C.;
and New York City, but the groups filled engagements throughout the country.

New York City's Gaston O. Sanders announced in early November 1939 that he would

> begin rehearsal . . . of a girls' orchestra within a few days . . . The
> orchestra, and all-symphonic combination, will be booked for ap-
> pearances in Harlem and on Broadway during the season.

Sanders would serve as supervisor and musical director, assisted
by the prominent local cellist Marion Cumbo, violinist Raymond
LeMieux, and concert harpist Gertrude Peterson, all black. The
project would be supported by the Metropolitan Music Society
("Begin Rehearsal for New York Girls' Ork," *Chicago Defender*,
November 4, 1939, p. 21).

J. T. Hailstalk led a girls' drum and bugle corps in New York
City, affiliated with Post 398 of the American Legion. This Harlem Rhythm Girls' Corps, made up primarily of teenagers, attracted widespread attention in the early 1940s. At the same time,
Earl D. Clenendon organized St. Paul, Minnesota's Sepian Lassies
of Harmony, a group that specialized in music "from spirituals to
swing." This novel string orchestra was composed of mandolins,
mandolas, mandocellos, and Hawaiian and Spanish guitars,
played by "race girls" all under sixteen years of age.

Donald E. Thornton, a janitor and bricklayer, was organizer of
The Thornton Sisters' Combo, known as the Thornettes, in Long
Branch, New Jersey. Comprised of Thornton's six daughters, the
group began performing professionally in 1955, shortly after an
appearance on Ted Mack's "Amateur Hour." According to Georgia Dullea:

> Every weekend, from kindergarten on through professional school,
> the Thornton Sisters hit the road in their big white van. Behind
> the wheel was Mr. Thornton, also the acoustical engineer, also the

manager. Mrs. Thornton [the wife and mother], who played bass, did double duty as wardrobe mistress ["Janitor Who Dreamed That His Daughters Would Be Doctors," *New York Times*, June 20, 1977, p. 22].

The group last appeared professionally in the mid-'70s, by which time five of the jazz/rhythm 'n' blues/rock performers were all medical or paramedical professionals. As Rita Thornton wrote, "Music was not to be our life's work, rather, a means of financing our education" (Personal Data Sheet—July 1977). For more on the Thornton family, see Yvonne S. Thornton, *The Ditchdiggers Daughters* (New York: Carol Publishing Group, 1995).

Female Leaders and Orchestras: 1880–1920s

Through the years black women have been supervising and guiding the proceedings of various musical aggregations. They have been musical pacesetters for all-male, all-female, sexually integrated, and, in more recent years, racially integrated ensembles (with the exception of the mid-1940s integrated International Sweethearts of Rhythm). Let us follow their individual musical activities and that of their groups chronologically.

Cornetist Viola Allen fronted East Saginaw, Michigan's, sixteen-piece Colored Female Brass Band in the late 1880s. Pianist/organist Hallie L. Anderson (b. January 5, 1885, Lynchburg, Virginia / d. November 9, 1927, New York City) alerted the community to the availability of her orchestras regularly in the *New York Age* in the first years of the twentieth century. Anderson offered New York City and environs "orchestras for all occasions." Festival, picnic, dance, and riverboat orchestras were probably male and/or male-female staffed, but she offered her ladies' orchestra for a 1906 Ladies Day Celebration at Hamilton Street Church in Albany, New York. Hallie Anderson always wielded the baton.

A member of Lafayette Theatre in Harlem's house staff, she led a five-piece male orchestra there in 1914. In the late teens and early '20s she served as organist at Harlem's Douglas Theatre, but turned up again as leader of the "lady band" playing at the Lafayette in 1919. Performing in the nation's capital between 1910

and 1920 was the Corda Club, a thirty-member ladies string orchestra. The group was founded and led by music educator Gre-
goria Fraser Goins (McGinty, p. 428). At Barron's Astoria Cafe,
also in Harlem, Ethel Hill led the Hill Astoria Ladies' Orchestra.
A 1914 advertisement labeled the cafe as "The Handsomest Ren-
dezvous of the Elite" and the orchestra as "Performers of that
'Real' Music."

The Lafayette Theatre conducting starlet was trombonist Marie
Lucas. Her affiliation with the theater began in early 1914. On
November 26 of that year the theater announced: "A bill of unusual excellence will be presented next week, . . . which will include Europe's Ladies Orchestra" (presumably James Reese
Europe, who may have provided the Personnel). It was announced the following week that the orchestra was under the direction of Marie Lucas.

The New York Age reported on January 14, 1915:

> At the Lafayette Theatre this week, a female orchestra, under the
> direction of Marie Lucas, is winning unstinted applause at each per-
> formance, and although not occupying a spot on the regular vaude-
> ville bill, the female musicians are engaged in a friendly rivalry
> with the acts for public approval.

In mid-May of the same year the *New York Age* reported:

> Marie Lucas, leader of the Lafayette Theatre Orchestra, distin-
> guished herself Tuesday evening by conducting the orchestra in the
> absence of the Smart Set Company's regular director, who was
> compelled to leave the city. Miss Lucas had never gone through the
> score of "His Excellency the President," prior to Tuesday evening.

In 1916 the same paper reported:

> Marie Lucas and her girls are playing as though inspired this week,
> and it is to be observed that the work of the orchestra calls for as
> much appreciation as the work on the stage. . . . The Ladies' Orches-
> tra is presenting some well-selected programs, classical and popu-
> lar selections being judiciously intermingled [November 2 and 16].

We will return to Marie Lucas later in this chapter.

Around 1915 violinist Mildred Gassaway Franklin directed

New York City's Martin-Smith School Ladies' Staff Orchestra. She led a ladies' orchestra at the Lafayette Theatre in 1919. Around the same time (1915–20), Madam Corilla Rochon, pianist, was leading a ladies' Symphony Orchestra in Houston, Texas. In this orchestra was the teenager E. Jessie Covington (Dent), later a recognized concert pianist, and her mother, Mrs. B. J. Covington, both on violin.

Though we recognize the danger of categorizing in terms of "first," we report journalist Grace Lucas-Thompson's statement that appeared in the *Indianapolis Freeman,* January 30, 1915:

> Miss May Moore was the first woman to start an orchestra at Cleveland, Ohio. Miss Moore is an accomplished pianist and usually has a violin, cornet and drum in the orchestra ["What Our Women Are Doing," p. 3].

In 1915 Chicago cornetist (and vocalist) Estella Harris was fronting The Harris Jass Band. A year later we discover that drummer Marian Pankey's Female Orchestra was "on the stroll" on the streets of Chicago. Around 1919 violinist Mae Brady fronted a ten-piece orchestra in Chicago, including clarinetist Buster Bailey and drummer Eddie Jackson. Pianist Lillian "Lil" Hardin Armstrong worked with Brady's group at the Dreamland Cafe in 1921. Though we are uncertain as to the specific dates of its existence, we speculate that the late 1910s or early 1920s is the time frame for the popular St. Suttles All Girl Jazz Band of Chicago.

In the early 1920s Washington D.C., pianist Gertie Wells led a band at one point made up of former members of The Eubie Blake Band. According to her husband, (guitarist) Elmer Snowden, "She was tearing up Washington and nobody could touch her band." Leading a small band in Norfolk, Virginia, in the early '20s was pianist Lil Jones. New Orleans pianist Dolly Marie Douroux Adams began leading her own group at about age sixteen (early '20s). The trumpet, violin, piano, and drum band played for about a year at the city's Othello Theatre.

Here let us recognize an important musical happening that took place in St. Louis, Missouri. Annie Turnbo Malone, of Poro Beauty Culture fame, was concerned with "enhancing the beauty of the Negro woman." This Lovejoy, Illinois, native opened her business in St. Louis, in 1902. She opened the million-dollar Poro College in 1918, training beauty operators and manufacturing beauty products to service black women throughout the United States. The three-story modern brick building that housed the College accommodated an auditorium that saw appearances of such outstanding black artists as Marian Anderson, Roland Hayes, Ethel Waters, and others. Annie Malone consecrated her program to

> dignity, grace, beauty, industry, thrift, efficiency, and goodliness—that these ideals be held aloft for the glorification of the women and girls of my race.

Culture and constructive use of one's leisure were major concerns. Early in the 1920s Malone personally organized a ladies' orchestra. Under the direction of Iola Cornelius, the group attracted national attention. Receiving front-page coverage in the *Norfolk Journal and Guide,* an article read:

> [I]t pays in dollars and cents, in increased efficiency and employee turnover to take more than a casual interest in their workers' leisure time and personal welfare. Poro College['s] . . . welfare program has been extensive, including a sick benefit association, rewards for special effort and progress and even a chapel service during the morning. . . . [T]he establishment of the Poro Girls' Orchestra was but another step to aid in the culture of the Poro family, and the promotion of the harmony in which they work together ["Poro College Ladies' Orchestra," May 2, 1925, p. 1].

Local people are uncertain as to how long the group existed, but the twenty-piece orchestra was still playing in 1927, at which time the "St. Louis musicians made a favourable impression" at Mother A. M. E. Zion Church, New York ("Poro Graduates Largest Class in Its History," *Norfolk Journal and Guide*," June 18, 1927, p. 5). Before leaving St. Louis, let us mention two theater orchestras of the same period that had as their leaders black women: the Star Theatre Orchestra, led by Birdie E. Doudy, and the Cornet Theatre Orchestra, led by Marie Harris Bradshaw.

A 1926 issue of the *Chicago Defender* provided a feature story on four black women band leaders in Chicago: Ida Mae Maples, Garvinia Dickerson, Lovie Austin, and Lottie Hightower, "all of whom [had] risen through their sheer grit and will to places of responsibility as leaders of outstanding organizations" (June 12, 1926, Music Section, p. 2).

Pianist Lovie Austin served as director of various theaters in the 1920s and '30s, the best known of which was the Monogram. According to the article, theater and vaudeville artists looked forward to their Chicago Theater engagements, "knowing well that their accomplishments [would] be well rendered." She also ranked with the best of the country's arrangers. Lovie Austin and Her Blues Serenaders specialized in backgrounds for blues singers Viola Bartlette, Edmonia Henderson, "Ma" Rainey, and Ida Cox. Her group was a popular backup for recording dates in the mid-'20s and included such veterans as clarinetist Johnny Dodds, cornetist Tommy Ladnier, and drummer Baby Dodds.

Lottie Hightower (b. Charleston, South Carolina, and educated at Boston Conservatory) led a popular Chicago group in the mid-'20s, which included her husband, trumpeter Willie Hightower. Lottie, the only female member, was a pianist. The group's banner displayed the label Lottie Hightower's Nighthawks Singing Orchestra. The 1928 edition of *The Official Theatrical World of Colored Artists the World Over* carried the name Hightower Nightingales. In a 1958 interview with jazz archivist William Russell, Willie and Lottie indicated that the group's real name was Lottie Hightower and Her Eudora Nighthawks Band. Lottie also held the position of financial secretary in Local 208 (Colored), American Federation of Musicians.

Pianist Ida Mae Maples led her own six-piece Melody Masters Orchestra, a group "much in demand" on the dance-academy circuit. According to the 1926 *Chicago Defender* article, Maples was a native of Paducah, Kentucky, and a product of the State University at Louisville (Kentucky) and Chicago Musical College.

Keyboardist Garvinia Dickerson served as leader of the seven-piece Gold Coast Syncopators, "favorites of Chicago's most exclusive social clubs and organizations." A native of Chicago, Dickerson received her training at the Chicago Musical College.

Irene Armstrong (Eadie/Wilson/Kitchings),[1] for a brief period Mrs. Teddy Wilson, was an active participant in the mid- and late 1930s South Side Chicago musical scene, as both pianist and orchestra leader. Her ensembles were generally all-male, but at one time included trumpeter Dolly Jones Hutchinson. At the same period, pianist Georgia Corham led a group called The Syncopators, also in the Windy City.

The most popular Chicago leader was pianist Lillian "Lil" Hardin Armstrong. In an interview with William Russell (July 1, 1959) Lil Armstrong stated that Tommy Rockwell of Columbia Records asked her to put together a band in the mid-'20s for the New Orleans Wanderers' recording sessions. She led a band at Chicago's Deluxe and Lorraine Gardens, which included trumpeter Freddie Keppard. It was her band (The Dreamland Syncopators) at the Dreamland that husband Louis joined following his stint with Fletcher Henderson. The band was called Lil's Hot Shots, recording for Brunswick and Odean. The group later became Louis Armstrong's Hot Five (1925 and '26). Musicians who worked with Lil were Manuel Perez (trumpet), Lorenzo Tio, Jr. (Clarinet), Kid Ory (trumpet), Johnny Dodds (clarinet), Johnny St. Cyr (guitar), and Baby Dodds (drums). Jazz historian Sally Placksin alerted us to the West Coast activities of pianist-leader Edythe Turnham in the 1920s and early 1930s (Spokane, Seattle, Tacoma, and Winnipeg, Canada). She and her Knights of Syncopation or Dixie Aces performed on the Orpheum and Pantages circuits and did club dates. She was leader of the staff bands at radio stations WFWB, WFOX, and KGFJ in Los Angeles (*American Women in Jazz*, pp. 47–49). Pianist Mary Lou Williams played with husband John Williams's band at the Pink Rose Ballroom, Memphis, Tennessee (1927). When he left, Mary Lou became the leader, during which time Jimmie Lunceford joined the band on alto saxophone. Offering a concert at the Washington, D.C., Metropolitan A.M.E. Church in the early 1920s was the Arabic Saxophone Band of Chicago, Illinois.

Madam E. M. Pratt, pianist, directed a "symphony" orchestra in Dallas, Texas, in the late 1920s. The group, primarily made up of young players, made its initial appearance in Fort Worth in 1929.

In New York City, also in the late 1920s (and early '30s), trombonist/violinist Della Sutton led her own ladies' band. In addition to the various school and federal-project instrumental groups that Isabele Taliaferro Spiller directed, she led The Women's Excelsior Temple Band. Rose Johnson made her debut in the "band leading" business in 1927, in Omaha, Nebraska. She was still creating a local sensation in the early 1940s.

Female Leaders and Orchestras: 1930s

Numerous black female musical activities took place in the early '30s. This is the period in which singer/dancer Blanche Calloway began her lengthy reign. This is the period in which Texas-born Victoria Spivey (vocal, piano, organ, and ukulele) began her own lengthy reign, directing Lloyd Hunter's Serenaders and Jap Allen's Cotton Pickers.

Tennessee-born trumpeter/vocalist Valaida Snow led Pike Davis's Continental Orchestra for Lew Leslie's *Rhapsody in Black*. Lil Armstrong directed her own all-girl orchestra. Records indicate that the group appeared at New York City's Lafayette Theatre in 1932 and the city's Apollo Theatre and Chicago's Regal Theatre in 1934. Known members of this group were Leora Meoux Henderson, trumpet; Alma Long Scott, tenor and alto saxophone; and Dolly Jones Hutchinson, trumpet. Trumpeter Leora Meoux Henderson fronted an all-female group known as The Vampires.

Cornetist Gertrude Irene Howard (Harrison), an N. Clark Smith protégée, directed the twenty-five-member Chicago Colored Women's Band in the early 1930s. Billie Bailey and Her Rhythm Girls were also active in the Chicago area. Creating a sensation in the windy city was cornetist/trumpeter Dolly Jones Hutchinson, leader of her Twelve Spirits of Rhythm. According to journalist Rob Roy,

The Savoy Ballroom drew our attention . . . last week for the reason . . . that we wanted to see what critics are finding to rave about in the work of Dolly Hutchinson. . . . She has an orchestra that features jazz à la Earl Hines and . . . ranks well with anything the ballroom has had in recent months. . . . They sing, play and cut up a religious fervor. . . . New Yorkers have been talking about their [Valaida] Snows, Blanche Calloways and others—but now Dolly Hutchinson is Chicago's own female maestro of Jazz ["Dolly Hutchinson's Band, Chicago's Latest Acclaim." *Chicago Defender*, July 30, 1932, p. 5].

It was with her mother Alma Long Scott's American Creolians Orchestra (all-girl) that pianist Hazel Scott made her ensemble debut at age fourteen. The New York-based group traveled throughout the East Coast and Caribbean in the early and mid-

1930s. Trumpeter Jonah Jones, reflecting on the early years of Jimmie Lunceford's Band, recalled for jazz historian Stanley Dance, "We had a chance to come down to New York [from Buffalo] and try out for a job, but we missed it because a girl called Cora La-Redd [primarily a vocalist] had a band they liked better." As the singing Mills Brothers were beginning their climb to world fame, sister Pauline Mills was making her mark as a conductor of a ten-piece orchestra in Cincinnati, Ohio.

Black female orchestral leadership and total black female organization continued throughout the decade. Pianist Jeri Smith led a dance band throughout the state of New Jersey. Pianist Cleo Brown fronted several small groups at Chicago's Three Deuces and Silver Frolics.

Appearing throughout the Pittsburgh, Pennsylvania, area was pianist Gertrude Long and Her Rambling Night Hawks. The *Pittsburgh Courier* reported:

> The greatest crowd in the history of the Monongahela went out to Olympia Park Tuesday midnight for the midnight-to-dawn "battle of music," featuring Bill Mears and his Sunset Royal Entertainers . . . and Gertrude Long and Her Rambling Night Hawks [July 7, 1934].

The group appeared regularly on radio station WWSW and was a favorite among local residents. Duke Ellington indicated in 1934 that the band was then "ready for the big time," but apparently its activities were confined to the Pittsburgh area and its monetary rewards sufficient.

According to a *Chicago Defender* report, Jean Calloway (no relation to Cab or Blanche) and her sensational band "echo[ed] through the southland on a successful trip in the states of Georgia, North and South Carolina" (June 1, 1935). Better known in the mid-1930s were the cross-country activities of The Harlem Playgirls and The Dixie Sweethearts. Leading the former were Mayme Lacy and Babe Briscoe, and the latter, Edna "Edie" Crump and Lela Julius. Also associated with The Dixie Sweethearts as fronts were Marjorie Ross and Madge Fontaine. Tenor/ baritone saxophonist Lorraine Brown (Guilford) fronted the eighteen-piece Darlings of Rhythm, but one of several spin-off groups from The Harlem Playgirls and The Dixie Sweethearts.

In 1935, Lil Armstrong led a band made up primarily of the personnel of violinist Stuff Smith's band, including trumpeter Jonah Jones. Her 1935 and '36 "big bands" played residences in Detroit, Buffalo, and other large cities. Recordings with Lil as leader (and pianist) included: "Lil Armstrong and Her Swing Band," Decca and Brunswick, 1937; and "Lil Armstrong and Her Orchestra," Decca, 1938.

Chicago pianist Mrs. Roberts Campbell fronted a band in the mid-and late '30s. Fronting an all-girl orchestra (carrying her name), also in Chicago, was Annie Harris. Selma (Alabama)-born and Detroit-educated Nora Lee King fronted her Rhythm Dandies for regularly scheduled Sunday afternoon intermission appearances at New York City's 1939 hockey games at Madison Square Garden. Under the caption "Heads Coast Band" the *Chicago Defender* announced in 1939 that pianist/singer Nellie Lutcher was leading the band playing nightly aboard the S.S. *Texas,* "the palatial pleasure ship that rides at anchor in Santa Monica Bay" (September 2, p. 21).

Directing the orchestra at Straight College in New Orleans, Louisiana, was M. C. Bigney. In late 1930, soliciting more members, the student newspaper raised this question, "Do you want Straight College to be well represented by an orchestra as she is in scholarship, athletics, and dramatics?" ("Music," *The Crimson Courier,* October 1930, p. 2). Leading the orchestra at New Orleans University in the same city during the late 1920s was Marion Dozier (Walker), popular piano instructor and mother of the noted author Margaret Walker (Alexander).

Popular singers' names have frequently been used to publicize an instrumental group. Such was the case with Mamie Smith and Her Jazz Hounds, Lucille Hegamin and Her Blue Flame Syncopators, "Ma" Rainey and Her Georgia Band and Her Tub Jug Washboard Band, Sara Martin and Her Jazz Fools; Ida Cox and Her Five Blue Spells, Lillyn Brown and Her Jazz Bo Syncopators, Ethel Waters and Her Jazz Masters and Her Ebony Four, and Billie Holiday and Her Orchestra. In each case the "name" fronted the group more than the musical personality.

An exception would be Ella Fitzgerald, who led the band of her "discoverer" Chick Webb for a period after his death in 1939, before taking off on her own. "Queen of Jazz Vocalists" Fitzgerald merits recognition as a "genuine" band leader if for no other reason than the players and the industry respected her as such.

According to jazz journalist George T. Simon,

> [She] came into the band in mid-1935. When she wasn't singing . . .
> she would usually stand at the side of the band, and as the various
> sections blew their ensemble phrases, she'd be up there singing
> along with all of them, often gesturing with her hands as though
> she were leading the band. . . . Ella's value to the band was tremen-
> dous. The guy's loved her; she loved the guys. . . . [Following
> Webb's death] [t]he band stayed pretty much intact for several years
> thereafter. Ella fronted it and two saxists . . . acted as musical direc-
> tors [Simon, *The Big Bands*, p. 442].

Female Leaders and Orchestras:
1940s, "The Golden Age of Black Female Involvement"

New York concert violinist Gertrude Eloise Martin served as conductor of the twenty-five-piece orchestra for Lew Leslie's 1939–40
version of *Blackbirds*. According to the *Chicago Defender*, "America's No. 1 Swingheart, Nina Mae McKinney, vivacious star of
stage and screen [(*Hallelujah*] and her orchestra, are all set for that
debut" (Yates, "Nina Mae in Debut," December 23, 1939, p. 21).
The group opened on December 28, at Columbia, South Carolina.
McKinney's tenure, however, was brief, for in early April 1940 it
was announced that she would return to New York City to star
in the World's Fair production of *Gay New Orleans*.

In 1940 pianist Una Mae Carlisle recorded with Her Jam Band,
including Benny Carter on trumpet, Slam Stewart on bass, and
Zutty Singleton on drums. In the same year, Gwendolyn More-
land fronted an all-male band in Toledo, Ohio. Georgia-born ac-
cordionist/vocalist Edith Curry fronted her Gentlemen of Swing
on a tour of one-nighters in her native state. The following year
she "invaded" Cleveland, and was billed as "America's Queen of
Swing." Louisiana native Bernice Rouse (Knighten) fronted Chicago's Paradise Syncopators.

In 1941 Joan Lunceford ("The Brown Bombshell") and Her
Dukes of Rhythm filled a lengthy assignment at New Orleans's
Rhythm Club. Violinist Angel Creasy, formerly with the song-
and-dance trio Three Little Words, announced that she would organize her own sixteen-piece swing band in New York City. Baby

Calloway and Her Rockin' Rhythm Orchestra were active in her native area of Tulsa, Oklahoma.

Pianist Mary Lou Williams led a six-piece band in the early '40s, with second husband Harold "Shorty" Baker on trumpet and Art Blakey on drums. For Decca she recorded under the name "May Lou Williams and Her Kansas City Seven" and for Varsity, "Six Men and a Girl." In 1946 she was one of five women—the others were nonblack—assembled for a recording date. This session has been preserved on a Stash recording ("Women in Jazz: All-Women Groups," ST-111), issued in 1978. The session included, in addition to Mary Lou, vibist Marjorie Hyams, guitarist Mary Osborne, bassist June Rotenberg, and drummer Rose Gottesman.

Returning to the early '40s, let us note that trumpeter Valaida Snow fronted The Sunset Royal Band at the Apollo Theatre. One critic wrote, "[The] boys carry the trademark of good musicianship which they probably get from their leader" (*Chicago Defender*, May 9, 1943). Alto saxophonist Irene Folks fronted a calypso group in and around New York City.

A 1940 recording carries the name of "Lil Armstrong's Dixielanders" and a 1945 recording carries the name "Lil 'Brown Gal' Armstrong and Her All Star Band," both Decca. Veteran of show business, pianist Julia Lee recorded with Her Boy Friends for Capitol Records in 1946 (Hollywood). In the early and mid-'40s Detroit harpist Clara Young Walker trained and directed an all-girl aggregation called The Coleridge-Taylor Harp (and Vocal) Ensemble. Pianist Camille Howard fronted a trio in Washington, D.C., appearing frequently at the Howard Theatre. Though few details are available, we can be certain that Anna Ray Moore led an orchestra in the 1940s. The group was managed by Orchestra Service of America, which was based in Houston, Texas.

The 1940s were the years in which the world came to know that black women were capable of orchestral participation, in terms of organization, membership and leadership. It was the decade when The International Sweetheart's of Rhythm were at their peak.

Of all the ladies' orchestras The International Sweethearts of Rhythm enjoyed the longest existence (c. 1937–48)[2] and acquired the most extensive recognition. It is appropriate then that we recognize this group, discuss its origin, and follow a few of its many activities.

Upon the retirement of Consuella Carter (b. April 16, 1902, Haynesville, Alabama; d. January 22, 1989, Clarksdale, Mississippi) in 1976 from Coahoma Junior College and Agricultural High School in Clarksdale, Mississippi, the institution's president wrote, "Your bands have been a reflection of your dynamic personality, your versatility and your love of excellence." The Coahoma County Teachers Association presented a plaque that read, "To Miss Consuella Carter who has been a Golden Ray of Light through the dark and lonely days in the birth of education in Mississippi." This genesis related to music as well.

Consuella's initiation into the business of band building and direction took place at Piney Woods Country Life School in Piney Woods, Mississippi, twenty-one miles southeast of Jackson, the state's capital. This was the school that provided Carter with an elementary and secondary education,[3] the school that encouraged female instrumentalists, and the school that granted Carter's first opportunity to test her band-building capabilities. Also tested was her ability to learn and teach every instrument in the orchestra.

Prior to Carter's initiatives Annie B. White (known as "Baby" White) made a significant contribution at the institution. According to the *Chicago Defender*, she was a composer, arranger, pianist, and guitarist and studied saxophone and trumpet with Jimmie Lunceford (July 1, 1939, p. 21).

At Piney Woods Country Life School "no one willing to better his or her condition in life" was ever turned away. The doors were open to the materially impoverished, the social misfits, the lame and the blind, as well as the more affluent applicant. Piney Woods was built on the personality and convictions of its 1909 founder, Laurence C. Jones,[4] who stressed the training of youth to use their head, heart, and hands. It was a "work your way through" situation, with stress on vocational education. One's work assignment might well have been in the music department.

Following in the tradition of Fisk, Hampton, and Tuskegee universities sending out musical messengers of goodwill and publicity, Dr. Jones began sending to all parts of the country various small vocal groups called The Cotton Blossoms early in the 1920s. As the financial needs and enrollment increased (and resources diminished) in the 1930s Jones began sending out more and more vocal groups. He also noted the great public response to the Hormel, Phil Spitalny, and Ina Ray Hutton all-girl, all-white orchestras. Jones then conceived the idea of glorifying "the girls of tan and brown" orchestrally.

As a *Chicago Defender* journalist wrote:

> For the band, Indian, Mexican, Chinese and Race girls were secured. Their native heritages—emotions, rhythmic sense and musical tendencies—found natural expression in swing music. As a result, they produced a new type of dance music, the "International" style ["Sweethearts of Rhythm," June 22, 1940, p. 20].

Consuella Carter, then Piney Woods's Band Director, had laid the musical foundation. A former Cotton Blossom singer and a dancer, she supplemented the girl's instrumental bandsmanship with vocal and dancing techniques. According to Consuella:

> All of the girls I had in the band could dance and play well. As the final concert every year, we had band music, floor shows and jokes. It was just like what you see in the movies [correspondence with the author, August 31, 1977].

A nationally competitive outfit was evident as early as 1937. Dr. Jones was convinced that this group should become the school's principal "traveling messenger." Organizer/promoter/director-general Jones sent to Iowa for Edna Williams, who took over as the fifteen-piece touring group's musical director. Trumpet player Williams was referred to as "the female Satchmo," was a respected accordion player, and was fully capable of "filling in" on any instrument in the band.

The girls' ages ranged from fourteen to nineteen, including high school enrollees and those from the school's junior college. Senstitive to the girls' youth, Jones secured the services of Nebraska-born Rae Lee Jones to act as chaperone and director of singing.

The year 1939 found the group appearing at dances, fundraisng events, conventions, winter resorts, and all-day frolics as far removed from Piney Woods as Florida and Texas. During the winter of 1940 the group completed a successful nationwide tour that carried it as far away as California. Laurence C. Jones remained the guiding hand and frequently appeared on the same bill, talking about Piney Woods and keeping the group on its mission of school publicity and fund raising.

The "girl music-makers" traveled via their own luxury liner, an ultramodern bus, fully equipped with pullman beds for the Sweethearts, chaperone, and driver; dressing and makeup rooms; bath and kitchenette; three clothes closets; storage area for instruments; and practice piano. A portable school was established, with Vivian C. Crawford (from Ohio) serving as instructor.

The fourteen-to-sixteen-piece orhestra made its theatrical debut at the Howard Theatre in Washington, D.C., during the late summer of 1940. So successful was its performance that a contract for a week's engagement at New York City's famed Apollo Theatre was instantly issued and signed. In August 1940 The International Sweethearts of Rhythm was one of thirty bands participating in the large-band division contest sponsored by *Swing* magazine and staged at the New York City World's Fair. The swingcopating group from Piney Woods placed third.

Much publicity followed: "a package of music wrapped in the cellophane of loveliness"; "no hotter bunch ever tooted a horn or beat a drum"; "the best playing, finest looking bunch ever to grace the stage or a cafe bandstand." Promoters and booking agents rated the swingerettes as "one of the nation's best draws—a sweetheart for the box office." Top prices prevailed. The group's September 1940 itinerary included Fredericksburg, Virginia (16th); Frederick, Maryland (17th); Alexandria, Va. (18th); Emporia, Va. (19th); Petersburg, Va. (20th); Martinsville, Va. (23rd); Statesville, North Carolina (24th); Charlotte, N.C. (25th); and Columbia, South Carolina (27th)—nine concerts in eleven days.

In early April 1941 the group severed its relationship with Piney Woods Country Life School and Laurence C. Jones. Amusement Enterprises in Washington, D.C., now had the booking rights. With sufficient verification from several of the original members and the original leader, we see merit in citing the following:

[W]hen announcement was made that an all-girl jazz band from Piney Woods (Mississippi) School was touring the nation's dance halls to raise money for that institution, we envisaged two problems. First: Whether the chaperonage was adequate and whether dance halls were the proper locale for a girl's activity which would aid a school. Second: How much these tours would interfere with studies. . . . [O]ur queries were justified. Eighteen girls of Piney Woods School band quit the school, took the school bus and, pursued by highway police, fled through seven States to Washington and freedom. . . .

Reason for their flight: they learned that eight of their members, who had been traveling for three years, would not graduate. Playing dance dates and sending funds back to the school had not taken the place of studying lessons. . . . Piney Woods School learns too late that jazz bands and studies do not mix. It is an experiment experienced educators do not make [McCarthy, "A Jazz Band Flees." *The Afro-American*, May 3, 1941, p. 13].

Dr. Jones would not be outdone. On April 17, 1941, he announced that on May 9, 1941, he would

for the first time in Mississippi history . . . bring the entire department of music [from] Piney Woods . . . to Jackson [Mississippi]. Swing bands will be there. . . . Then will be heard the Orange Blossoms, Magnolia Blossoms, and Cotton Blossoms ["Piney Woods to Present School Bands." *Pittsburgh Courier*, April 19, 1941, p. 23].

On the same day, it was announced from Washington, D.C., that

the girls [The International Sweethearts of Rhythm] are now on their own, . . . and are busy rehearsing in order to fill the big-time contracts which they have tucked under their wings ["17-Girl Band Which Quit School at Piney Woods, Rehearses for Big Time," *Pittsburgh Courier*, April 19, 1941, p. 21].

In late May 1941 theatrical editor Billy Rowe wrote the following for the *Pittsburgh Courier:*

The center of much controversy since leaving their home ground. . . . the girls are . . . dreaming dreams of big times. . . . In hopes of starting out on the best note, $30,000 has been spent to tighten up the loose ends that are usually found in aggregations mastered by women. . . . [U]pwards of ten-thousand dollars has been spent to house the girls. . . . The new home [in Arlington, Virginia] is a ten-room affair with recreation facilities and two bedrooms arranged dormitory style.

Continued Rowe:

> Since leaving school, the band has been incorporated, making each
> member a co-owner. . . . [T]he band rehearses six hours each day.
> . . . [Y]ou can hear them as individuals rehearsing all over the place,
> their music . . . echoing for miles around. But noboby ever kicks as
> the girls' coming to Arlington is considered as somewhat of an
> event by the plain folks living around them, for they feel that at last
> this city will be made famous by the living instead of the dead, who
> thru the years have fertilized its soil ["All Girl Orchestra Is Getting
> Prepared to Crash the Big Time," *Pittsburg Courier,* May 31, 1941, p.
> 20].

By June 1942 "the darlings of swing" were booked solid
through North and South Carolina, New Jersey, and Pennsylvania. From Omaha, Nebraska, had come singer Anna Mae Winburn to front the band. In October 1942 the group's one-week
engagement at Chicago's Regal Theatre broke all attendance records, exceeding those previously held by Count Basie and Louis
Armstrong.

By early 1943 "the group from Washington, D.C.," was in the
"big times"; the association of music directors and arrangers
Eddie Durham, Jesse Stone, and Maurice King had begun. Trade
magazines and local newspapers spoke of them in the same con-
text as bands fronted by Duke Ellington, Count Basie, Earl Hines,
Andy Kirk, Louis Armstrong, Fletcher Henderson, Erskine
Hawkins, and others.

Many new faces were added to the Sweethearts' roster, including those of several whites. During the course of its eleven-year
existence the group traveled to Mexico, Canada, France, Germany, and almost every state in the Union. Its decline might be
attributed to several causes, uppermost being "changing times
and changing interests." Other causes that have been advanced
are 1) the loss of members to marriage and no interested replace-
ments, 2) the failing health of chaperone/teacher/leader/man-
ager Rae Lee Jones, and 3) the desire of key members to establish
their own groups.

It was in early April 1941 that The International Sweethearts of
Rhythm and Piney Woods Country Life School "parted ways." In
January 1941 Laurence C. Jones, in an exclusive interview with a
Chicago Defender representative, had talked about The Swinging

Rays of Rhythm, which was originally the training group for the Sweethearts—when the latter group defected, the former group became its replacement.

> It's the largest "all-girl" sepia dance band in the world. The Rays have seventeen girls—a saxophone sextet . . . [and] a brass sextet. . . . The most versatile group of girls of the day. . . . All of the Rays are versatile and full of their music. They are still happy little sepia junior debs, growing and developing in a school atmosphere and already called the greatest of all girl bands [" 'Swinging Rays of Rhythm' Is Newest, Hottest Band on Tour," *Chicago Defender*, January 21, 1941, p. 20].

In August 1941 The Swinging Rays of Rhythm served as guest artists for a National Association of Colored Women's meeting in Oklahoma City. In November 1941 the group appeared at the Dallas State Fair. The Earl Hines Band was touring the same area, and Dr. Jones managed to have the group photographed with the keyboard whiz himself. A few months later Earl Hines visited with the band at Piney Woods and while on the scene, reportedly rehearsed the group. Instruction and arrangements for the all-girl group were provided to male students Laurence C. Jones, Jr. (trumpet/piano), James Polite (saxophone) and Leon Span (bass). Polite was the principal leader and coach. Fronting the group was Nina de la Cruz.

In a 1941 "Band of the Year" Contest, sponsored by the *Chicago Defender*, twenty-seven band names were submitted. Sixteenth was The Swinging Rays of Rhythm, in advance of Tiny Bradshaw, Coleman Hawkins, Lucky Millender, Earl Hines, Claude Hopkins, and others.

In February 1942 it was announced that the number of members would be increased to twenty-eight and the concept would be that of "symphonic swing." In April 1942 it was announced that the Rays had been divided into two groups, "because of the wide-spread demand for the girl's band." The senior group would be under the direction of Thelma Perkins and Myrtle Polite and the junior group, under the direction of Ione and Irene Grisham and Afro-British musician Yvonne Plummer (Terrelongue). All except Plummer were Piney Woods students.

Just when Jones's Swinging Rays of Rhythm were phased out

has not been determined. What has been determined is that Piney Woods Country Life School (and Laurence C. Jones) had a second all-girl's swing band that traveled extensively and was well respected in musical circles, but never achieved the status of Piney Woods's original instrumental group, The International Sweethearts of Rhythm.

Following her early- and mid-'40s membership in The Swinging Rays of Rhythm and The International Sweethearts of Rhythm saxophonist Myrtle Young formed a five-piece group called The Rays. The group was extremely popular in Baltimore and was featured in a 1954 *Our World* article entitled "They Make Music in Baltimore." In the late 1980s Young was still a "union card holder" and musically active in Philadelphia.

Former Sweethearts saxophonist Viola (Vi) Burnside led an orchestra, active in the early and mid-'50s. Its activities were frequently reported in the *International Musicians' Monthly* section entitled "Where They Are Playing." Former Sweethearts bassist Edna Smith fronted a trio that worked out of New York City for about four years. The press referred to Smith, who also played trombone and guitar, as "Miss Calypso." Other members of the group were Carline Ray (Russell) on piano and Pauline Braddy on drums, both Sweethearts veterans.

Beginning in the late '40s popular Pittsburgh pianist/organist Ruby Young[5] led a trio (first piano/saxophone/drums; then organ/trumpet/guitar) carrying her name. The group played at Pittsburgh's select lounges exclusively, with only one out-of-state engagement (upstate New York). According to a still-active Ruby in the late '70s,

> I was always fortunate to make a very good living in my profession here in Pittsburgh, therefore I did very little traveling to other cities, even though I had many offers [correspondence February 3, 1978].

According to a 1950 *Our World* article entitled "Boss Lady," "Lady bass players and band leaders are a rarity, but Lucille [Dixon] takes it all in stride." A 1949 *Chicago Defender* caption to a photograph read,

> LUCILLE DIXON, attractive leader and stellar performer on the bass, is leading her all-male star sextette at the Club Savannah, in

New York. Direct from an eight-month engagement at the 845 Club in New York City, Lucille Dixon is now in her seventh month at the Club Savannah [April 23, 1949, p. 25].

A reflective Lucille Dixon stated in 1975,

> The Lucille Dixon Orchestra was in full operation close to fourteen years, from 1946 to 1960. Some of the musicians who played in my band were Tyree Glenn and George Matthews, trombone; Taft Jordan, trumpet; Buddy Tate, saxophone; Sonny Payne and Bill Smith, drums. These guys were some of the best in the business and the only reason I was able to get them was because they were black. . . . Had they been white musicians, they could have found excellent jobs because they were so highly qualified [Handy, "Conversation with Lucille Dixon," *Black Perspective in Music,* Fall 1975, pp. 303–304].

Female Leaders and Orchestras: 1950s–1970s

The 1950s brought some conducting recognition to composer Julia Amanda Perry (1924–79), who frequently stated that conducting was her most rewarding performing medium. "Elite art" composer Perry received her conducting training at Westminster College and the Accademia Chigiana in Siena, Italy, and utilized her skills primarily in the performance of her own instrumental and vocal works. In 1957 she conducted a series of concerts in Europe, under the auspices of the U.S. Information Service.

Pianist Beryl Booker began leading a tremendously popular "all-girl jazz trio" in 1953, including bassist Bonnie Wetzel and drummer Elaine Leighton, both white. This group went abroad with the Jazz Club U.S.A. Show in 1954. In 1955 there appeared on Ted Mack's "Amateur Hour" The Thornton Sisters, a six-piece combo from New Jersey. This was followed by appearances at New York City's famed Apollo Theatre. Then followed two decades of weekend appearances at various Ivy League colleges. Additionally, the group worked as a backup group for varying East Coast rhythm 'n' blues concerts ("Janitor and His Six Daughters Prove 'We Can.' " *Ebony,* September 1977, pp. 33–42).

Several veteran New Orleans pianists began leading groups in the 1960s. The Dolly Adams Band, including three of Dolly's sons, played for the city's Creole Spring Fiesta Ball, May 1966. The 1960 popularity of Emma Barrett ("Sweet Emma the Bell Gall") made it commercially feasible to center a group of New Orleans traditionalists around her name. Lady Charlotte's Men of Rhythm came into existence in 1965. Olivia Charlotte Cook said of her role with this much-sought-after New Orleans group, "I've been leading my own combo for the last twelve years. When I say leading, I mean just that—no smoking and drinking on the band stand" (correspondence with the author, June 30, 1977).

Pianist Daphne Weekes ("Queen of Calypso and Rock and Roll") and Her Caribbean Versatile Orchestra were active in New York City throughout the 1970s. The sexually mixed group specialized in Caribbean and Latin music. Leading a quintet in the late '70s, also in New York City, was pianist/composer Dona Summers. The Peace Makers' leader described the group's music as "contemporary acoustic jazz." Also in the jazz metropolis, during the same period, joint group leadership was assumed by two brass players, French hornist L. Sharon Freeman and trombonist Janice Robinson fronted a quartet (occasionally quintet) carrying the name of the group's two female leaders.

An outgrowth of chamber musicales held in cellist Carlotta Gary's New York City residence, a group carrying the name Mixtures began concert appearances in 1977. According to leader Gary, "The group is a multi-ethnic ensemble of outstanding instrumentalists, vocalists and dancers dedicated to integrating all art forms." Also in the late 1970s pianist/composer Amina Claudine Myers expanded her musical activities to include the five-piece (otherwise all-male) instrumental ensemble Amina and Company, working out of New York City. Fronting the seventeen-piece (primarily instrumental) "Big Apple Jazz Women" group performing at the 1979 Women's Jazz Festival in Kansas City was bassist Carline Ray.

The 1970s found harpist Ann Hobson leading the New England Harp Trio (flute, Lois Schaefer; cello, Carol Procter), composed of three Boston Symphony members. Guitarist/vocalist/composer Monnette Sudler Honesty fronted her own jazz quartet in Philadelphia. Violist J. Darlene Toliver brightened the Pittsburgh musical listening horizon with her freelance quartet Strings 'N' Things, "versed in jazz, classical, pop, improvisational and ethnic music for all occasions."

In the one-time jazz metropolis Chicago trumpeter Ernestine "Tiny" Davis fronted a three-piece ensemble, specializing in performances for senior citizens and hospital patients. Sitarist Shanta Nurullah fronted an eight-piece instrumental ensemble. While in her senior year at Livingston College (Salisbury, North Carolina), Portsmouth (Virginia)-native Jessie Jeanette Harris conducted the Salisbury Symphony Orchestra during its 1976 Young People's Concert.

On the West Coast accordionist Ida Guillory fronted Queen Ida's Bon Temps Zydeco[6] Band. A native of Lake Charles, Louisiana, she moved with her family first to Texas and then to San Francisco (1946), where the family remained. She drove a school bus while raising her family of three children. Then Ida Guillory was on the road, giving over two hundred concerts yearly. According to Guillory,

> I'm a missionary of Zydeco. I want to play this music in every country in the world. . . . When I started out with this music, it was virtually unknown outside the bayou of Louisiana. . . . Now Zydeco's nearly a household word. [Todd Klein, "Queen of the Road," *Philip Morris Magazine,* Winter 1988, pp. 10, 12].

She considered herself a spiritual descendant of the great female blues artists of the 1920s and 1930s.

In addition to the accordion (played by "Lady Fingers" Ida), the Bon Temps Zydeco Band included guitar, bass, drums and washboard, tambourine, and other miscellaneous percussion instruments played by Queen Ida's youngest son. Partially a family affair, her brother is featured on washboard and her husband is the road manager. She and the band have crossed the Atlantic more than a dozen times.

The band was featured at the 1976 Monterey Jazz Festival and the 1978 San Francisco Blues Festival. It is a regular at the New Orleans Jazz and Heritage Festival. Her many albums (selling between 15,000 and 25,000 copies) have received several Grammy nominations. She won the Grammy in 1983 for her album *Queen Ida and the Bon Temps Zydeco Band On Tour.*

The sensation of the early 1980s was Oklahoma native Linda Twine, conductor-pianist-composer-arranger. Since Twine worked as assistant conductor and pianist for Broadway musicals

The Wiz, Ain't Misbehavin', and *Bring Back Birdie*, it stands to reason that the incomparable Lena Horne engaged her to conduct
her sixteen-piece orchestra for the show *Lena Horne: The Lady and
Her Music*, both on Broadway and on the road (Ruthe Stein,
"Lena's Conductor," *Ebony*, December 1982, pp. 46–40). Fronting
her own group in Washington, D.C., was pianist Maria Rodri-
guez. Her personnel were all male.

   In early 1993, *Symphonium* alerted its readers to the fact that
Yvette Devereaux was the newly appointed conductor and music
director of the Southeast Symphony Orchestra in Los Angeles.
She was the first woman to hold this position in the community
orchestra's forty-five-year history. The first African-American
woman to receive a master of music degree in orchestral conducting from Peabody Conservatory, she immediately launched into
a Ph.D. program at UCLA. (See "Ms. Devereaux Gets California
Conducting Post," *Symphonium*, Winter 1993, p. 3.)

Profiles

MARIE LUCAS
conductor (trombone, piano)
b. c. 1880, Denver, Colorado; d. April 26, 1947, New York
   City (?)

The daughter of celebrated minstrel star Samuel Lucas enjoyed
an enviable reputation during her lifetime. She first appeared
with her father on a public concert in Boston, as a singer, in 1883.
Sam Lucas, "dean of the colored theatrical profession," secured
for his daughter the best musical instruction this country could
afford and sent her abroad to acquire the finishing touch.

   Dahl Thomas, first black manager of Harlem's Lafayette Theatre, remembered her as a fantastic musician and sensational performer. She led various groups, trained new members, performed
with the groups, and soloed with them. According to Thomas,
her affiliation with the Lafayette began around 1913 (telephone
conversation with the author, June 27, 1978). Veteran performer
Tom Fletcher remembered Marie in his publication *The Tom*

Fletcher Story: 100 Years of the Negro in Show Business (pp. 76–78), confirming the opinions of Dahl Thomas.

In January 1915 a ladies' orchestra under her direction was "installed as a permanent fixture to the house [Lafayette] by the management" (Lester A. Walton, "Theatrical Comment," *New York Age*, January 14, 1915). Soon after, advertisements circulated announcing Lucas' availability to teach and train "all young women with even a slight knowledge of music" for female theater orchestras in Boston, Baltimore, Philadelphia, and Washington, D.C. Female orchestras under her superb direction performed between the years 1915 and 1920.

Jazzmen Elmer Snowden and Duke Ellington wrote of her 1919–20 activities at D.C.'s Howard Theatre. According to Snowden,

> Marie Lucas's band [male] would come out into the pit, and she had sent down to Cuba or wherever it was [Ellington said Puerto Rico] and got all those musicians like Juan Tizol and Ralph Escudero and had enlarged her band. They would play the show, and we'd [Louis Thomas's Band] come back and play the intermission and exit music [Dance, *The World of Swing*, p. 47].

In his book *Music Is My Mistress* Ellington indicated that a group under Lucas's direction played the TOBA[7] circuit as well as the Howard Theatre. He indicated that the group was very impressive "because all the musicians doubled on different instruments, something that was extraordinary in those days" (p. 34).

One Marie Lucas was listed as a "composer and arranger" in *The Official Theatrical World of Colored Artists the World Over*, giving as her address the Lincoln Theater, Louisville, Kentucky. The last account that this writer was able to find of Marie Lucas's musical activity was in 1931, at which time the *Chicago Defender* reported, "Lucas of New York and Her Merry Makers are leaving a smoking trail for the gang who are behind her band . . ." ("Orchestras," January 3, 1931, p. 5).

BLANCHE DOROTHEA CALLOWAY (JONES)
conductor (singer, dancer)
b. 1903 (?), Baltimore / d. December 16, 1978, Baltimore

There was a period when Cab Calloway was known simply as "Blanche's younger brother." It was the older Calloway who assisted the younger in his show-business breakthrough, though she advised against it. Cab's book *Of Minnie the Moocher and Me* (1976) is dedicated to his wife and family and "sister Blanche who introduced me to the wonderful world of entertainment."

In the mid-1920s Blanche Calloway toured extensively with various traveling revues, as singer and dancer. She fronted Andy Kirk's band in 1931, for a residency at Philadelphia's Pearl Theatre. Subsequently she fronted her own bands. Records indicate that the Blanche Calloway Band (all-male) appeared at New York City's Lafayette Theatre ('31, '32, and '34), Harlem Opera House ('34 and '35), and Apollo Theatre ('35, '36, '37, '38, and '41).

Blanche's band once made a five-band tour with Bennie Moten, Andy Kirk, Chick Webb, and Zack Whythe's bands. Blanche Calloway and Her Joy Boys recorded extensively in 1931 (Victor) and again in 1934 and '35. Bands under her leadership played in all parts of the United States, including New York City, Baltimore, Boston, Atlantic City, Indianapolis, Cleveland, Cincinnati, St. Louis, Kansas City, and Pittsburgh. Playing under her direction were such jazz stalwarts as Cozy Cole (drums), Andy Jackson (guitar), Vic Dickenson (trombone), and Ben Webster (tenor saxophone).

A 1931 *Pittsburgh Courier* Band/Orchestral Survey listed thirty-eight "leading Negro Orchestras" nationally. Blanche's band (the only one led by a woman) ranked ninth, only five points less than Louis Armstrong and well in advance of bands fronted by Jimmie Lunceford, Chick Webb, Bennie Moten, Claude Hopkins, and several others that made jazz history.

In an article entitled "Dance Bands That Made History" (*International Musician*, October 1950), seven female orchestra leaders were singled out for recognition. Blanche Calloway, the only black, was included in the list. A 1932 *Pittsburgh Courier* article referred to Blanche as "one of the most progressive performers in the profession," acknowledging the ownership, management, and directorship of her then-popular band ("Blanche Calloway," January 16, 1932).

Calloway studied piano and voice with Llewelyn Wilson, prominent Baltimore music teacher and conductor of the Baltimore City Colored Chorus and Orchestra. She also attended Morgan State College.

She made a mid-1940 appearance with an all-girl orchestra at

Club Harlem in Atlantic City, New Jersey. But the success of this group and others failed. For a brief period she worked as a solo artist, then settled in Philadelphia and became active in community and political affairs. She later moved to Florida, where she served as executive director of Miami's radio station WMBM. Subsequently, she founded and served as president of Afram House, Inc., a firm specializing in cosmetics and cosmetic aids for blacks.

Calloway spent the last six years of her life in Baltimore. She was eulogized as the 1930s' and early '40s' "Queen of Swing"— "the leading female band leader rotating on the Chitterlin' Circuit, playing the Lafayette Theatre on 7th Avenue; the Apollo in Harlem; the Regal in Chicago; the Royal in Baltimore and the old Howard Theatre in Washington" ("Remembering Blanche Calloway," *Richmond Afro-American,* December 30, 1978, p. 19).

AVRIL GWENDOLEN COLERIDGE-TAYLOR
conductor (composer)
b. 1903, S. Norwood, England

The Etude, a prestigious musical publication (1883–1957), announced the following in 1939, under the headline "The Daughter of a Famous Father":

> One of the most noted English composers of the past century, Samuel Coleridge-Taylor (1875–1912), whose "Hiawatha's Wedding Feast" has been sung around the world, was of part African descent. . . . His daughter, Miss Averil [sic] Coleridge-Taylor, . . . is also an able conductor. *She is this year touring America and is scheduled to lead the Boston Symphony Orchestra* [*The Etude,* May 1939, p. 305; emphasis added].

This announcement justifies the inclusion of Avril Gwendolen Coleridge-Taylor and a review of her conducting career, though she was born in England and spent most of her life there.

At age twelve Avril won a scholarship for composition and pianoforte to the Trinity College of Music. She also studied violin and conducting with Albert Coates. She made her conducting debut in 1933, conducting The Band of H.M. Royal Marines, the only woman to enjoy this honor. Avril is one of the few women to have conducted the BBC Symphony Orchestra.

In memory of her father she organized the Coleridge-Taylor Symphony Orchestra in 1941. The group existed for a decade. In 1971 she organized the Malcolm Sargent Symphony Orchestra. Throughout her conducting career she appeared on symphony orchestra programs as conductor/composer, her most frequently performed work being the *Piano Concerto in F Minor*. Other conducting specialties were performances of her father's compositions and works by British composers.

She was often written about in the British press, and the comments were always laudatory: "a pioneer of women conductors"; "her conducting style is a model of grace and clarity"; "technical firmness and interpretive skill"; "a talent far above the average"; "strangely unfeminine"[!]. In the late 1970s Avril Gwendolen Coleridge-Taylor was still musically active, serving as curator of the Colt Clavier Collection in Kent, England.

ANNA MAE DARDEN WINBURN
conductor (guitar, vocals)
b. August 13, 1913, Port Royal, Tennessee

The International Sweethearts of Rhythm turned professional in April 1941. Joining the group soon thereafter was Anna Mae Winburn, who served as both leader and vocalist until the group's demise in 1948. She and her second husband (Duke Pilgrim) soon reorganized the band, continuing under the name of Anna Mae Winburn and Her Sweethearts of Rhythm.

Winburn was a seasoned performer when she joined the Sweethearts. Prior to completing high school (and one year into marriage) she won an amateur contest at the Isis Theatre in Kokomo, Indiana—at age sixteen. The prize presentation featured Winburn singing the popular tune "Little Joe from Chicago," accompanying herself on guitar.

There followed a brief period as vocalist on radio station WOW, Fort Wayne, Indiana. During the mid-1930s Winburn was associated with Frank Shelton "Red" Perkins's Dixie Ramblers and Lloyd Hunter's Serenaders, as vocalist and/or leader. Both bands worked out of Omaha, Nebraska. In the late '30s Winburn fronted the former Blue Devils of Oklahoma City, of which the most illustrious member was guitarist Charlie Christian. He left this band for New York City and Benny Goodman.

Winburn wrote:

> World War II came along, so I lost most of my musicians to the army and others to Fletcher and Horace Henderson's Bands. Jimmie Jewel, who owned the Dreamland Ball Room in Omaha, recommended me to The International Sweethearts of Rhythm, then ready to hit "the big times." I stayed with them until the death of the group's manager Rae Lee Jones. The reorganized Anna Mae Winburn and Her Sweethearts of Rhythm existed from 1950 until 1956, working out of New York City with Universal Attractions serving as the booking agency [correspondence with the author, April 8, 1980].

Though not one of the original Sweethearts, Anna Mae Winburn was one of fifteen Sweetheart honorees at the Third Annual Women's Jazz Festival, March 1980. The retired and widowed mother of four journeyed to Kansas City, Missouri, from her home in Louisville, Kentucky, still physically capable of fronting any band—with an abundance of charm, elegance, and style.

*JOYCE BROWN
conductor (pianist, composer, arranger)
b. December 1, 1920, New York City

Critics wrote of Joyce Brown that she was "the first black woman to conduct the opening of a Broadway musical." The date was March 15, 1970; the production was *Purlie*. Journalist John S. Wilson quotes Brown regarding the experience:

> The men in the orchestra respected my musicality. We communicated immediately. "I know what I'm doing," I told them, "and I'm sure you know what you're doing. Let's do it." There were never any problems [*International Musician*, December 1970, pp. 8, 24].

The daughter of West Indian parents (Montego Bay, Jamaica) and the oldest of six children, Brown's first instrumental involvement was with the family orchestra, playing classical and liturgical music. She started on the piano at age three and later began formal study of the violin, cello, trumpet, saxophone, organ, and voice. She studied at the New York College of Music, Columbia University Teachers College, and New York University.

Conducting experience came from the choir and various instrumental ensembles of Salem Methodist Church in New York City. From there she moved to the city's Latin Quarter, playing the piano, arranging, and conducting the nightclub's shows for eleven years. When the Latin Quarter closed she began traveling with Lou Walters Enterprises.

Brown's musical flexibility, thorough musicianship, and "no nonsense" approach led to a variety of experiences, serving as musical director for singers Napoleon Reed, Joyce Bryant, Norman Atkins, and Diahann Carroll and dancers Marge and Gower Champion. For a period she served on the staff of CBS. Other assignments included tour conductor for the musical *Bye Bye Birdie;* assistant conductor of the Broadway shows *Golden Boy, Hallelujah Baby,* and *How Green Was My Valley;* and musical director of the Alvin Ailey Ballet Company.

> MARGARET (Rosiezarian) HARRIS
> conductor (pianist, composer)
> b. September 15, 1943, Chicago

Margaret Harris made her debut as a pianist at age three. A Juilliard School of Music graduate (B.S. and M.S.), she made her Town Hall (New York City) debut in 1970 and subsequently appeared as piano soloist with the Great Neck Symphony and the Los Angeles Philharmonic, performing her own piano concerto with the latter. Included on her Town Hall debut recital was her own "Collage One." Of this composition she stated,

> It's how I feel as a black woman living in America. I may not be able to walk out tomorrow and say I'm going to play with the New York Philharmonic, but still I'm [not] giving up that passport. All colors of people have to live as one in a collage, otherwise we're going to destroy ourselves like the "gingham dog and the calico cat" [Mary Campbell, "A 'Hair' Raising Conductor," *News and Observer,* June 13, 1971, p. 4-V].

It was the musical *Hair* that brought Harris to national prominence as a conductor. The 1968 production that brought rock, nudity, and youth to Broadway, in 1971 brought along "vivacious, young enough to be in the 'Hair' generation," and black Margaret Harris as the production's musical director (*ibid.*). Previously she served as musical director for the European tour of *Black New World*. Returning to the States, she served as musical director of the New York City Shakespeare Festival's production of *Sambo* and *Two Gentlemen of Verona*. For several of the productions, she doubled as company pianist.

Other conducting experiences included the St. Louis, Minneapolis, San Diego, Los Angeles, and Chicago symphony orchestras. In the early '70s Harris served as musical director of a Mississippi-based Opera/South production. In the mid '70s she became general director of the Philadelphia-based National Opera Ebony. For several years conductor/pianist/composer Harris served on the faculty of the Harlem School of the Arts, as chair of the piano department.

Recent conducting experiences include appearances with the Winston Salem Symphony Orchestra, the Dayton Philharmonic, and the Bronx Arts Ensemble. In her personal "Career Highlights" she lists "Raisin," "Guys and Dolls," "Amen Corner," "I Love New York" (France, Italy, and Spain), and "My Heart Belongs to Broadway" (Israel); "Raazzmatazz," a CBS-TV Emmy Award-winning series; and "The Shape of Things," a CBS-TV special. Harris has been featured on "Today Show" (Los Angeles), "The David Frost Show," "The Joe Franklin Show," "The Will Rogers, Jr. Show," and "Like It Is" (New York City). As to her personal conducting identity, Harris emphatically wrote, "I am an American Black Female Conductor." Her advice to aspiring black conductors, male and female, was, "Be good at your craft, learn as much as you can, and have faith." (Questionnaire, January 21, 1989).

She is extremely proud of having had the distinction Dame of Honour and Merit, Order of St. John, Knights of Malta, bestowed upon her in 1987. In the early 1990s, Program Corporation of America announced the availability of Harris for lecture/demonstrations, piano recitals, master classes in piano and choral literature, and as artist-in-residence. Lecture topics include such insightful titles as "The Business of Being an Artist," "The Black and Minority Artists in the United States," and "Affirmative Action: Friend or Foe to the Black/Minority Artist."

TANIA (Justina) LEON (Ferran)
Conducting (Composition, Piano)
b. May 14, 1943, Havana, Cuba

According to freelance writer Angela Iadavaia-Cox, Leon's

> grandmother was a slave in Cuba and her mother carried sugarcane
> on her head. By the age of 20 she was a solo pianist in Cuba's Na-
> tional Philharmonic Orchestra and a conductor of the Alicia Alonso
> Ballet Company. . . . [Her] grandmother lost her job scrubbing
> floors in a mansion because she played the piano one day. She knew
> though from those few notes that someone in her family would
> play the piano, be famous and travel ["The Tug Between Conduct-
> ing and Composing," *Essence,* December 1976, p. 72].

Leon was enrolled as a conservatory piano student by her grandmother at age four and was composing by age thirteen. She received the B.A. degree in piano and theory from Carlos Alfredo
Peyrellade Conservatory, the M.A. in Music Education from the
National Conservatory, and the B.A. in Accounting/Business Administration from Havana University, all in her native Cuba. Arriving in the United States, she enrolled at New York University,
receiving both the bachelor's and master's degrees in composition. Leon continued the matriculation, in pursuit of the Doctorate in Science (Acoustics) degree.

Her list of awards has included the Bronze, Silver, and Gold
Medals in the Carlos Alfredo Peyrellade Piano Contests and First
Prize—Young Composers, National Council of the Arts, Havana,
Cuba. "Outstanding achievement" recognition continued as she
was selected "Best Student" in the Music Education Division,
New York University (1968). Leon was the recipient of the Alvin
Johnson Award, American Council for the Emigres in the Profession (1971). She received the CINTAS Award in Composition
(1976 and 1978–79) and the ASCAP Composers Award in Composition (1978–79). For the Bicentennial Celebration she received
a commission for an original composition from the National Endowment for the Arts (1975).

Tania Leon's affiliation with the Dance Theatre of Harlem
began in 1968, as staff pianist. In 1970 she established the DTH's
music department and in 1975 the DTH Orchestra, serving as di-

rector of both. Guest-conducting experiences included the Buffalo Philharmonic, Concert Orchestra of Long Island, BBC Northern, Royal Ballet Touring, and Halle orchestras.

At the famous "Festival of Two Worlds," Spoleto, Italy, Leon served as director of the Juilliard Orchestra (1971). She conducted the Genova (Italy) Symphony Orchestra at the Nervi Festival (1972). In 1978 she served as conductor/musical director of the popular Broadway musical *The Wiz*. Maestra Leon served as conductor/music director of WNET's "Dance in America" Special in 1977. In 1978 she was appointed conductor/musical director of the Brooklyn Philharmonic Community Concerts, while of course continuing her affiliation with the Dance Theatre of Harlem.

Leon's eclectic musical tastes and her fluency in many genres reflect a myriad of musical influences—Latin, Asian, African-American; jazz and popular music; opera, dance, and other music for the theater; western European (particularly impressionist and postimpressionist). She has appeared as guest conductor with the Buffalo Philharmonic, Cologne and Sadler's Wells Orchestras, and the orchestras of the Kennedy Center Opera House and the Metropolitan Opera. She served briefly as music director for the Alvin Ailey American Dance Theatre and *The Wiz* (Broadway). She composed commissioned works for the Brooklyn Philharmonia, the Whitney Museum, Lincoln Center Institute, the Bay Area Women's Philharmonic, and the American Composers' Orchestra.

Since 1992, Leon has served as artistic adviser to the American Composers Orchestra's Latin American Project. In 1993 she was appointed to a two-year term as Charles H. Revson Composer Fellow with the New York Philharmonic. She was on the podium, conducting the Munich Biennale Festival Orchestra when her opera *Scourge of Hyacinths* was premiered in Munich, Germany, on May 1, 1994.

> *D. JERLENE HARDING
> conductor (saxophone)
> b. June 21, 1933, Portsmouth, Virginia
> d. December 20, 1995, Portsmouth, Virginia

For D. Jerlene Harding, a twenty-year dream was realized in 1975, when she organized the Tidewater Area Musicians (TAM) Youth

Orchestra. She assembled the group of Tidewater youngsters to perform at the Regional Conference of the National Association of Negro Musicians, Inc. Harding's son was at the keyboard, while her daughter enhanced the ensemble's flute section.

The graduate of Central State College was always fascinated by "classical music" and the orchestral sound. She wrote:

> I developed a love for classical music as a child. I would drop every-thing (even outside activities) to listen to the old Longine Whit-nauer Music Hour which came on radio every Sunday [correspondence with the author, March 1979].

Though principally a saxophonist, she developed sufficient string skills to teach the recruited black string players in the junior and senior high school orchestras that she directed. According to jour-nalist Wilma Tillis,

> Before schools were integrated, many blacks didn't think they could identify with playing [string] instruments. . . . But Mrs. Har-ding changed those attitudes and helped students realize string in-struments have a close tie to all cultures ["With Her Help, Students Hit High Note," *Currents*, December 12–13, 1978].

TAM, originally a fifteen-to-eighteen-member string ensemble, within three years grew to a forty-eight-member ensemble, in-cluding nineteen females (all black). Membership in the commu-nity orchestra remained open to all Tidewater youth, the only requirement being "membership in a Tidewater orchestra and student string experience."

In keeping with the times the group's repertoire ranged "from symphony to soul." TAM's publicity material stated:

> The versatile group presents a program that includes something for everyone, e.g., symphonies, string quartets, chamber music, gospel, jazz, and standard pop tunes [TAM brochure].

A smaller string ensemble provided music for various occa-sions, including weddings, luncheons, banquets, receptions, church services, and chamber concerts.

Comprised of students from local high schools and colleges (Norfolk, Portsmouth, and Chesapeake), the group filled local assignments and traveled to other cities, including Indianapolis, Philadelphia, Kalamazoo, Detroit, and New York City. Moving into the eighth decade of the twentieth century, the group was still in operation, with a steadily increasing membership. The black female contingency kept pace.

Well into the ninth decade, TAM continued to perform for special events in the Tidewater area and throughout the country. The group became the principal orchestral arm at annual conferences of the National Association of Negro Musicians (NANM). Harding put to rest the notion that "black children are not suitable to play string instruments." Supported by donations, the group became Portsmouth's most effective ambassador, retaining that position until Harding's untimely death. (See Vernon Kitabu Turner, "T.A.M. Youthful Artists Create the Music of Love . . . ," *New Journal and Guide,* October 26–November 1, 1994, p. 1.)

> *MARSHA (Eve) MABREY
> conductor (violin, viola)
> b. November 7, 1949, Pittsburgh, Pennsylvania

Mabrey's interest in music was sparked in the fourth grade, when she was introduced to the violin. She was only a seventh grader when she decided to become an orchestra conductor, "one who shapes the symphonic whole." Her family was supportive but initially had some reservations. Serious violin study was understandable, but the idea of serious conducting study seemed somewhat unrealistic. "How would she support herself?"

Says Mabrey,

> I was aware at an early age that the conductor was an important catalyst in bringing many musicians together to create the whole picture of music. As a violinist, I was involved with just one line. Conducting came to me quite naturally and the analysis and challenge of communication with other musicians was very exciting. I enjoyed the exchange of energy between conductor, musicians, and audience in helping to convey the composer's ideas [Questionnaire, December 1987].

She received the B.Mus. (1971) and the M.Mus. (1972) degrees from the University of Michigan School of Music, majoring in instrumental music education and minoring in violin/viola. She worked toward the D.M.A. at the University of Cincinnati College Conservatory of Music (orchestral conducting/viola cognate) between 1973 and 1976. Her instructors were Elizabeth A.H. Green, Theo Alcantara, and Louis Lane. She participated in conducting workshops with Richard Lert, Maurice Abravanel, and Otto-Werner Mueller.

Her educational affiliations include instructor of music and conductor of the University Symphony, Winona State University in Winona, Minnesota (1978–80); assistant professor of music and conductor of the university symphony, Grand Valley State University in Allendale, Michigan (1980–82); and assistant professor of music and conductor of the university symphony, University of Oregon school of music in Eugene, Oregon (1982–89). She left the faculty position at the University of Oregon School of Music to accept an assistant dean position.

Mabrey has also taught elementary and secondary school in Ann Arbor, Michigan (1972–73, 1976–77), and Denver, Colorado (1977–78). But conducting has always been her major interest, and she has been involved with all-state, honors, and youth orchestra, including the Interlochen National Music Camp (Interlochen, Michigan), conducting the all-state intermediate division, all-state and honors orchestras, Oregon Music Educators Association (Eugene, Oregon), guest conductor and clinician, and Pennsylvania Music Educators Association (Wilkes-Barre, Pennsylvania). She had similar responsibilities with the Utah Music Educators Association (Salt Lake City, Utah), Arkansas Music Educators Association (Pine Bluff, Arkansas), and the Miami Dade County Public Schools Music Festival (Miami, Florida). Mabrey has also guest conducted the Greater Twin Cities Youth Philharmonic.

In 1988 she guest conducted the Sinfonietta Frankfurt in Frankfurt, Schwalbach, Offenbach, and Hanau, West Germany. She also guest conducted the Oregon Symphony Orchestra (Portland), participating in the New Music Reading Program of the American Symphony Orchestra League. Mabry conducted the Savannah (Georgia) Symphony in 1991 for the orchestra's Black Heritage Concert Series and the Women's Philharmonic (San Francisco, California) in 1994 for its fourth annual New Music Reading Session. In 1996 she conducted the Seattle Philharmonic Orchestra (Seattle, Washington) as one of five finalists being considered for the position permanently.

Between 1991 and 1993, Mabrey was vice president for educational affairs with the Detroit Symphony Orchestra (Michigan). The following year, she was interim director of education with the Philadelphia Orchestra (Pennsylvania). As a music education consultant (1993–present), she has worked with the San Jose Symphony Orchestra (California), New World Symphony (Miami, Florida), Duke University, and St. Augustine's College. Long remembered will be the two symposia that she developed and directed at the University of Oregon (1985–86): West Coast Women's Conductor/Composer Symposium and the American Women's Conductor/Composer Symposium.

KAY GEORGE ROBERTS
conductor (violin, education)
b. September 15, 1950, Nashville, Tennessee

Kay George Roberts is one of a select group of black female symphony orchestra conductors. Roberts is the first woman and second black to earn the doctor of musical arts degree in conducting from Yale University. In 1972, she entered the Yale University School of Music, working toward a master's degree in violin performance, which she received in 1975. Enrollment in a conducting class and the opportunity to conduct the graduate school orchestra brought about a shift in Robert's career choice.

Violin study began when Kay was in the fourth grade, thanks to black Nashville public schools pedagogue Robert Holmes. Five years later she joined the Nashville Youth Symphony and then the Peabody Demonstration School Orchestra. Membership in the Nashville Symphony began during her senior high school year. She soon graduated from the second- to the first-violin section and remained with the group through her undergraduate years at Fisk University.

In 1971 Nashville Symphony conductor Thor Johnson recommended Roberts to be the orchestra's representative in Arthur Fiedler's World Symphony Orchestra. She admirably represented her hometown ensemble in the first-violin section of Fiedler's touring orchestra.

While enrolled at Fisk University, the young violinist was an associate fellow at Tanglewood in Lenox, Massachusetts. Other significant violin affiliations included the Yale Collegium Orches-

tra, Philharmonic Orchestra of Yale, Institute des Hautes Etudes
Musicales (Montreaux, Switzerland), Festival Orchestra of Two
Worlds (Spoleto, Italy), Chamber Orchestra of New England,
New Haven Symphony, Nashua Symphony Orchestra, and the
Indian Hill Chamber Orchestra. In 1976 she received the master
of musical arts degree in both conducting and violin perform-
ance.

Conducting instructor Otto-Werner Mueller customarily took a
student along when he made guest conducting appearances and
allowed his better conducting students to share the rehearsal podium. During the 1975–76 season, Mueller permitted Roberts to
rehearse both the Atlanta and Nashville Symphony Orchestras in
Gustav Mahler's Symphony No. 1. During the same season, she
made her conducting debut as guest conductor of her hometown
orchestra, the Nashville Symphony.

She received the Doctor of Musical Arts in Conducting in 1986,
having met Yale's requirements of "demonstrating her qualifica-
tions through distinguished achievement." Roberts participated
in conducting workshops, seminars, and choral institutes: Aspen
(Colorado) Music Festival Conductors Program and American
Symphony Orchestra League (ASOL) Conducting Workshops.
Conducting instructors included Murray Sidlin, Gustav Meier,
and Margaret Hillis (choral). She participated in master classes
conducted by Seiji Ozawa, Andre Previn, Leonard Bernstein, Edo
de Waart, and African-American Denis de Coteau.

Roberts accepted the position of assistant professor of music
and conductor of the university orchestra at the University of
Lowell (now the University of Massachusetts at Lowell) in 1978.
She retains her position at the university (where she is now a full
professor), while continuing to build a solid conducting career.
She was assistant conductor of the Mystic Valley Chamber Orchestra (1983–84) and the Greater Boston Youth Symphony Orchestra (1984–85). She assumed leadership of the New
Hampshire Philharmonic in 1982 and the Cape Ann (Mass.) Symphony in 1986. She held the New Hampshire position until 1987
and the Cape Ann position until 1988. Currently she is music
director of a new chamber orchestra, String Currents.

Now under management of Shaw Concerts, her guest conducting appearances have become quite impressive. Bangkok Symphony Orchestra (Thailand), New York Housing Authority

Symphony Orchestra, Women's Philharmonic, Cairo Conservatoire Orchestra (Egypt), Black Music Repertory Ensemble, Haddonfield (N.J.) Symphony, Dayton Philharmonic, Louisiana Philharmonic, Detroit Symphony, Chattanooga (Tenn.), Dallas, Cleveland, Louisville, and Chicago Symphony Orchestras. During the summers of 1994 and 1995, she guest conducted the Orchestra Svizzera Italiana at the Lugano Jazz Festival. Return engagements are frequent.

Roberts's list of honors and awards is quite impressive and includes the National Fellowship Fund for Black Americans, Bates Junior Fellow, Jonathan Edwards College of Yale University; Woman of Promise, *Good Housekeeping;* Distinguished Alumna of the Year, National Association for Equal Opportunity in Higher Education (NAFEO); Distinguished Alumna Award, University School of Nashville (formerly Peabody Demonstration School); and Outstanding Woman in the Performing Arts, League of Black Women (Chicago).

*(Georgianne) ANNE LUNDY
conductor (violin/viola)
b. October 18, 1954, Houston, Texas

Lundy's conducting activities have primarily involved black community orchestras. For her work with the Scott Joplin Chamber Orchestra (formerly Community Music Center of Houston's Orchestra), Lundy was designated an Outstanding Texan by the black caucus of the Texas House of Representatives in 1989.

She received the B.Mus.Ed. and performance certification (violin) from the University of Texas at Austin in 1977 and the M.Mus. in conducting from the University of Houston in 1979. She studied conducting with Igor Buketoff at the University of Houston. Between 1981 and 1989 she enrolled in numerous master conducting classes with instructors such as Harold Farberman, Herbert Blomstedt, Paul Vermel, Hugo Jon Huss, Elizabeth Green, and Jon Robertson. In order to acquire additional experience, she founded the Mountain Chamber Orchestra while attending the Aspen Music Institute during the summer of 1983. Anne Lundy held membership in the Austin and San Angelo Symphony Orchestras and the Abilene Philharmonic, playing violin and viola.

The Community Music Center of Houston was founded in 1979

and is devoted to "promoting music (through five music ensembles—orchestra, chorus, string quartet, brass quartet, and chamber singers) often overlooked [and to] exposing and involving all children in appreciating and participating in the art of music making (Barbara Karkali, "Black Community Music Center Finds Home Where Its Heart Is," *Houston Chronicle*, October 14, 1984, p. 6).

Lundy became executive director of the center in 1983. Concerned that the music of black composers was seldom performed, Lundy organized the William Grant Still String Quartet in 1981 and played viola with the group. Shortly after joining the staff, she organized an orchestra, commenting, "I just started calling up string players I knew and I found a number of people out there, teaching school, working in banks and elsewhere. Then I went to Wheeler Ave. Baptist Church, where they were planning a performance of Handel's 'Messiah,' and said, 'Hey, how would you like to do this with an orchestra?' (Carl Cunningham, "Sound of Music: Young Conductor's Ambition Leads to Black Chamber Orchestra, New Arts Enterprise," *Houston Post*, October 16, 1985, p. 14E).

The group performs for various community and church activities. The Scott Joplin Chamber Orchestra joined with the Houston Symphony during the summer of 1989 to perform a tribute to the black composer William Dawson, celebrating his ninetieth birthday. Leading the combined orchestral forces was Maestro Anne Lundy. She spent seven years as an orchestra and general music instructor in the Houston school system. Between 1982 and 1984, she conducted the Houston All-City Youth Orchestra. Between 1985 and 1987, Lundy was a string instructor at Texas Southern University. Sharing her artistic concerns for the music of black composers and black participation in the music-making scheme of things, she contributed articles to *The Black Perspective in Music* and *American String Teacher*.

Notes

1. Irene Armstrong Eadie is best remembered as a composer and personal friend of singer Billie Holiday. One of Billie's favorite tunes was

Eadie's "Some Other Spring." For more on Irene see Dance, *The World of Earl Hines*, pp. 179–182.

2. Around 1948 the International Sweethearts of Rhythm disbanded. Leader Anna Mae Winburn then organized her own Sweethearts of Rhythm, providing a popular attraction until about 1954.

3. Consuella Carter completed college (Rust) and graduate work (Vandercook) following her stay at Piney Woods. Though retired, she remains musically active in Lyon, Mississippi. Always a capable trumpet player, her teaching of many instruments continues. When this writer visited her during the summer of 1979 she found her still playing, still teaching (privately)—clarinet, saxophone, trumpet, and percussion—and leading a rhythm band of senior citizens. (Deceased.)

4. The school received its Charter of Incorporation in 1913. Dr. Jones and Piney Woods Country Life School were the topic for a Ralph Edwards *This Is Your Life* television production in 1954.

5. In 1948 Ruby Young was the first woman to serve on the Board of Directors of Pittsburgh's Musicians Protective Union, Local 471 (Black), American Federation of Musicians. She then served as Secretary-Treasurer of the same local. She was still in office in 1965, when the black and white locals merged, and served until 1970 on the merged Board of Directors.

6. "Zydeco" is described as a heavily syncopated, ethnic, and danceable kind of music, blending cajun, reggae, calypso, western swing, dixieland jazz, blues, rock, and Latin music.

7. Theater Owners Booking Association, a management agency providing black shows for black audiences throughout the South and Midwest. TOBA also stood for "Tough On Black Artists."

III.

String Players

Strings represent the backbone of symphony and theatrical orchestras and the "added touch" in all other instrumental ensembles. Black women string players have been active participants in the business of "group music-making" in America at all levels and in a variety of settings. Their choice of instruments has ranged from the ukulele to the string bass; indeed, no instrument has appeared unattractive to them or incapable of mastery.

Early Dance and Minstrel Bands

One of the earliest black woman string players of whom we have some details was Myrtle Hart of the Henry Hart Family Orchestra. This group furnished the best possible music for dances in the state of Indiana, from the last decade of the nineteenth century until the father's death in 1915. Based in Indianapolis, the group entertained political dignitaries visiting the city, played for "the bloods" locally and worked plush summer resorts throughout the Midwest ("Henry Hart and His Family of Musicians Always in Demand," *Indianapolis News*, April 6, 1901).

Myrtle Hart (Frye) started out in the Hart ensemble as pianist in a piano-violin duo while still in her teens, but before long performed professionally as harpist with her violinist father. Her sister Willie also started out as pianist in the ensemble, but as other daughters were born (and soon brought into the musical fold) she was shifted to the cello. Myrtle was apparently the principal feature of the "father-plus-five-daughters" orchestra. She studied with Edmond Schnecker, solo harpist with the Theodore Thomas Orchestra. Her "elite' musical involvements were primarily as so-

loist. She performed at the British exhibit of the Chicago World's
Fair in 1893 and played solo recitals in black churches in the same
city and in Washington, D.C. She appeared with a small vocal
and instrumental ensemble at Philadelphia Odd Fellows' Temple
in 1903.

Myrtle's training and experience suggest that she was the harpist whose services were utilized whenever "highbrow" instrumental music making called for her instrument. But in 1915
Myrtle Hart Frye was a harpist in the orchestra of one of the leading theaters in Chicago (*Indianapolis Freeman,* February 13, 1915,
p. 3).

Several additional names have come down to us from the nineteenth century. In the early 1800s Mrs. Jesse Scott was one of the
fiddlers in the Scott Band, which played around Charlottesville,
Virginia. Florence Givens Joplin, mother of rag king Scott Joplin,
was both a singer and a banjo player. It may be that she occasionally joined her violin-playing husband Giles in supplying plantation entertainment in the mid-1800s. At the same period Carrie
Melvin (Lucas), wife of famous minstrelman Samuel Lucas,
played both violin and cornet in minstrel bands. There were violinist Adaline Talbot of Portland, Maine, and guitarist Clara Mon-
teith Holland (daughter of guitarist/composer/pedagogue Justin
Holland), active in the mid- and late 1880s, respectively. Surely
all performance was not solo.

Elizabeth Foster, sister of jazz bassist George "Pops" Foster,
alternated on mandolin, violin, and bass with The Foster Trio and
band, a late-nineteenth-century family group that specialized in
quadrilles, polkas, and rags in Donaldsonville, Louisiana. The
three-piece Wiley Family String Band of South Carolina in the
early twentieth century included Fanny Wiley on guitar and Alice
Wiley on string bass.

Theater Orchestras

When the present writer thinks of theater orchestras, she thinks
of the Lafayette Theater in New York City, since it was there that
black-women orchestras and theater were almost synonymous,
from 1914 to 1920. A ladies' orchestra under the direction of

Marie Lucas made its debut at the Lafayette in late 1914. Included in the personnel were Marie Wayne (Townsend) and Mildred Franklin, violins; Maude Shelton, viola; percussionist Alice Calloway, cello; and Nellie Shelton, bass violin—all musicians far above the average and experienced (*New York Age,* December 3, 1914). Minnie Brown's name appeared on the projected list of participants, as cellist (*The New York Age,* November 26, 1914).

A later member of Lucas's Lafayette Ladies Orchestra was Olivia Porter (Shipp), and Maude Shelton played violin as well as viola in the ensemble. Other string players in the Lucas Colonial Theater Orchestra in Baltimore, Maryland, and the Howard Theater Orchestra in Washington, D.C. (1916–17), were Evangeline Sinto, violin, and Santos Riviera, bass violin.

Black composer/critic H. Lawrence Freeman was impressed with the Lafayette Ladies Orchestra and praised the group in an article for the *Indianapolis Freeman.* He commented on one string player:

> [T]he smallest lady of the organization, and the one to handle the largest instrument therein, namely, the bass violin, is the happy possessor of all the elements that go to make up the unit of successful manipulation of the apparently cumbersome piece of mechanism . . . Miss Shelton meets [the instrument's] demands with authority, piquancy or delicacy, as the occasion requires. Her tone is always vibrant, true and decisive ["A Review of the Two Leading New York Orchestras—The Lafayette and New Lincoln," January 20, 1917].

Gertrude H. Martin (registrar at the Martin-Smith Music School and wife of the School's founder-director) played bass with the predominantly male seven-piece orchestra that played at the New Lincoln Theater in New York City during the same period. And, finally, let us note that Mildred Frankin was also a violinist in Hallie Anderson's Ladies Orchestra and Will Marion Cook's Ladies Orchestra, which worked at the Lafayette in 1919. Olivia Porter (Shipp) was bassist with both orchestras. Kathryn Revy, a New York City violinist, was the only woman listed in the 1928 edition of *The Official Theatrical World of Colored Artists the World Over.*

Jazz Ensembles and Big Bands

Proceeding chronologically, we can identify black female string players associated with the earliest jazz ensembles and big bands. The first names are those of Maude Shelton, Nellie Shelton, and Mildred Gassaway Franklin, all violinists. These three women covered the Harlem club circuit in the latter part of the second decade of this century, playing with combos of all conceivable combinations. At the same time, in Chicago violinist Gertrude Palmer played "on the stroll" with the five-piece Harris Jass Band. During the same period and well into the next decade Mae Brady played violin in Chicago clubs on Thirty-first and Thirty-fifth Streets.

During the late 1920s and early 1930s the Negro Women's Orchestral and Civic Association in New York City included Mazie Mullen, violin; Betty Lomax, guitar; Gertrude H. Martin and Olivia Shipp, string bass. Other string players in this group that specialized in syncopated music remain anonymous.

The Harlem Playgirls were active in the Midwest during the mid- and late 1930s, and included violinists Lelia Julius, Pamora Banks, Pamela Moore, and Jean Taylor and string bassist Marge Backstrom. The name Gwenn Twiggs, bassist, comes down to us from The Dixie Sweethearts.

In the mid-1930s harpist Olivette Miller caught the attention of the listening public. She appeared as a jazz harpist in top theaters, hotels, and lounges throughout the United States and Europe. Daughter of actor/writer Flournoy Miller, Olivette did not initially follow the "short-haired" harpist's route. After receiving the instrument as a Christmas gift from her father at age seven she studied traditional harp repertory for many years and played the conventional church and school recitals. Following the suggestion of her mother that she learn to play "St. Louis Blues," Miller said that "everything changed for me . . . I was on my own playing jazz music, for there are no rules in it for the harp to go by" ("Jazz Harpist," *Ebony*, April 1952, 97–99).

Her group involvements included performance with Noble Sissle's band and her own trio. During World War II she completed a fourteen-month tour of Europe. Following many years of residency in Chicago, she and her dancer husband, Freddie Gordon, moved to California, where she continued to perform. Betty Tillman was another harpist who occasionally played with Noble Sissle's band and with various pick-up orchestras in the area of Washington, D.C., during the 1940s.

"Talented and versatile" violinist Angel Creasy worked the Harlem club circuit as both singer and violinist before joining Earl Hines in 1943. The International Sweethearts of Rhythm and The Swinging Rays of Rhythm carried the following string players' names on their rosters: Roxanna Lucas, Carline Ray, and Chela Vegas, guitar; Bernice Rothchild, Lucille Dixon, Trump Margo, Edna Smith, and Lillian Carter, string bass. When the need arose Yvonne Plummer played guitar with the Swinging Rays.

In the early 1940s Earl D. Clendenon programmed a repertory ranging "from spirituals to swing" for his Sepian Lassies of Harmony, working out of St. Paul, Minnesota. The roster included Antoinette Morris, Janet Armstrong, and Mercedes Morris on mandolin; Dorothy Munson and Donna Guy on guitar; Ruth Davis on Hawaiian guitar; and June Morris on string bass.

For his 1943 big band pianist/leader Earl "Fatha" Hines brought in seven black women string players. The press hailed Hines's decision as "one of the most revolutionary steps ever taken by a colored bandleader" ("Earl Out to Prove Value of Mixed 'Ork' Personnel," *Pittsburgh Courier*, September 11, 1943, p. 20). The group made its first public appearance at the Apollo Theatre in New York City, September 10, 1943.

The seven women were violinists Angel Creasy (featured also as a solo artist with the band), Helen Way, and Sylvia Medford; cellist Ardine Loving; guitarist Roxanna Lucas; bassist Lucille Dixon; and harpist Lavella Tullas. Both Lucas and Dixon had been members of The International Sweethearts of Rhythm. Creasy had already established a reputation as a respectable jazz performer and band leader. Cellist Ardine Loving had been recognized as an outstanding "elite artist" talent in her native Detroit prior to joining the band. She had held membership in the Detroit Negro Symphony and the black Lyric String Ensemble and was a respected cello soloist and radio personality. Harpist Lavella Tullas had also established a name for herself in Detroit's "elite art" instrumental circles.

In the late 1940s and '50s New Yorker Gloria Bell was string bassist with the Myrtle Young and Her Rays combo, which worked throughout the East Coast. The string players with the Long Branch, New Jersey-based Thornton Sisters Combo (mentioned in Chapter II) were Jeannette Thornton on electric guitar and Itasker Thornton (her mother) on electric bass.

The youthful Cremona Strings of Nashville, Tennessee, offered a diversified repertory. Organized in 1958 by Robert Holmes, then a string teacher in the Nashville Metropolitan Schools, the group's roster featured these names during its more than a decade of existence: violinists Lyndell Barton, Rosalyn Baxter, Denise Bentley, Lynn Ellison, Harriette Green, Sandra Harris, Princess Maclin, Donna Phillips, Kay Roberts, Vanessa Spells, Vivian Stevenson, Lajuanda Street, Jo Ann Sweeney, Lucretia Walker, and Phyllis Woods; violists Daphne Brady, Beth McClain, Allison Scott, Lisa Spells, and Renee Vincent; and cellists Dianne Couch, Patricia Leonard, and Patricia Yeargin. Both Green and Roberts early "graduated" to membership in the Nashville Symphony.

In New York City during the mid- and late 1970s the name of cellist Deidra Murray (Johnson) was as frequent on the roster of the Jazz Composer's Orchestra and The Marvin Hannibal Band as it was on the roster of the Dance Theatre of Harlem Orchestra and other "elite art" ensembles. She is credited with having pioneered the cello as an improvisational instrument.

EAR Magazine, in its October 1987 issue, featured Murray as one of its "new faces," focusing on Deidra Murray the composer. As she states, "I would like to do larger works, and I want to spend more time with experimental electronic music. I want to get higher up into technology than I am now." Her heights have certainly been elevated in recent years. Murray's music dancescape "Mu Lan Pi" was featured at Dance Theater Workshop's (New York City) "Big City Music 1993." The work explores pre-Columbian images by Africans in the 1300s to the Americas and featured Murray as both composer and cellist.

Another freelancer in New York City during the same period who also played with a wide variety of groups was violinist Barbara Thornton. Detroit harpist Onita Jackson Sanders played with groups that specialized in gospel, rock, jazz, pop, and "classical" music. She performed in opera-theater orchestra pits, recorded with such performers as Stevie Wonder and Marvin Gaye, and in the late 1970s played five nights a week at the Hyatt-Regency Hotel in Dearborn, Michigan ("Working World," *Essence,* May 1979, p. 36).

Finally, the 1970s brought to the public's attention the string-bass work of Dorothy Horney (who doubled on organ in The Ernestine "Tiny" Davis Trio) of Chicago; the guitar work of Monnette Sudler Honesty (also a leader, singer, and composer) of Philadelphia; and guitarist Hazel Payne and bassist Janice Johnson, both members of the award-winning, four-member A Taste of Honey ("Best New Artists," Grammy, and Tokyo Festival Gold Prize, 1979).

The late 1980s and 1990s brought forth the names of two impressive female jazz violinists: Sonya Robinson and Regina Carter. Miles Davis once said of Robinson, "If you have an ear for creativity, listen to Sonya." Currently guest soloist with the Lincoln Center Jazz Orchestra (1997 winter tour), Regina Carter studied European, Classical, and African-American music at New England Conservatory and Oakland University where she earned the Bachelor of Arts degree in performance. She was voted first in the category "Violin Talent Deserving Wider Recognition" in *DownBeat*'s forty-fourth annual critics poll. Both Robinson and Carter have distinguished themselves as recording artists as well.

The 1980s and 1990s brought to our attention the name of violinist Theresa ("Terry") Jenoure. She worked with some of the most inspired experimentalists of the period, such as Leroy Jenkins, Henry Threadgill, and Brandon Ross, and recorded with John Carter, Marion Brown, Leroy Jenkins and Archie Shepp. She is also a vocalist and composer and leads her own ensemble. For a period she served as artist in residence at Hampshire College and a fellow in the music program of the National Endowment for the Arts. She is a former executive director of Outward Visions (a performing arts organization) of New York City.

Another violinist of the same period is Kathy Grayce Kelsh, a native of Washington, D.C. She performed with such groups as the Boston Opera Company Orchestra, The Reger Quartet, Concerts in Black and White, the Nashua Philharmonic, and the Frankie Avalon Orchestra. Kelsh also performed in the duo "Shantih" (violin and cello). The duo appeared in concert throughout Europe. She played with the Ja-Ka-Scha Show Band, Neophelia Jazz Band, and the Chamber Orchestra of the Musikschule Kreuzberg in Berlin. As with Jenoure, Kelsh is also a vocalist and composer.

"Elite Art" Instrumental Ensembles

Irene and Jeanette Lambert were vocalists in the respected Richard Lambert Family musical dynasty, which existed in New Orleans from 1840 to 1880. The father and four sons were the family professionals, but on some occasions the string bass, cello, and harp talents of the two daughters (Irene and Jeanette) were utilized. Lillian and Jamesetta Humphrey, of the Humphrey musical dynasty in New Orleans, were both string bassists. Lillian Humphrey was on the roster of the twenty-two-piece Bloom Philharmonic Orchestra, which performed four "highbrow" concerts in New Orleans in 1903 (Charters, *Jazz: New Orleans*, p. 53). Clarinetist Willie Humphrey assured this writer that Jamesetta's name also appeared on various "elite art" instrumental-ensemble rosters (conversation with the author, December 2, 1978, New Orleans).

The Nickerson Ladies' Orchestra of New Orleans at the turn of the century consisted of nine female members (males supplemented on certain occasions), but only four of the six string players' names have come down to us: violinists Marie Guilbeau, Emma Harris, Florence Lewis, and Julia Lewis Nickerson, who doubled on cello. The name Alberta Riggs can be recalled as a violinist in N. Clark Smith's Ladies Orchestra of Chicago, founded in 1904.

In Houston string players on the roster of Madam Corilla Rochon's Ladies Symphony Orchestra of 1915 were E. Jessie Covington, Daisy McGee, Mrs. B. J. Covington, and Mrs. J. L. Blunt, violins; Mrs. A. E. Butler, cello; and Mrs. Frank Martinere, string bass. In New York City the Martin-Smith Music School Symphony Orchestra included the names of many black female string players during the years 1916–20: Marie Wayne (Townsend) and Mildred Franklin, violins; Maude Shelton, violin and viola; Alice Calloway, cello; and Nellie Shelton, Gertrude H. Martin, and Olivia Porter Shipp, string bass—all members of the Lafayette and New Lincoln theatre orchestras as well. Other known string players with the Martin-Smith Music School Symphony Orchestra during this period were: Angelina Riviera and Ruth Jackson (Jimbefume), violin, and Minnie Brown, cello.

Early in the 1920s Annie Malone, founder of the Poro School of Beauty Culture, organized the Poro College Ladies' Orchestra in

St. Louis "to aid in the culture of the Poro Family." Though the city was a center for "hot music" at the time, the prevailing attitudes among "cultured" blacks suggest that this group's repertory was limited to the more "elite" literature. The twenty-piece ensemble included Hattie McAllister, Elizabeth Carter, Rowena Slaughter, Johnetta Bell, Artechia Charleston, Naomi Coates, Dorothea Scott, Zenobia Carr, Beatrice Dunlap, and Goldie Copher, violins; Ida Phelps, cello; and Lillie Martin, string bass.

In Chicago Harrison Ferrell organized and directed a symphony orchestra during the 1920s and early '30s that included Marjorie Ferrell (Lewis), concertmistress, and Irene Britton (Smith), Grazia Bell (Ferrell), Michaeli Davila, Ruth Sarver, and Willa Belle Jones, violinists. The names of the five females noted in the string section of the Baltimore City Colored Orchestra, organized in 1929, are not known. Male leader B. L. Graves specified that his mid-1930s group of Baltimore, Maryland, concentrated on the "classical" literature, tolerating "jazz on rare occasions." His eleven-piece Colonial Park String Ensemble included Viola Cobham on violin.

Personnel listed on a 1935 program given by the Martin-Smith Music School Symphony Orchestra included Gertrude E. Martin, concertmistress; Leola Armstrong, Thelma Burns, Helen Harris, Catherine Hunter, Penelope Johnson, Elizabeth Sloane, Cora Stout, and Lillian Sykes, violins; Laura Jenkins, cello; and Gertrude H. Martin, bass. In New York City during the years 1950–65 the Gladys Seals Symphonette included on its roster the names of Helen Peterson and Clementine Thomas, violinists.

It should be pointed out that until the 1960s the basic source of "highbrow" orchestral music for the southern black community were the black colleges, whose orchestras reached their audiences through tours, radio broadcasts, and campus concerts. Among those active with such orchestras were violinist/violist Margaret Davis; violinists Gretchen Branch, Wilhemina Patterson, and Emma L. Cannon; and violist Evelyn Carter West, with the Hampton Institute Orchestra in the early 1930s. During the same period violinist Lawsona Collins's name appeared on the roster of the Tuskegee Institute Orchestra, and in the early 1940s the names of Ruth McArthur, violin, and Sue Whitfield, cello, appeared. Harpist Catherine Moton Patterson (wife of Frederick D. Patterson, the Institute's president), though primarily a solo harpist, also played occasionally with the school's orchestra. Violinist Ruth McArthur and cellist Sue Whitfield were also members of Tuskegee Institute's string quartet.

Morehouse and Spelman College were represented by the Kemper Harreld String Quartet, which included cellist Geraldine Ward in an otherwise male ensemble, on its tours in the late 1930s. In the late 1930s the twenty-one-piece orchestra at Dillard University of New Orleans included one female (name unknown), who also served as the group's concertmistress.

The West Virginia State College Strings, organized in 1939, included during the course of its seven-year existence Delores Mercedes Henri, Finneater Irene Braithwaite, Christine Williams, and Lucy Ann Morrow, violins, and Joyce Lillian Coe and Elizabeth Wilcox, cellos. The Bennett College (Ladies) Symphony Orchestra at Greensboro, North Carolina, included in the early 1940s as many as twenty-four players, although only the name of violinist Mildred Gatlin, wife of founder/director F. Nathaniel Gatlin, is remembered today.

Prior to the 1970s the number of black performers in traditionally nonblack orchestras throughout the country was extremely limited, and the number of black women was even more limited. Nevertheless, a few names of string players can be cited. Violinist Dorothy Smith made history when in 1937 she became "the only colored member" in the Cleveland Women's Orchestra. She was joined at a later date by harpist Vivian Weaver. Violinist Sylvia Medford also made history when she was selected as the only black to be a member of the eighty-five-player Brooklyn Symphony Orchestra in 1949. Wrote *Musical America*, "The democratic makeup of the group is indicated by the presence of fourteen women, one of them a Negro, . . ." (Eaton, "Brooklyn Hears Its Own Orchestra for the First Time," March 1949, pp. 3–4).

Violinist Joella Hardeman Gipson kept musically active on the West Coast with various community orchestras in the Los Angeles area during the 1950s. In the late 1950s violinist Barbara Campbell was the only "race girl" playing with the Little Orchestra Society in New York City. Cellist Carlotta Gary played with the same organization at a later date. Violinist Campbell was one of the earliest blacks to play with the Radio City Music Hall Orchestra, also in the late 1950s.

Violinist Sylvia Medford and bassist Lucille Dixon were permanent members of the "slightly" integrated Orchestra of America, organized in New York City in 1959. Violinist Maurine Francisco made history when she was invited to join the Oklahoma City Symphony Orchestra in 1962. History was made in the early '60s in El Paso, Texas, when violinist/violist Carlotta Washington (Scott) was invited to join the local symphony. In 1963 violinist Carole Anderson was invited to join the Oak Park (Illinois) Symphony Orchestra, but was denied membership. The orchestra's conductor, Milton Preves of the Chicago Symphony Orchestra, resigned in protest after being "over-ruled in the hiring of a Negro violinist." Let us indicate however that in early August of the same year, the *New York Times* reported,

> The New Symphony Orchestra in Oak Park and River Forest announced . . . that membership would be based "entirely on musicianship" and auditions would be conducted with a screen between judges and prospective players. The New Symphony replaces one that was recently disbanded following a controversy over the hiring of a Negro violinist . . . ["Chicago Suburb Orchestra Moves to Bar Hiring Bias," August 2, 1963, p. L17].

Finally, let us note that in the mid-1960s bassist Lucille Dixon (along with timpanist Elayne Jones) played with the Boston Women's Symphony, serving in the capacity of section leader.

Other associations between black women string players and the traditionally white orchestra began taking place in the 1970s, as the Profiles included in this chapter will reveal. To these let us add the following data: Dianne Gary (Kelly) was bassist with the Erie (Pennsylvania) Philharmonic in the early 1970s. Following a summer experience with the Colorado Philharmonic voilist Arecia Stephen joined the North Carolina Symphony for the orchestra's 1971–72 season.

Violist Norma Stanford auditioned during her senior year in high school (1975) for the Norfolk Symphony and was notified of her acceptance the same day. A student of the violin and viola since elementary school, Stanford received additional orchestral training and experience during the summers at the Eastern Music Festival in Greensboro, North Carolina, as a scholarship recipient from the Norfolk Committee for the Improvement of Education.

In the late 1970s violinist Patricia Ashford (Wilson) held membership in the Cleveland Civic Orchestra, and bassist Laura Hendricks Snyder held membership in the Milwaukee Symphony Orchestra. This second edition finds her enjoying more than a quarter of a century with the orchestra. Snyder's extensive vocal talents have been utilized by the orchestra. She presents clinics throughout the Milwaukee area and addressed the convention of the American String Teachers Association/Music Educators National Conference (Cincinnati). The Petersburg Symphony Orchestra, organized in 1979, included several black female string players, many of them in their late teens and early twenties: Mildred Gatlin, Teresa Sessoms, Samelia Spicely, Evanne Tucker, violins; Alice Brown, viola; and Sharon Chambliss and Martina Dawson, cellos.

Those orchestras that were all-black or primarily black (with a concern for integration) included many black female string players. Best known of such orchestras was the Symphony of the New World, organized in New York City in 1965. The following black female string players' names appeared on its roster: Valerie Bynum, Doreen Callender, Gayle Dixon, Marie Hense, Sylvia Medford, and Harriette Watkins, violinists; Marilyn Gates, Judith Graves, Betty Perry, and Maxine Roach, violists; Akua (Patricia) Dixon, Carlotta Gary, Clarissa Howell, Esther Mellon, Edith Wint, and Ann Taylor, cellists; Lucille Dixon, bassist; and Sarah Lawrence, harpist.

The Harlem Philharmonic (formerly the Harlem Youth Symphony), organized in 1968, included on its roster: Gayle Dixon, Valerie Bynum, Harriette Davison Watkins, Sylvia Medford, and Lois Reid, violinists; Sandra Fernandez, Marilyn Gates, and Maxine Roach, violists; and Akua (Patricia) Dixon, cellist. The writer was successful in obtaining only the name of cellist Naomi Millender as a member of the all-black Chatham Village Symphony Orchestra, organized in Chicago in 1974.

Since the first edition of this publication, we have been made aware of several black women string player's important activities. Lynne Richburg, a student of viola since age ten, played a summer season with the New York Philharmonic in the early 1990s. Shortly thereafter, she became principal violist with the Sacramento Symphony. She was soloist with the Savannah Symphony Orchestra in 1987. Another Sacrament Symphony violinist during the same period was Annie McClasky. Nora Bailey Lorberbaum was violinist with the El Paso (Texas) Symphony Orchestra, and Robin Burwell was a member of the violin section of the Austin (Texas) Symphony (having joined the orchestra in 1982). The 1990s find harpist Arcola Clark a member of the ORF Symphony Orchestra in Vienna, Austria.

Violist Regina Calloway joined the Detroit Symphony for the 1992–93 season. She was one of two African-Americans participating in the orchestra residency program to enhance the career development of African-American orchestral musicians. Also in the early 1990s, University of Michigan graduate Gwen Laster founded the Legacy String Quartet and was one of the group's violinists. She was also a member of the Flint (Michigan) Symphony. In her jazz role, where she plays a five-stringed white electric violin. She headed a group that in 1992 won the $10,000 grand prize of the Cognac Hennesy best of Detroit jazz search.

Washington, D.C., native Pamela Barr, a cellist, earned her B.Mus. from Catholic University and her M.Mus. from New England Conservatory. A mid- and late-1980s member of the Richmond Symphony, Barr performed extensively as a solo recitalist and chamber musician, including appearances at the National Gallery of Art, the Phillips and Renwich Galleries, the Smithsonian Institution, and the Kennedy Center Terrace Theatre.

Worth noting is the following list of black female string players, under regular contract, included in the American Symphony Orchestra League's 1990 *The Participation of Blacks in Professional Orchestras*: violin—Karen Walker (Midland-Odessa Symphony Orchestra), Amie McClasky (Sacramento and Stockton Symphony Orchestras), Audrey Lipsey (Kalamazoo Symphony Orchestra), Cheryl Lawhorn (Columbus, Georgia) Symphony Orchestra), Irenee Johnson (Evansville Philharmonic), Dianne Howard (Northeastern Pennsylvania Philharmonic), Mary Corbett (The Florida Orchestra), and Michelle Bluford (Sioux City Symphony Orchestra); viola—Deborah Dansby-Wells (Brevard Symphony Orchestra) and Nina Cottman (Delaware Symphony Orchestra); cello—Dawn Foster Dodson (San Jose Symphony Orchestra); and bass—Angela Jones (Kalamazoo Symphony Orchestra) and Ida Bodin (Cabrillo Music Festival Orchestra). On the mid- and late-1990s roster of the Mississippi Symphony was violinist Dorothea Wilson.

Most noteworthy are the achievements of the Anderson String Quartet (formerly the Chaminade Quartet), composed of three females—Marianne Henry and Marisa McLeod, violins, and Diedre Lawrence, viola—and one male. As winner of the Cleveland Quartet Competition in 1990, the Anderson was in residence at the Eastman School of Music. It has since moved on to other residences and is quite visible on the concert circuit, always receiving rave reviews.

Profiles

JULIA LEWIS (Nickerson)
violin, cello
b. 1878 (?) New Orleans / d. December 17, 1908, New
    Orleans

According to the New Orleans *Daily Picayune,* Julia Lewis was

> a woman of many talents—cultivated to benefit her race. . . . [H]aving studied in the New England Conservatory of Music, she shone as an accomplished scholar and musician. Her talent as a violinist and cellist was recognized, and on many an occasion in church and in public concerts, she appeared and gained merited applause [December 18, 1908, p. 13].

A Straight University (New Orleans) and New England Conservatory graduate, "Miss Julia" (as she was known throughout Louisiana) was the second wife of distinguished New Orleans violinist/teacher/orchestra leader William J. Nickerson. Following graduation from the Conservatory she was appointed supervisor of music and drawing (for "colored") in the New Orleans Public Schools. Following marriage she assisted her husband in his work as chair of the department of music at Southern University.

The Nickerson Ladies' Orchestra (New Orleans) was Miss Julia's principal group affiliation, where she held the positions of concertmistress, tutor, assistant director, and cellist.

Julia was the daughter of Colonel James Lewis and Josephine Joubert, "two families that rank[ed] high in the annals of the respectable element of their class. [Her early death] removed from the prominent colored circles of New Orleans one of its brightest ornaments" (*ibid.*). Those who recall Miss Julia support the *Picayune's* assessment—but oppose the racial restriction.

OLIVIA SOPHIE L'ANGE (Porter) SHIPP
cello, string bass (piano)
b. May 17, 1880, New Orleans / d. June 18, 1980, New York City

In the late teens various orchestra rosters in New York City included the name Olivia Porter. From the 1920s onward the name Olivia Shipp appeared. The name "Porter" was adopted to avoid the stigma attached to show business—a forbidden profession for the two daughters of the L'Ange household. The name change was out of respect for her father and, according to Olivia, her religion.

Olivia's sister May (May Kemp, a member of the popular Bob and Kemp vaudeville team) was an actress, her talents having been recognized by a group of New Englanders visiting New Orleans in the 1890s. When the Black Patti Troubadour Company visited the city, sister May joined and finally settled in New York City, promising an always encouraging and supportive mother that she would "rescue" the younger sister at some future date. The promise was kept: Olivia arrived in the big city around the turn of the twentieth century.

She arrived in New York City with both pianistic and vocal abilities. Of her early musical experiences Olivia recalled:

My first musical instrument was a comb and tissue paper. My sister and I celebrated my father and mother each evening after dinner, getting all conceivable harmonies and rhythms. As for the keyboard, the family acquired an old pump organ from a local minister's wife. They were moving to a country assignment and didn't have the money to move the organ. I got the gist of the thing and proceeded to teach myself. I soon began helping out at a local church, playing for the junior choir.

She continued:

The nearest to any teacher in music was Abbey Lyons of the Fisk Jubilee Singers. She married a New Orleans minister. But it was not the instruments; it was the voice that she taught [conversation with the author, February 22, 1979, New York City].

Once in the big city Olivia began working in vaudeville shows—"in order to make ends meet"—and studied the piano seriously with a Madam Harper, "colored." It was at one of these performances that she heard a British brother-and-sister team play a cello and piano duo. Olivia Porter decided that the cello was "the sweetest instrument ever heard" and that someday she would master it.

Porter began "trading" lessons with one of the several cellists whom she was then accompanying. An unevenness of exchange was soon evident. So, with money saved from piano lessons that she was offering and accompanying fees, she soon acquired her own cello and the tutoring services of Professor Turkisher, a renowned Hungarian cellist.

When Turkisher left the city she began studying with the black cellist Wesley Johnson and, finally, with black cellist Leonard Jeter, a member of the "Shuffle Along" Orchestra (1921). Porter began her affiliation with the Martin-Smith Music School in the early teens, serving as Jeter's assistant and a member of the school's orchestra. Chamber music had become a medium of musical expression, as she performed on radio with black violinist Charles Elgar and his ensemble, including two violins, piano, and cello. She also performed on various occasions with an all-female trio, with Marie Wayne (Townsend) on violin and Pearl Gibson on piano.

Cellist Porter was not one of the original members of the popular Lafayette Theatre Ladies' Orchestra led by Marie Lucas, but joined the group later as string bassist. A close friend of Marie Lucas, Porter was the orchestra's replacement for bassist Nellie Shelton. She recalled:

> Mr. Jeter arranged for me to study with a bassist from the New York Philharmonic, Mr. Buldreni. My fix and his were the same. When he came to this country, he was a cellist. But there was no vacancy. So, he made the switch and saw to it that I did the same. People use to say, "I played like a man and played bass like a cello. Buldreni taught me to play every note, including cues" [*ibid.*].

Olivia Porter, the bassist, became a permanent member of the Lafayette Orchestra and the Marie Lucas Orchestra that per-

formed at D.C.'s Howard Theatre (1917). Because of her solid musicianship she was a favorite with top male bands in the New
York area, both as regular and substitute. She was a frequent orchestral supporter of rag pianist/band leader Charles Luckyeth
"Luckey" Roberts and violinist/pianist/band leader Allie Ross.

But her real concern was for holding together a ladies' orchestra. Announcing "Music for All Occasions," she formed the
Olivia Shipp's Jazz-Mines—Famous Female Orchestra in the late
1920s. With the help of Local 802, American Federation of Musicians, and U.S. Representative (and subsequent New York City
Mayor) Fiorello La Guardia, an associate of her athlete husband,[1]
she organized the city's first civic orchestra, the Negro Women's
Orchestral and Civic Association. When Chicago pianist Lillian
"Lil" Hardin Armstrong accepted the offer of bringing a ladies'
band into Harlem's Apollo Theatre in the early 1930s (but had
not the band), Olivia Shipp supplied many of the ladies from her
Negro Women's Orchestral and Civic Association.

When asked at age ninety-eight if music had been her sole life's
work, she responded,

> Yes—I didn't come up just given things. I worked hard; I sacrificed.
> I had good teachers. For my lessons, I would take something out of
> my home and pawn it, because study was important to me. I never
> worked at anything but music. I played the best of shows; I worked
> with the best of them [*ibid.*].

At peace with self and the world, Olivia Shipp was radiant with
love, happiness, and fond memories of a glorious musical past.[2]

MINNIE "MEMPHIS MINNIE" DOUGLAS (McCoy)
guitar, vocals
b. June 3, 1896, Algiers, Louisiana / d. August 6 (?), 1973,
Memphis, Tennessee

Memphis Minnie is best remembered as a solo and duo performer. But in August 1930 she recorded in Chicago with a jug band
carrying her name (*The Great Jug Bands: 1927–1933*, Origin Jazz
Library, OJL4, Liner Notes by Sam Charters).[3] A 1954 Job recording carried the name "Memphis Minnie and Her Combo" (two
guitars, piano, and drums); a 1952 Checker recording carried the

name "Memphis Minnie with Little Joe and His Band" (guitar, piano, harmonica, and drums).

The Louisiana native moved to Walls, Mississippi, at age seven or eight, which placed her only a few miles from Memphis. She started playing the banjo around age ten and soon thereafter began playing the guitar. By age fifteen "Kid Douglas" was a popular Memphis street attraction, occasionally displaying her singing and playing talents in barber shops and at house parties.

Following a brief stint traveling all over the South with the Ringling Brothers Circus she returned to Memphis. The first of three marriages followed. All three husbands (Casey Bill Weldon, Joe "Kansas Joe" McCoy, and Ernest "Little Son Joe" Lawler) were, like Minnie herself, fine blues singers and guitarists. She collaborated with each mate, in live and recorded performances. Her greatest successes were in collaboration with "Kansas Joe."

In typical fashion, she was described as "a female Big Bill Broonzy." Regardless, she was acknowledged to be "the equal of the best among blues guitarists—superb, fluent, formidable technician, and consistently good." According to blues enthusiast Barbara Dane, her

> drive and finesse on the guitar, never approached by any other woman in the idiom, gave even male exponents . . . a tough time. . . . A legend . . . everywhere her records sold, she spread her special optimism, grit, swing and sensuality liberally for thirty years ["It's Hard to Be Mistreated," *Sing Out*, No. 3, 1966, p. 25].

Minnie moved to Chicago early in the 1930s, remaining in the Windy City until 1957. The Memphis country style of singing and playing gradually became more and more sophisticated. Returning to Memphis, she suffered a stroke in 1960 and remained paralyzed until her death.

A prolific recording artist (1929–59), Memphis Minnie was a best-seller for Vocalion, Columbia, Decca, Regal, Chess, and Job. In 1931 alone she appeared on fourteen records. During her thirty recording years the number of titles reached close to two hundred. For the best of Memphis Minnie, highly recommended are "Memphis Minnie With Joe McCoy" (Blues Classics No. 13) and "Memphis Minnie" (Blues Classics No. 1).

LAURA DUKES
ukulele, banjo (vocals)
b. June 10, 1907, Memphis, Tennessee

In the late 1970s Laura Dukes was helping to keep alive remnants of the once-vibrant city of Memphis, appearing regularly at Blues Alley, "night capital of downtown Memphis." A longtime favorite of Memphis audiences, Laura during this period was featured as a vocalist only, rocking the place nightly with oldtime blues hits and the more recent pop tunes.

The walls of Blues Alley were covered with photographs, plaques, and newspaper articles recalling the exciting career of Little Laura Dukes. She was especially proud of the plaque that read:

Beale St. Music Festival

LITTLE LAURA DUKES

In Appreciation for
Outstanding Contributions
to the World of Music

Memphis in May
1977

The powerful singer's adult weight was always less than one hundred pounds, distributed over a 4'7" frame. Occasionally referred to as "Little Bit," Laura Dukes never appeared concerned over her membership in the family of "Little People."

Little Laura's career began at age five, when her father lifted her to the stage of the Laura Smith Show. As she recalled, "I started to dance and sing. I could always dance and sing. I don't think I ever learned. I just could" (James Cortese, "Little Feet Keep On Dancing, Big Voice Keeps on Singing," *Commercial Appeal*, September 20, 1976). As she furthered recalled:

> I grew up running up and down Beale Street. My daddy [Alexander Dukes] used to play with the W. C. Handy Band. He taught me show business. This fella by the name of Robert McCollum taught

me to play the guitar. But with my little bitty hands, the uke became my instrument [conversation with the author, May 28, 1979, Memphis, Tennessee].

With her ukulele (occasionally banjo), her voice, and her dancing feet, Little Laura traveled with the J. A. Gentz and Frank Sutton carnivals and various minstrel shows. In the late 1920s she toured with blues singer Effie Moore. In the mid-1930s she joined The Will Batts Band, traveling throughout Mississippi, Arkansas, and Indiana. Following a brief period with trumpeter Son Smith's band, Little Laura played (sang, and danced) with the Memphis Jug Band from the late '40s through the '60s. She joined Charlie Banks and the Beale Street Originals in the mid-1960s, continuing the relationship through the early 1970s.

Little Laura was featured on Televista's videotape "Memphis South Side Blues," filmed in 1978. Blues Alley owners, employers, and guests celebrated her seventy-second birthday in 1979, recognizing close to seventy years of stellar performance. Signs of decline were in no way evident.

> VANZULA ("Van") CARTER HUNT
> guitar (piano, washboard, jug, vocals)
> b. September 1, 1909, Sommerville, Tennessee

Van often recalled her state of shock when she first learned of Bessie Smith's accident and subsequent death (1937). Van appeared regularly on the same bill as the "Empress of the Blues" and was a part of the show that Bessie was appearing with at the time of her death.

Sommerville native Van moved to Memphis during her teen years. The musical foundation was laid by family members, with whom she began playing at an early age. During the 1920s and '30s Van toured with various medicine shows, circuses, and carnivals, including Barnum and Bailey, Silas Green, Jessie Shipp, and the Hunt Brothers (no relation).

As a vocalist, she recorded in the '30s with the Tennessians, working under the name of The Carolina Peanut Boys (Victor). She was a respected composer; her "Selling the Jelly" can be heard on the reissued album "More of That Jug Band Sound,"

Origin Jazz Library, No. 9, featuring harmonica player Noah Lewis.

Van also played (and sang) with a W. C. Handy Band, one led by Howard Yancey and the Memphis Jug Band (fronted by several). Guitar was her principal instrument, though she was also quite proficient on piano, washboard, and jug. Singing was always a part of her professional assignment.

It was during the '30s that she put together her own touring show, including a band that she fronted. Through the musically lean years she coasted along singing and playing at Memphis vicinity clubs and house parties. Still active in the late 1970s, Van sang and played guitar at the 1978 Beale Street Festival and was featured on Televista's videotape "Memphis South Side Blues," also a 1978 production. In 1979 she journeyed to Louisville, Kentucky, to perform with The Beale Street Jug Band and participated in the Memphis Music Heritage Festival with the same group.

GERTRUDE ELOISE MARTIN
violin
b. 1910, New York City / d. September 6, 1945, New York City

Alain LeRoy Locke, spokesman for black contributions to American art and culture, in his 1936 listing of competent violinists who "warrant the expectation of full recognition and acclaim when opportunity comes," included the name Gertrude Martin (*The Negro and His Music*, p. 126). Violinist Martin was a member of the famous David I. Martin family, founders and directors of the Martin-Smith Music School. The youngest of three children (all fine string players), Gertrude had innate talent and musicianship. Following in the family tradition, she studied with her father (beginning at age six) and later with the noted Czech violinist/pedagogue Otakar Sevcik. Study with Professor Sevcik took place in Boston, where upon completion of the six-month course she received the master teacher's Artists Certificate.

Solo recitals were frequent for the talented violinist, in both America and the West Indies. Following a February 1936 concert at Howard University one reporter stated that Gertrude Martin is one of the most brilliant of our present day musicians (and the most brilliant of our violinists, if many personal opinions are accepted). Her playing is acclaimed as perfect in technique by those versed in the ways of violins, and the music she coaxes from that instrument—of which we, the unversed, are more sure—is full, vivid, moving. It is the sort of music which seems to strike a responsive chord within and hold one warmly breathless [Pitts, "Gertrude Martin, Violinist: An Opinion," *Negro Woman's World*, March 1935, p. 5].

Martin was concertmistress of the Martin-Smith School's Symphony Orchestra and before her early death was active in various local orchestras, including several sponsored by the Federal Music Project of the WPA. Her ability with the baton was an added source of musical recognition.

> MARGARET ("Peggy") PHILLIPS DAVIS
> violin, viola
> b. 1912, Hampton, Virginia

Violinist/violist Margaret Davis integrated the Peninsula Symphony Orchestra in the early 1960s. In the late '70s "Peggy," as she was known to her friends and associates, was continuing as a permanent member of the Tidewater, Virginia, organization.

Though enthusiastic over her orchestral association, Davis wanted most to be remembered as one who spent her professional life "getting string beginners started—encouraging and helping them to find themselves and develop as musicians." The inspiration for this notable endeavor came from I. Wesley Howard and Clarence Cameron White, two prominent black violinists and teachers.

The Howard/White encounter was the result of enrollment at Hampton Institute, where both her keyboardist mother and horn-playing father received their musical training. Prior to Howard and White, Peggy studied with German-born bandmaster W. O. Tessman, also at Hampton Institute. She graduated in 1933, a schoolmate of concert soprano Dorothy Maynor. According to Davis,

> Music was important at Hampton Institute. The music program was a busy one. Everyone in the department was required to play

in the orchestra [telephone conversation with the author, February 9, 1979].

Violinist/violist Davis gave thirty-three years to music education in the public schools, teaching for one year in Tucson, Arizona, and the remainder in three Virginia cities—Blackstone, Hampton, and Newport News. The teaching years were interrupted only long enough to complete the master's degree at Pennsylvania State University (1957).

Virginia's Tidewater area honored Davis on many occasions, in recognition of her having launched the careers of many Tidewater musicians and having established the string program in Newport News, where she gave twenty-three years of service. The final ones were spent as head of the String Program in Newport News. Retirement (1972) was only in the formal sense, for she continued as a studio teacher, instructor of violin and cello at the Virginia School (for the Blind) at Hampton, and violist with the Peninsula Symphony. A source of real pride was welcoming to orchestral membership some of her former students. Another source of pride was relinquishing her Head of Strings' position to one of her former students (see Dianne Chapman, later in this chapter).

DOROTHY E. SMITH
violin
b. Cleveland

The Cleveland Women's Orchestra, founded in 1935, had the distinction of being the oldest, continuously existing symphony orchestra in America composed entirely of women. One woman with a twenty-five-year affiliation with the organization (1937–65) was violinist Dorothy Smith (see "Member of All-Women's Band Barred from Hotel," *Chicago Defender*, August 5, 1939, p. 3). Her tenure was interrupted only by a three-year instructorship of violin and theory at Knoxville College (1942–45).

Smith's self-taught violin/mandolin-playing father led the turn-of-the-century Smith Quartet (violin-mandolin, viola, cello, and guitar) prior to the increase of his family to a wife and nine children; he consequently resorted to barbering. However, the father's influence was strong. According to Smith,

> I was just a dutiful little daughter, . . . afraid to tell Papa I wanted
> to quit. The teacher he had secured was wrong, practically starting
> all over at about age nineteen [correspondence with the author, De-
> cember 3, 1978].

Poor beginning-corrective measures taken, she enrolled at the
Cleveland Institute of Music, where for three years she was the
recipient of a Rosenwald scholarship. The list of new instructors
included André de Ribaupierre, Josef Fuchs, and Louis Persinger.
In later years she studied the Suzuki method of teaching violin at
Oberlin Conservatory.

Dorothy shared her skills with students at the Music School
Settlement of the Phillis Wheatley Association and taught privately. Performance centered around the Cleveland Women's Orchestra. Stated the violinist,

> I was a loner [racially] for many many years in the orchestra. Later,
> I had company—mostly high school students who played unusual
> instruments such as tuba, bassoon and tympani [*ibid.*].

Never having joined the musicians' union and facing a financial crisis after completion of graduate courses at Western Reserve
University, Smith took a civil-service examination and was soon
"locked into a Social Work position." However, she never completely divorced herself from music. A reflective violinist in 1979
wrote, "I turned down two offers to teach in the South . . . I have
felt real guilty for not following my profession more" (*ibid.*).

PENELOPE JOHNSON (RUFFIN)
violin
b. November 13, 1916, Columbus, Ohio / d. March 5,
    1979, New York City

A privileged few will recall the virtuoso playing of concert violinist Penelope Johnson. The Juilliard School of Music scholarship
student made frequent solo appearances in New York City and
toured the black-college circuit in the 1940s. Her commitment to
musical excellence was an inspiration to all who heard her.

In the mid-1940s Johnson organized a string quartet that performed frequently for church and community affairs. A Harlem
resident since graduation from high school, she joined the first-

violin section of the area's Martin-Smith Music School Symphony Orchestra while still a teenager. She was the first black female scholarship student on her instrument at the prestigious Berkshire Music Festival, in Lenox, Massachusetts. When Southern University (Baton Rouge, Louisiana) performed large choral works, such as oratorios and cantatas, during the 1950s, limited available instrumental forces were supplemented by outside players. Violinist Johnson joined the group of players that traveled to the southern college from New York City.

Quoting from "The Obituary":

> Thwarted in her quest for enduring success in her chosen field of music because of her ethnic origin, the strong influence of Dr. Adam Clayton Powell, Jr. (her minister) began to evidence itself. Penny, as she was now familiarly known, overcame monumental obstacles to become the first black person to be granted a license to operate a sightseeing agency in New York City ["Obsequies for Penelope Ruffin," Abyssinia Baptist Church, New York City, March 9, 1979].

Penelope operated tours throughout Manhattan and Harlem, being the first to bring tourists into the latter area. Soon Harlem became her exclusive concern. The tours continued after her death, as a living monument to her achievements in the field of tourism, a second professional choice.

VIVIAN LaVELLE WEAVER
harp (piano, organ)
b. August 18, 1918, Cleveland

Norman Nadel of the Columbus (Ohio) *Citizen* wrote the following after hearing harpist Weaver in recital:

> She has a thorough understanding of her instrument and obviously sincere responsiveness to the music she plays. A mature, confident, technically skilled musician, she drew from her harp an amazing variety of tone colors, exceptional volume range and exquisite and sensitive interpretations. She knows the secrets of effective phrasing of contrast, delicacy and grandeur in music [January 31, 1948].

Weaver was born into a family where music was important. Her trumpeter father led many local bands; her sister studied vio-

lin and piano (although she eventually chose another profession);
and a brother was a promising classical and jazz musician. She
received the B.Mus. Ed. Degree (cum laude) from Howard University and a master's degree in public school music from Western Reserve University. Additional study was pursued at the
Cleveland Institute of Music, with Cleveland Symphony harpist
Alice Chalifoux.

As a solo harpist, Weaver covered the black-college circuit and
toured for two years with the Nobel Sissle Concert Varieties (doubling as harpist and pianist), along with a singer and violinist.
Orchestral/ensemble affiliations included three years of permanent membership in the Cleveland Women's Symphony Orchestra, harp-ensemble appearances with the Cleveland Symphony,
Mount Pleasant (Ohio) Symphony Orchestra, and The Duke Ellington Band for the show *My People*.

Though primarily a harpist, Weaver was rated as a fully competent pianist and organist. A woman of varied talents, she
trained and directed many school and church choral groups and
played lead and supporting dramatic roles with the Howard University Players and the Gilpin Players of Cleveland's famed Kar-
amu House. She was affiliated with the Cleveland Public Schools
(as vocal/instrumental music teacher and director of dramatics)
and taught privately.

A woman of diverse interest and skills, Weaver was the Cleveland representative for Motown Attractions, Queen Booking
Agency, and the Shaw Theatrical Agency. A member of the
American Guild of Variety Artists, Weaver for a period directed
her own theatrical booking agency, Erieview Attractions. Respected and honored for her many accomplishments, she has
been the recipient of many honors and awards, including Delta-
Sigma Theta Sorority's Outstanding Achievement Award, the
Artha-Jon Ukaya Outstanding Talent and Achievement Award,
and the Cleveland Howard Alumni Club's Outstanding Alumnus
Award.

SYLVIA MEDFORD
violin
b. New York City

The mid- and late 1970s found New York City violinist Sylvia
Medford realizing some of the playing satisfaction and security

that she once thought had eluded her. In the late 1960s the violin case was closed for one solid year, as Medford worked as a sales-clerk at Stern's Department Store in New York City. She hesitated to talk about the past, recalling the many indications of listener disbelief when she related her musical experiences to others. Said Medford,

> Sometimes when you are so honest, it sounds like fantasy—make believe. Yet, I've always wanted to tell my story, for posterity's sake [conversation with the author, New Rochelle, New York, July 9, 1976].

Of her early musical training. Medford said,

> I began studying violin at age five, after hearing my cousin play in a student recital. He recommended his teacher, John Richards [black]. Limited funds were stretched to include the cost of private instruc-tion for me and my sister [piano], because music was important in the Medford household [*ibid*.].

The daughter of West Indian parents (mother from St. Kitts and father from Barbados), she gave her first full-length recital at age twelve. Now a promising student of Russian pedagogue Vladimir Graffman (father of pianist Gary Graffman), with one recital com-pleted, she began preparations for the next. Performance sites in-cluded reputable Aeolian, Masters Institute, Steinway, Carnegie Recital, and Town halls.

Medford's first orchestral involvement was with the National Youth Administration Orchestra, a musically and economically rewarding (for a high school student) but socially degrading ex-perience. Of the many visiting conductors, one was not receptive to the idea of "up-front" seating for a black—the black being the only nonwhite player. She was reassigned to the rear of the sec-tion. Regardless, Medford remained with the group throughout its existence, retaining the fondest memories of guest conductors Leopold Stokowski and Dean Dixon. She stated that Dean Dixon remained uppermost in her memories, "because of his ability to teach from the podium." It was Dixon who recommended her next teacher, Mario Viletto of Arturo Toscanini's NBC Symphony.

Other persons and groups that Sylvia recalled with affection were Congressman/minister Adam Clayton Powell and Abyssinia Baptist Church, trumpeter/composer William C. Handy, The Monarch Band, and the Urban League of Greater New York. All provided assistance (moral and financial), consistent encouragement, and performing opportunities.

Following the years at Manhattan's Washington Irving High School Medford entered Brooklyn College, where she received the B.A. in Music Education. During her last college year she participated in The Earl Hines Band (1943). Later she toured Europe with USO Camp Shows.

Upon her return to the States, hopes for a solo career were abandoned as she began concentrating on orchestral career opportunities. Along the way, she played with black conductor Dean Dixon's American Youth Orchestra and black conductor Everett Lee's Cosmopolitan Orchestra. A successful audition for the Brooklyn Symphony Orchestra, created in 1949, brought on words of gratitude for auditioning conductor Herbert Zipper. Responded the maestro, "Don't thank me. You are here because of your talent." For the eighty-five-player orchestra maestro Zipper auditioned seven hundred players. Unfortunately, the orchestra's existence was brief.

"One shot" and "occasional" orchestral associations were in abundance throughout the 1950s and early '60s, including the Municipal Concert Orchestra, Brooklyn Philharmonic, Orchestra of America, and Radio City Music Hall Orchestra.

The mid-'60s brought on affiliation with the newly formed Symphony of the New World and the beginning of several seasons with "Soul Brother No. 1," James Brown's touring orchestra. The late '60s and early '70s comeback trail offered promise, with employment opportunities in the New Jersey, Westchester, Puerto Rico, Dance Theatre of Harlem, and American Symphony orchestras and several Broadway pit orchestras. Additionally, Medford spent a few years teaching privately in her own studio and gave about five years of service to singer Dorothy Maynor's Harlem School of the Arts.

In 1977 her years of "outstanding musical achievements and cultural contributions to the community" were recognized by the New York Chapter of the National Association of Negro Musicians. Most New York musicians agreed that despite the lack of full recognition violinist Medford remained one of the city's finest—technically reliable, musically sensitive, and tonally superior.

LUCILLE DIXON (ROBERTSON)
string bass
b. February 27, 1923, New York City

A mid-1970 résumé for Lucille Dixon listed under "Professions": Musician/Double Bassist, Symphony Manager, and Realtor. To these might have been added orchestra leader, organizer, artistic activist, music commentator, typist, receptionist, and supervisor of press-release information (war department).

Lucille Dixon's career has been a most exciting one, filled with the routine challenges and epitomizing the added burdens of femininity, blackness, and forthrightness. She studied piano with her mother before enrolling in New York City's Carmen Sheppard School of Music (a black institution). With an eye on her only brother's beautiful saxophone, she began playing clarinet in high school but was soon "conned" into playing bass. Before long, P. K. (preacher's kid) Dixon successfully auditioned for the exclusive All-City High School Orchestra. Shortly thereafter she began studying with the New York Philharmonic's principal bassist, Fred Zimmerman, and was the second of two black females admitted to the National Youth Administration Orchestra. As a clearinghouse for orchestras throughout the country, the NYA practiced six hours a day, five days a week. A small salary was paid each member.

While participating in the NYA she was enrolled at Brooklyn College (1941–43) and playing bass with the Juilliard Orchestra. In the meantime all-girl orchestras in the national market were becoming quite fashionable. But Dixon's requests for auditions were denied, even with groups designed for radio broadcasting (and where color was not discernable).

By 1943 employment in a symphony orchestra appeared to be an unrealistic pursuit. As she pointed out,

> I became well aware that no blacks were playing in any of the nation's symphonies, and it was obvious that none were going to be placed through the NYA orchestra. As long as the symphony was in existence, I continued to play. But after it was over [1942], I decided that I had to make a living and would just have to go into some other kind of music [Handy, "Conversation with Lucille Dixon," *Black Perspective in Music,* Fall 1975, p. 305].

The result was a turn to jazz, a decision easily reached when an offer to tour with Earl "Fatha" Hines presented itself. Additionally, she had spent the summer of '42 touring with The International Sweethearts of Rhythm. Touring became a way of life for two years. In 1946 she formed her own orchestra as a means of terminating the constant travel.

As a jazz bassist, Dixon gained and maintained tremendous respect. But as jazz historian Frank Driggs wrote, in laying his claim that women in jazz had not received their deserved recognition:

> Who remembers the promising bassist Lucille Dixon who made such a bright beginning in 1943? In order to keep working steadily, she wound up leading a nightclub band in Greenwich Village for many years. She is still working [1977], but the kind of recognition she should be getting today has passed her by [Driggs, *Women in Jazz: A Survey*, p. 4].

The idea of playing in a symphony orchestra remained. Between 1960 and 1964 Dixon was a member of New York City's National Orchestra Association (another symphony orchestra clearinghouse), learning more symphonic orchestral repertory and winning the association's achievement awards in 1961 and 1962. But the picture for black membership in professionally secure American orchestras remained essentially unchanged. Dixon, now past forty, joined ranks with other concerned musicians in 1964. The result was formation of the Symphony of the New World. She explained her affiliation:

> I should like for the children of today to have a choice. If they want classical, there's a place for them to go. If they want jazz, they can go into jazz . . .
> I am . . . determined to see that the Symphony of the New World succeeds. I don't want black youth of this and future generations to experience some of the things that I experienced [Handy, "Conversation . . ., p. 305].

Let us note here that it was Lucille Dixon who organized and spearheaded the activities of the Concerned Musicians Association (1969), in support of two young black men who brought charges of discrimination against the New York Philharmonic before the state's Division of Human Rights (see Eleanor Wehle, "Music Still Sounds Sour When It Comes to Color," *Standard-Star*, July 10, 1970, p. II-1). It was Lucille who challenged the "artistic judgment/artistic discretion rights" and "can't find any qualified" claims of symphony orchestra hiring agents and agencies (1971). She expressed her views in a "letter to the editor" and later in a guest music commentator column—both in the *New York Times* (Lucille Dixon, "Put Down," *New York Times*, May 30, 1971, p. D12; "Is It 'Artistic Judgement' or Is It Discrimination?," August 1, 1971, pp. 11, 18).

Other orchestral affiliations of Lucille Dixon included: National Symphony of Panama (1954–56), Radio City Music Hall (1960), Boston Women's Symphony (principal) and Orchestra of America (1964–65), Dimitri Mitropoulos Competitions (1965–67), Westchester Philharmonic (1962–72), Ridgefield Symphony (1972–73), and Scranton Symphony (1970–72). Her relationship with the Symphony of the New World ended in 1976, but not prior to her having served as the orchestra's manager (see Chapter VI). The mother of three children was still very active in the late 1970s. A veteran of the business, six nights a week she served as trio bassist in a Westchester, New York, dinner theater. As concerts occurred for the Bridgeport, Connecticut and Westchester orchestras, Dixon's schedule was arranged so as to accommodate participation. Additionally, she was only a few credits away from receiving a degree in business management from Iona College.

The degree has now been received. For a number of years (in the mid and late 1980s) Dixon was a member of the Executive Board of Local 802 (New York City), American Federation of Musicians. Performance was soon restricted to an Evening Dinner Theatre in Elmsford, New York. Also during the late 1980s and early 1990s, Dixon served as a panelist of the National Endowment for the Arts.

HARRIETTE DAVISON WATKINS
violin
b. December 11, 1923, Newark, New Jersey/d. June 16,
1978, Newark

A child prodigy, Watkins enjoyed a full and exciting career. Following years of local recognition in her native Newark she began to gain national recognition in 1941, when she made a solo appearance at the Twenty-First Annual Convention of the National Association of Negro Musicians' meeting in Pittsburgh.

Watkins received the bachelors degree from Oberlin Conservatory and studied further at the Cleveland Institute of Music, Juilliard, and Columbia. She was a founder of the chamber group known as Music Among Friends, sharing the enthusiastic spirit of "musical togetherness" with her French-hornist husband Julius Watkins. Other group affiliations were the Harlem Philharmonic and the Symphony of the New World.

EDNA MARILYN SMITH (Edet)
string bass
b. January 16, 1924, Boston

Between 1956 and 1961 Smith earned the B.Mus., M.Mus., M.A., and Ed.D. degrees, the first two from Manhattan School of Music and the latter two from Teachers College, Columbia University. During these years she worked in the New York City Public Schools, at both the elementary and the secondary levels. From 1961 to 1967 she lived in Africa, serving as a lecturer at the University of Nigeria.

Returning to the States, Smith served on the faculties of Queens and Medgar Evers colleges. Research on the subject of African and Afro-American music led to the publication of articles in scholarly journals and appearances on radio and television.

History will no doubt register Smith's major contribution as that of a music educator. However, it must also register her name as a major contributor to the history of jazz. She performed primarily in the 1940's and '50s, first with The International Sweethearts of Rhythm, then with The Vi Burnside Orchestra, and finally, with The Edna Smith Trio. Edna Smith [Edet] "speaks out" on her career and black womanhood in Shanta Nurullah, "The Family Struggles of Sisters Makin' Music" (*Black Books Bulletin*, Vol. 6, No. 2, 1978, pp. 20–27).

CARLINE RAY (Russell)
string bass, guitar, piano, vocals)
b. April 21, 1925, New York City

Music was in Carline Ray's blood; the acquisition of superior training was a family tradition. Ray's father was a first-class brass man, graduating from Tuskegee Institute and the Juilliard School of Music. Her mother (Mary Catherine Baker) was a freelancing pianist with various New York City ensembles. When Ray took a mate, she selected the remarkable pianist/band leader Luis Russell (1902–63).

She received the B.S. degree in piano and composition in 1946 from Juilliard; ten years later she received the M.Mus. in voice from the Manhattan School of Music. She was a student of Metropolitan Opera's John Brownlee; her superb musicianship and a marvelous contralto voice justified her classification as one of the nation's finest concert choristers.

Spanning a quarter of a century, her choral affiliations (both in concert and recording studio) included the Schola Cantorum, Musica Aeterna, Camerata Singers, and the Bach Aria Group. When listening to the Metropolitan Opera recording of *Carmen*, with Marilyn Horne, James McCracken, and Leonard Bernstein (Deutsche Grammophon), be aware that one voice heard is that of Carline Ray. On the recording "Mary Lou's Mass" (Mary Records, M 102), be aware that Carline Ray was present, in the double role of vocalist and bassist.

As vocal soloist, Ray worked with trumpeter/band leader Erskine Hawkins (1948). Sometime during the early 1970s she produced for *Music Minus One* the album "Music for Contralto and Piano," Carline Ray and Bruce Eberle. In the mid-70's Ray served as an adjunct instructor at New York City's Medgar Evers College and as director of the college choir.

As a pianist, they called her "Queen of the Keyboard." She worked with The Edna Smith Trio (piano, drums, bass) for about two years in the mid-1950s. Ray's performing skills already included the guitar when Edna Smith's mastery of the Fender bass encouraged her to expand still further instrumentally.

As a guitarist, she worked with The International Sweethearts of Rhythm and as bassist with Skitch Henderson's Band, as well as those fronted by Peter Duchin, Sy Oliver, and Frank Anderson (Latin and calypso). In 1976 she toured as bassist with The Duke Ellington Band, covering the western USA, Canada, and Japan. Throughout the 1970s Ray "the bassist" worked as a regular with the Alvin Ailey Dance Company and for brief periods with the

American Ballet Theatre, Royal Ballet, and Pennsylvania Ballet orchestras.

She appeared as bassist with the six-piece all-women's jazz band (three blacks, three whites) for the Calvert Extra Sunday Concerts at New York City's Jazz Museum in 1973. She was most visible (and audible) at both the 1978 and 1979 Women's Jazz Festivals in Kansas City. At the former she was the featured bassist in a performance of "Mary Lou's Mass" for the Premiere Concert. According to journalist Cathy Lee, "Carline's almost baritone vocal about Lazarus' triumph over the rich man who refused his calls for material help was a highlight" ("First Women's Jazz Festival KO's Kaycee," *Sojourner* [Jazz Supplement], May 1978, p. 11).

At the 1979 event Carline Ray was the bassist (and only black) for Aerial, the group that won the Combo Tape Contest (piano, flute, bass, and drums). She also served as bassist and leader of the seventeen-piece performing group Big Apple Jazz Women, representing the New York-based Universal Jazz Coalition. Finally, Ray "the singer" emerged as one of the Festival's top vocalists, performing Emme Kemp's "Tomorrow's Woman."

Her more than half a century of performance now includes jazz, R&B, classical, and pop styles. Most recently she was bassist in the backup group for R&B diva Ruth Brown. Currently she is bassist with the New York City based group of four black women, Jazzberry Jam. The late 1980s and early 1990s saw Ray serving as a panelist for the National Endowment for the Arts.

VIOLET ("Vi") M. WILSON
bass (string and Fender) (piano)
b. December 16, 1925, Los Angeles, California

Wilson has been playing jazz bass for half a century, mainly on the West Coast. Though she spent a lot of time on the road with various bands (large and small), Los Angeles, where she grew up and received her training, was home. She was introduced to the bass in junior high school by teacher Mrs. Bignel. High school and college instructors figured importantly in her development as a musician.

Wilson also came under the influence of Alma Hightower (percussionist and piano player), who worked diligently with young music students. Wilson's talent brought her invitations to play with all the important women's groups that visited the city. She played briefly with the International Sweethearts of Rhythm and spent time with the Darlings of Rhythm and Frances Gray's Queens of Swing (West Coast). Between 1948 and 1953, she worked in Chicago with pianist/organist Sarah McLawler's popular Syncoettes. Before long the group was brought east by the Moe Gale Agency. Amid all of her musical activities, Wilson trained and apprenticed to be a barber and became a qualified master barber.

In 1976–77 she sang with the Interdenomination Choir under the direction of Joseph Westmoreland of the Los Angeles Philharmonic. The choir made a three-week tour of Israel, Jordan, and other countries in the area with maestro Zubin Mehta. Wilson indicates that this was an unforgettable experience. Currently Wilson is active with church choirs and the Most Worshipful Sons of Light (Grand Lodge), Queen Ada Division (a fraternal organization). A member of Trinity Baptist Church, she contributes her piano skills to the work of the church.

Wilson's message to the world is, "Women musicians should be given more credit for the contribution they have given to the music world." This message is shared on behalf of the many who never got the recognition that they deserved (telephone conversation with author, July 8, 1996).

MAURINE ELISE MOORE FRANCISCO
violin
b. March 14, 1929, Oklahoma City / d. March 1978,
   Oklahoma City

The Oklahoma City Symphony Orchestra's first black member was violinist Maurine Francisco. She joined the ensemble in 1962 and was a charter member of the Oklahoma City Chamber Orchestra. For many years she headed the string department at Langston University, where she was also assistant professor of theory. Francisco was serving in this capacity at the time of her death. During her final years she was a member of the Lawton Philharmonic Orchestra (Oklahoma), along with her son, who was a member of the orchestra's bass section.

A frequent recitalist, Francisco attributed her success to "parental interest—their constant encouragement and financial back-

ing, good teachers providing good foundations, and practice."
She listed as problems encountered during her training period:
1) inability to join community student orchestras due to race[4] and
2) having to travel out of the local area for instruction since no
Negro instructors in strings were available.

When asked what problems she encountered while in pursuit
of professional status, she responded, "Limited openings for
Negro teachers in local areas" (survey, Handy, "Black Music and
Black Musicians," 1971). Nevertheless, Francisco maintained a
private music studio in Oklahoma City, teaching string instruments and piano, and was a teaching fellow at the Interlochen
(Michigan) Arts Academy.

Francisco received the B.Mus. from Howard University and the
M.A. from Teachers College, Columbia University. Additional
studies took place at the Juilliard School of Music, Northwestern
University, and the University of Michigan. At the time of her
death she was a doctoral candidate at the University of Oklahoma. For a period of time she worked in the music department
at Tennessee State University, teaching strings and music theory.
She was an original member of the University's Mells Memorial
String Quartet.

GERMAINE BAZZLE
string bass (piano, vocals)
b. March 28, 1932, New Orleans

Visitors to the Mardi Gras City in the late 1970s probably encoun-
tered Germaine Bazzle the vocalist, appearing with The Original
Tuxedo Jazz Band (continued by Bob French, drummer, son of
Albert "Papa" French), June Gardner, or Red Tyler and The Gen-
tlemen of Jazz. Earlier in the '70s privileged students encountered
Germaine Bazzle the educator, as she served on the faculty of
Xavier Preparatory High School, also in the Crescent City.

During the early 1960s students at Washington High School in
Thibodaux, Louisiana, also encountered Bazzle the educator. The
local community encountered Germaine Bazzle the bassist—the
youthful member of Earl Foster's five-piece band, which specialized in dixieland. According to Bazzle

The experience was tremendous. There were no rehearsals; you
learned on the bandstand. The leader called a tune; your ears [plus

fingers, hand, and bow] went to work [telephone conversation with the author, December 2, 1978].

This experience lasted for six or seven years.

Bazzle started playing bass when she was fourteen, participating in Xavier University's Junior School of Music Orchestra. Though the group's repertory was of the "elite art" type, as she once stated to journalist James Borders,

> Sister Mary Letitia [her teacher] never put thumbs down on the kind of music that I liked. She knew that I had a leaning toward what we called jazz because she used to hear me singing it a lot, but she never discouraged it ["Jazz Singer's Career Started Off Bass," *New Orleans States Item,* April 10, 1976].

The period with Earl Foster's band followed graduation from Xavier University. Between the bass-playing years and the era of vocal specialization Bazzle engaged in professional duo-piano playing, primarily in the Thibodaux vicinity.

> DOROTHY JEANNE ASHBY (Thompson)
> harp (piano, vocals)
> b. August 6, 1932, Detroit / d. April 13, 1986, Santa
>   Monica, California

Harpist Ashby studied at Cass Technical High School and Wayne State University (harp, piano, and voice). Early instruction came from her self-taught, jazz-guitar-playing father Wiley Thompson. She served as harpist in the Wayne State University Orchestra and filled assignments as choir pianist and studio accompanist. She was featured folk singer on Detroit radio station WJR and for a while hosted the station's jazz discussion show "The Lab."

When the Detroit Public Schools began its harp program in 1969 Ashby played a very active role. Her lecture-demonstrations were frequent. In the 1970s she began spending much of her time on the West Coast. Television viewers occasionally glimpsed the virtuoso harpist as a member of various orchestral ensembles, but in many instances she was recognized only aurally.

The Dorothy Ashby Trio won accolades internationally, performing in concert halls, night clubs, and on television and radio shows. The bands with which the trio performed included Duke

Ellington's, Louis Armstrong's, and Woody Herman's. Larger group participation was represented on the 1965 Atlantic album "The Fantastic Jazz Harp of Dorothy Ashby" (1447), with the number of ensemble members reaching seven. A master musician, virtuoso harpist, and authoritative jazz exponent, obviously she surrounded herself with musicians of a similar caliber, for example, trombonists Jimmy Cleveland, Quentin Jackson, Sonny Russo, and Tony Studd; bassist Richard Davis; drummer Grady Tate; and percussionist Willie Bobo.

Jazz commentator Bob Rolontz stated the case well when he wrote,

> To achieve fame as a harpist is not an easy task. To achieve fame as a jazz harpist is infinitely more difficult. She has become famous as America's foremost jazz harpist . . . She is the first harpist ever to be chosen by readers of *Down Beat* in the Down Beat Reader's Jazz Poll. She was also chosen by the critics in the Down Beat International Critic's Jazz Poll in 1962 [liner notes for the album "The Fantastic Jazz Harp of Dorothy Ashby"].

When she moved to California in the early 1970s, her reputation remained intact. She also became a much sought after studio musician.

> JESSIE MAE HEMPHILL (Brooks)
> guitar, bass drum (tambourine, piano, organ)
> b. October 18, 1932, Senatobia, Mississippi

One ambition of Jessie Mae's was "to keep the Hemphill name alive" (conversation with the author, June 1, 1979, Memphis, Tennessee). Her great-grandfather was a performing fiddler. Grandfather Sid Hemphill (d. 1961) was a popular musician in the Senatobia area, specializing on the fiddle, but also playing drums, guitar, mandolin, banjo, fife, quills, and harmonica. As her Aunt Rosa Lee Hill (a guitarist) related to blues enthusiast George Mitchell,

> My daddy [Sid] played everywhere . . . Play for white till ten o'clock and then play for colored till twelve at night. And he play music from Monday till Monday again . . . Everybody in my family played. My mother, my daddy, my auntie, and my grandpa played, all my

cousins and sisters played. The whole Hemphill band played music—all of 'em [*Blow My Blues Away*, pp. 62–65].

Jessie Mae took her place in the family band at age eight, joining musical ranks with her mother (Virgie Lee, guitar and drums), aunts, grandfather, sisters, brothers, and cousins. She was already a show-business veteran, however, having won several singing, dancing, and drumming competitions. On one occasion she took the prize for beating and shaking the tambourine.

Through the years Hemphill never left music, though the financial rewards were minimal. Her two specialties were guitar and bass drum. Her style of guitar playing called for making the strings say what she was saying, "in the Hemphill manner."

Performance sites varied from house parties to church socials to area festivals and community get-togethers; her repertory varied from gospel to blues to boogie-woogie. She liked to be called "boogie-woogie woman." Home base was Panola County, Mississippi, but musical travels occasionally carried her into Tennessee, Alabama, Kentucky, and Virginia.

The 1970s offered musical promise, particularly during the latter part of the decade. She appeared at Memphis' Beale Street Music Festival and the Second Annual Delta Blues Festival in Greenville, Mississippi, both in 1979. Her participation was both as soloist (guitar) and as a member of The Beale Street Jug Band and The Napoleon Strickland Fife and Drum Band (guitar, vocals, and bass drum). Hemphill was prominently featured at the 1979 African-American Crafts Conference/Jubilee Memphis, appearing in duo with hat-box/washtub–playing Compton Jones and as bass drummer with the Fife and Drum Band. During this visit to the blues capital she made her debut at the popular club Blues Alley. Musical travels of early 1980 brought Hemphill to Richmond, Virginia, and Washington, D.C., performing in the latter city for the Folklore Society of Greater Washington and at the Smithsonian Institution.

Hemphill performed her own compositions almost exclusively. Since the first edition of this book she has performed in over twenty states and nine foreign countries. She was the recipient of the 1987 and 1988 Handy Award for traditional female blues artist of the year.

MARIE HENSE
violin
b. July 2, 1937, Trenton, New Jersey

Violinist Hense arrived in New York City in the fall of 1960, having only recently completed her undergraduate and graduate studies at Boston's New England Conservatory. Participation in Yale University's Summer Music School followed a June '60 graduation. It was there that she met Visiting Artist Julius Baker (flutist). The popular New York freelancer (subsequently principal flutist of the New York Philharmonic) convinced Hense that the time was ripe for her to tackle the city that she desperately feared.

The twenty-three-year-old violinist had been studying the instrument for almost two decades. It was her pianist/piano-teacher mother who decided that the violin was the appropriate instrument for young Marie. One year prior to her beginning the violin Marie's name appeared on her mother's piano roster.

A product of the Trenton Public Schools, Hense's exceptional ability netted her a place in the Trenton Youth and New Jersey All-State orchestras. Entering New England Conservatory in 1954, Hense soon began to take advantage of freelancing opportunities. Additionally, she became a regular with the Springfield (Massachusetts) Symphony Orchestra. The summers of '56 and '58 were spent acquiring experience and exposure at Tanglewood (Lenox, Massachusetts), participating in the Boston Symphony-sponsored Berkshire Music Center's summer school for advanced musical training.

In 1960 violinist Hense arrived in New York City with not only the proper training but also the necessary professional experience. Lodging was provided by a great-aunt, in Brooklyn. Employment was at a Fifth Avenue bookstore (Doubleday)—selling records, with an occasional extra dollar coming in from babysitting. She began spreading the word, "Violinist Marie Hense is in town and is available for employment." Quite a pronouncement, in view of the fact that the city was already accommodating several thousand violinists, all Local 802 AFM card holders. But, said Hense, "I could feel it in my bones. I would survive and I would survive as a musician" (conversation with the author, July 9, 1976, New York City).

Word of Hense's availability began to circulate, and by summer

'60 several "pick-up" orchestras included the name Marie Hense on their rosters. This continued during all subsequent summers, but to a lesser extent as more permanent playing opportunities increased. During her first year in the city she was a commuting member of the Springfield Symphony's string section. She played regularly with the Symphony of the New World during the first few years of its existence. Additionally, Hense was a member of the pit orchestra of such popular Broadway shows as *Carnival, Oliver, Fiddler on the Roof, Cabaret, Mame, Happy Times,* and revivals of *Annie Get Your Gun* and *Lost in the Stars.* But Hense's major impact on the city of New York was as a contractor—serving as musical employer, supervisor, and musicians' union liaison rather than as musical employee.

CARLOTTA GARY
cello
b. November 29, 1940, Buffalo, New York

After graduating from high school Gary enrolled at the University of Buffalo, in pursuit of a degree in Business Administration. She soon abandoned this idea for a degree in Music Education from Fredonia College, SUNY (1964). She went on to receive the MSLS from Syracuse University (1966). Additional training was received at the Juilliard School of Music (music calligraphy) and New York University (Performing Arts Administration). A student of New York Philharmonic solo cellist Lorne Munroe, she was twice the recipient of a New York Philharmonic scholarship to defray the cost. Juilliard study was made possible by a scholarship from the New York Public Library.

Gary's work as a librarian begun in 1964, moving up to the position of Senior Librarian in charge of the New York Public Library's Orchestra Collection at Lincoln Center. Her responsibilities included "liaison for the library with conductors, orchestra managers and librarians, music service organizations, orchestra collections, music schools and conservatories and music publishers." Between 1963 and 1974 Gary taught at the elementary, junior high, and college levels (Mannes College of Music).

As a solo cellist, Gary appeared with the Huntington Philharmonic, Yonkers Civic Philharmonic, New York City Housing Authority Symphony, Greenwich House Orchestra, Crossroads

Chamber Orchestra, and Shenandoah Valley Music Festival Orchestra. Her ensemble affiliations included the Fredonia College Symphony and Faculty Chamber Orchestra, American Broadcasting Company Studio Chamber Orchestra, Municipal Concerts Orchestra, Shenandoah Valley Music Festival Orchestra, New York Lyric Opera, Westchester Symphony, Symphony of the New World, Alvin Ailey Dance Theatre Orchestra, and the Little Orchestra Society. In 1977, she added to her group affiliations the popular New York City-based ensemble known as Mixtures, a group that she organized and managed.

DIANNE HUGHES CHAPMAN
viola
b. January 28, 1942, Newport News, Virginia

An appropriate place for a school system's string and orchestra department coordinator is in the orchestra. That is where violinist Chapman was to be found in the mid- and late '70s, interestingly enough, sitting next to her retired predecessor, Margaret Davis, in the same position. Chapman was a permanent member of the Peninsula Symphony Orchestra and various "occasional" orchestras for special performances. She also lent her talents to the Hampton Institute Community Orchestra and String Quartet and the Faculty Ensemble of the Newport News Schools.

Chapman was musically influenced by her church-organist father. Following the elementary and secondary years in Newport News Public Schools she enrolled at Virginia State College, for both the undergraduate and graduate degrees. She was the college's first recipient of the M.Mus. Ed. degree. Her list of string instructors included Raymond Montoni, Thomas C. Bridge (of the Richmond Symphony), and Margaret P. Davis. She was District Chairman of Strings, Virginia Band and Orchestra Directors Association, and at one point served on the Board of Directors of the National School Orchestra Association.

VALERIE COLLYMORE (BYNUM)
violin
b. March 9, 1942, Bronx, New York

Collymore attributed her success to "strong parental influence, an equally strong desire to play, and a willingness to work." The discouraging experiences but "despite-it-all" accomplishments of her violinist father, Winston Collymore, played a meaningful part in the younger violinist's development.

When asked, "What problems did you encounter during your training period?," her response was: "None really serious enough to cause a major setback. Though I was sometimes seated in 'the back of the bus,' my confronting the conductor and/or challenging [an earlier decision] produced results." Asked what problems she encountered while in pursuit of professional status, she responded "None that so stymied me that I couldn't look for another way 'in' " (survey, Handy, "Black Music and Black Musicians," 1971).

Violinist Collymore received the B.S. in Music Education degree from Ithaca College in 1963. She was a regular member of the Radio City Music Hall Orchestra from 1963 to 1965. Membership in the Symphony of the New World began during the orchestra's initial year, 1965. Other orchestral involvements included The String Reunion, Urban Philharmonic, Metropolitan Opera, Westbury Music Fair, Russian Ballet, studio, and Broadway pit orchestras.

ANN (Stevens) HOBSON-PILOT
harp
b. November 6, 1943, Philadelphia

The real orchestral breakthrough for black female string players took place in Washington, D.C., when Ann Hobson became principal harpist of the National Symphony. The year was 1966; the National Symphony Orchestra's principal harpist had met with a finger accident. With insufficient time for advertising and auditioning, a master harpist (who was also a master musician) was needed at once to fill a one-year assignment. The orchestra's management contacted harp authority Alice Chalifoux of the Cleveland Symphony Orchestra, who in turn contacted her student Ann.

The recent Cleveland Institute of Music graduate had acquired the necessary experience—as substitute second harpist with the Pittsburgh Symphony during her final year of academic study (1965–66); with various pick-up orchestras in her native Philadelphia (including the all-black Philadelphia Concert Orchestra);

and with Philadelphia's All-City High School Orchestra, while still enrolled at Girls High School in Philadelphia. She had also engaged in serious study and performance at Camden, Maine's Salzedo School for Harpists and Marlboro Music Festival.

The one-year assignment with the National Symphony lasted for several additional seasons. In 1969 an opening for second harpist occurred in one of America's "Big Three" orchestras, the Boston Symphony. A decision had to be made—principal in the National or second in the Boston? Competing for the latter position with approximately thirty other harpists, twenty-five-year-old Hobson emerged the undisputed winner. To make the decision easier, the Boston position was upgraded from second harpist to associate principal—and she would serve as principal harpist with the Boston Pops Orchestra.

Hobson began studying the piano at age six. Her mother trained to be a concert pianist, but only partially realized her ambitions through piano teaching. Mrs. Hobson's two daughters were included in her list of students. Then, the family's three and a half years in Germany (while father Hobson filled a military assignment) provided continued cultural exposure and private piano instruction with German tutors for young Ann.

Practice at home permitted interruptions from a perfectionist mother—"E flat, not E natural," "Watch the pedal," "Check your key signature," and similar pedagogical directives not necessarily welcomed by an early music student. Said a reflective Hobson:

> The thought occurred to me to take up an instrument that my mother could not tell me what I was doing wrong. Philadelphia's Girls High School had a strong music program. I approached the music chairman about participating. My first choice was the flute, but there were already too many. The Chairman suggested that I consider the harp, in view of my strong piano background [conversation with the author, September 26, 1975, Brookline, Massachusetts].

From the beginning (age fourteen), harp and Ann Hobson seemed to mesh perfectly. As she explained:

> First of all, I loved it, took to it immediately, and all the blisters, having to keep my nails cut short and lugging it around, that never bothered me. I knew it was what I wanted to do [Meritt, "Harpist

Says Her Profession Worth Trouble," *Richmond Times Dispatch*, January 23, 1978, p. B6].

Early in Hobson's senior high school year Philadelphia Symphony harpist Marilyn Costello (who taught harp in the city's schools) indicated that the young harpist was "concert caliber." Hobson then enrolled at the Philadelphia Musical Academy. At the end of her second year she spent the summer at the Maine Harp Colony. It was there that she met the noted harpist/teacher Chalifoux, a meeting that prompted the decision to transfer to the Cleveland Institute of Music.

Earlier, teacher Costello had scheduled an audition for the Maine Harp Colony's founder/director Carlos Salzedo. Costello was aware of the unwritten racial ban, but hoped that Salzedo would be so overwhelmed with Hobson's talent that the rule would be suspended. Though very impressed, the master harpist/teacher pointed out that since participants lived in Camden homes, he did not believe the townspeople would accept a black. Hobson recalled:

> This was hard for me to accept. This place was like a summer camp.
> You paid your money and you enrolled, even if you couldn't play.
> I was rejected only because of race [conversation with the author].

But now Salzedo was deceased and the walls of segregation were beginning to collapse. As the nineteenth century black preacher John Jasper proclaimed to his Baptist congregation, "De Sun Do Move," and mid-twentieth-century black music critic Nora Holt once proclaimed to her readership, "De World Do Move," both "de sun" and "de world" moved because of harpist Ann Hobson.

Beyond her National and Boston Symphony/Boston Pops memberships, Hobson's performing brilliance began to beam through her associate membership with the Boston Symphony Chamber Players, with whom she recorded on the Deutsche Grammophon label (Claude Debussy 2530 049 ST33); the New England Harp Trio (harp, flute, cello), which she founded; and solo appearances with the National, Boston, Boston Pops, Springfield (MA), St. Trinity Orchestra of Port-Au-Prince (Haiti), Wichita (Kansas), and Richmond (Virginia) symphony orchestras.

Following her 1977 appearance with the Wichita Symphony a local critic wrote:

> Miss Hobson is an incredible technician, but more, she is able to tear the harp out of its traditional raiment and give it new and vital voices. Certainly one will be convinced after hearing her that she not only knows as a musician what the harp is capable of with its present limited repertoire, but also what it may be required to explore in the future. If so, she is the artist to take us into that future [*Wichita Eagle*].

In June of 1966 Hobson appeared as soloist at the American Harp Society's National Conference in Boston. She was a part of the Spring 1979 "Musical Diplomacy" trip that took place in Shanghai and Peking, China, with the Boston Symphony, performing and conducting one of the orchestra's master classes. By the mid-'90s, Hobson-Pilot had made numerous trips to Hong Kong and Japan with the Boston Symphony.

Ann Hobson has had musical impact through her many students, teaching privately and at the Philadelphia Musical Academy, Temple University Music Festival at Ambler, New England Conservatory and Boston Symphony Orchestra's Tanglewood Music Center. She often conducted clinics for school harp students, recalling that she got her start in the public schools.

She has been principal harpist of the Boston Symphony since 1980, the same year that she married R. Prentice Pilot, a freelance string bassist, regular performer with the Boston Pops Esplanade Orchestra, and former teacher in the Boston public schools. She and her husband have conducted a concert series on the Caribbean Island of St. Maarten. Together they direct a music program in the Boston public schools, and she teaches troubadour harp at one of the city's middle schools.

Hobson-Pilot's first solo compact disc was released in 1991 and included works of the African-American composer William Grant Still. She followed this with a CD that included works by Bach, Debussy, Hindemith, Salzedo, Faure, Ravel, Pierne, and Malotte. In 1993 Hobson-Pilot made concerto appearances with the New Zealand Symphony and the English Chamber Orchestra in London.

Hobson-Pilot's talents and accomplishments have been ac-

knowledged by the Pro Arte Society of Philadelphia, the Boston
Chapter of Girl Friends, and the music sorority Sigma Alpha Iota.
Both the Philadelphia College of Performing Arts (1992) and the
Cleveland Institute of Music (1993) have bestowed their Alumni
Achievement Award on her. She received an honorary doctorate
degree in music from Bridgewater State College in 1988.

BETHANY HARPER BERNSTEIN
viola
b. July 10, 1944, Washington D.C.

Bethany Bernstein received the B.Mus. and M.Mus. in viola performance from Duquesne University. An only child, she cited as
her musical influences, "Mother's love for music, early exposure
to opera and symphonic recordings, and a love for ballet and
ballet music" (Personal Data Sheet, 1978).

A pupil of Raymond Montoni and Richard Goldner, in the mid-
and late 1970s Bethany and her cellist husband (Martin) were
members of the Wheeling (West Virginia) Symphony Orchestra.
Both held principal positions in the organization and were members of the Dumas String Trio and the Nova String Quintet.

Prior to joining the Wheeling Symphony Bernstein was a member of the Johnstown (Pennsylvania) Symphony, the Youngstown
(Ohio) Philharmonic, and the Shenandoah Valley Music Festival
Orchestra (Virginia). Membership in the Wheeling Symphony
Orchestra called for her to fill several other assignments: Coordinator of the Wheeling Symphony's Training Ensemble and adjunct instructor at West Liberty State College, where she taught
string-related courses and music theory. Her duties at West Liberty also included leadership of the string orchestra.

The development of young string players was always of paramount interest to violinist Bernstein. A highly respected pedagogue, she taught strings in several government-sponsored
programs in Pittsburgh, directed a string orchestra in East Allegheny School District, and taught in the laboratory school at Pittsburgh's Point Park College. For four years she was a teacher of
string-class methods at her alma mater, Duquesne University.

JOYCE RENEE COBB
guitar (harmonica, conga, vocals)
b. June 2, 1945, Okmulgee, Oklahoma

Joyce Cobb's only formal musical study was piano, pursued while growing up on the campus of Tennessee State University, where both her mother and father were employed. She prepared to be a social worker, having received the B.A. degree in Social Welfare from Central State University. For two and a half years she worked in the field in Dayton, Ohio, but the call of the musical art persisted.

Between 1969 and 1971 Cobb was on Ramada Inn's Midwest circuit, performing in duo under the name "Joyce and William [Temme] Duo." The two broke all attendance records during their first weekend, both singing and playing guitars, bongos, and congas, and Joyce coloring William's guitar solos with sounds from the flute and tambourine.

Moving back to Nashville in 1971, she became featured vocalist for WSM-TV, while playing with the WSM-TV and Radio Studio Orchestra. A quality country-music singer, Cobb was voted Opryland's Most Outstanding Performer in 1974. *Billboard* Magazine selected one of her Stax releases as the best potential single hit in the Country Division, May 1975.

When Cobb appeared with groups she was generally the featured vocalist, but she often effectively played one of her instruments for musical emphasis or embellishment. Groups with which she performed included the Avery Richardson, Bill Easley, Rick Christian, Ray Reach, and Herman Green and the Green Machine bands; The Thomas Cain Trio; and The Sidney Kirk Quartet. In the late 1970s much time and effort was being devoted to her own instrumental and vocal group, Hot Fun. She shared billings with such popular show-business personalities as Bill Cosby, Jerry Butler, Muddy Waters, Jerry Lewis, Buddy Rich, Woody Herman, and Taj Mahal.

Cobb appeared as harmonica soloist with the Nashville Symphony in 1977. That same year she was a part of the Beale Street Music and Memphis Music Heritage festivals. The key word in describing the work of Joyce Cobb is versatility. She is a skilled jazz, blues, latin, country, pop, and rock 'n' roll performer, and critics have found difficulty in labeling the artist. *Living Blues* critic Jim O'Neal, following a Joyce Cobb appearance at Memphis' Blues Alley (with Herman Green and the Green Machine) in 1978, simply said, "phenomenal" ("Blues for the Tourists at Blues Alley in Memphis," November–December 1978, p. 29).

CHARLOTTE ANNE DAVIS-PARAMORE
violin
b. August 19, 1945, Columbus, Ohio

A permanent member of Washington, D.C.'s National Symphony Orchestra in the late 1970s was violinist Charlotte Davis. Prior to joining the National, Charlotte was a permanent member of the Columbus (Ohio) Symphony Orchestra. With her mother a well-respected church organist, Charlotte (and music-educator sister Carolyn) received a solid music foundation and consistent encouragement.

Davis received the B.Mus. Ed. and M.Mus. degrees from Ohio State University. Her teachers included Lloyd Elliott, George Hardesty, and Vida Reynolds. Performance awards were received from Ohio State University and the Allegheny Music Festival.

CHARLENE K. CLARK
violin
b. November 6, 1945, Litchfield, Illinois

Joining the St. Louis Symphony in 1968 was violinist Charlene Clark, a graduate of Southern Illinois University (B.Mus. in Music Education). Her teachers included Charles Slavish, Russell Gerhart, and Jerome Rosend.

Violinist Clark was a scholarship student at Southern Illinois and was the recipient of an award to participate in the AF of M String Congress. She taught instrumental music in the St. Louis County School System. In addition to her St. Louis Symphony participation, Clark performed with St. Louis Casa Chamber Group, appeared as soloist with the St. Louis Little Symphony, and participated in the "Rarely Performed Music Series." In 1977 she wrote:

> I believe that the time has finally come for qualified black musicians. If you have the basic skills and a strong foundation, you can become a qualified musician in any orchestra [correspondence with the author, April 1977].

Clark is currently in her twenty-sixth season with the St. Louis Symphony, enjoys membership in the Amichi Quartet, and performs frequently in a solo capacity.

PATRICIA TERRY-ROSS
harp
b. January 2, 1947, Detroit, Michigan

Patricia's parents "made a conscious decision not to have any more children after I was identified as musically gifted by several music teachers" (author's questionnaire). Both parents are musical but neither pursued a career in music. Terry-Ross indicates that her parents taught her to "practice by the goal, not the clock." Other influences were her childhood piano teacher, Maxine Skelton Zeite, Velma Froude, her first harp teacher, and Lucile Lawrence, with whom she studied at Tanglewood.

Harpist Terry-Ross began studying harp with Froude at Cass Technical High School, where she currently teaches harp and voice. She is also affiliate professor of harp at Wayne State University. She earned a bachelor's degree and a master's degree in music from the University of Michigan, where she studied harp with Ruth Dean Clark. She undertook additional study at the Tanglewood Institute. She received the Teacher of the Year Award from the Detroit public schools and was considered for the Michigan Teacher of the Year Award (1992–93).

Extremely active as a solo and chamber harpist throughout the metropolitan Detroit area, she is principal harpist with the Michigan Opera Theatre, the Michigan Chamber Orchestra, and the Dearborn Symphony. The Detroit Symphony Orchestra has utilized her skills on many occasions, in concert and on recordings. One exciting recording experience with the orchestra was the 1982 Grammy-nominated recording of Stravinsky's *Firebird*, under the direction of Antal Dorati. She also performed for two Open Sky recordings, where she is featured along with actor John Carradine, jazz flutist Bud Shank, and actress Loretta Swit.

A few of the artists with whom Patricia Terry-Ross has performed are Dame Joan Sutherland, Luciano Pavarotti, Leona Mitchell, Sammy Davis Jr., Cleo Laine, and Johnny Mathis. Most memorable was the 1994 performance at a private reception for the president of the United States, Bill Clinton; members of his cabinet; and foreign ministers and diplomats attending the Group of Seven conference in Detroit. To those considering or preparing for a career in music she says, "All of your inspirations may not come in positive packages. However, if you want to be successful, you can learn something even from those whose vision is limited. If you don't learn anything else from them, learn that you don't want to be like them and work hard not to be" (author's questionnaire).

KAREN ANDUZE ATKINSON
string bass
b. Bronx, N.Y.

Karen majored in flute at both City College of New York (B.A., 1972) and Columbia University Teachers College (M.A. in music education, 1978). Her instructors were Andrew Lolya, John Wummer, and Frank Wess. Just before she entered graduate school, she began taking lessons on the string bass. A student at New York City's Jazzmobile, she received instruction from bassist Lisle Atkinson, who eventually became her husband. The bass soon became her primary instrument.

Karen is cofounder, manager, and bassist (the only female) with the unique ensemble Neo-Bass, which includes five acoustic basses. One bassist keeps the rhythm while the other four bow the melody. A very popular group, the Neo-Bass Ensemble has been performing in the New York tristate area since 1988 and can be heard on the album *Bird Lives!* (Karlisle Records). Bassist Karen Atkinson has performed with Evelyn Blakey, Stella Mars, Carmen McRae, Dizzy Gillespie, Marian McPartland, and the Bergen Philharmonic Orchestra.

AKUA (Patricia) DIXON
cello
b. July 14, 1948, New York City

A New York City native, Dixon's years of development and professional activity took place in the same city. She graduated from the city's High School of Performing Arts and the Manhattan School of Music, where she studied with Bernard Heifetz.

Akua was primarily a freelance cellist, filling studio assignments and Broadway pit orchestra engagements. Additionally, she was a member of the Symphony of the New World and The String Reunion, which she cofounded with her sister, Gayle Dixon, and Noel Pointer, both violinists. Composition and arranging also occupied Dixon's interest. She received a composition grant from the National Endowment for the Arts in 1974.

During the 1970s Akua Dixon taught voice and cello in the public schools of Harlem and at Brooklyn's New Muse Community Museum. She was an "Essence Woman" in the November issue of *Essence* magazine, 1979 (pp. 30, 32).

LINDA KAY SMITH
violin
b. July 7, 1949, Kansas City, Kansas

Linda Kay Smith, one of nine children, was fortunate enough to have come under the influence of Sumner High School's black band director Leon Brady (Kansas City, Kansas). She wrote:

> He was my teacher in grade school, junior high and senior high school. Though he was a percussionist, he helped to stir up a lot of interest in good music. He was able to impress on my parents the importance of private music lessons and to get me going to summer music camps. He went over and beyond the call of duty. He cared [correspondence with the author, August 3, 1979].

Another significant influence was her mother, who "taught herself to play piano by note and ear when she was a young girl." The mother provided consistent encouragement and also piano accompaniments for the beginning violinist. Her first violin was purchased with money won from a Kansas City Beautification Contest, at age eleven.

In 1965 Smith won the Kansas City Local's scholarship for participation in the AF of M String Congress, in Michigan. She was a member of the Kansas City Youth Symphony for two seasons (1969–71), serving during the latter season as concertmistress. She twice won the orchestra's Concerto-Aria Contest and appeared as soloist with the group in 1970. She participated in the Blossom Festival School Orchestra in 1971, again on scholarship.

Violinist Smith attended the Kansas City Conservatory and the University of Missouri at Kansas City, receiving the B.Mus. from the latter in 1971. Always an honor student, she was selected for membership in the national honorary society Pi Kappa Lambda. Her list of teachers included Joseph Landes, Jaime Laredo, Frank

Hauser, Tiberius Klausner, and Richard Burgin. She joined the Atlanta Symphony in 1972 and remained with the orchestra for three seasons. Her Atlanta assignment included a three-year membership in the Little Symphony Orchestra and during the final season membership in the Symphony Quartet.

During the summer of 1974 Smith was a member of the Dorset (England) Festival Orchestra and during the summers of '75, '76, and '77, the Roehampton Festival Orchestra in London. She was violinist with the American Quartet for the Winter Roehampton Music Festival. Smith freelanced in London throughout the 1976–77 season, becoming almost a regular with the Hammersmith Orchestra, teaching and doing back-up recordings as a vocalist. While in England she studied with the world-famous violinist/pedagogue Kato Havas. Following the London experience she settled in Washington, D.C., freelancing and preparing for another permanent symphony assignment.

In review of the past, Smith wrote:

> If anything has been lacking in my experiences, it was an image. There was no violinist to pattern myself after. I was pretty old before I ever heard someone play the violin well. . . . I was in college before I heard my first violin soloist. That had a strong negative affect—like trying to build a swimming pool in a desert [*ibid.*].

OLA VERINE JONES (WHITE)
string bass
b. December 28, 1949, Indianapolis

In the late 1970s Jones joined the Cleveland Civic Orchestra (formerly the Cleveland Philharmonic) as principal bassist. Previous professional orchestral affiliations included the Indianapolis Philharmonic and the Nashville, New Haven, Winnipeg, Canton (Ohio), and Bridgeport (Connecticut) Symphony orchestras. School instrumental affiliations included the Indianapolis High School Symphony, Indiana University Symphony, and Yale Collegium and Philharmonic Orchestras. While pursuing the M.A. degree from Fisk University, Jones gave cello assistance to The Orchestrated Crowd, the University's jazz ensemble.

Bassist Jones received the B.S. in Music and Spanish from Indiana University, the M.A. in Ethnomusicology from Fisk University, and the M.Mus. degree in Double Bass from Yale University School of Music. In addition to mastering the double bass, Jones specialized in the areas of Afro-American folk music and African music and musical instruments. Her instructors included Murray Grodner, Lawrence Angell, and Gary Kerr. Jones was a string assistant at Fisk and Tennessee State universities; taught strings in the public schools of Darien, Connecticut; and taught privately.

> MAXINE (Lorna) ROACH
> viola (composition)
> b. May 12, 1950, Brooklyn, New York

Only a few are fortunate enough to develop under the influence of such a musician (and person) as drummer Max Roach, father of violist Maxine. This positive influence was reflected in Maxine's attitudes concerning music. As she stated:

> Music must be functional. It cannot exist in a vacuum. Music should convey social and political messages—make statements about and to people, society and one's self [Personal Data Sheet, 1978].

Obviously then, one of her most exciting group affiliations was with the mid-1970s New York City-based The String Reunion, a group that shared Roach's musical philosophy. Fifteen years later, she would not hesitate to say that her richest group experience is affiliation with the Uptown String Quartet, a unique string ensemble conceived by her father, Max Roach. The group is a direct outgrowth of the Max Roach Double Quartet. Its independent career began with the debut CD *Max Roach Presents the Uptown String Quartet.* The disc includes Maxine Roach's "Extensions," for which she received a Grammy Award nomination.

Maxine Roach was a product of Oberlin Conservatory (B.A.) and the Institute for Advanced Musical Studies in Switzerland. A student of Emanuel Hirsh, Heidi Castleman, and Jesse Levine, coached by William Primrose, Paul Doktor, and Bruno Giuranna, Roach is extremely qualified to offer the following advice: "For young black string players, study hard and make an effort to find out about other string players who are black professional musicians. If possible, ask them questions—get all the information you can from them. Never discard what you are taught or told; just keep adding to your skills, your musicianship, and your knowledge (author's questionnaire, July 1996).

Roach is currently a member of the board of directors of Chamber Music America. Freelancing in New York City, her performing credits include the Brooklyn Philharmonic, American Symphony, Dance Theatre of Harlem, Joffrey Ballet, Symphony of the New World, and numerous Broadway shows (*Dream Girls, Kiss of the Spider Woman,* and *Into the Woods,* to name a few). She has worked with recording artists such as Aretha Franklin, Johnny Mathis, Frank Sinatra, Shirley Bassey, and Sarah Vaughan and with the Max Roach Double Quartet and Uptown String Quartet in concert halls, night clubs, and music festivals across the country and throughout Europe.

SHANTA SABRIYA FERMIYE NURULLAH
sitar, electric bass
b. June 16, 1950, Chicago

Included in Nurullah's list of musical influences are God and black people. The message she wanted to get across was "Let's use our talents to change the condition of our people" (correspondence with the author, February 2, 1979). Shanta's personal and musical philosophies were closely allied to those of Alice Coltrane, who is another of her musical influences. In the late 1970s she began expressing her beliefs most profoundly in articles appearing in *Ebony, Jr., Black Books Bulletin,* and *Black News.* Her principal research and writing area was "Women in Music."

During Nurullah's third year at Carleton College, where she majored in English, she went to India to complete a political-science project on the Untouchables. Shortly after her arrival she heard the sitar and decided instantly that she had to learn to play the instrument. Despite a piano background (eleven years with Nannie S. Reid), she had never considered music as a career.

Sitarist Nurullah studied in Poona, India, with world-renowned sitarist Ravi Shankar's protégé Bhaskar Chandavarkar, and upon her return continued to advance the sitar cause, both in solo and ensemble. She continued her sitar studies in Chicago with Ramrao Bhatodekar, theory and composition with Phil Cohran and Muhal Richard Abrams, and electric bass with Pete Cosey.

Beginning in 1971 Nurullah filled many lecture and teaching assignments at such institutions as Malcolm X and Olive-Harvey colleges, University of Illinois/Chicago Circle, Northeastern Illinois University, and New Concept Development Center, Chicago. As a bassist, Nurullah performed with the Mod Hatter Disco House Band (Hammond, Indiana), Harry Hill's Invincible Artiste (Chicago), Jimmy Ellis's Big Band (Chicago), and Phil Cohran's Black Music Workshop (Chicago). With Cohran's group she doubled as sitarist, the musical role of uppermost satisfaction. She performed regularly as sitarist with Amina and Company and as sitarist and leader of her own eight-member group, billed simply as Shanta Nurullah.

To journalist Aquil Nurridin she once stated:

> I have a strong spiritual attachment to the sitar . . . I've made a commitment not to take that instrument into nightclubs or places where alcohol is served. . . . One of my goals is to play music that is healing and soothing . . . making art accessible to the public . . .
>
> In India, the sitar is played in the home . . . remind[ing] me of rent parties. It comes out of the attitude of making sure that the artists survive and that they're provided for . . . I'd like to see that happen here ["Shanta Nurullah: The Sister with the Sitar," *Bilalian News*, September 2, 1977, p. 29].

By the mid-1990s, she was divorced and devoting all of her energies to her children, storytelling, and performing solo and with the group SAMANA, of which she is one of the three founders (1981). Ranging in size from a duo to a large ensemble of female vocalists, instrumentalists, and dancers, SAMANA "combines eastern and western instruments, ancient and modern musical concepts into a presentation that soothes, inspires, heals and excites" (SAMANA publicity document). It is the first all-women ensemble of the Association for the Advancement of Creative Musicians (AACM). The group merges traditional West African musical language with experimental jazz.

Shanta Sabriya Fermiye Nurullah (still Chicago based) is now known simply as Shanta. Her performing instruments now include the mbiras (thumb pianos), four-string harp, and reed zither (all West African), in addition to the sitar and electric bass. She is owner of Storywiz Records, which has to date produced three recordings: *The Adventures of Shedoobee, Light Worker,* and *Samana.* Shanta has made several radio and television appearances, including the Oprah Winfrey Show (1993). For six years, she was a member of the Columbia College faculty.

In Chicago, Shanta Nurullah, mother of three children, was known as "The Sister with the Sitar." By late 1970 evidence of her expanding reputation was clearly evident.

ROSALYN MARIE STORY
violin
b. July 31, 1950, Kansas City, Kansas

Rosalyn Story was another student who came under the influence of black band director Leon Brady at Sumner High School in Kansas City, Kansas. High standards became a part of Story's musical existence from junior high school onward.

Always an honor student, Story was the recipient of the Youth Symphony of Kansas City Music Award and a scholarship from the Thomas Presser Foundation. She received the B.A. degree from the University of Missouri at Kansas City in 1972 and during that summer represented the state of Kansas at the AF of M String Congress at the University of Southern California and the Wolf Trap Music Festival in Washington, D.C.

In 1972 Story joined the Kansas City Philharmonic, where she remained for six seasons. The preceding years were musically occupied with membership in the Kansas City Youth Symphony (1964–70) and the Civic Orchestra of Kansas City (1968–72). She accompanied the Youth Symphony on its 1969 European tour.

During the summers of 1974 and '75 Story participated in the Purbeck Music Festival Chamber Orchestra in Dorset, England, and in 1977, the Roehampton Music Festival Chamber Orchestra in London. She relocated in 1978, first to the New York area, where she played with the New Jersey State Opera Orchestra and the South Bronx Chamber Orchestra, and finally to Washington D.C., where freelancing became a way of life.

The next move was to Fort Worth, Texas, where she became a member of the Fort Worth Symphony. She also performed with the orchestra of the Dallas Opera and served on several occasions as an orchestra category panelist for the National Endowment for the Arts.

Story received training in journalism at Tulsa University and has contributed articles to several publications, including the *Dallas Morning News*, *Dallas Observer*, and *Essence* magazine. Most outstanding was her 1990 book, *And So I Sing: African-American Divas of Opera and Concert* (Wagner Books). This publication has become a standard reference volume.

Instructors through the years have included Tiberius Klausner, Samuel Thaviu, Kato Havas, and black violinist Sanford Allen. Also worth noting is the fact that Story taught violin at the Charlie Parker Music Foundation in Kansas City, Missouri. Her affiliation with this federally funded program, providing music instruction for inner-city youth, lasted for five years (1972–77). Story's orchestral experiences included a few jazz and rock engagements, performing with such artists as Isaac Hayes, Barry White, Hubert Laws, Freddie Hubbard, Ray Brown, Bob James, and Stanley Turrentine.

ESTHER LOUISE MELLON
cello
b. September 17, 1950, Pittsburgh

Esther Mellon joined the Buffalo Philharmonic in 1976 and the Baltimore Symphony in 1977. During the 1975–76 season she was a member of the New England Conservatory String Quartet (faculty assistant). Despite her many accomplishments prior to reaching age thirty, Mellon viewed her musical position as "in the early stages." She wished to involve herself in more solo and chamber-music playing, in addition to the orchestra (correspondence with the author, August 6, 1979).

Superior training supported the above positions: Mellon received the B.A. degree from Swarthmore College (1971) and the M.Mus. from New England Conservatory (1975), studying at the latter institution with Laurence Lesser and David Soyer. She participated in the Preparatory Division of the Juilliard School and at age sixteen, a seminar conducted by the Budapest String Quartet at the University of Buffalo. Additionally, she studied cello with Orlando Cole and chamber music with the Curtis String Quartet at Philadelphia's New School of Music (1969–72).

In 1977 Mellon was one of fifteen cellists selected to participate in the University of Southern California's Piatagorsky Seminar, benefiting from master classes conducted by Gabor Reita, Laurence Lesser, Lorne Monroe, Nathaniel Rosen, and Stephen Kates. She also benefited from her household environment: Her father was a pianist and her mother a public-school music teacher. Though born in Pittsburgh, she grew up in New York City.

Between the years 1972 and 1976, Mellon freelanced in the New York City and Boston areas. Her associations included several Broadway shows, the Symphony of the New World, Dance Theatre of Harlem (principal cellist), Fine Arts Chamber Orchestra, Henry Street Settlement Faculty Chamber Players, Associate Artist Opera (principal cellist), Springfield (Massachusetts) Symphony, New England Opera, New Hampshire Sinfonietta, and a Young Audiences String Quartet. She was principal cellist with the Royal Winnipeg Ballet Touring Orchestra during the 1973 season and played with the Spoleto (Italy) Festival Orchestra during the 1974 season and the Eastern Philharmonic at the Eastern Music Festival in Greensboro, North Carolina, during the 1975 season.

PHYLLIS MCKENNY SANDERS
violin (piano)
Chicago

A native of Chicago, Illinois, Sanders received a bachelor's degree in music education from Chicago Conservatory College and pursued graduate study at Northwestern University (1974–75). Her areas of concentration were music history and violin performance and her instructors include Alsa Crane, Nesta Smith, George Perlman, A. Ghertovichi, and Samuel Thaviu. She currently offers violin instruction at the Beverly Arts Center in Chicago.

Professional activity began in 1971 with orchestral membership, chamber music affiliation, Broadway shows, ballet orchestras, recording, and touring. She has worked and toured with such artists as Nancy Wilson, Johnny Mathis, Sarah Vaughan, and Frank Sinatra, to name a few. She has recorded with Ramsey Lewis, Earth, Wind, and Fire, Della Reese, Peabo Bryson, Obert Davis, and others.

Sanders plays chamber music with the Connoisseur Musica Ensemble. Her show list includes *Hello Dolly, Gigi, Dreamgirls,* and *Porgy and Bess.* Her ballet affiliation is with the American Ballet Theatre (ABT). After graduating from high school, she was accepted into the Civic Orchestra of Chicago, a training orchestra under auspices of the Chicago Symphony (1971–76). Subsequent orchestral associations included the Chicago Festival Orchestra (1976), the Festival de Musique (Neuchatel, Switzerland, 1977), the Illinois Philharmonic (1980, 1991, 1994), the Orchestra of Illinois (1981–86), the Elgin Symphony (1989), the Lake Forest Symphony (1991), the Kenosha Symphony (1994), and the Illinois Chamber Orchestra (1996).

Phyllis McKenny Sanders joined the Chicago Sinfonietta in 1986 and the Fox Valley Symphony Orchestra in 1993 and maintains her affiliation with both orchestras into the present.

JUANITA DARLENE TOLIVER
viola
b. December 20, 1951, Pittsburgh

Violist Toliver was a product of Duquesne University (B.Mus. in Performance). Her teachers included Aaron Chaifetz, Richard Goldner, Charmian Gadd, Harold Coletta, and Geraldine Lamboley. During the summer of 1970 she participated in the AF of M String Congress and in 1971 the Composer's Conference and Chamber Music Center at Bennington, Vermont.

While enrolled at Duquesne, Toliver served as principal violist with the University's Chamber Ensemble and Symphony Orchestra. In the summer of 1972 she toured Europe with the Pittsburgh Youth Symphony, also as principal. During the same summer she served as assistant principal violist with the International Festival of Youth Orchestra ensemble.

Throughout the Duquesne years (and several subsequent ones) Toliver was assistant principal violist with the Wheeling (Pennsylvania) Symphony Orchestra. In the late 1970s talented violist Toliver kept herself musically active with the Westmoreland (Pennsylvania) Symphony Orchestra (assistant principal) and her own freelancing quartet, Strings 'N' Things.

Toliver once stated as her life's objective, "becoming a well-rounded, versatile professional musician." Toward achieving this goal, in addition to the above, she filled orchestral assignments with groups accompanying such artists as The Temptations, Dionne Warwick, Diana Ross, Melba Moore, Ben Vereen, Sammy Davis, Jr., Tony Orlando and Dawn, Smokey Robinson, and Lou Rawls. She was also a regular member of the Jack Purcell Orchestra. In early 1978 she began serving as production director of Pittsburgh's radio station WAMO.

MELANIE PUNTER
string bass
b. February 1, 1952, New York City

"Solid training, good opportunities (at an early age), hard work and a good ear" were the explanations for Punter's New York City popularity throughout the 1970s. She graduated from the city's High School of Music and Art and continued at the Manhattan School of Music. Her list of teachers included Alvin Brehm, Homer Mensch, and the phenomenal black bassist Richard Davis. Punter stated:

> I overcame the obstacles of a "man's" instrument and the public's attitude. I set out to prove nothing, but appreciated the respect received from fellow musicians [Personal Data Sheet, 1978].

Punter performed with the Spoleto (Italy) Festival Orchestra, 1971–73. A member of the Symphony of the New World during the 1976–78 seasons, she served as assistant principal. Other orchestral associations included the Dance Theatre of Harlem, Alvin Ailey and Eric Hawkins dance companies, Scholar Cantorum, The String Reunion, New York Housing Authority Orchestra, American Symphony Orchestra, Radio City Music Hall, and the National Afro-American Philharmonic.

HARRIETE (Patricia) GREEN-HURD
violin
b. February 22, 1952, Nashville, Tennessee

A veteran of Nashville's Cremona Strings, which went on to noteworthy orchestral accomplishments, Harriette Green was a member of the Nashville Youth Symphony and recipient of the parent organization's Guild Scholarship. Her first permanent orchestral membership was in the Nashville Symphony, where between the years 1970 and 1974 she received both orchestral experience and constant encouragement from conductor Thor Johnson.

The Nashville Symphony assignment was carried out while Green was a student at George Peabody College for Teachers, where she received the B.Mus. degree in 1974. In 1976 she received the M.Mus. in Performance from Indiana University, where she played in the Indiana University Philharmonic Orchestra.

While completing her undergraduate studies Green played with the University Center Orchestra and during her final year served as the orchestra's concertmistress. Her instructors included Stephen Clapp, Christian Teal, James Buswell, Patricia Harada, and black pedagogue Robert Holmes.

During the summer of 1973 Green participated in the Aspen Music School's Philharmonic Orchestra. She substituted with the Nashville Symphony during the '75 and '76 summers and became a permanent member of the Louisville Symphony Orchestra in 1976.

With a love for teaching, Green was a part-time faculty member at Nashville's exclusive Blair Academy of Music and also held a teaching assistantship at the same institution, where she provided instruction to preschoolers, using the Suzuki Violin Method. Green continued to foster the Suzuki approach at the University of Louisville's preparatory school, while meeting her obligations as violinist in the Louisville Symphony.

Green noted:

> In playing with the various orchestras (symphonic or otherwise), I'm usually among a small number of blacks, often numbering no more than five. Of that sum, the "female number" equalled "one"—me. Despite the novelty of it all, I found it rather disconcerting. I live for the day when the number of [black females] increases and the novelty of it all disappears [correspondence with the author, July 6, 1976].

Finally, it should be noted that Green's orchestral involvement was not limited to those groups specializing in the "elite art" repertory. In 1975 she toured with the Barry White Love Unlimited and Henry Mancini orchestras. The summer of 1976 found

Green substituting with Nashville's Opryland USA Show Orchestra.

During the 1978–79 season, Green-Hurd performed with the Kentucky Opera Association. During the 1982 and 1984 seasons, she was a member of the Bridgetower String Quartet. Always a studio teacher, she was director of orchestra sectionals for the Sidwell Friends School in the nation's capital from 1979 to 1981.

Other performing experiences in the Washington D.C. area (in more recent years) include Washington Bach Consort, Baltimore Opera Orchestra, Summer Opera Theatre Company, Wolf Trap Farm Park Orchestra, and National Theatre. She is also affiliated with the Concert Artists of Baltimore. She toured East Germany with the Washington Bach Consort in 1985. Green-Hurd occasionally substitutes with the National Symphony Orchestra and currently is involved in small ensembles performing in elementary schools, primarily in Washington, D.C. The Back to School program introduces children to music and musical forms of the Baroque, Classical, and Romantic periods.

INDIA COOKE
violin, composition
b. 1953 (?), Durham, North Carolina

The late 1980s and early 1990s saw increased activity and publicity for violinist India Cooke, primarily in the San Francisco area. Her early dream was to obtain an orchestral position, but toward the close of the 1970s she found herself drifting toward improvisational music. Cooke is a native of Durham, North Carolina, and received her secondary and college training at the North Carolina School of the Arts. She earned a master's degree from the University of Michigan. Her interests broadened when she moved to San Francisco in 1978.

A recording by jazz violinist Michael White influenced her to pursue something other than orchestral music making. According to Cooke, "I said, Aha! There's something else that's possible. I no longer saw everything from a strictly classical perspective. I realized I could play violin and tap my toes at the same time."

She received her orientation into jazz from George Sams's quartet, Middle Passage. At the same time, she was artist in residence in the public schools and taught at San Francisco State University and at the East Bay Center for the Performing Arts. She also performed with the Oakland Opera and the Oakland and Berkeley Symphony Orchestras. She played in the pit orchestra for such Broadway productions as *Pal Joey, Timbuktu,* and *Showboat* and performed in the string section for recording sessions with Diana Ross, Smokey Robinson, Gladys Knight and the Pips, and others.

In the late 1980s, she formed the New World Trio. The trio has performed in Carnegie Hall's Weill Recital Hall and throughout the Bay area, always to rave reviews. Most exciting was her European trip with Sun Ra. But most of her energies were devoted to the New World Trio, which performed blues, jazz, gospel, and classical. The repertoire frequently included compositions by violinist Cooke. According to one San Francisco writer, the New World Trio is "without question the freshest and most spontaneous." (See David Rubien, "Classical Violinist Cooke Lights a Jazz Fire," *San Francisco Chronicle/Datebook,* July 28, 1991, pp. 34–35.)

> MARILYN E. THORNTON TRIBBLE (Mett)
> violin (storytelling)
> b. April 7, 1953, Washington, D.C.

In the words of her publicist, "Marilyn E. Thornton Tribble is a musician and educator whose interests and training cover two distinct cultural traditions, Western music and African American culture, bi-cultural skills in a multi-cultural world." Trained at Howard University (B.Mus., music history) and the Peabody Conservatory of Johns Hopkins University (M. Mus., violin), she is a student of Berl Senofsky.

Tribble is an adjunct professor of violin at Tennessee State University and an instructor in African-American and Native American folk literature at East Literature Magnet School (both in Nashville, Tennessee). She acquired pedagogical experience with the D.C. Youth Orchestra, Howard University; the Evanston, Illinois, Special Recreation Department; and Croton-on-Hudson, New York. Arriving in Nashville in 1992, she has enjoyed playing with chamber ensembles, orchestras, jazz ensembles, and various church ensembles. She has previously performed with the Georgetown Symphony, Elizabeth Greenfield Chamber Ensemble, Brother Ah and the Sounds of Awareness, all in Washington,

D.C., and the Evanston Symphony Orchestra, Morris Ellis Jazz Orchestra, and the Bridgetower Quartet in the Chicago area. Also since 1992, she has been a member of an innovative musical partnership, the New York City-based Sisters' Grace Chamber Ensemble (violin, cello, piano, and string bass). The multitalented Tribble is also an official storyteller for the Metro Public Library System (Nashville).

Tribble's performance programs include classical music, jazz, spirituals and/or storytelling. Her consulting activities include workshops and lectures on the African-American perspective in literature, history and music. She also gives private lessons in violin, piano, African-American folklore, and African-American history.

BELINDA DIANNE SHAW
string bass
b. February 1, 1954, Richmond, Virginia

While in high school Shaw was a member of the Richmond Youth Orchestra and during her senior year served as a regular substitute with the parent organization. During the summer of 1971 she received a scholarship to American University's Music Institute at Wolf Trap Farms.

Recipient of a performance scholarship, Shaw enrolled at Indiana University School of Music. While there she served as a permanent member of the Owensboro (Kentucky) Symphony Orchestra and during the summer of 1974 participated in Temple University's Music Festival at Ambler. She was one of the select members of Alexander Schneider's Christmas Orchestra appearing at Carnegie Hall in 1974.

Shaw joined the Richmond Symphony as a permanent member upon completion of her B.Mus. degree from Indiana University in 1975. She remained with the orchestra for one season, departing then for New York City to begin preparing for a career in arts management.

Between 1976 and 1978 Shaw was employed as business manager for the Rod Rodgers Dance Company and completed an internship in administration with the New York City Opera Company. During the summer of 1977 she returned to Richmond, her native city, to serve as box-office manager of the new

Empire Theatre, planning and coordinating its first season of classical-music concerts. In addition to these many activities she was successful in completing the requirements for the M.A. degree in Arts Administration from New York University in 1978. In the fall of '78 Shaw returned to Indiana University to coordinate the Afro-Arts Institute's three performing ensembles and direct the booking arrangements. Orchestral involvements were sure to continue: Shaw had been prepared as a performer by Delbert Williams, Murray Grodner, Roger Scott and Anthony Bianco and had orchestral experience dating back to her teenage years.

Equally skilled in the financial world, Shaw left her music profession for a field that brought a great deal of personal satisfaction. One meaningful contact with the music business, however, was serving as a lay panelist for the National Endowment for the Arts's Orchestra category in the late 1980s and early 1990s.

DIANE MONROE
violin (composition)
b. March 15, 1954, Philadelphia, Pennsylvania

The author became acquainted with the name Diane Monroe when seeking a "female/minority/solo recitalist/string player" to serve on a solo recitalist panel at the National Endowment for the Arts. The chairperson had mandated that there be total representation (race, gender, and geography) on all panels, in addition to expertise. The year was 1989. As we were about to abandon our efforts (solo recitalists are a rare breed), I suddenly recalled a Pro Musicis brochure that focused on a beautiful black female violinist. Though she did not serve on the solo recitalist panel, she did serve on a chamber/new music panel. I never forgot the face, the tape, or the impressive write-up about her.

Monroe began studying the violin in Philadelphia when she was eight years old. At sixteen, she entered the Drexel Music Awards competition and won first place. At seventeen, she received the American Federation of Musicians Congress of Strings Award. In 1983 she won the coveted Pro Musicis Foundation Award. The foundation's "sponsorship award provides the needed public exposure to advance the professional careers of exceptional, talented, emerging concert solo artists. According to the *New York Times*, Monroe was "a vibrant, assured, young violinist," needing (for a solo career) only what the Pro Musicis Foundation could provide.

Monroe is a student of some of the nation's finest teachers, including Ivan Galamian, Charles Castleman, David Cerone, and Joyce Robbins. She attended Oberlin College (1971–73), Philadelphia Musical Academy (1973–75), Michigan State University (1975–76), and the Curtis Institute of Music (1976–80). She received a bachelor of music degree from the Philadelphia Musical Academy and a certificate of performance from Curtis Institute. She was appointed concertmistress of the Pennsylvania Ballet Company Orchestra in 1980, where she was a frequent soloist.

Her group affiliations, including permanent and substitute memberships, are numerous: Reading (Penn.) Symphony, Concerto Soloist of Philadelphia, St. Luke's Chamber Ensemble, Orpheus Chamber Ensemble, Solisti of New York, Garden State Chamber Orchestra, Concordia Orchestra, Relâche, Odyssey Chamber Players, Kasimir String Quartet (founder), Amabile Piano Quartet (cofounder), Contrasts Chamber Artists of Philadelphia (cofounder), Beaumont String Quartet, and the Lark String Quartet (as a touring substitute). As soloist, she has appeared with several symphony orchestras: the Curtis, the Old York Road, the Marion, and the Jupiter. She has participated as soloist at the following festivals: New Music America, Black Arts Festival (Atlanta), Mellon Jazz Festival, May Music in Charlotte, Sitka Chamber Music Festival (classical and jazz), the Bach Aria Festival and Institute, and Carnegie Hall's 1993 FiddleFest. Monroe participated in the following festivals as a chamber artist: Marlboro, Caramoor, Sitka, and the Craftsbury Chamber Music Festival. For the Network for New Music, Monroe did the world premiere of Steven Dempsky's Violin Concerto; with Orchestra 2001 she did the Philadelphia premiere of Anthony Davis's Violin Concerto "Maps."

Diane Monroe reached a wider audience when she affiliated with the Uptown String Quartet, a direct outgrowth of the Max Roach Double Quartet. Monroe is the principal violinist, sharing the honors with three other impressive women. The group's repertoire emphasizes music of the African-American cultural heritage and includes several Monroe originals and arrangements. Through the Uptown String Quartet's many television appearances (*Today Show, Cosby Show, CBS Nightwatch*, and others), CD releases, and extremely successful concert appearances, its reputation will continue to grow.

Monroe was a member of the Oberlin Conservatory faculty for two seasons (1984–86) and for four years, adjunct faculty member at Swarthmore College (1987–91). At Swarthmore, Monroe was also chamber music coach. Since 1993, she has been an adjunct faculty member in the Department of Music at Temple University and has been artist in residence at Lafayette College. Violinist Monroe list as her musical influences Oscar Schumsky, Karen Tuttle, Miles Davis, and Aretha Franklin. Her words of wisdom are, "With faith and courage, it is highly possible to fulfill our creative dreams" (author's questionnaire, July 1996).

ELAINE (Beatrice) MACK
cello
b. November 20, 1954, Chicago, Illinois

Achievement is important in the Mack family. Elaine Mack's father, James L. Mack, a flutist, composer, and arranger, is currently chairman of the humanities department at Harold Washington College in Chicago. Mother Beatrice Mack is a retired teacher from the Chicago public school system and is currently studying piano. One sister is a cultural anthropologist at Northwestern University, and another sister is a planned giving manager and accountant with the American Heart Association in Chicago. A third sister is a premed student at Loyola University in Chicago. An autistic brother lives "well and happy in a stable home environment" (author's questionnaire).

Elaine Mack received both a bachelor's degree in music (1978) and a master's degree (1980) from Roosevelt University. She is a student of Karl Fruh (Roosevelt University) and William Stokking (principal cellist, Philadelphia Orchestra). She was the recipient of a Music Assistance Fund Fellowship in 1979, which provided a seven-month residency with the Indianapolis Symphony Orchestra.

As a freelancing cellist in Chicago, she performed with many different groups: the Civic Orchestra, the Chicago Chamber Orchestra, the Orchestra of Illinois, and the Milwaukee Symphony Orchestra. In 1981–82, she was in Caracas, Venezuela, as a member of the Philharmonic of Caracas. Since 1987, Mack has been a member of the Black Music Repertory Ensemble, which completed its first American tour in February 1996.

Mack attended the Grand Teton Orchestral Seminar in Jackson Hole, Wyoming, in 1990. She spent two years as a member of the Bridgeton Symphony in Bridgeton, New Jersey, as both a full-time member and a regular substitute. For the past seven years, she has been associate principal cellist with the prestigious Orchestra Society of Philadelphia, where she currently resides. She has appeared as featured soloist on four different occasions.

During the summer of 1996, she spent one month in Sienna, Italy, participating as a student at the Sienna Summer Institute. She is preparing for publication a book on black classical musicians in Philadelphia and has recently begun a project in conjunction with the West Philadelphia Cultural Alliance that will feature the talents of black musicians in the Philadelphia area. The program is scheduled to begin in the Fall of 1996. To those who follow, she advises,

> Have faith in your talents and always keep learning. Do not be afraid to go to different countries to perform. Attend as many music festivals as you can. Learn a foreign language or languages. Keep your mind open and positive, and avoid *all* negative people of any color. Don't try to change the world; just be your best self.

KAREN (Lynette) LOWRY
violin
b. May 4, 1955, Louisville, Kentucky

Lowry is currently a violinist with the Kennedy Center Opera Orchestra, a position she has held since September 1992. With a wealth of experience, she was well qualified to fulfill the assignment. Orchestral experience includes the Louisville Orchestra (1975–77), Aspen Festival Orchestra (1977), Austin Symphony Orchestra (1977–79), Munich Chamber Orchestra (Germany 1979–81), Atlanta Symphony Orchestra (1982–83), National Symphony Orchestra (1983–85), Knoxville Symphony Orchestra and Knoxville Chamber Orchestra (assistant concertmistress, 1985–89), North Carolina Symphony (1989–91), and Grant Park Symphony Orchestra (summer 1990–91).

Atlanta and National Symphony Orchestra membership came

through the Music Assistance Fund. Lowry performed with the National Symphony as a substitute and accompanied the orchestra on its 1993 tour to Russia and its 1994 tour to Japan. Violinist Lowry received a bachelor's degree in music education from the University of Louisville (1977) and a master's degree in performance from the University of Texas at Austin (1979). She is a student of Stephen Clapp, Paul Kling, and David Cerone.

She has been an instructor in the University of Louisville's Preparatory Department and has participated in the University of Texas at Austin's String Project and the Eastern Music Festival. Since arriving in Washington, D.C., in 1991, she has served as a violin instructor at Peabody Institute's Preparatory Department. Lowry's professional activities have been documented in the publication *Symphonium*.

> CLARISSA HOWELL
> cello
> b. May 22, 1955, New York City

An alumna of retired soprano Dorothy Maynor's Harlem School of the Arts, Clarissa Howell continued at the Mannes School of Music, where she received the B.Mus. Her list of instructors included Jean Goberman, Martha Williams, Roy Christensen, Jonas Starkas, and black concert cellist Kermit Moore.

In the late 1970s she returned to the Harlem School as instructor and supervisor of the piano laboratory. Orchestral affiliation, as cellist, was confined to New York City and environs and included the Harlem Philharmonic, New York Housing Authority Orchestra, Dance Theatre of Harlem, Urban Philharmonic, Queens Symphony Orchestra, and the Symphony of the New World. Additionally, she was a frequent substitute in Broadway pit orchestras. Howell was cellist in the Chaminade Ensemble (quartet), from the group's inception in 1986.

> LESA TERRY
> violin, composition
> b. December 30, 1955, Pasadena, California

Lesa Terry's father is a tuba player and her mother is a pianist, violinist, and singer. Her sister is Zela Terry, principal cellist with the Nice (France) Philharmonic. It has been said that Lesa is an artist whose voice is certain to shape the future of the music field. Terry is an innovator and is helping to expand awareness in the field of jazz, blues, and the Negro spiritual.

She received a B.Mus. degree from California State University at Northridge and is a student of Robert Gross, Manuel Compinsky, Endre Granaul, Naomi Fischer, and William Precell. Between 1982 and 1987, Terry was a member of the Atlanta and Nashville Symphony Orchestras. While in Atlanta, she served as a faculty member at Spelman College and subsequently taught improvisation at the Louis Armstrong Middle School in New York City. She is currently a guest lecturer at New York University, where she presents a series on the African-American experience in music based on the Negro spiritual. Her Negro spiritual presentations have been enjoyed at the World Expo in Stuttgart, Germany, and Maison de Seminar in Nice, France. With a concern for the educational benefits of Negro spiritual enlightenment, she has presented concerts, workshops, master classes, and residencies at the University of Massachusetts, New York University, Rutgers University, Alabama State University, and the Quad City Arts organization, to name a few sites.

Terry's compositions (and arrangements) have been heard on a number of recordings and are heard regularly on Uptown Strings Quartet concerts. In 1995 Terry produced, composed, orchestrated, directed, and performed the premiere performance of her "Reflections of Ellington" at Aaron Davis Hall in New York City. Assisting performers were jazz legends Clark Terry (her cousin), Kenny Burrell, Sir Roland Hanna, Al Grey, and Ray Drummond, as well as a full string orchestra. For this production she received a Meet the Composer grant and benefits from the Fund for New Work.

A noted performer on Broadway, she has been engaged for the following shows: *Show Boat, The Phantom of the Opera, Les Miserables, Miss Saigon, Black and Blue, Camelot, My Fair Lady,* and many others. She is heard on several motion picture soundtracks, most notably Spike Lee's *School Daze, Do the Right Thing,* and *Jungle Fever.*

She is a member of the very popular Uptown String Quartet and the Double Quartet founded by Max Roach. The group has been acclaimed as a "dynamic ensemble with a distinctive per-

sonality . . . bristling with energy." Appearing throughout the
world, they have been seen and heard on numerous radio and
television broadcasts, including the *Cosby Show,* the *Today Show,*
and *CBS Sunday Morning.* The group recently appeared at the
Mary Lou Williams Women in Jazz Festival produced by Billy
Taylor (Kennedy Center) and at the "Sung and UnSung: Women
in Jazz" symposium and concerts produced by the Smithsonian
Institution/651 Brooklyn, NY. Her popular "Midnight Child"
and "Sugar Shuffle" can be heard on the quartet's recordings,
along with several other compositions and arrangements.

> EILEEN (Maria Garden) FOLSON
> cello, composition
> b. October 22, 1956, Philadelphia, Pennsylvania

Five of the six Garden children (four girls and two boys) are involved with music. One sister is a soprano and another is a music
teacher and choral director; one brother is a drummer and another a guitarist/composer. Eileen Maria Garden Folson received
both the B.Mus. and M.Mus. degrees in cello performance from
the University of Michigan, where she was inducted into the honorary music fraternity Pi Kappa Lambda. Her instructors included Samuel Mayes, David Guggenheim, David Baker, and
Barry Harris.

Folson was soloist with the Philadelphia Orchestra in 1978, performing Saint-Saens's Cello Concerto. Upon completing her degrees, Folson headed for New York City, where she spent two
years as a Music Assistance Fund fellow with the New York Philharmonic. Other orchestral memberships included the Flint and
Saginaw Symphony Orchestras (principal); the Williamsburg
(Brooklyn) Composers Orchestra; and substitute affiliation with
the Toledo Orchestra, the Brooklyn Philharmonic Orchestra, and
the Philharmonic Orchestra of New Jersey.

Broadway associations include pit orchestra membership for
many shows: *Sunday in the Park with George, Sweet Charity, Smile,
Into the Woods, Carousel, The Knife, The Wind in the Willows,* and
The Red Shoes. She held substitute membership with *Zorba, The
Rink, Phantom of the Opera, Cats, Les Miserables, Kiss of the Spider-
woman, Beauty and the Beast, How to Succeed in Business, Grand
Hotel, Sunset Boulevard, Gypsy,* and *Tommy.* She was a substitute

musician for Whitney Houston at Radio City show and for Stevie Wonder also at Radio City Orchestra. In 1995 she completed the Luther Vandross Orchestra Tour. While she has enjoyed membership in the Black Swan Quartet, Folson's best-known chamber affiliation is with the Uptown String Quartet. Many of Folson's compositions were performed (and recorded) by the group. Her composition "Hello Joy" (for the quartet) was commissioned by the 92nd Street Y New York Chamber Symphony and was featured on *CBS Sunday Morning*. Her "JJs Jam" was featured on *The Cosby Show*.

When asked to identify who and what has influenced her, she responded, "Everything I ever heard has influenced me: the great jazz artists, the great European classical artists, the great pop artists." This message she sends to those who follow: "Practicing is like putting money in the bank."

ZELA TERRY
cello
b. January 18, 1957, Pasadena, California

At age twenty-one Zela Terry joined the cello section of the Pittsburgh Symphony; at age twenty-two she joined the cello section of the New York Philharmonic. Terry was reaping the benefits of symphony-orchestra affirmative-action programs. Preparation came by way of her selection to participate in the Los Angeles Philharmonic's Orchestral Training Program for Minority Students (OTPMS), 1974–77. Between 1973 and 1979, four OTPMS "graduates" were awarded positions in major symphony orchestras ("Reaching Out to Minority Musicians," *Symphony News*, April 1979, pp. 16–17).

The Pittsburgh Symphony assignment took place in 1978 and the New York Philharmonic assignment in 1979. Both orchestras were participants in the Orchestral Fellowship Program sponsored by the Music Assistance Fund, with supporting grants from the National Endowment for the Arts and the Exxon Corporation. With both orchestras Zela Terry was an Orchestral Fellow, not a student or a trainee. She had the experience of playing with a major orchestra and an opportunity to learn major orchestral routine and discipline.

Terry's father played the tuba (though not professionally), and her mother taught the violin and piano in her private studio. Zela attended Pasadena City College and California State University. During her Pittsburgh residency she matriculated at Carnegie Mellon University. Her teachers included Jeffrey Solow, Ronald Leonard, Jennifer Langham, and Nathaniel Rosen.

Professional experience included the American Youth Symphony (1974–77); Idyllwild Music Seminar, USC (1975); San Gabriel Symphony (1975–76); Northridge String Quartet (1975–78); Hidden Valley Seminar (1976); and the International Music Program, North Carolina School of the Arts (1976–77). Terry was assistant principal cellist with the American Youth Symphony and principal cellist with the Idyllwild and Hidden Valley seminars.

RENEE CLARK BAKER
viola (violin)
b. May 28, 1957, Washington, D.C.

Violist Baker is currently principal violist with the Chicago Sinfonietta and the Fox Valley Symphony Orchestra, where she also serves as personnel manager. She has also played with the Youngstown Symphony (Ohio), the Dubuque Symphony (Iowa), and the Springfield Symphony (Ill.), as well as the New Philharmonic, the Chicago Chamber Orchestra, the Illinois Chamber Symphony and Philharmonic, and the Civic Orchestra of Chicago. She has participated in festival orchestras at Eisenstadt and Graz, Austria; Martigues, France; Aspen, Colorado; Rochester, New York (Gateways Festival); and Ravinia (Evanston, Ill.).

A resident of Bolingbrook, Illinois, the Washington, D.C., native is one of the Windy City's busiest freelance artists, fulfilling assignments with various symphony and festival orchestras, as well as chamber ensembles. Baker is founder and artistic director of the Connoisseur Musica String Ensemble, a group of fine string players from the Chicago Sinfonietta. The core group consists of four players (two females and two males, all black) and performs in the Chicago area for churches, receptions, conventions, and private affairs.

An active recording artist, she enjoys session work with Orbark Productions, working out of Universal Studios. Baker has backed such artists as Nancy Wilson, Smokey Robinson, and Harry Connick Jr. and played in orchestras accompanying Ben Vereen and Najee.

Renee Baker began her music studies when she was in the first grade. Having heard (and observed) a visiting string quartet at school, she knew then and there that she wanted to become a musician. Thirty-odd years later, preparation and determination have paid off. Only one ultimate goal remains—a position in a major symphony orchestra. She tried for several years to "give it up" and worked in the area of retail management. But she soon learned that music making was too important and she could not give it up.

The violist/violinist matriculated at the University of the District of Columbia, Thomas A. Edison State College, and received the B.F.A. degree in viola performance from Pacific Western University. She is a candidate for the M.M.A. degree from National Louis University.

Baker shares her talent and enthusiasm with students at the College of DuPage and Sherwood Conservatory, in addition to maintaining a private teaching studio (viola/violin). She offers the following "words of wisdom":

> We must avail ourselves of all opportunities. Involvement of minorities in the classical field is key. We must push with all of our energies, whether on the instrument or in the classroom, to not only foster a love of music in our youngsters but utilize all resources—instruments, teachers, and so on [correspondence with author, April 18, 1996].

BEVERLY (Jean) KANE BAKER
viola
b. June 23, 1957, Newport News, Virginia

When Beverly Jean Kane enrolled at the University of Missouri in 1975 she was already a veteran of the symphony orchestra, as both a "member of the ensemble" and as soloist. She began studying the violin at age seven with string teacher Margaret Davis. The native of Newport News and resident of Hampton continued her violin study with Elizabeth Chapman. By 1973 her interest had shifted to viola, and she then became a student of violist Raymond Montoni.

During her third year in high school she attended the Juilliard School of Music in the precollege division, studying with Christine Dethier. The same year, she was selected "Most Outstanding Musician" from two hundred participants in the Eastern Music Festival (Greensboro, North Carolina).

Her "member of the ensemble" orchestral affiliations have included the Norfolk and Peninsula Symphony Orchestras (on a permanent basis) and the faculty orchestra at Eastern Music Festival. Kane also enjoyed the experience of playing in back-up orchestras of Tom Jones, Gladys Knight and the Pips, Ella Fitzgerald, and Pat and Debby Boone. Her solo appearances were with the Eastern Symphony Orchestra, Richmond Youth Symphony, Peninsula Youth Symphony, and the Purbeck Festival Orchestra (Dorset, England).

With all this behind her, Kane enrolled at the University of Missouri to work for a B.Mus. in viola performance. There she studied with Carolyn Kenneson and enjoyed membership in the University Symphony Orchestra. Soon after enrollment violist Kane began teaching privately and offering instruction through the Missouri String Project for third and fourth graders.

Kane reflected on her early years:

> When I was small, I got some pressure being black and playing violin. This wasn't the "cool" thing to do. But when I got older, my friends became very encouraging and supportive. When I set my mind to it, that's when my friends began taking me seriously. When they saw how excited and interested I was, they realized how important it was to me. They saw that this "classical" thing was not just for white people, but that blacks could dig it too [correspondence with the author, February 1979].

Baker joined the Virginia Symphony Orchestra in 1983. In 1992, she was promoted to the position of principal violist. According to the music director JoAnn Falletta, "[Baker's] a terrific principal, and in the last couple of years the section has responded to her leadership and understanding" ("Potpourri," *Symphonium*, Spring 1994, p. 2).

NORMEARLEASA (Norma) THOMAS
cello (vocals)

b. July 17, 1957, Bronx, New York

Norma Thomas secured her training at the High School of Music and Art (New York City) and Nyack College (B.A. in Music Education). She cited as her musical influences black cellist Marion Cumbo (who shared his library of cello compositions by black composers) and the National Association of Negro Musicians. A serious student of the cello since age twelve, she included among her teachers Marion Feldman, Mary Conberg, Christine Saffidi, and Louis Luigiea.

Even prior to her 1979 graduation from Nyack College Thomas enjoyed extensive orchestral experience. She was a permanent member of the Ridgewood Symphony and Chamber Ensemble and the Bronx Philharmonic. She substituted with the Rockland Choral Society Orchestra and the predominantly black String Reunion (New York City). She also played with Philip Rogers's Oral Caress, an orchestra of predominantly black musicians from Harlem, playing Rogers's original compositions and arrangements of popular ballads and dance tunes (disco).

During the summer of 1978 she toured with the Continental Ministries Orchestra. Thomas explained:

> It is a Christian Orchestra of very fine players. Our tour took us across the U.S., from California to New York, then overseas to Wales, London, Belgium and Holland. We did a full two hour concert every night and usually two or three on Sundays [correspondence with the author, July 24, 1979].

With the exception of The String Reunion and Oral Caress, Thomas was always the only black participant. Rather than serving as a source of discouragement, this superminority status inspired her to continue, work harder, and encourage others.

JACQUELINE PERRY
violin, orchestra administrator
b. Anderson, South Carolina

Jacqueline Perry joined the Mississippi Symphony as a violinist in 1992. The Anderson, South Carolina, native currently holds the position of education director and membership in the first violin section of the orchestra. As education director, she oversees the orchestra's Family Fun Concerts, Children's Concerts, Kinder-concerts, Young Artist Recital, Young Artist Concerto Competition, Mississippi Symphony Orchestra's String Institute, Youth Symphony Orchestra, and fifteen string teachers in the Jackson and Clinton public schools. Perry is also conductor of the Mississippi Youth String Orchestra.

Educated at the University of Southern Mississippi, she holds degrees in music education and music performance. Perry also teaches violin and viola privately. She was president of the American String Teacher Association and is an active member of the Mississippi Educational National Conference.

CECELIA ANN HOBBS
violin
b. August 21, 1959, Newport News, Virginia

The experiences of violinist Cecilia Hobbs with American and European orchestras were rare. Prior to high school graduation young Cecelia had to her credit nine years of membership in the Peninsula Youth Orchestra (under black conductor Roland M. Carter), several years with the Peninsula Symphony, and several summer seasons with the Purbeck Music Festival Orchestra in Dorset, England. She had already spent six summers in England with the outstanding Hungarian violinist and pedagogue Kato Havas; four summers at the Eastern Music Festival in Greensboro, North Carolina, on a Ford Foundation Scholarship; and two academic terms of study in the precollege division of the Juilliard School of Music. Cecelia began studying the violin at age five with violinist/violist Margaret Davis. Her instructor after Davis was violinist/pedagogue Elizabeth Chapman. Both Davis and Chapman are of African descent.

Cecelia's solo performances included appearances with the Academy National Youth Orchestra at Wolf Trap Farms (Virginia); Richmond, Peninsula, and Norfolk Symphonies (also in Virginia); Cosmopolitan Young Peoples Symphony (Philharmonic Hall, New York City, Leon Thompson conducting); and the Purbeck Music Festival Orchestra. Her appearance with the Norfolk Symphony Orchestra in early 1970 resulted in *Jet* magazine citing her action photograph as one of "The Week's Best."

Norfolk Symphony conductor Russell Stanger described young Cecelia Hobbs as a "Cadillac engine in a Volkswagen body." The Norfolk press labeled the talent as "rare . . . as the Hope diamond" (*Jet*, January 21, 1971, p. 33).

Upon graduation from high school Hobbs received a scholarship to the Conservatory of Music of the University of Cincinnati. There she remained for two academic years, studying with Henry Meyer of the famed LaSalle String Quartet. During the summer of 1978 she attended the University of Maine's Chamber Music School, studying with the director Joseph Fuchs. In September 1978 violinist Hobbs matriculated at the Juilliard School and continued the positive student/teacher relationship with master teacher Fuchs.

She remains active today in New York as a free-lance violinist, playing in pit orchestras for successful Broadway shows and in local chamber groups. She performs regularly, moreover, with the Opera Orchestra of New York under the baton of conductor Eve Queler, as well as with the Bronx Arts Ensemble, the American Symphony Orchestra, the New Jersey Symphony, the Brooklyn Philharmonic, and the New York City Housing Authority Orchestra.

MARION (Tecumseh) HAYDEN (Gardner)
bass violin, composer, leader
b. October 13, 1959, Detroit, Michigan

Detroit's tradition of producing fine jazz musicians (both male and female) continues. With extensive performing outreach, Hayden nevertheless remains a part of the local Detroit scene. The name Marion Hayden reached national attention through the group that she cofounded, Straight Ahead, a quintet/quartet of females that is based in Detroit. As a quintet, the group was one of the highlights of the 1994 International Association of Jazz Educators meeting in Boston. It has produced three recordings on the Atlantic Jazz label, and a fourth is in process.

According to the *Ann Arbor News*, "[Marion] Hayden is the most 'in demand' bassist in Detroit." As early as 1982, Hayden's talent was recognized when she was named "best bassist" in the *Detroit Metro Times* annual music poll. She was similarly recognized in 1991, 1992, and 1993. Hayden and members of Straight

Ahead were finalists in the 1989 Sony Innovators Award contest. In 1990 they represented the Detroit jazz community at the Montreux Jazz Festival. In 1991 Hayden received a U.S. Congressional Commendation from Congressman John Conyers.

In 1993 *Down Beat*'s critic's poll designated her as a "talent deserving of wider recognition." The *New York Times* wrote, "Strength and facility have always been the touch stone of Hayden's virtuosity and she regaled the audience with her manner of running the full gamut of her instrument." The *Detroit Free Press* wrote, "Acoustic bassist Marion Hayden swings to the updated sound with no-nonsense muscularity."

Marion is the daughter of a veteran jazz pianist, the late Herbert Hayden. She came under the tutelage of trumpeter Marcus Belgrave, whose teachings and preachings have influenced a generation of jazz musicians, at the age of fifteen. Classically trained, Hayden received the B.A. from the University of Michigan and the M.S. from Michigan State University. Though influenced by Ron Carter, Ray Brown, Charles Mingus, and Paul Chambers, her teachers have been Ernest Rodgers, Andrew White, Stephen Molina, Virginia Bodman, Ray McKinney, and Will Austin. Before committing her energies to jazz, Hayden played with the Detroit Youth Symphony, the Detroit Civic Orchestra, the Detroit Metropolitan Orchestra, the Flint Symphony, the Meadowbrook Festival Orchestra, and the Detroit Symphony Orchestra (as a regular substitute).

Bands and individuals with whom she has performed—all "top of the line"—include Marcus Belgrave, Lionel Hampton, Ellis Marsalis, Geri Allen, Donald Byrd, Joe Williams, Barry Harris, David Murray, Bobby Hutcherson, Dorothy Donegan, Jon Faddis, Hank Jones, David Baker, Josh White Jr., and Martha Reeves. In addition to offering private instruction, Hayden has served on the faculties of Cuyahoga Community College, University of Michigan (adjunct instructor of jazz studies), and the Detroit public schools. She has been a jazz clinician at Michigan State University. Currently she is a participant in the Sisters in Jazz pilot program in Michigan, mentoring and creating opportunities for young female jazz musicians. The program matches a professional woman musician with a young aspiring jazz musician in the locale.

Hayden's recording output is quite impressive. It includes

three albums on Atlantic with Straight Ahead and personal recordings with Wendell Harrison and the Clarinet Ensemble and Marcus Belgrave with Detroit's Jazz Piano Legacy, the Michigan Jazz Masters, and the best of the Montreux-Detroit Jazz Festival (1982). She has contributed expertise to panels for Meet the Composer, Detroit Council for the Arts, and the Detroit Historical Museum. Finally, she has been cited in Royal Stokes's *Jazz Profiles* and Leslie Gourse's *Madame Jazz*, both Oxford University Press.

Hayden offers the following words of wisdom for younger aspiring musicians:

> Always believe in yourself, your abilities. Know what you do well! Black women must document their musical ideas and interpretive skills by composing and recording far more than we do [correspondence with author, October 8, 1996].

JACQUELINE L. PICKETT
string bass
b. April 15, 1960, Somerset, Pennsylvania

Pickett is a perfect example of a late-twentieth-century musician who is ready to move into the twenty-first century. She is well trained and capable of doing it all, and she is willing to do it all. The Atlanta, Georgia, resident is a symphony musician, chamber musician (including "new" music), jazz musician, and university professor. She is artistic director of the Price Ensemble, a chamber society of African-American classical musicians and advocates that was named in honor of composers Florence B., John E., and soprano Leontyne Price.

Since 1988 she has been principal bassist of the Columbus (GA) Symphony. Pickett spent one season as an orchestral fellow with the Detroit Symphony Orchestra (1986–87, Music Assistance Fund) and one season as section bassist with the Jacksonville (Fla.) Symphony Orchestra (1987–88). She was a substitute bassist with the Savannah Symphony Orchestra between 1988 and 1991. She continues to do substitute work with the Alabama Symphony (1991 to date) and the Charlotte Symphony (1993 to date). For three summers (1982–85), Pickett was section bassist with the Mineria Symphony in Mexico City. During the summer of 1996, she served as principal bassist with the same orchestra. Pickett has been a core member of the contemporary music ensemble Thamyris in Atlanta since 1993 and the Quartet Alabama in Birmingham, Alabama, since 1994. She was a founding member of the latter group.

In 1992 she performed in Washington, D.C., with the Royal Ethiopian Philharmonic, and in 1993 she toured Italy with minimalist composer Terry Riley and Ensemble Khayal. A popular Atlanta bassist, Pickett participated in the Music Alive series of the National Black Arts Festival (1990) and the Fresh Images series at Spelman College (1991). She was a featured chamber musician on *Performance Today* for National Public Radio (1992). Recently she has made solo appearances at Auburn and Tuskegee Universities and at Spelman College.

A double bass student of Julius Levine, Warren Benfield, Homer Mensch, Jeffrey Mangone, Tyrone Greive, and Richard Davis, as well as a conducting student of Gunther Schuller, Pickett has consistently sought out master teachers as well as master classes at the Institute of Sandpoint, University of Wisconsin, and the Juilliard School of Music. She received the B.Mus. from West Virginia University (magna cum laude, 1982) and the M.Mus. from Yale University (1984). She received the D.M.A. from the University of Wisconsin-Madison in December 1996.

Working frequently as a clinician, she has also taught privately since 1979. She has held academic positions at Columbus College (Columbus, Ga., instructor), 1988–91, Clark-Atlanta University (adjunct professor of music), and Auburn University (assistant professor of music), 1991 to present. She has also taught for brief periods at the West Virginia Fine Arts Camp, in the Detroit public schools, and at the City Stages Festival (Birmingham, Alabama). She has shared her artistic insights with the American Symphony Orchestra League, the Kentucky Arts Council, the Southern Arts Federation, the Atlanta Bureau of Cultural Affairs, and the Georgia Council of the Arts.

PRUDENCE MCDANIEL
cello
b. February 5, 1962, Des Moines, Iowa

When world-renowned cellist Janos Starker appeared in McDaniel's hometown (and she had the pleasure of hearing him), she decided that music would be her chosen profession and cello would be her chosen instrument. She began piano lessons at age five and cello lessons at age eight. Many years later (during the course of an interview), she said, "I would like to have an orchestra job, maybe take a month for solo recital tours, and fit teaching into the regular orchestra season" (Sharon McDaniel, "Winning the Audition," *about . . . time*," June 1991). All of her training and experiences pointed her in these directions.

McDaniel received the B.Mus. in Performance degree from Drake University, the M.Mus. from the Manhattan School of Music, and an artist diploma from Duquesne University. She has been a resident of Pittsburgh, Pennsylvania, since 1992, when she entered Duquesne. She is a student of John Ehrlich, Raya Garbousova, Nathaniel Rosen, Jennifer Langham, and Karl Fruh. Other musical influences include Janos Starker, Anthony Elliot, Armenta Adams Hummings, Awadagin Pratt, Andre Watts, and Jesse Norman, to name a few. She relates best to "classical, jazz, R&B, Latin, traditional and modern Middle Eastern, rock, reggae, and bluegrass."

Her orchestral experience includes performing with the Des Moines Symphony (1980–84), the Chicago Civic Orchestra (Summer 1984), the Illinois Philharmonic Orchestra (1985–86), the Harlem Festival Orchestra (substitute, 1986–88), the Cedar Rapids Symphony (1988–89), the Houston Symphony (1989–90), the New York Philharmonic (1990–91), the Orchestra Nova (1991–94), the San Damiano Consort (1993–95), the Western Maryland Symphony (1995–96), and, since 1991, the Wheeling Symphony. She affiliated with the Houston and New York Symphony Orchestras as a fellow through the Music Assistance Fund. She has opera experience with the Houston Symphony and the Houston Grand Opera, as well as with the Dobbs Ferry, Regina, Piccolo, and Cedar Falls-Waterloo Opera Companies. McDaniel has appeared as soloist with the Illinois Philharmonic Orchestra, the Des Moines Community Orchestra, and the Drake University Orchestra. She has chamber experiences with the Des Moines Symphony's Meredith Quartet, the Cedar Rapids Symphony String Quartet, the San Damiano String Quartet, and the Sisters' Grace Piano Trio.

McDaniel conducts a private studio for children and adults, ranging from thirteen to sixty, and she serves as president of Sol

La Te Do Productions, based in Pittsburgh. To fellow musicians she states:

> When times are difficult, as they now are, it may seem necessary, for survival, to turn away from your calling. I ask everyone (musicians and non-musicians alike) to be Creative Survivalists. Find your strengths, figure out how to combine them, and make your art and creativity work with and for you. It has been said that in time of social unrest (and chaos), the "rules" do not necessarily work the same. This is when the artist is most free! It continues to be as it has been since ancient times . . . We are the healers of the spirit; without us society will lose the beauty of hope. Stay strong!" [author's questionnaire, July 18, 1996]

RACHEL (Wylene) JORDAN
violin
b. July 3, 1966, New Orleans, Louisiana

Rachel Jordan is a member of the famous Jordan clan, which includes Edward Jordan, a jazz saxophonist/educator (Southern University in New Orleans); Kent Jordan, a jazz flutist; and Marlon Jordan, a jazz trumpeter. Daughter Rachel elected to follow another course. She attended Benjamin Franklin High School and the New Orleans Center for Creative Arts (NOCCA) from 1980 to 1984. Rachel Jordan departed immediately for Peabody Conservatory, receiving the B.Mus. in violin performance in 1988 and the M.Mus. from the same institution in 1990.

Currently Jordan is a member of the Louisiana Philharmonic Orchestra (successor to the New Orleans Philharmonic) and concertmistress of the Gateways Music Festival Orchestra (summer 1995), the Eastman School of Music. She teaches a string methods course at Southern University in New Orleans and shares her talents with students at the Country Day School. For two summers she taught at the Children's String Workshop at Mount Holyoke College. Her plans for the future include composing and arranging for various string ensembles.

Notes

1. The son of Jessie Shipp, who was stage manager of the racially mixed Primrose and West Minstrel Company, a significant contributor

to the development of Negro musical comedy and a member of *The Green Pastures* cast.

2. Just after the first edition of this publication went to press (1980), the writer was notified of her death.

3. Charters indicates that some have suggested that the group's leader was Jed Davenport. Regardless of the leader, Memphis Minnie was a group affiliate—as an instrumentalist.

4. Francisco was recommended for membership in the Oklahoma City Junior Symphony while in high school (mid-1940s), following an audition for the conductor. She was denied membership "because of pressures from protesting white parents."

IV.

Wind and Percussion Players

Winds

"Girls who want to be musicians should stick to instruments such as piano, violin, harp, or even accordion—any instrument the playing of which doesn't detract from their feminine appeal." This statement was made by Lorraine (Mrs. Xavier) Cugat, in a *Down Beat* article entitled "Mrs. Cugat Can't See Gals as Tooters; Kills Glamor" (May 4, 1959, p. 13). Mrs. Cugat was only reflecting the common historical attitude toward women who play wind instruments.

People said that corset tightness prevented deep breathing and the proper flow of air from the diaphragm. They also said that the accompanying facial distortions of those who played winds were unbecoming to the gentler sex. Undoubtedly these ideas are true to some extent, but we must remember that tight-fitting undergarments have never been the vogue among black women. Also, facial distortions are the exception rather than the rule, and at any rate, are not a part of the physical adjustments required of a wind player—black or white, male or female.

Historically, black women wind players have been associated with minstrel, circus, and vaudeville bands; marching and concert bands; theater orchestras; small jazz ensembles and big bands; and chamber groups and symphony orchestras. Many have remained anonymous. For example, two unidentified females, playing mellophone and baritone, appear in a 1916 photograph of Sidney G. Paris's Family Band (New Orleans), a carnival band featured with Roy Gray's Amusement Company.

Minstrel, Carnival, Vaudeville, and
Marching-Concert Bands

Many names of wind players have come down to us. We know that cornetist Mattie Simpson (b. Harrisburg, Pennsylvania) traveled with The Mahara Minstrels in the late 1890s. According to the *Indianapolis Freeman*, Simpson appeared daily in free concerts "on the principal and prominent streets of each city [and] did solo work from the stage at each performance" (July 22, 1985). Bluesman William C. Handy recalled in his autobiography the name of trombonist Nettie Goff, also a member of The Mahara Minstrels in the last decade of the nineteenth century. Irma Young, sister of tenor saxophonist Lester Young, played saxophone in The Young Family Carnival Band during the first decades of the twentieth century.[1] A 1933 issue of the *Baltimore Afro-American* stated, "If Louis is king, she's queen of trumpeters when it comes to blowing high C's. She started her career with W. C. Handy 30 years ago" (January 21, 1933, p. 12). The "she" was Mrs. Lourie Johnson.

The Musical Spillers, a vaudeville group active at the beginning of the twentieth century, included saxophonists Alice Calloway, Mildred Creed, Helen Murphy, Leora Meoux Henderson, May Yorke, and Maydah Yorke. These women generally doubled on trombone or trumpet. Isabele Taliaferro Spiller, wife of the organizer and codirector of the group, played both saxophone and trumpet.

As for early marching and concert bands, leader Viola Allen was the featured cornetist in a Colored Female Brass Band of East Saginaw, Michigan, during the 1880s. The *Indianapolis Freeman* also tells us that cornetist Carrie Melvin (wife of minstrel Sam Lucas) was "a splendid musician, rendered difficult selections," and appeared with Professor Henderson Smith's superb military band (November 14, 1896). The roster of George Bailey's Female Brass Band of Indianapolis, organized in 1910, included Mrs. Roper Johnson and Nettie Lewis on cornet; Hattie Hargrow on saxophone; Susie Stokes and Anna Wells on trombone; Ada Low on baritone; and Ella Clifford on tuba. A marching and concert band in New Orleans during the twenties, called The Tonic Triad Band, included saxophonists Gertrude Grigsby (Dailey) and Ophelia Grigsby and clarinetists Geneva Moret and Bea Acheson.

Ophelia Grigsby also played in The Masonic Brass Band during the 1930s.

Listed as wind players with the early-1940s Sunday School Congress Band, made up of employees of the National Baptist Publishing Board, were Sadie Lindsley, Georgella Downey, Lillian McAdoo, and Martha Thompson. Saxophonist Gladys Seals was listed as the only female member of New York City's Prince Hall Marching (and Concert) Band in the early 1960s.

Theater Orchestras

Turning to theater orchestras, we note that Marie Lucas's 1914–15 orchestra at the Lafayette Theatre in New York's Harlem included cornetist Maude Shelton and trombonist Mazie Mullen Withers (b. Denver, Colorado/d. October 14, 1921). Lucas herself occasionally performed with the group on trombone. In her training orchestra were Ruth Reed on cornet, Nettie Garland on trombone, and Emma Thompson on clarinet. Reed, Garland, and Thompson played in Lucas's Colonial Theater Orchestra in Baltimore in 1916. Reed's name was also included on the roster of Lucas's Howard Theatre Orchestra of Washington, D.C., in 1917, along with that of Mazie Mullen Withers.

In 1919 Hallie Anderson's Lafayette Theatre "Lady Band" included Leora Meoux Henderson on cornet and Della Sutton on trombone. And in 1919 the Lafayette Ladies' Orchestra, directed by Will Marion Cook, included trombonist Mazie Mullen Withers, doubling on saxophone.

Four women wind players were listed in the 1928 edition of *The Official Theatrical World of Colored Artists the World Over:* saxophonists Madeline Vaughn (Chicago), Mrs. Bert Adams (Omaha), and Cleo Good (Columbus, Ohio) and trombonist Pearl Vuse (Martin's Ferry, Ohio). All were members of the American Federation of Musicians.

Jazz Ensembles

Several of the early jazz ensembles, which were generally small, included black female wind players. Chicago bandleader Estella

Harris not only sang but also played cornet with her group during the years 1916–19. Eddie Lange was the featured cornetist in Marian Pankey's Chicago female group, active during the same period. Elizabeth King played saxophone with small jazz ensembles during the 1920s in Norfolk, Virginia. This no doubt is the same Elizabeth King who played saxophone with The Harlem Playgirls in the mid-1930s.

We know that saxophonist Alma Long Scott and cornet/trumpet players Leora Meoux Henderson and Dolly Jones Hutchinson appeared on the roster of Lil Hardin Armstrong's All-Girl Orchestra in the early 1930s. It should be observed here that Jones also appeared in the late 1930s with white clarinetist Milton "Mezz" Mezzrow's Disciples of Swing in New York City, a fifteen-piece, all-star mixed band. This band of "seven whites, seven colored and Dolly" has been referred to as the band that put a dent in the Great White Way—Broadway.

Dolly was the daughter of trumpeter Dyer Jones and for a brief period was the wife of saxophonist "Hook" Hutchinson. The "wonderful sensational colored female trumpeter" Dolly was the cornetist featured on trombonist Albert Wynn's Okeh recordings in 1926. She can be heard with Wynn's group on the Stash record "Jazz Women: A Feminist Retrospective" (ST-109).

Saxophonist Gladys Seals and trombonists Leila Gibson and Thelma Patterson were regulars in Richard Baker's popular 1940s New York City dance band. During this same period Chicago trumpeter Ann Cooper was the only female member in Oliver Bibbs's Swing Orchestra. The *Chicago Defender* wrote:

> Ann, who plays a plenty hot "Bugle," . . . not only does . . . specialty trumpeting and singing, but she has her rightful place in the band and plays all the music along with the other swingsters [February 17, 1940, p. 20].

Moving into the 1950s, we note that wind personnel in the Thornton Sisters' six-piece band were saxophonists Donna Lee Thornton (Nelson), tenor, and Yvonne Thornton, alto. Also during the same decade Myrtle Young and Viola "Vi" Burnside fronted combos with their powerful tenor saxophone playing.

Toward the end of the decade singer Maxine Sullivan (née Marietta Williams, 1911, Homestead, Pennsylvania) expanded her performing skills to include the valve trombone. She appeared primarily with The World's Greatest Jazzband in concerts and festivals, in the 1960s and early '70s, both here and abroad.

At present, of course, black female wind players in small jazz ensembles are no novelty. In the 1970s The Jazz Sisters of New York City (six pieces), led by white pianist Jill McManus, included Willene Barton on tenor saxophone and Jean Davis on trumpet. This group performed at the New York Jazz Museum, Village Gate, Storyville, Five Spot Cafe, and other clubs and colleges in the New York metropolitan area.

Trumpeter Davis played with the jazz sextet featured in late 1973 at the New York Jazz Museum in what was "believed to be the first major presentation of an all-women's jazz band in twenty-five years . . . [and which featured] top professionals specifically selected for the occasion" ("Women's Lib in New York," *Black Perspective in Music,* Spring 1974, p. 197). Davis, a respected composer/arranger as well, also participated in the Universal Jazz Coalition's "Salute to Women in Jazz" at Casa Blanca 2 (formerly Birdland) in New York City during the summer of 1978 and, along with Willene Barton, participated in the Universal Jazz Coalition's "Big Apple" Jazz Women Ensemble, featured at the Kansas City Women's Jazz Festival in 1979.

Big Bands

Now let us turn to the black all-female big bands. Cellist/bassist Olivia Shipp's late-1920s and early-1930s Negro Women's Orchestral and Civic Association included saxophonists Gladys Bell (Seals), Minette Fraction, Lula Richardson, and Leora Henderson (primarily a trumpet player); trumpeters Edna Buchanan and Hilda Magingault; and trombonist Della Sutton. The mid- and late-'30s Harlem Playgirls included Lula Edge, Lorraine Brown (Guilford), Margaret Backstrom, Elizabeth King, and Viola "Vi" Burnside on saxophone and Mary Shannon, Ernestine "Tiny" Davis, and Gene Ray Lee on trumpet. The mid- and late-'30s Dixie Sweethearts included Alice Proctor on trumpet.

The 1940s and '50s saw several of these bands on the scene. Wind players with The Swinging Rays of Rhythm were Estelle Bluitte, Leaster Bethea, Marion Bridges, and Leora Bryant on trumpet; Myrtle Polite, Myrtle Young, Lou Holloway, Dora Henderson, Ora Dean Clark, and Marion Simms on saxophone; and Sammie Lee Jett, J. Stagg, Doris Nicholson, Corine Posey, Mary Stuart, and Lena C. Posey on trombone. Playing any instrument in the band, including winds, was Yvonne Plummer (Terrelongue). Plummer's principal instrument was the bagpipes, the instrument with which she made history when she arrived in this country (from her native England) in 1936. Playing twenty different instruments (including accordion, xylophone, and Hawaiian guitar), sixteen-year-old Afro-British Plummer immediately won a spot on the Major Bowes "Amateur Hour." As winner, she became a part of the impresario's touring company ("Race Amateurs Capture Places on Bowes' Hour," *Chicago Defender,* January 11, 1936, p. 9).

The more popular and longer surviving International Sweethearts of Rhythm carried the following wind players' names on its roster: Ernestine "Tiny" Davis, Jennie Lee Morse, Sadie Desmond Pankey, Nova Lee McGee, Jean Starr, Ray Carter, Terry Texara, Johnnie Mae Stansbury, and Edna Williams on trumpet; Viola "Vi" Burnside, Marge Pettiford, Carlene Murray, Frances Gaderson, Myrtle Young, Amy Garrison, Lou Holloway, Helen Saine, Grace Bayron, Lucy and Ernestine Snyder, Willie Mae Wong, and Lorraine Brown (Guilford) on saxophone; and Lena C. Posey, Jean Travis, Ina Bell Byrd, Helen Jones (Woods), Judy Bayron, Ione Grisham (Veal), Esther Louise Cooke, and Irene Grisham on trombone.

Sweethearts of Rhythm trumpeter Jean Starr later joined The Jimmie Lunceford Band. She was also prominently featured in a 1945 eight-piece, all-female pick-up group. The latter can be heard on the 1978 reissue by Stash Records, "Women in Jazz; All Women Groups" (ST-111). A former Sweethearts leader, "any instrument in the band" performer Edna Williams, was the featured trumpeter on a 1946 five-piece, all-female pick-up group available on the same Stash recording.

The tenor saxophonist "Vi" Burnside of 1945 can be heard on the 1978 Stash reissued recording "Jazz Women: A Feminist Retrospective" (ST-109). Jazz authority Mary Lou Williams stated in the jacket notes, "Vi really plays fine. That's strong, good tenor . . . She was really tough." She was also featured on the "Women in Jazz" album. For the liner notes Art Napoleon wrote, "[Her]

ORCHESTRAS AND ORCHESTRA LEADERS

Marie Lucas and her Band, c. 1916. Courtesy, William L. Dawson

The Christian Endeavor Orchestra, Central Congregational Church, New Orleans, 1905; violinist Emma Harris, organizer/director. Courtesy, Amistad Research Center.

The Seven Musical Spillers, including Helen Murphy (left) and Isabele Taliaferro Spiller (right). Courtesy, Moorland-Spingarn Research Center, Howard University.

Little Laura Dukes and Will Batts's Memphis Blues Band. Courtesy, Blues Alley, Memphis.

Prof. Nickerson's Ladies Orchestra and Concert Company, 1902

Virginia State College "Symphony" Orchestra, 1918

Marion Dozier (Walker) (right), director and mother of writer Margaret Walker (Alexander) with the New Orleans University Orchestra, late 1920s. Courtesy, Dillard University.

Ferrell Symphony Orchestra, Chicago 1930–31. Female members: pianist Lethia Johnson; violinists (left to right) Irene Britton Smith, Grazia Bell Ferrell, Marjorie Ferrell Lewis, Willabelle Jones, Ruth Sarver. Courtesy, Grazia Ferrell.

Lillian Harding and Joe "King" Oliver's (trumpet) Creole Jazz Band. Harding's future husband Louis Armstrong poses with a slide trumpet.

Sweet Emma and Her Preservation Hall Jazz Band. Left to right: Alcide Pavageau, Jim Robinson, Emanuel Sayles, Willie Humphrey, Josiah "Cie" Frazier, Percy Humphrey, Sweet Emma Barrett (piano). Courtesy, Preservation Hall Archives.

Billie and De De and their Preservation Hall Jazz Band. Left to right: George Lewis, De De Pierce, Billie Pierce (piano), Josiah "Cie" Frazier, Louis Nelson, Narvin Kimball, Chester Zardis. Courtesy, Preservation Hall Archives.

Gladys Seals's Symphonette, 1950–65, New York City. Female members: Mabel Billings, piano; Freddie Mae Baxter, tenor saxophone; Clementine Thomas and Helen Peterson, violins; Gladys Seals, alto saxophone (behind violins); Thelma Patterson, trombone; Alice Aiken Pinkney, trumpet. Courtesy, Gladys Seals.

Major N. Clark Smith's Mandolin and String Instrument Club, Chicago, 1904. Courtesy, Vivian G. Harsh Collection of Afro-American History and Literature, Woodson Regional Library, Chicago.

Richard Baker's Dance Band. Female members: Leila Gipson, trombone; Thelma Patterson, trombone; Gladys Seals, alto saxophone; Belle Durham, bass; Judy Defere, piano. Courtesy, Gladys Seals.

Though principally a guitarist, Jessie Mae Hemphill also plays bass drum in the Napoleon Strickland Fife and Drum Band, Second Annual Delta Blues Festival, Greenville, Mississippi, 1979. Photo by Cheryl T. Evans.

Major N. Clark Smith's Mandolin and String Instrument Club, Chicago, 1904. Courtesy, Vivian G. Harsh Collection of Afro-American History and Literature, Woodson Regional Library, Chicago.

Madame Corilla Rochon's Ladies Symphony Orchestra, Houston, Texas, 1915. Corilla Rochon seated fourth from left. Courtesy Jessie Covington Dent, seated first on left.

Poro College Ladies' Orchestra, St. Louis, Missouri, c. 1922. Annie Pope Malone in dark dress. Courtesy, Thomas Jefferson Library, University of Missouri, St. Louis.

Blanche Calloway, Chicago, n.d. Photo by Maurice. Courtesy Schomburg Collection, New York Public Library.

Olivia Porter Shipp's Negro Women's Orchestral and Civic Association, New York City, late 1920s to early 1930s. Front row, left to right: Bell, Mannie Mullen, unknown, unknown, violins; Della Sutton, trombone; Hilda Manigault, Edna Buchanan, trumpets; leader unknown; Betty Lomax, guitar; Gladys Bell (Seals), Minette Fraction, Lulu Richardson, unknown, Leora Meoux Henderson, saxophones. Back row, left to right: Dillion, piano; Gertrude Martin, Olivia Shipp, bass; Corinne Schyver (Shipp's daughter), drums; Alberta Conklin, unknown, piano.

Excelsior Temple Band, Brooklyn, New York, late 1920s to 1930s. Isabelle Taliaferro Spiller, leader. Courtesy, Moorland-Spingarn Research Center, Howard University.

NYA Colored Girls' Orchestra, Mobile, Alabama, 1937. Courtesy, National Archives.

Bennett College Orchestra, Greensboro, North Carolina, early 1940s. F. Nathaniel Gatlin, director. Courtesy, F. N. Gatlin.

The Vi Burnside Combo: Pauline Braddy, drums; Flo Dryer, trumpet; Vi Burnside, tenor saxophone; Edna Smith, bass; Shirley Moore, piano. Courtesy, National Archives.

Anna Ray Moore. Courtesy, Orchestra Service of America.

Margaret R. Harris

Tania Leon

Marsha Mabrey

Anne Lundy

Kay George Roberts conducting the Cleveland Orchestra, January 1993. Photo by Jack Van Antwerp. Courtesy, Kay George Roberts

The International Sweethearts of Rhythm

International Sweethearts of Rhythm, early 1940s.
Anna Mae Winburn, leader.

The Thornton Sisters

Calvert Extra Sunday Concerts, Jazz Museum, New York City, 1973. Left to right: Dottie Dodgion, drums; Carline Ray, bass; Julie Gardner, accordion; Renee Berger, trombone; Hilary Schmidt, flute; Jean Davis, trumpet. Courtesy, The Black Perspective in Music.

The Helen Cole Quartet. Helen Cole, drums; Maurine Smith, piano. Courtesy, Helen Cole

STRING PLAYERS

An early start: Robert L. Holmes and string students of the Nashville Public Schools

The Cremona Strings, essentially a female outfit, Nashville, late 1950s. Robert L. Holmes, director. Photo by Casey Walton.

The Uptown String Quartet. Lesa Terry and Diane Monroe, violins; Maxine Roach, viola; Eileen Folsom, cello. Photo by Nina D'Alessandro.

*New England Harp Trio,
all members of the Boston
Symphony Orchestra. Ann
Hobson, harp, leader; Lois
Schaefer, flute, Carol
Procter, cello.*

*Gateway Festival
Orchestra. Concert mistress
Rachel Jordan shakes the
hand of female soloist
Eleisha Nelson. Photo by
James Montanus.*

Harpist Myrtle Hart, attracting the press as early as 1895. Courtesy, Illinois State Historical Library.

Harpist Vivian LaVelle
Weaver

Harpist Patricia Terry-Ross

Harpist Anne Hobson-Pilot, Boston Symphony Orchestra

"Memphis Minnie" Douglas

Shanta Nurulla, the "Sister with the Sitar." Photo by Kofi Moyo.

Guitarist Joyce Cobb, 1979

Bassist Carline Ray

Gertrude Eloise Martin

Karen Lowry. Photo by
William Haroutounian.

Lesa Terry, violinist

*Harriette Patricia Green,
violinist*

Margaret P. Davis and her student Dianne H. Chapman, both violists in the Peninsula Symphony (Virginia)

Beverly Kane Baker, violinist

Cellist/violinist Julia Lewis Nickerson

Carlotta Gary, cellist

Prudence McDaniel, cellist

Elaine Mack, cellist

Lucille Dixon, from her Sweethearts of Rhythm days

*Olivia Porter
Shipp, cellist/bassist*

*D. Antoinette Handy
and cellist/bassist
Olivia Porter Shipp,
New York City,
February 1979*

Bassist Jacqueline Pickett

Bassist Marion T. Hayden

WIND AND PERCUSSION PLAYERS

*Melba Liston. Courtesy,
Johnson Publishing Co., Inc.*

*The Arabic Court
Saxophone Band,
Chicago, 1922.
Courtesy,
Schomburg.*

Valaida Snow

Clora Bryant

Bassoonist Gail Hightower

Judy Dines, flutist, Houston
Symphony Orchestra

Flutist Dottie Anita Taylor

Valarie King

Fostina Dixon

E. Diane Lyle-Smith

Saxophonist Evelyn Marie Young at Blues Alley, Memphis. Photo by Cheryl T. Evans.

Della Sutton. Courtesy, Moorland-Spingarn Research Center, Howard University.

L. Sharon Freeman

Bassoonist
Margaret "Peggy" Dudley

Janice Robinson. Photo by Yasuhisa Yoneda.

Alice Calloway, percussionist, Lafayette Ladies Orchestra

Timpanist Barbara Burton

Timpanist Elayne Jones

KEYBOARD PLAYERS

Auzie Russell Dial

Ruby Young

Dolly Marie Douroux Adams. Courtesy, Preservation Hall Archives.

Johnnie Mae Rice, pianist, Sweethearts of Rhythm

Patricia "Pattie" Brown

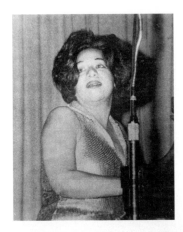

Dorothy Donegan.
Courtesy, Johnson Publishing.

Rose Murphy

Olivia "Lady Charlotte" Cook

Jeanette Salvant Kimball.
Courtesy, Preservation
Hall Archives.

Author D. Antoinette Handy and Cleo Patra Brown in Denver, Colorado, 1986

Julie Gardner

Frances Elaine Cole

Patrice Rushen

Terri Lyne Carrington

Amina Claudine Myers

Mary Lou Williams, "First Lady of Jazz," at a lecture/demonstration for Richmond, Virginia, public school students, December 1979. Photo by Samuel Banks.

D. Antoinette Handy and Mary Lou Williams, Richmond, Virginia, December 1979. Photo by Samuel Banks.

Valerie Capers

*Patricia Prattis
Jennings*

NON-PLAYING ORCHESTRAL AFFILIATES

Jackie Banks, Fort Worth Symphony Orchestra

Clarissa Wilhelmina Cumbo, Symphony Orchestra devotee and board member

Juanita Wallace Jackson, National Symphony and American Symphony Orchestra League

Carol Porter, Mississippi Symphony

*Hansonia Caldwell,
Los Angeles
Philharmonic. Photo
by Bill Doggett.*

Armenta Adams Hummings, Gateway Music Festival

work has both drive and substance, and the temptation here is to say virility."

"Elite Art" Instrumental Ensembles

Female wind players were as active in "elite art" instrumental ensembles of an earlier age as they were in minstrel, vaudeville, and jazz groups—despite the barriers raised against them. As historian James Monroe Trotter reminded us:

> [T]he gentler sex are only behind the other in possessing a knowledge of music, to that extent which has been caused by those unreasonable, unwritten, yet inexorable rules of society, that have hitherto forbidden women to do more than learn to perform upon the pianoforte and guitar, and to sing [*Music and Some Highly Musical People*, pp. 346–347].

By the turn of the twentieth century black women had developed their musical and performing skills to the extent that they were able to organize (or have organized) their own ensembles. Several examples come to mind: The turn-of-the-century Female Symphony in Cambridge and the Nickerson Ladies' Orchestra in New Orleans. "Serious" literature was the concern of both groups. Madam Corilla Rochon's Ladies' Symphony Orchestra, active in 1915 in Houston, was unique for its inclusion of so many wind players. Included on Madam Rochon's roster were Mrs. Milton Griffin on flute; Virgie S. Cornish and R. O. Smith on clarinet; E. M. Johnson and B. F. Barlow on cornet; and M. E. Isaac on trombone.

And then there were women who played with predominantly male groups. In Chicago during the 1920s Gertrude Irene Howard (Harrison) played cornet with a twenty-four-piece community orchestra, under the direction of Robert E. Giles and sponsored by the Metropolitan Church. Cornetist/leader Howard, a Chicago Musical College graduate, gave much credit to band/orchestral leader N. Clark Smith for the orchestral knowledge she gained while in his ladies' orchestra in the first decade of the century (*Chicago Defender*, July 9, 1932, p. 7). Wind players with the 1920s' Poro College Ladies' Orchestra in St. Louis were

Madie Jones, Blanche Valentine, and Ida Johnson on saxophone, and Thelma Tibbs and Sarah Brooks on trumpet.

One female woodwind player appears in a 1932 photograph of the Baltimore City Colored Orchestra. There was a black flutist noted in Boston's Commonwealth Women's Orchestra (WPA) of the late '30s. Members of Dean Dixon's American Youth Orchestra and Everett Lee's Cosmopolitan Little Symphony, both active during the 1940s, cannot recall the participation of any black female wind players; but a photograph made in 1954 of the sixty-five-piece "all-colored" Philadelphia Concert Orchestra includes a black female trombonist.

An opportunity to play "serious music" was the concern of saxophonist Gladys Anderson Seals when she organized her Symphonette in 1950 in New York City. Involved wind players included (in addition to Seals) Freddie Mae Baxter on tenor saxophone, Alice Aiken Pinkney on trumpet, and Thelma Patterson on trombone. Librarian-cellist Carlotta Gary's group of instrumentalists, vocalists, and dancers, one of the most refreshing ensembles in New York City during the late '70s, included clarinetist Deborah Pittman and bassoonist Gail Hightower.

The several all-black, predominantly black, and/or "integration-concerned" orchestras organized in the late 1950s and '60s brought about an acceleration of black female wind participation. For example, New York City's Symphony of the New World included on its roster Deborah Pittman on clarinet, Portia Smith and Rhina Cuevas on flute, Gail Hightower on bassoon, Sharon Johnson on French horn, and Janice Robinson on trombone. New York City's Harlem Philharmonic Orchestra included on its roster flutist Yvette Thomas and Portia Smith, oboist Tresa Elvy, bassoonist Gail Hightower, and French hornist L. Sharon Freeman.

One black female wind player affiliated with the New York City Housing Authority Symphony Orchestra was trombonist Janice Robinson. Two affiliated with the 1970s organized Dance Theatre of Harlem Orchestra were trumpeter Marilyn Reid and bassoonist Gail Hightower. Affiliated with Philadelphia's 1970s National Afro-American Philharmonic and New York City/Washington, D.C.'s Urban Philharmonic Orchestra were oboist Ada Delores Saunders and bassoonist Gail Hightower.

A review of orchestra rosters in the 1970s revealed the following as regular or substitute members with various traditionally nonblack orchestras throughout the country: flutist Linda Parker in the Richmond (Virginia) Symphony; flutist Thelma Karen Elliott in the Corpus Christi (Texas) Orchestra; flutist Doris Spooner Hall in the Huntsville (Alabama) Symphony Orchesta; and bassoonists Anguenette Simmien in the Beaumont (Texas) Symphony Orchestra, Florence Bowser in the Nashville (Tennessee) Symphony, and Jo Ann Caldwell in the Compton (California) Symphony. The Petersburg (Virginia) Symphony Orchestra, organized in 1979, included flutists Karen Cosby, Brenda Lundy, Maggie Powell, and Robin Tillar; oboist Dorothy Davis; clarinetists Francine Hawkins, Delores Hembrick, and Angelique Robinson; and French hornist Debra Clemons.

Two additional black female wind players were discovered as a part of the New York Housing Authority Orchestra in the late 1980s and early 1990s: Linda Blacken, French horn, and Amy Fraser, bassoon.

Second flutist in the Houston Symphony, beginning in the early 1990s, is Judy Dines, a Washington, D.C., native. She began playing the flute at age six. For several seasons, Dines participated in the National Symphony Orchestra's Youth Fellowship Program and is the first graduate of that program to be hired by a major American orchestra. On two occasions, she appeared as soloist with the National Symphony, having won the orchestra's Young Soloist Competition. She received her training at Temple University and the Peabody Conservatory (*Symphonium*, Spring 1994, p. 3).

Profiles

ISABELE TALIAFERRO SPILLER
saxophone, trumpet (piano)
b. March 18, 1888, Abingdon, Va./d. May 14, 1974, New
    York City

Isabele Taliaferro Spiller received her first music instruction from her mother Josephine Benjamin Outlaw Taliaferro. Her early years were spent in Philadelphia, where she regularly attended concerts at Wanamaker's Department Store, the Academy of

Music, St. Peter Claver's, and Willow Grove Park. She graduated from the New England Conservatory and the Juilliard School of Music and studied further with Madam Azalia Hackley (voice) and organist Melville Charlton (theory), both black.

While in her youth Spiller played organ, piano, and mandolin in the family orchestra, along with her mother on guitar, a family friend on harp, and another family friend on violin. In 1912 she joined The Musical Spillers, a vaudeville group organized in Chicago by her husband William Newmeyer Spiller, about 1906. Her primary instrument was the tenor saxophone, but she also doubled on alto and baritone and occasionally trumpet. As pointed out earlier, she served the group as codirector for a period of time.

In 1926 Isabele left The Musical Spillers and organized the Spiller School of Music in New York City. During the same period she played with Della Sutton's All Girls' Band. But from the late 1920s until her death her major musical impact was as a teacher and musical director. For a number of years Spiller was affiliated with the music programs of the Harlem Evening School and Wadleigh High School. She supervised the Woodwind, Brass and Percussion Institute of New York City's Federal Music Project (WPA) and supervised the instrumental program for the New York World's Fair, 1939, both on the grounds and on the airwaves.

LEORA MEOUX HENDERSON
trumpet (saxophone)
b. late 1890s, Louisville, Kentucky/d. 1958(?), New York
  City

Leora Meoux is remembered primarily as the wife of pianist/arranger/orchestra leader Fletcher Henderson, receiving along the way some recognition as a performing musician in her own right. She and Fletcher met while both were playing on a Hudson River boat. She was a "schooled" player, and her early years were confined to the classics. She credits her husband with teaching her to play jazz and "go beyond the printed page" and Louis Armstrong with teaching her to play "hot trumpet" (Shapiro and Hentoff, *Hear Me Talkin' to Ya*, pp. 218–223).

Her marriage to Fletcher took place in 1924, after a divorce from trumpeter Russell Smith, a member of Fletcher's famous band. Leora Meoux occasionally substituted with the Henderson band, but her permanent group affiliations were with The Musical Spillers, the Negro Women's Orchestral and Civic Association, Lil Armstrong's All-Girl Band, and her own small combo, called The Vampires. She also was a member of the orchestra that played for *The Blue Pearl* at the Lafayette Theatre, under the direction of Hallie Anderson (1919) and of a later group playing at the same theater, under the direction of Mildred Franklin Gassaway.

In the late '20s and early '30s the Henderson house on 139th Street served as the meeting place for many of the world's jazz greats, including Bessie Smith, Clara Smith, Cab Calloway, and white jazzmen Bix Biederbecke and Joe Venuti. Some were boarders; others came for rehearsals or simple fellowship. According to Calloway, "Usually Lee [Leora] cooked . . . All ate together before going their separate way to gigs . . . That included Lee, because Mrs. Henderson was a fine trumpet player in the pit orchestra at the Lafayette Theater" (Calloway, *Of Minnie the Moocher and Me*, p. 70). Mrs. Henderson's affiliation with Lafayette Theatre House Orchestras spanned a period of nine years. According to trumpeter/saxophonist Leora herself, she never suffered from a lack of musical employment.

VALAIDA SNOW (EDWARDS)
trumpet (vocals)
b. June 2, 1905, Chattanooga, Tennessee/d. May 30, 1956, New York City

Trumpeter, singer, actress, dancer, and band leader Valaida Snow was noted for her versatility. Her trademark was superior musicianship; with her numerous worldwide billings, she was "Queen of the Trumpet." Both her mother and father were performers and it was her Howard University-trained mother who taught her to play cello, guitar, accordion, harp, saxophone, clarinet, bass violin, banjo, mandolin, and trumpet. She was a close friend of theatrical personalities Sophie Tucker, Ethel Waters, Josephine Baker, and Maurice Chevalier. She once sat in as second trumpeter to Louis Armstrong in Chicago.

Valaida Snow made her debut in show business at age three. Her first national recognition resulted from an appearance at Barron Wilkins's Harlem Cabaret in 1922. A New York City paper reported on April 1950 that "Valaida Snow played real pretty at the Alhambra last week and has dates for Buffalo and Montreal." The same paper reported that the following month she would "entertain at the Waldorf . . . for the benefit of the Hebrew Home for the Aged. . . ." Six years later another New York City paper gave front-page coverage to the announcement of her death. The lengthy article was captioned "Valaida Snow, Ex-Blackbirds Star, POW Dies." A second article in the same paper read, "Death of Valaida Snow Leaves Void in Theater" (*New York Amsterdam News*, June 9, 1956).

The former performing events are particularly noteworthy in view of the fact that Valaida Snow was imprisoned for more than a year, having been captured by the Nazis while performing in Denmark just prior to World War II. Bayoneting and robbing her of expensive furs and jewelry, her captors also took her golden trumpet, a gift of Queen Wilhelmina. Released in a prisoner-of-war exchange in 1942, the superstar, reduced to sixty-eight pounds, resumed her career at New York City's Apollo Theatre in May 1943, fronting the Sunset Royal Band. She continued to perform until the time of her death.

In the course of her career she appeared in Lew Leslie's Broadway stage shows *Rhapsody in Black, Chocolate Dandies,* and *Blackbirds*; Will Masten's *Revue*; and various Noble Sissle stage productions. In the late '30s Snow appeared in the American films *Take It from Me* and *Irresistible You,* and the French film *Alibi*.

Journalist Rudolf Hopf paid tribute to her memory in an article entitled "Valaida Snow, Queen of [the] Trumpet" (*Jazz Podium*, October 1972, pp. 8–9). Hopf pointed out that Snow's trumpet playing was inventive, effortless, highly stylized, and exceptionally improvisational. He acknowledged a strong Louis Armstrong influence (in Europe she was referred to as "Little Louis"), but asked, who of that period (1930s) was not influenced (and judged) by Armstrong? Her treatment of lyrical themes was suggestive of Billie Holiday—highly personal and reflective.

There are those who believe that Valaida Snow was as much an American jazz ambassador of enormous importance abroad as Coleman Hawkins, Fats Waller, Bill Coleman, or Benny Carter. Her honorary title, "Queen of the Trumpet," was earned in Europe (primarily England).

Between 1936 and 1941 Snow recorded more than forty titles

for companies in England, Denmark, and Sweden. Hopf expressed the opinion that her recordings were comparable to those of her contemporaries, made with European musicians.

Valaida was at some time associated with the bands of Earl Hines, Jack Carter, Teddy Weatherford, Willie Lewis, and Fletcher Henderson. She can be heard with the Henderson Orchestra on the 1977 reissue by Stash Records, "Jazz Women: A Feminist Retrospective" (ST—109). "Miss Show Biz" can be heard on fifteen cuts from 1936–44, rereleased in 1982 by Rosetta Records (album *Hot Snow, Valaida Snow, Foremothers*, vol. 2, Women's Heritage Series, RR 1305). Extensive notes accompany the album.

She toured the Middle East, the Far East, and Europe (several times). She was briefly married to the dancer Ananias Berry and later to performer and producer Earle Edwards.

ERNESTINE "TINY" DAVIS
trumpet
b. August 5, 1907, Memphis, Tennessee/d. 1994, Chicago, Illinois

Trumpeter Davis said that her "formal" musical training acquired at the Booker T. Washington High School in Memphis supported a career that spanned more than forty years. In the mid-'30s "Tiny" played with the popular Harlem Playgirls. She established herself on the national and international scene with the still-more-popular International Sweethearts of Rhythm, in the mid-'40s, reigning as a featured performer with the group both here and abroad.

Following The Sweethearts' USO tour abroad in 1945 "Tiny" formed her own six-piece group, called The Hell Divers working out of Chicago. Active for about six years, the group was managed by Joe Glaser, agent for the extremely popular trumpeter Louis Armstrong. Consequently The Hell Divers frequently appeared on the same bill, covering the East Coast and the Caribbeans. "Tiny" then settled permanently in Chicago, where she continued to perform (as she moved into her seventies), primarily with her own trio, which included her daughter Dorothy on keyboard and bass.

(Cassandra) GLADYS O'FARRELL (Bell/Anderson)
   SEALS
saxophone (clarinet, flute)
b. New York City

In 1979 Gladys Seals gave as her age—"senior citizen." From the
standpoint of musical activity, she was a mere teenager. Since the
early '60s Seals was the only female member of New York City's
Prince Hall Marching and Symphonic Bands. For a number of
years she served as treasurer of the organization, implying more
than musical respectability.

Seals was very active in the affairs of the New Amsterdam Musical Association from the late 1930s onward. She was a regular
at the Association's "through the years" Saturday Night Jam Sessions and with various pick-up bands. As late as 1970 she and
her colleagues were conducting a community music school at the
Association's Harlem headquarters.

Music was a serious lifetime business for Seals. Her first instrument was the violin, which she started at age four under the tutelage of her father. Instruction soon included piano, saxophone,
and clarinet, with the German tutor Johann Rudolph. All music
instruction was private.

Group affiliations included membership in the early-'30s
Negro Women's Orchestral and Civic Association and Richard
Baker's early-'40s dance band. One of her most interesting orchestral affiliations lasted from 1950 until about 1965: the Symphonette, "a classical orchestral pride of Harlem" and a pride of
Gladys Seals. "Serious music" was the group's specialty. Seals
was the group's organizer, leader, and general manager. The thirteen-piece Symphonette was well-integrated sexually. But according to Seals,

> The middle-age membership began dying out. Finally I had to close
> it out. It was then that I began devoting much of my performing
> time to the Prince Hall Band—no longer leader, but a member of
> the ensemble. I've enjoyed it [telephone conversation with the au-
> thor, July 5, 1979].

In 1979 Seals was a "senior citizen," but she had a date book
filled with playing commitments.

GERTRUDE HUGHES (White)
trumpet
b. September 5, 1913, San Francisco

San Francisco, Tacoma, Oakland—this was the route followed by trumpeter Gertrude Hughes before arriving in Nashville for enrollment at Tennessee State College. Financing a college education through musical performance was automatic for Gertrude, daughter of concert violinist Virginia Moore.

In the early '30s trumpeter Hughes fronted her own band in Nashville and substituted with those led by Don Redmond and Fletcher Henderson. Her band once shared the spotlight with one led by Joe "King" Oliver. The Gertrude Hughes Band worked primarily on weekends in Nashville, but also in other Tennessee cities, such as Knoxville, Memphis, and Chattanooga. During the summer months "heavy earnings" were acquired in points as far away as Denver (Colorado), Jacksonville (Florida), and Shreveport (Louisiana).

Returning to her native California in 1935 (following graduation), Hughes assembled a five-piece combo that remained at San Francisco's Bon Ton Nightclub for one year. During the summer of 1939 she was featured trumpeter with a Chicano band in the same city. Around this time she met her drumming/banjo-playing/tap-dancing husband, Bill White. Of this union was born two children, the younger of whom was the bassoonist/actress/director/tap dancer Terri White. The result, of course, was formation of the White Quartet, composed of guitar/drums/banjo, played by the father; piano and flute, played by the six- or seven-year-old daughter; bass/tuba/trombone, played by the son; and trumpet/guitar/piano, played by Gertrude. The group performed mostly in the Bay Area.

Hughes eventually abandoned music as a profession. She went on to receive a master's degree in English Literature; in 1978 she retired as librarian (Current Periodicals) from Stanford University.

BERT ETTA DAVIS
alto saxophone
b. December 12, 1923, San Antonio, Texas; d. 1982, San
    Antonio, Texas

Already a rather skilled player, Bert Etta Davis entered Prairie
View College confident of her abilities. When tryouts were held
for the Prairie View College Collegians, an all-male outfit, Davis
entered the competition. Though she was the twenty-seventh saxophone auditioner (and the only female), consent was given for
her to occupy the third stand; but the all-powerful Dean of
Women objected. Not only was the idea of a female participating
in an all-male band in poor taste, but Bert Etta was a freshman.

World War II was at hand; the draft was soon to reveal the
attractiveness of female instrumentalists. The Prairie View College Co-Eds was organized. Following a successful year of on-
campus performance the group took to the road for a summer
tour. Under management of Moe Gale Agency (New York City),
the Co-Eds covered all the big Eastern theatres, including the
Apollo. Bert Etta was in her glory, generally as a featured soloist.

The group completed another school year, with all expenses
paid through the previous summer's earnings. The following
summer's tour duplicated the first; but at the end of this tour the
Co-Eds (and its director William Henry Bennett) decided not to
return to the Prairie View campus.

As the Big Band era began drawing to a close the group disbanded. On Bert Etta's initiative a combo was formed, enjoying a
brief stay in Houston, another in Detroit, and finally Peoria (Illinois). Davis then joined trumpeter Ernestine "Tiny" Davis's Hell
Divers. Touring the States and the Caribbean, she remained with
the six-piece all-female group for approximately three years.

In 1951 Davis departed for Chicago, which was home base until
1970. First she fronted her own all-male combo, then joined a five-
piece combo fronted by pianist Memphis Slim (Peter Chatman).
She then became a featured soloist on the road show of songstress
Dinah Washington. It was "Miss D" who bestowed upon Bert
Etta the name "Ladybird."

In the early 1960s "Ladybird" completed a nine-month residency in Sweden. The group consisted of all black females, with
the exception of the group's leader, Swedish pianist/arranger
Mary Hemmenson. Back in Chicago in the mid- and late '60s
Davis fronted an organ trio, as well as the Ladybird Band.

The failing health of her parents required that she, an only
child, return to San Antonio in 1970. But her jazz-loving minister
seized the opportunity and persuaded the alto saxophonist to

share her talents with the congregation in St. Paul United Methodist Church. According to Davis,

> At first I wondered how the congregation would accept the idea. But they were so fascinated that there are few Sundays that I have missed playing the Offertory since 1970 [conversation with the author, March 23, 1980].

Unable to make a living from music alone, Davis's financial mainstay was management and supervision for San Antonio's Salvation Army.

Sunday mornings found "Ladybird" wailing through such favorites as "Amazing Grace," "It Pays to Serve Jesus," and "My Tribute," backed by organ, piano, and choir. Other evenings found her working with local jazz groups. She (one of two minorities) joined Houston's six-piece jazz ensemble "Ad Lib" in 1980 and accompanied the group to Kansas City, Missouri, for an appearance at the Third Annual Women's Jazz Festival.

MELBA (Doretta) LISTON
trombone, arranging
b. January 13, 1926, Kansas City, Missouri

Liston is virtually the only woman brass player to work for big bands such as those led by Gerald Wilson, Count Basie, Quincy Jones, Dizzy Gillespie, and Duke Ellington and to write for an equally impressive array of musicians. Her outstanding talent and her gifts to the field of jazz were recognized with an American Jazz Masters Award from the National Endowment for the Arts in 1987. Born in Kansas City, Missouri in 1926, she moved with her mother to Los Angeles eleven years later. She became a member of Alma Hightower's band as a young teen and joined the pit band of the Lincoln Theater at age sixteen. She began arranging at this time as well. During her years as trombonist with Gerald Wilson, she recorded several historic tracks (on trombone) with tenor saxophonist Dexter Gordon. The Southern tour that Wilson put together to accompany Billie Holiday was disastrous.

Artists with whom Liston played or recorded include Quincy Jones, Clark Terry, Freddie Hubbard, Cannonball Adderley, Eddie "Lockjaw" Davis, Dinah Washington, Sarah Vaughan,

Betty Carter, Milt Jackson, Art Blakey, J. J. Johnson, Billie Holiday, and Budd Johnson. She arranged for such stellar artists as Benny Goodman, Mary Lou Williams, Elvin Jones, Johnny Griffin, Dakota Staton, Billy Eckstine, Gloria Lynne, Junior Mance, Solomon Burke, Tony Bennett, Abbey Lincoln, Charles Mingus, Diana Ross. She also acted as musical director for Eddie Fisher. Since 1958 she has collaborated with pianist/composer Randy Weston. This composer/arranger relationship has often been compared to the one between Billy Strayhorn and Duke Ellington.

Liston toured with Dizzy Gillespie in the Near East and Latin America in 1956–57 and toured Europe with the Quincy Jones Orchestra in 1959, acting and playing trombone in the Harold Arlen/Johnny Mercer musical *Free and Easy*. During the early 1950s, Liston worked for the L.A. Board of Education. In the mid-1950s, she performed bit parts in movies that included *The Prodigal* (1955) and *The Ten Commandments* (1956).

In June 1977 *Ebony* magazine asked, "What happened to Melba Liston?" The article began, "To the serious fan of Afro-American music, the name Melba Liston immediately recalls the image of a young talented trombonist and composer who, from the mid '40s to the late '50s, was one of the few female musicians to make a significant impact on the jazz world" (p. 122). This opinion was seconded by Leonard Feather in his 1970 *Encyclopedia of Jazz*, describing Liston as a "fine musician, the only outstanding feminine trombonist in jazz." In the late 1960s and 1970s, she worked as a staff arranger at Motown. During a trip to Jamaica with Weston in the early 1970s, she elected to remain on the island, having been recruited to establish the popular music studies program at the University of the West Indies and to head the African-American music division of the Jamaica School of Music.

Liston returned to the States in 1979, appearing at the Kansas City Women's Jazz Festival. Settling in New York City, she began touring with her own band. The world of jazz was saddened in 1985 when she experienced a stroke. She had to give up playing the trombone, but she was finally able to resume her composing and arranging (with the help of a computer). In recent years, she has done arrangements for Abbey Lincoln and Ronnie Matthews. The Liston/Weston collaboration continues in Los Angeles.

CLORA (Larea) BRYANT (Johnson)
trumpet, flugel horn (drums, piano, vocal, composition)
b. May 30, 1927, Denison, Texas

A mid-1980s press release announced that Bryant was "lost out there in the stars" but her feet were on the ground and "she'd be blowing her horn, singing and entertaining for a long time to come, on her own terms." When she experienced her busiest and most musically fulfilling period, her friends commented, "It's about time." She had just returned from a successful tour of the East Coast and was making her maiden voyage to Europe.

The East Coast tour included appearances at Carnegie Hall and Saratoga, New York, for the Kool Jazz Festival. The European experience was with the Johnny Otis Show and included festival stops at Pori, Finland; Vienne and Nice, France; Montreux, Switzerland; and The Hague. Yet, as Leonard Feather often remarked, "Clora Bryant is one of the most underrated jazz trumpet players in Los Angeles or anywhere else for that matter." Most of Bryant's friends and acquaintances shared Feather's opinion.

Bryant has been paying her dues in show business for close to half a century. Jazz historians, with the exception of Linda Dahl (*Stormy Weather*, 1984) and Sally Placksin (*American Women in Jazz*, 1982), have ignored her. Feather continued to foster her career in his book *The Jazz Years* (1987) and often wrote about her in his *Los Angeles Times* column. In recent years, she has received a performance Award from the University of Massachusetts and has been included in the Smithsonian Institution's jazz oral history project. In 1990, the Prairie View College (University) Alumni Club featured Bryant and a twelve-piece band that she assembled at the Wilshire Ebell Theater in Los Angeles.

Bryant attempted to assist herself in 1988 when she wrote a letter to Soviet leader Mikhail Gorbachev requesting an opportunity to perform in his country. Addressed simply "Kremlin, Moscow, U.S.S.R.," the letter read,

> Dear Party Leader Gorbachev: When I was young, my father always said "nothing ventured, nothing gained," so I am venturing, and hopefully will gain a line of communication to you that will result in my being the first lady horn player to be invited to your country

to perform, and maybe a friendship will blossom, because it seems that this is the time to open our hands and our hearts to each other [Leonard Feather, "Letter-Writer Clora Bryant: To Russia with Trumpet," *Los Angeles Times*, December 3, 1988, p. 54].

The letter was in Russian.

She received a reply from the Soviet cultural agency's Gosconcert U.S.S.R. offering her up to five concerts in Moscow and Leningrad, paying a thousand rubles a concert. This translates to almost $1,600 per event. They would also provide an orchestra, an interpreter, and transportation between Moscow and Leningrad. All she had to do was provide her own transportation to and from the Soviet Union. She sought assistance from the State Department, but to no avail. With the help of friends and a Russian-American organization called the Society for Cultural Relations, she and her two sons (drummer Kevin and singer Darrin) were able to make the trip (Carolyn Mitchell, "Woman's Trip to Russia to Perform in Concert Will Be a Dream Come True," *Wave*, January 4, 1989, pp. 1, 3). This was quite a feat for an artist who had not had a manager or an agent since the 1950s.

Determination came naturally to Clora, whose mother died when Clora was two. Reared by her father, Clora never forgot her father's belief in letter writing. Charles Bryant communicated regularly with his childhood friend Sam Rayburn, Speaker of the House, prior to the family's move to California in 1945. She began playing the trumpet when her brother departed for military service and left his trumpet behind. She managed to teach herself until school instruction became available to her. She was determined to be in the high school marching band.

When it came time to enter college, she was offered scholarships to Oberlin, Bennett, and Prairie View. She selected the latter because it had an all-girl band, the Prairie View College Coeds. Playing lead trumpet with the group, she saw parts of the country she never dreamed of and played in theaters she had only read about previously: D.C.'s Howard Theater, Baltimore's Royal Theater, Chicago's Regal Theater, and New York City's famous Apollo Theater. Along the "chitlin' circuit," there were many one-nighters as well as appearances at various military camps and bases.

In terms of orchestral (group) affiliations, Bryant recalls the following: Billy Williams Revue, Cheathams Sweet Baby Blues Band, Bill Berry Big Band, Bill Cosby's Proteges, Watts 103rd Street Rhythm Band, Charles Wright's Wright Sounds, Ben Pollacks Sextet, Teddy Edward's Band, Hollywood Sepia Tones, Roger Jamison's New Orleanians, Mickey Evans Swing Band, Jay Hodge Band, Trumpet Summit (octet organized by Bryant as a tribute to Dizzy Gillespie and made possible by a National Endowment for the Arts grant), Floyd Ray's All-Girl Band, Queens of Swing, Clora Bryant and Swi-Bop, and for a brief period, the International Sweethearts of Rhythm. She has guested with Count Basie, Duke Ellington, Dizzy Gillespie, Stan Kenton, Lionel Hampton, Metropole All-Stars, Harry James Orchestra, Art Blakey, and the Lighthouse All-Stars and has jammed with Dexter Gordon, Sonny Criss, Charlie Parker, and Clark Terry.

Bryant appeared on the *Ed Sullivan* and *Tonight* Shows and has worked on the cruise ships *S.S. Norway* and *S.S. Southward*. In 1953, she was the only female horn player to tour with the *Joe Louis Show*, with a five-piece band. Bryant's solo album, *Gal with the Horn*, was released in 1957.

In 1960, while Bryant was playing at the Flamingo Hotel in Las Vegas with Maurice Simon's Band, she met Harry James and Sammy Davis Jr. They helped her get into the movie *Pepe*, as a member of the big band. The following year, Bryant appeared in a single act with the Billy Williams Revue at the Riviera Hotel. She included her impersonation of Louis Armstrong (for which she has since become quite famous). The trumpet celebrity, who was performing with his band in the big show room (Williams Revue was in the lounge), brought his entire band into the lounge and played three numbers with Bryant and expressed his admiration and respect for the "trumpetiste." Dizzy Gillespie presented Bryant as his protégé at El Camino College.

In the early 1990s, Bryant was diagnosed with chronic bronchitis and was unable to play her horn. Nevertheless, she continued to teach college jazz history classes and private trumpet lessons, producing jazz concerts and writing her autobiography (*Trumpetistically Speaking, Love, Clora Bryant*). In early 1996, Bryant underwent heart surgery and was expected to make a full recovery (correspondence with author, May 26, 1996).

EVELYN MARIE YOUNG
saxophone (alto/tenor), clarinet, piano
b. March 24, 1928, Memphis, Tennessee; d. October 2,
1990, Memphis, Tennessee

Routinely the only female band member, Young nevertheless held her own, whether on the bandstand or in the recording studio. A veteran of Memphis's blues, jazz, and R & B bands, she produced a sound that was refined, a technique that was solid, and interpretations that were ethereally musical. She was recognized as one of the best ensemble players in the business.

The extent of Young's formal training was the high school band in Memphis under the direction of Professor W. T. McDaniels. She began claiming professional status at about age fifteen. Shortly thereafter she began touring and recording with B. B. King's band, fronted by Bill Harvey. Young's place in the twenty-one-piece band was as secure as that of any other. Her musicianship ensured full participation.

She has been home based since the early '60s. Some of the other bands with which she has played are The Rhythm Bombers, The Club Paradise Orchestra, and The Rufus Thomas Bearcats. As she pointed out, "Many of the bands were just put together for the job. They didn't have a name" (conversation with the author, May 28, 1979, Memphis, Tennessee).

In early 1978 Young began playing with the six- to eight-piece horn-oriented Blues Alley All Stars, a group that served primarily as back-up for featured vocalists Ma Rainey No. 2 (Lillie Mae Glover) and Little Laura Dukes. But often the "sidepersons" took the spotlight, with Young assuming her responsibilities both instrumentally and vocally.

Evelyn Young was a participant in the 1978 Memphis Music Heritage Festival and the 1979 Beale Street Music Heritage Festival. As *Living Blues* critic Jim O'Neal wrote in 1978:

> There's a new approach to the blues underway in Memphis: blues—in particular, "Beale Street Blues"—as tourist trade. . . . Memphis' civic pride in the Beale Street heritage is gaining momentum ["Blues for the Tourists at Blues Alley in Memphis," November-December 1978, p. 28].

Her days of traveling ended, Evelyn Young was a part of the heritage and was both musically and emotionally prepared to assume her place on the new Memphis scene.

ESTHER LOUISE COOKE
trombone, trumpet
b. January 1, 1929, Atlanta, Georgia

Esther Cooke was trombonist with The International Sweethearts of Rhythm from May 1947 through September 1948. She was one of the few who remained in the music business (following the group's demise), acquiring additional formal education and imparting her knowledge and skills to the younger generation. Cooke's other group affiliation was with the Howard (University) Swingmasters, a coeducational group started around 1949 composed of Howard University upperclass members and sponsored by the school's chapter of the Alpha Phi Alpha Fraternity.

Cooke began studying the trombone while in the fourth grade. She stated, "My arms were not long enough to reach the seventh position. So I had to start off with an extension." Attending the Atlanta University Laboratory High School, she was introduced to piano, violin, and cello by the school's music teacher, Lillian Webster. While in high school she played cello in the school's string quartet.

Enrolling at Howard University as a music major, she studied trombone with Bernard Lee Mason and piano with Francesca Alfreda Dixon. She received the B.Mus. from Howard University, the M.Mus. from the Eastman School of Music, and a certificate in composition from the Juilliard School of Music.

Cooke was a full-time professor of music from 1953 on, teaching music theory and strings at Tennessee State University and theory and brass-winds at Grambling University. She served as band director at Edward Waters College, assistant band director at North Carolina A & T University, and instructor of theory and orchestra director at Saint Augustine's College. In the late '60s Cooke accepted the position of Supervisor of Music in the Wilkes County, Georgia, public-school system. In the late '70s she was preparing to enter Emory University as a doctoral candidate in musicology (correspondence with the author, September 28 and November 8, 1978).

ELVIRA ("Vi") REDD
saxophone (vocals)
b. September 30, 1930, Los Angeles

Vi Redd was acknowledged as the leading female saxophonist to
have emerged in the history of jazz. A graduate of California State
(Los Angeles) and recipient of a teaching certificate from the University of Southern California, Redd's basic musical instruction
came from her great-aunt, Alma Hightower, and her father, Alton
Redd, a drummer from New Orleans. Primarily an alto saxophonist, Vi Redd performed on soprano saxophone as well and
acquired wide recognition for her vocals. She has appeared in
every major jazz festival in the world (Monterey, Newport, and
Antibes, for example). Her ten-week appearance at Ronnie Scott's
Club in London in 1967 was the longest of any American instru-
mentalist/vocalist to date.

Redd's group affiliations included bands fronted by Max
Roach, Dizzy Gillespie, and Count Basie (she toured Europe and
Africa with the latter in 1968). She was guest artist at UCLA's
Royce Hall in 1974, appearing with Rahsaan Roland Kirk. She
participated in the 1970 Charlie Parker Memorial concerts in Chicago. The five concerts were recorded by Cadet, and preserved
from the first concert was the solo playing of Vi Redd. The liner
notes referred to her as "the beautiful lady-progenitor of the Parker style . . . as creative and facile as any male counterpart."

National television viewers were exposed to her artistry frequently in 1977. In the television epic *Roots* Vi Redd was a member of Lou Gossett's band, which played during the wedding
scene. Morning viewers saw and heard the saxophonist when she
appeared with jazz pianist Marian McPartland on NBC's *The
Today Show* in 1976. Another McPartland-arranged event was *At
the Top,* featuring a five-piece female jazz ensemble, with Vi Redd
on alto saxophone (PBS). This 1977 session was recorded live at
the Monticello Room in Rochester, New York, for release on McP-
artland's record label Halcyon ("Now's the Time," HAL 115). A
"charming, vivacious, and articulate lady," she served on the Jazz
Panel of the National Endowment for the Arts and maintained a
position in the Los Angeles City Schools.

Redd was the headliner at the Tucson Primavera Jazz Fest in
1985. She also delivered "a little sermon" on women in the arts,

while her trio (John Larkin, pianist; Redd's son Randall Goldberg, drummer; and Jeff Littleton, bassist) comped quietly. Reporter Allen Scott reminded readers that Redd had "long since assured her status as perhaps the finest and certainly one of the first women saxophonists to reach prominence in jazz." With "Shadow of Your Smile," "Speak Low Misty," "I've Got It Bad," "Mister Magic," and a few other tunes, she "roused the audience," offering "a tandem which brought the crowd to its feet, roaring" (Allen Scott, "Primavera: A Celebration of Women in the Arts," *Jazz Beat*, May–June 1985).

DOROTHY ("Dotti") ANITA TAYLOR
flute, piano, composition, arranging
b. October 5, 1942, New York City

Dotti Anita Taylor is the daughter of John Taylor Jr. (d. 1972), second tenor in the Southernaires (a men's quartet), and Dorothy Marks Taylor, a mathematician/violinist who currently teaches piano and violin. A sister (d. 1973) also studied piano and theory. During the 1940s and 1950s, the sisters performed together in recital halls and churches, playing solos and duets. Dotti began studying piano when she was three and gave her debut piano recital at age seven (Carl Fisher Recital Hall). She played piano on WABD television and WNYC radio's Young Artists series.

A math teacher in the New York City public school system, Dotti Taylor also enjoys a very busy musical career, playing flute and piano, accompanying vocalists, choruses, and instrumentalists, and serving as music director of the Theatre of the Living Word. She performs and works with the International Women in Jazz, leads Moment of Truth, her seven-piece women's ensemble, performs with the Dotti Anita Taylor Quartet (Flute), the World Flute Orchestra, the New York Flutet, the Roy Prescott Orchestra, and the Ben Jackson Big Band (jazz pianist). She composes and teaches flute, piano, and voice. She performed at the 1995 National Flute Association Convention and the First Mary Lou Williams Women in Jazz festival at Kennedy Center (1996).

Taylor received her training at the Caputo Conservatory of Musical Arts (1946–49), the Juilliard School of Music (Preparatory Department, 1949–60), and Syracuse University (1960–63). She participated in various jazz workshops: Barry Harris Workshop (flute, piano, and voice), Jazzmobile (flute and arranging), and the University of Massachusetts Jazz in July (flute, piano, and arranging). From Queens College she received a bachelor of arts degree in music and math (1971) and a master of arts degree in music (1976). Her instructors include Frank Wess, Yusef Lateef, Barry Harris, Billy Taylor, Ted Dunbar, Frank Foster, Jimmy Heath, Fred Tillis, John Stubblefield, Ron Bridgewater, Jimmy Owens, and Doug Harris.

Taylor works with her quartet in various clubs and churches and performs two-piano classical compositions with pianist Helen Rutledge. Since both were born under the astrological sign Libra, they took on the name The Libran Duo. Taylor was an understudy for the pianist/conductor of the Broadway musical revue *Black and Blue*. Taylor cites Frank Wess (flute), Barry Harris (piano), and Bobby Shoe (trumpet) as her strongest influences. Her message to the younger generation is, "Always pursue your dreams and fulfill your purpose here in the universe" (author's questionnaire, May 1996).

GAIL HIGHTOWER
bassoon
b. March 29, 1946, Jamaica, New York

Gail Hightower has received numerous honors, grants, and awards. A graduate of New York City's High School of Performing Arts, Hightower received a study scholarship from the New Amsterdam Musical Association and grants from the Rockefeller Foundation, North Carolina School of the Arts, and the National Endowment for the Arts (Jazz/Folk/Ethnic). She attended the Manhattan School of Music, where she studied bassoon with Robert Sensale and Stephen Maxym. Further study was with the black bassoonist Fred Alston.

After receiving the B.Mus. and M.Mus. she taught instrumental music in the New York public school system, during which time she served as the founder/executive director of the Performing Arts Workshop of Queens. Subsequently she joined the faculty of Queens College and served as Chair of the college's Special Programs and as lecturer in music.

Her performing affiliations included the Great Neck Symphony, Festival Orchestra in Siena (Italy), North Carolina School of the Arts Festival Orchestra, Symphony of the New World, Urban Philharmonic (New York City and Washington, D.C.), Harlem Philharmonic, and the instrumental ensembles of the Dance Theatre of Harlem. Chamber affiliations included Suite Five, Zenith Bassoon Quartet, Euphorium, and Mixtures.

Hightower made her New York debut at Carnegie Recital Hall in late 1979, using the concert as a benefit for the Universal Symphony, which she founded in 1978. Of one performance, *New York Times* critic Peter G. Davis wrote:

> Miss Hightower certainly showed herself to be a deft, skillful performer, adapting smoothly to her various roles of soloist and chamber-music colleague. Her tone has an especially pleasant reedy tang that never gets out of control, while her technical facility proved to be more than proficient to support her end of the proceedings handsomely ["Gail Hightower Gives Recital on Bassoon," December 23, 1979, p. 32].

*SHERRY WINSTON
flute
b. February 15, 1947, Queens, New York

"Windsurfing in the summer. Skiing in the winter. Scuba diving during Caribbean getaways. A little mountain climbing for good measure. Now throw in a half-mile swim every morning, and some tennis, and you've got a woman for all seasons!" (Allyson Reid-Dove, "Lifestyles of the Bold and Daring," *Black Enterprise*, June 1988, pp. 332–33).

This woman for all seasons is Sherry Winston. The physical challenges that she pursues help build stamina for her performances as a jazz flutist.

A native of Queens, New York, Sherry Winston was born into a musical family. Her father, Charles Winston, was a professional saxophonist/clarinetist and band leader and her mother, Jocelyn, was an amateur classical pianist. Sherry began taking piano lessons at age eight but switched to flute in junior high school because jazz was the genre that appealed to her.

A student of John Dennis (National Symphony Orchestra), Julius Baker (New York Philharmonic master class), Hubert Laws, and Jimmy Heath (flute and saxophone), Winston received the

B.Mus. degree from Howard University (1968). Upon graduation, she worked as director of recreation and arts at two senior centers in Flushing, New York (while steadily practicing, studying, and "gigging"). Between 1974 and 1977, she was a freelancing flutist on the New York City club scene. Around this time, she formed the Sherry Winston Band.

Following a four-month tenure as administrative assistant at Warner Communications (learning the business), she worked as national director of college promotion for Elektra Records. Between 1980 and 1982, she worked as jazz and progressive promotion manager for Arista Records. In 1982, she established Sherry Winston Enterprises, handling major accounts for GRP, Elektra, and Island Records. In the meantime, Winston was realizing more and more that the marketing and promotional skills she had used for others (Hubert Laws, Chuck Mangione, Grover Washington, Branford and Wynton Marsalis, Kenny G., and Harry Connick Jr., to name a few) could be used to foster her own career.

She formed Sherry Winston Enterprises in 1982. Her client list includes AT&T, *Black Enterprise* magazine, the Coca Cola Corporation, the Coalition of 100 Black Women, the Congressional Black Caucus, the Jackie Robinson Foundation, the World Conference of Mayors, the NAACP, the National Bar Association, the United Negro College Fund, the Black Expo, the Charles Ives Center for the Arts, *Emerge* magazine, and numerous others. Winston classifies the Sherry Winston Band's music as "jazz-fusion with a bent toward the pop side of jazz."

Her debut album, *Do It for Love* (1986), included six of her own compositions and was a home-based, mail-order operation. Nevertheless, it rose to number one on the industry's black recording excellence (BRE) chart and to number two on the radio and records (R&R) chart. Her second album, *Love Madness* (1989), was released on the K-Tel label and made the top 10 on the *Billboard* contemporary jazz album chart. Her third album, *Love Is* (1991), Warlock Records, reached the top 10 on the jazz chart. In 1991, she was nominated for a Grammy in two categories: best contemporary jazz performance and best instrumental solo.

Venues for appearances of Sherry Winston (solo or with her band) include the Apollo Theater, Village Gate, Carnegie Hall, Metropolitan Museum of Art, and the United Nations (New York

City); Blues Alley, Howard University, and the Carter Baron Amphitheater (Washington, D.C.); San Diego Convention Center; Savannah Jazz Festival; Orlando Jazz Festival; Jackie Robinson Jazz Festival; and the Charles Ives Center for the Arts (Danbury, Conn.). Some of the artists with whom she has performed are Roberta Flack, Herbie Mann, Hubert Laws, Arthur Prysock, Phyllis Hyman, Ahmad Jamal, Quincy Jones, Grover Washington, Regina Bell, and Peabo Bryson.

Sportswoman, businesswoman, band leader, composer, arranger, and jazz flutist, Winston has received ample recognition for her many achievements, including the NAACP Arts and Humanities Award, Howard University Alumni Award, Eubie Blake Award, and the Serwa Award from the Coalition of 100 Black Women of Richmond, Virginia. Publications as diverse as *Japan Times* and the *Washington Post* have run feature articles describing Winston's musical diversity.

L. SHARON FREEMAN
French horn, piano
b. February 26, 1949, Brooklyn, New York

In the late 1970s Sharon Freeman was equally adept on both French horn and piano and was steadily acquiring joint performing recognition. Freeman graduated from New York City's High School of Music and Art and Manhattan School of Music (B.Mus. in Theory and French Horn). Band/orchestral affiliations included Gil Evans Orchestra, Sam Rivers's Harlem Ensemble, Charles Mingus's Big Band, Kenny Dorham Quintet, New York Jazz Repertory Company, Jazz Composers' Orchestra Association, McCoy Tyner's Big Band, the French Horn Ensemble (of which she was organizer/leader), Collective Black Artists' Ensembles, and the Harlem Philharmonic (of which she was one of several cofounders).

Her most exciting group involvement during the late 1970s was with the Sharon Freeman/Janice Robinson Quartet and Quintet. The Universal Jazz Coalition's "Salute to Women in Jazz" in June 1978 prominently featured the group, with Freeman as French hornist, pianist, and composer.

Freeman was the French hornist on recordings made by Carla Bley, Gil Evans, Don Cherry, Leroy Jenkins, Roswell Rudd, and

Charles Sullivan. In 1975 and 1976 she served as Artist-in-Residence and Team Coordinator in East Harlem District 4, under the auspices of the Emergency School Aid Act (ESAA), Special Arts Project (U.S. Office of Education). She taught piano, theory, and sight singing in various New York City schools and for several years was a member of the Henry Street Settlement music faculty. During the summer of 1973 she taught jazz improvisation at the Manhattan School of Music, and beginning in 1974 she served as piano, theory, and ensemble instructor at New York City's Jazzmobile. Freeman was a frequent panelist for the music program of the National Endowment for the Arts during the late 1980s and early 1990s.

MARGARET DUDLEY
bassoon
b. September 21, 1949, Detroit

Margaret Dudley followed her pianist/music-teacher mother into the profession. Her list of bassoon instructors included Charles Sirard and Lyell Lindsey (Detroit Symphony), Stephen Maxym (Metropolitan Opera Orchestra), Assaf BarLev (Lausanne Chamber Orchestra), and John Price (Royal Philharmonic, England).

A 1973 scholarship to the Institut des Hautes Etudes Musicales (IHEM) in Montreux, Switzerland, was to have provided only a six-week European musical experience for Dudley. But having emerged as first bassoonist with the Orchestre de IHEM and having received playing offers from various European orchestras, she decided to remain. The way of musical life abroad was far more attractive than a clerical existence in New York City, where playing opportunities were few and far between.

According to Dudley,

> [While in New York], I auditioned for one of America's leading music festival orchestras. One official, who had not heard my audition, said that I could get a scholarship if I applied as a student, because they were given out to black students who hadn't had the right education. This, despite my holding degrees from America's leading schools of music. There followed soon after a similar experience. In this case, I was told that if my teacher had interceded, I

would have gotten the position. By this time, I was finished with New York City [correspondence with the author, September 28, 1978].

The bassoonist's bitterness was justified. She received the B.Mus.Ed. from the University of Michigan in 1971. During her final two years she held the position of first bassoonist with the school's symphony orchestra and symphonic band. From 1967 to 1970 she served as rotating bassoonist with the Meadow Brook Summer Orchestra. Other pre-European orchestral experiences included the Detroit Women's Symphony (1971–72), Detroit Metropolitan Orchestra (1971–72), Colorado Philharmonic (1972–73), and Teatro Lirico Opera Company of New York (1972–73), all in the position of first bassoonist. Additionally, Dudley had been a member of the Haydn-Mozart Society Chamber Players (1970–71) and the New York Bassoon Quartet (1972–73).

After spending several musically rewarding seasons in Europe Dudley wrote,

> It's a refreshing change to be discriminated against not for color but for being a foreigner. I'm grouped with all Americans. Actually [in Europe], being a black woman is more difficult than being black [*ibid.*].

Discrimination (sexual or racial) notwithstanding, Margaret Dudley added the following to her impressive vita since the summer of 1973: solo bassoon, Bad Wiesse Kammerorchester (Germany, 1974); first bassoon, Bavarian Sinfonie (Germany, 1975–77); and assistant first bassoon, Nürnberg Philharmonic (1977–   ). A very special affiliation was with the New York Kammermusiker, a touring quartet (two oboes, English horn, and bassoon) that performed throughout Europe, South America, and New York City.

BARBARA ANN ("Bobbi") HUMPHREY
flute
b. April 25, 1950, Marlin, Texas

Primarily recognized as a solo flutist, Bobbi Humphrey played often enough with groups to justify inclusion here. The promise of Humphrey's flute talent was recognized by her band director at Lincoln High School in Dallas. From here she went to Texas Southern University (1968–70) and then transferred to Southern Methodist University (1970–71).

When one is arriving in the city of New York it is tremendouly beneficial to have a contact. When the contact is a relative (Eddie Preston) who plays trumpet with The Duke Ellington Band, the perfect introduction is at hand. Such was the case in 1971 for the arrival of flutist Humphrey. On the second day she was "sitting in" with Duke's band. She had come to "test the waters"; she had also come to study with her idol, black flutist Hubert Laws. The waters were receptive and so was flutist/coach Laws.

The Ellington experience was the first of many for Humphrey within the first few months of her arrival in the musical metropolis. There followed playing experiences with Rahsaan Roland Kirk, Cannonball Adderley, Pharoah Sanders, and Dizzy Gillespie, to name a few. The young flutist, who arrived in New York with only a few demonstration tapes but with a wealth of talent and confidence, secured her first recording contract with Blue Note Records during the second week of her residency. Shortly thereafter she was on tour with the popular jazz flutist Herbie Mann.

The contract with Blue Note extended from 1971–76. In a 1977 interview with *Afro-American* music journalist Frederick L. Douglass, commenting on her first release on the Epic Label, Humphrey said,

> I hope that the music on the album will show that I haven't made it this far just because I'm a woman who is supposedly invading territory that belongs exclusively to men—playing Jazz music ["Bobbi Reads the Afro," *Richmond Afro-American*, November 19, 1977, p. 23].

During the early months of New York City residency Humphrey competed in one of the Apollo Theatre's celebrated amateur shows. She emerged the winner—first time around, second time around . . . seventh time around. Seven years later, for the official reopening of Harlem's Music Showcase, flutist Humphrey was in the lineup of "friends" whom headliner Ralph MacDonald brought along. Critic John Rockwell commented, "But the highlight was two numbers featuring Bobbi Humphrey. . . . Miss

Humphrey's personal and musical charm made the whole evening very much worthwhile ("The Apollo Theatre Reopens with Ralph MacDonald," *New York Times*, May 7, 1978, p. 70).

Bobbi Humphrey made television appearances on *The Barbara Walters Show* and Johnny Carson's *Tonight Show*; she participated in the Newport, Montreaux, Schaefer, and Hampton jazz festivals; and she piled up the honors: "Number One Flutist," *Ebony* magazine Music Poll; "Female Jazz Performer of the Year," *Record World* magazine; and "Best Female Instrumentalist," *Billboard*— all during the mid- and late 1970s.

PORTIA SMITH
flute
b. May 8, 1950, Brooklyn, New York

Portia Smith, a graduate of New York City's High School for the Performing Arts and Manhattan School of Music (B.Mus. and M.Mus.), studied her instrument with Harold Bennett, Howard Harris, and Paige Brooke. After completing her formal training she became a music instructor in the Bronx, New York, Public Schools and director of the Worldwide Church of God Choir. Her band/orchestral affiliations included the Queens Symphony, Brooklyn Philharmonic, Symphony of the New World, and the Harlem Philharmonic. She also substituted with the New York Philharmonic and The Goldman Band.

JANICE ELAINE ROBINSON
trombone
b. December 28, 1951, Clairton, Pennsylvania

According to jazz journalist Cathy Lee, trombonist Janice Robinson "exhibited incredible range, from openbell soulful shouting to mute work that was visually as well as acoustically sensual," at the First Women's Jazz Festival, held March 1978 in Kansas City ("First Women's Jazz Festival KO's Kaycee," *Sojourner* [Jazz Supplement], May 1978, p. 12). Jazz critic John S. Wilson praised the "rich, full brilliance of her tone," when she (along with other members of The Sharon Freeman/Janice Robinson Quartet) participated in the June 1978 "Salute to Women in Jazz" (*New York Times*, June 28, 1978, p. C19).

A graduate of the Eastman School of Music (B.Mus. in Music Education), she received scholarships to the Pennsylvania Fine Arts Camp for Gifted Students and jazz clinics of the National Stage Band Camps. While a student at Eastman, Robinson served as principal trombonist in the Philharmonia, Eastman School Orchestra, Jazz Lab and Jazz Ensemble, Studio Orchestra, Wind Ensemble, and Trombone Choir. Before entering Eastman she was principal trombonist with the Pittsburgh Youth Symphony and the recipient of several awards from solo festivals at Carnegie-Mellon University.

In 1967 Robinson was soloist on the Ted Mack *Amateur Hour*; in 1968, soloist on the first Bill Cosby Special (NBC); and in 1969, soloist with the Nipsey Russell USIA Show. During the summer of 1970 she was coprincipal trombonist in the American Wind Symphony and during the summer of 1971, principal. During the summer of 1972 she toured Europe with the Pittsburgh Youth Symphony and participated in the International Festival Youth Orchestra in Lausanne, Switzerland.

Petite and soft spoken, Robinson's powerful personality surged forth when she spoke through the trombone. Evident at all times was outstanding musicianship and musical adaptability. Her professional group affiliations have included the New York Repertory Company and the Chuck Mangione, Clark Terry, Gil Evans, and Thad Jones–Mel Lewis bands. With the latter group, she toured Scandinavia in 1975. Of her "only girl" status, the Stockholm, Sweden, press said, "It is clear . . . that the girl sitting second from the right among the four trombone players is definitely not there for decoration and/or tour hostess" (Fridlund, "The Only Girl in a Big Band," *Expressen*, September 2, 1975). She was a popular Broadway-theater-orchestra trombonist and a member of the late-'70s Slide Hampton and the World of Trombones and Frank Foster's big band called The Loud Minority.

Robinson is equally at home in the symphonic orchestral setting, having performed with the Rochester Philharmonic and the Symphony of the New World, of which she was a permanent member. Additionally, she has played with the St. Luke's Chamber Ensemble and the New World Brass Quintet. According to trombonist Robinson, there was a consistent desire to "experience playing in a variety of musical settings . . . but I chose to be truthful with myself. I really wanted to become a so-called 'jazz musician.' I wanted to be a creative force in black music" (correspondence with the author, September 10, 1976). In the late '70s her desire was fulfilled, not only as a trombonist but also as a dynamic composer/arranger.

ADA DELORES SAUNDERS
oboe
b. September 17, 1952, Washington, D.C.

First there was a courtship with the flute, then the double bass, and finally, the oboe. But there was little in the form of serious oboe study prior to Saunders's enrollment at the Cleveland Institute of Music. There she studied with John Mack, principal oboist of the Cleveland Symphony Orchestra, receiving the B.Mus. degree in 1974. While enrolled, she served as second and principal oboist with the Canton (Ohio) Symphony.

Upon graduation Saunders returned to her native D.C., opening her own oboe studio and serving as oboe instructor in the D.C. Youth Orchestra Program and at the Duke Ellington School of the Arts. Professional orchestral affiliations have included the Lake George Opera Festival Orchestra (principal); Annapolis and Arlington Symphony Orchestras (principal); National Gallery Orchestra (second and assistant principal); John F. Kennedy Center Opera House Orchestra (assistant principal); Filene Center (Wolf Trap Farm Park) Orchestra (assistant principal); and the Urban Philharmonic (principal).

By the late 1980s, she was the principal oboist with the Virginia Pops Orchestra at Virginia Beach and was the oboe soloist with the United States Army Band, "Pershing's Own." Saunders continued her quest for a position in the American orchestral "big times."

(Eva) DIANE LYLE-SMITH
trumpet and flugelhorn (conducting)
b. May 14, 1953, St. Louis, Missouri

Lyle-Smith is an educator with a passion for personal performance. Currently she is an instrumental music teacher and a band director in the Camden, New Jersey public schools and is the former executive director of the Camden School of Musical Arts.

Lyle-Smith received a bachelor's degree in music edution from Hampton (Institute) University (1975), a master's degree from Bowling Green State University (1977), and a doctorate (jazz education, music supervision, and brass pedagogy-trumpet) from the University of North Texas (1993).

Teachers who influenced her include Earl O'Hare Spearman, John A. Taylor, Chelsea Tipton, Blonnie Tipton, Consuela Lee Moorehead, Edwin Betts, John Haynie, Christopher Vadalla, Dan Hearle, Neil Slater, George Hudson, and John "Johnny" Coles. All were important in shaping who and what she has become. She has taught at Fayetteville State University (1977–80), Xavier University in New Orleans (1980–85), Bishop College (1985–86), and Ursinus College (1996), as well as at Navarro College (Texas), Lincoln University (Pennsylvania), and Valley Day School on a part-time basis.

Lyle-Smith became the first woman to play with the Young Tuxedo Brass Band in New Orleans. She played with groups pulled together for Mardi Gras festivals and balls, appeared regularly at Snug Harbor Jazz Club, and performed with the Billy Eckstine Big Band in 1984. Lyle-Smith has appeared at the New Orleans Jazz and Heritage Festival since 1980 and was musically visible at the World Exposition Fair in 1984. She has appeared with such artists as the Marsalis Family, Randy Weston, Cassandra Wilson, John Faddis, Dirty Dozen Brass Band, Allen Toussaint, Fats Domino, Diane Reeves, and Hank Crawford. She has also performed with members of the Fort Worth Symphony, the New Orleans Philharmonic, the North Carolina Symphony, and the Peninsula Opera Orchestra. She was a part of the instrumental ensemble for the musicals *We Love Your William* (Anthony Bean and Allen Toussaint) in New Orleans in 1984 and *King Buddy Bolden* (Joseph Walker) at Rutgers University in 1995.

Not limited to any one musical style, Lyle-Smith toured the United States and Canada with Burning Spear (reggae) in 1988. She joined the Keystone Band of Philadelphia in 1990, becoming its first female band member. She has directed groups appearing in the Bahamas, Canada, South America, and Europe (Italy). She led the presidential jazz festivals in Philadelphia and Wilmington (Delaware)—"A Tribute to Miles Davis, Lee Morgan, and Clifford Brown" (1992–94)—and made a winning appearance at the Apollo Theater in New York City. She was leader of Philadelphia's Mill Creek Community Jazz Orchestra in 1991–93 and directed Women in Jazz Orchestras in Louisiana, Texas, New Jersey, and Pennsylvania (1980, 1986, 1988, 1991, and 1994).

A popular radio personality, she has appeared on WRTI (Temple University) on several occasions and appeared on *The Philadelphia Jazz Showcase* in June 1996. She also appeared in "A Tribute to Ella Fitzgerald" at Fairmount Park, Philadelphia, in 1996. Lyle-Smith's honors include Governor's Teacher of the Year Award, Camden (N.J.) Board of Education; Outstanding Young Woman in America (1985); *Who's Who of International Musicians* (1985); Photo Exhibits—*Wavelength*—Women in Jazz and "Hot Days, Cool Nights," Painted Bride Theatre. Articles by E. Diane Lyle-Smith have appeared in the bulletin of the Historical Research in Music Education, *Second Line,* and *Southern Black Culture: The African Heritage and the American Experience* (a syllabus for undergraduate courses in the humanities, National Endowment for the Humanities Institute, Spelman College, 1982).

> VALARIE KING (Lozano)
> flute
> b. December 30, 1953, Bridgeport, Connecticut

King studied flute with Roger Stevens (Los Angeles Philharmonic) and David Shostac (Los Angeles Chamber Orchestra). After she graduated from the University of Southern California (B.A., music), her interest turned to commercial music. She trained in recording techniques with woodwind specialists Bill Green and Buddy Collette.

Of her style, King says, "I play contemporary R&B jazz." She is comfortable working in recording studios and on the live stage. King has a command of all the literature, regardless of style. She has performed with the San Francisco Ballet, the Los Angeles Chamber Orchestra, the Pasadena Orchestra, Glendale Orchestra, and the Pacific Orchestra, as well as Opera Pacific and the American Jazz Orchestra.

She has shared the Hollywood Bowl stage with legendary flutists Hubert Laws and Jean-Pierre Rampal for a history-making concert and tour. King has played to sold-out audiences with such artists as Ella Fitzgerald, Stevie Wonder, Luther Vandross, Tony Bennett, John Denver, Robert Goulet, and Ray Charles.

Active in television and film, King has worked with such artists as Harold Wheeler, Patrice Rushen, Herbie Hancock, and Marvin Hamlish. Her recording credits include Whitney Houston, Barbra Streisand, Natalie Cole, Madonna, Michael Jackson, Tony Bennett, Paula Abdul, Patti Labelle, Nina Simone, Patti Austin, Kenny Rogers, Dolly Parton, David Benoit, Grover Washington Jr., Johnny Mathis, George Benson, Dionne Warwick, Sheena Easton, and numerous other distinguished artists.

Show credits include Emmy, American Music, Billboard, Newsweek, and People's Choice Awards. King is currently preparing to release her own CD as leader of the Valarie King Band. She is married to the outstanding West Coast flutist Danilo Lozano. The couple resides in Altadena, California.

FOSTINA (Louise) DIXON
baritone, alto, soprano saxophones; flute and clarinet
b. August 16, 195?, Wilmington, Delaware

The uniqueness of Fostina Dixon is apparent in her resume: instrumentalist, vocalist, composer, arranger, lyricist, actress, teacher. She describes her employment objective as "to combine musical and educational experience in an educational setting. Background and experience suitable for teaching masters in music classes, adult education, and cultural enrichment workshops." She also continues to pursue a career with her band, Winds of Change, as bandleader, composer, and arranger.

Dixon has been referred to as "a rare musical treasure," "charismatic and multitalented," "a musical powerhouse," "a performer with impeccable control and skill, with a distinctly individual sense of musical time and space and highly independent ideas," "saxophonist extraordinaire," "a prodigious writer and arranger," and "Delaware's best-kept secret." In the business, she is known as a true original.

A native of Wilmington, Delaware, her musical roots were in the African-American church. She began studying the clarinet at age five. As a junior in high school, she was playing the baritone saxophone. She developed her own musical talent, except for some study and coaching with such pros as Frank Foster, Buddy Collette, Victor Morosco, Joe Viola, Andy McGhee, Robert Lowery, and William Bowie.

Upon leaving Wilmington, she enrolled in a premed program at Boston University but soon switched to the Berklee College of Music, which granted her several awards for excellence in jazz performance. While she was still in high school, she was first clarinetist for the Delaware All-State Band and was clarinetist for the American Youth Symphonic Orchestra that toured Europe. She received a Bachelor of Fine Arts degree from California Institute for the Arts in the late 1970s, by which time she had settled in Los Angeles. She returned east for graduate study at Jersey City State College.

Teaching experiences began in her hometown, where she was a member of the music faculty at Christina Community Center (1975–76). In 1978 Dixon was a music instructor at Adam and Clay Junior High School and Washington High School, both in the city of Los Angeles. Private instruction has also been one of her pedagogical activities.

Dixon toured the United States and Japan with Marvin Gaye between 1977 and 81. She was a member of Gerald Wilson, Jimmy Cleveland and Leslie Drayton Big Bands (1980–81) and led Collage, a group that she organized (1979–81). Featured as baritone and alto saxophonist, singer, flutist, composer, lyricist, and arranger, she was backed by piano, guitar, bass, drums, congas, and two male backup singers. The group was appropriately named, since it was an artistic assembly of musical diversity—funk, pop, rock, reggae, and jazz.

Arriving in New York City in early 1980, Dixon organized the group Winds of Change. She enjoyed a five-year, record-breaking engagement at Harlem's Baby Grand Club. Concert performances included appearances with Melba Liston, Slide Hampton, Frank Foster, Sammy Davis Jr., Joe Williams, Nancy Wilson, Gil Evans, Cab Calloway, Charlie Persip, Prince, Andrew Cyrille, Roy Ayers, and Abbey Lincoln, to name a few. Dixon and her group, Winds of Change, have appeared at every major festival on the East Coast, always receiving rave reviews. During 1991–92, she engaged in a five-month tour of the U.S. Virgin Islands.

Her television appearances include WNYC *Perspective in Jazz* and *Today in New York* with Billy Taylor. She was twice featured on "Showtime at the Apollo" (1992). In 1996, she appeared (as a saxophonist) on *New York Undercover Cop*. Dixon's honors and awards include a National Endowment for the Arts grant (1980) and the Eubie Blake Emerging Artist of the Year Award (1986). She was a panelist for the National Endowment for the Arts Music Program in 1989.

She has recently participated in two very significant festivals: the Mary Lou Williams Women's Jazz Festival at Kennedy Center in Washington, D.C., and "Sung and Unsung: Jazz Women" in New York City, sponsored by the Smithsonian Institution (Washington, D.C.) and 651 Majestic Theater (New York City). Dixon has given private instruction and woodwind instruction and has taught at the Manna House Music School (1984–85), the New School (1990), New York University (1990–92), the Jackie Robinson Center for Physical Culture (1992). She has also served as a woodwind consultant for the New York City public schools (1992–94).

ADELE STEPHANIE SEBASTIAN
flute (vocals)
b. August 14, 1956, Riverside, California

For the Sebastian family, music making was a way of life. Mother Jacquelyn was a pianist and vocalist in the Albert McNiel Jubilee Singers; father Malvin was a professional saxophonist; and brothers Joseph and Malvin, Jr., were both singers. Adele chose the flute as her primary source of musical expression.

The late '70s found Sebastian enrolled at California State University/Los Angeles, where she majored in Theater Arts, minored in Pan Afrikan Studies, and became involved in professional music activities. Her group affiliations included the West Coast's Frank Morgan Band, The Creative Arts Ensemble, Acknowledgement, and The Pan Afrikan People's Arkestra. She also led her own group, including vibes, drums, acoustic guitar, saxophones/English horn, and flute.

Multitalented flutist Adele Sebastian coauthored lyrics for songs performed and recorded by Gloria Lynne, Friends of Distinction, and the Pan Afrikan People's Arkestra. Her poems appeared in *Soulword* magazine. In 1973 she coauthored, staged and choreographed a black-history musical entitled *It's a Brand New Day*. Sebastian appeared on The Pan Afrikan People's Arkestra recordings "Flight 17" and "The Call" (Nimbus Records) and Perry Productions recording "Smokin" (RCA).

A religious and sensitive individual, Adele Sebastian wrote about herself and her career:

> I want to be an inspiration to all people, . . . inspiring someone to write, sing, play or pick up a paintbrush—especially the children. Everyone has creative energy. . . . I strongly believe in, contribute to and support the preservation and education of the black arts. For these are my people and our contributions are priceless. . . . I believe artists should use music not only for entertainment but for inner attainment. I have been blessed with God's gift of music and it is only fair that I give due praise. I desire to be a vehicle for God's love to flow to earth (correspondence with the author, February 27, 1979).

ELRETA DODDS
clarinet (bass/soprano) saxophone (tenor)
b. June 5, 1957, Greensboro, North Carolina

Clarinet study for Elreta Dodds began in elementary school. The shift to bass-clarinet specialization began in junior high school. In senior high she followed the vocational music curriculum and played in the jazz ensemble, symphony, and concert bands and the symphony orchestra. Dodds also sang in the concert choir. At Wayne State University, she participated in the symphonic, concert, and marching bands, though she received the B.A. degree in Psychology.

While a college enrollee Dodds participated in an eight-piece Experimental Instrumental Music Arrangement Workshop conducted by Leroy Jenkins and an Experimental Big Band Workshop conducted by Anthony Braxton, both held at the University of Michigan. During this same period Dodds worked with such bands as the Creative Art Ensemble, Neptune Divine, Harleque, and Onyx, and once "sat in" with Rahsaan Roland Kirk, all in the city of Detroit.

In 1976 bass clarinetists Elreta Dodds joined The Griot Galaxy Ensemble, an eight-piece instrumental group for which she wrote several compositions. Griot Galaxy was a regular on Detroit's radio station WDET and performed frequently at the city's finest "hot spots." The National Conference of Artists cited Griot Galaxy for "Artistic Excellence in the Field of Music" (1978).

In 1977 Dodds began affiliation with Detroit's Chalameau

Wind Ensemble, "a classically oriented clarinet quartet" that was
a part of Harris/Watkins and Company. She was occasionally
hired for recording dates at Motown Productions.

Percussion

Percussion playing for women is considered as "unladylike" as
wind playing, with the exception of keyboard percussions, for
example, glockenspiel, marimba, vibraphone, and celesta,[2] and
"color" percussions, like triangle, castanets, tambourine, and
woodblocks.[3] Traditionally, percussion instruments were associated with volume and sound reinforcement; the gentler sex was
deemed devoid of sufficient strength and stamina to meet the
challenge. As one male conductor generally "tolerant toward
women orchestral membership" stated, "Instruments requiring
physical force are a dubious choice, partly because women lack
the strength for them [and] partly because the spectacle of a girl
engaging in such physical exertion is not attractive" (Paige,
"Why Not Women in Orchestras?," *The Etude,* January 1952, pp.
14–15). Tradition also associated percussion instruments (particularly drums) with the military, until very recently, "off-limits" for
females.

   But as many came to discover, strength was of less significance
than precision, finesse, and solid musicianship. These and agres-
siveness, a percussive requirement, properly asserted themselves,
despite the female's assumed role of submission.

Early Dance Orchestras, Marching and Concert Bands

A black Female Drum Corps existed in Pittsburgh in the late
1880s, providing a societal/musical contradiction of the highest
order. Percussionists with the popular turn-of-the-century Henry
Hart Family Orchestra in Indianapolis were Hazel Hart on trap
drum, xylophone, and bells and Clothilde Hart on bass drum.
According to the *Indianapolis News,* not to have danced the two-
step to the Hart sisters' drumming was like unto missing one of
life's joys (April 6, 1901, p. 24).

   The next percussive involvement of a black woman that this

author could find dates back to 1911, when Maggie Thompson served as a drummer with George Bailey's Female Brass Band in Indianapolis. In the early 1920s Beverly Sexton served as drummer with Everett White's four-piece combo in St. Louis. Then, beginning in the late '60s, guitarist Jessie Mae Hemphill took over the bass drum in Mississippi Delta's popular Napoleon Strickland Fife and Drum Band—the only woman in the group.

Theater Orchestras

Turning to theater orchestras of the early teens, the drummer in Marie Lucas's Lafayette Theatre Orchestra was Lottie Brown and, later, Florence Sturgess. Both Sturgess and former saxophonist Alice Calloway (Thompson) were drummers in Lucas's Colonial Theatre Orchestra (Baltimore) in 1916. The name Florence Washington appeared as drummer on the roster of Lucas's Howard Theatre Orchestra (Washington, D.C.) in 1917. It is an assumption that Florence Sturgess and Florence Washington were one and the same. Alice Calloway (Thompson), encountered earlier as a saxophonist with The Musical Spillers and as a cellist with Marie Lucas's Lafayette Theatre Ladies' Orchestra in late 1914, was the drummer listed with Hallie Anderson's "Lady Band" at the Lafayette Theatre in 1919. Listed as "available drummers" in the 1928 edition of *The Official Theatrical World of Colored Artists the World Over* and holding full American Federation of Musicians' membership were Shirley Kennedy in Omaha, Nebraska, and A. Patty Carter and Leota Hunt in New York City.

Small Jazz Ensembles and Big Bands

In terms of early jazz ensembles, Chicago leader Marian Pankey was the drummer with her female orchestra in the late teens. New Orleans pianist Dolly Adams was known to double occasionally on drums (as well as bass). During the late '20s and early '30s Corrine Schyver (director Olivia Shipp's daughter) was drummer with the New York City Negro Women's Orchestral and Civic Association. In the late 1930s pianist Mary Alice Clarke doubled on vibes in Fess Whatley's Vibra Cathedral Band, based in Birmingham, Alabama.

Presently anonymous (to this writer) are drummers with the all-girl jazz bands of Lil Hardin Armstrong, Alma Long Scott, Leora Meoux Henderson, et al., and the 1940s "male plus one woman drummer" combos, The Harlemaires and The Lucien-aires. Known is the name of Jennie Byrd, serving as drummer with The Dixie Sweethearts (mid-'30s). Drummers with the Swinging Rays of Rhythm and The International Sweethearts of Rhythm, both 1940 "big bands," were Thelma Perkins and Paul-ine Braddy, respectively. Also known are the names of mid-cen-tury drummers Linda Thornton, with The Thornton Sisters' Combo, and Matty Watson, with The West Coast Hollywood Sepia-Tones (1950s). Though treated in this book as keyboard players, we must recall the vibraphone work of Detroit natives Terry Pollard and Alice McLeod Coltrane, both performing with Terry Gibbs in the mid- and late 1950s.

In the 1970s the name Paula Hampton emerged as a popular New York City drummer, appearing regularly with The Jazz Sis-ters. Hampton was prominently featured as drummer (and vocal-ist) at the 1978 "Salute to Women in Jazz" in New York City. She was also drummer in the Universal Jazz Coalition's "Big Apple" Jazz Women Ensemble, featured at the Kansas City Women's Jazz Festival in 1979.

Jazz pianist, proselytizer, and author Marian McPartland listed drummer Pola Roberts as one who made "a unique contribution to music" ("You've Come a Long Way Baby," *Esquire's World of Jazz*, 1975). Music journalist and "catalytic agent" John Ham-mond once referred to Roberts's work as "first class in every re-spect." It should be observed that Ernestine "Tiny" Davis's late-'70s Chicago-based trio included Renee Phelan as drummer. In recent years, a listening and viewing public has become familiar with two black female percussionists associated with late night television: Terri Lyne Carrington—the *Arsenio Hall Show* (see pro-file that follows) and Vickie Randall—*Tonight Show*. Randall's in-strument is congo primarily. Her vocals are frequently shared as well.

"Elite Art" Instrumental Ensembles

Turning now to groups concerned with the more "serious" litera-ture, anonymous are the percussionists with Cambridge's Female

Symphonette and Chicago's Ladies' Orchestra led by N. Clark Smith, both turn-of-the-century organizations. We note, however, that Corine Wright was the percussionist with Madam Rochon's 1915 Ladies' Symphony Orchestra in Houston, and that Bernice Williams was the percussionist with the Poro College Ladies Orchestra in St. Louis in the 1920s.

Attracting much attention in Pittsburgh in 1924 was twelve-year-old xylophonist Bernice Butler. Despite her youth, public appearances included both solo and ensemble work. In the late '40s New Yorker Jean E. Campbell (Moore) served as timpanist with the Philadelphia Concert Orchestra. Timpanist with Dean Dixon's American Youth Orchestra and Everett Lee's Cosmopolitan Orchestra (also late 1940s) was New Yorker Elayne Jones, marking the beginning of one of the most exciting careers in the area of symphonic orchestral music. Jones's pupil Barbara Burton began filling significant East Coast symphonic assignments upon her New York City arrival in the late 1960s. Apparently, the 1950s–1970s establishment of all-black, predominantly black, and/or "integration-concerned" "elite art" instrumental ensembles did not produce an acceleration of black female percussion participation.

Profiles

PAULINE BRADDY (Williams)
percussion
  b. February 14, 1922, Mendenhall, Mississippi/d. January
    28, 1996, Braxton, Mississippi

Pauline Braddy was referred to by the press as "Queen of the Drums," "one of the best female drummers in the country," and "a second Chick Webb." She received all of her training (musical and otherwise) at Piney Woods Country Life School. Her drum foundation was laid by the school's master teacher Consuella Carter, who though a trumpeter, of necessity taught all the instruments in the orchestra (see above, pages 46–47). Braddy, the pulse-beat of The International Sweethearts of Rhythm, was a member of the group from its Piney Woods beginning (c. 1939) until shortly before its demise (c. 1955). She remained musically active until the late '60s, serving as drummer with The Vi Burn-side Orchestra, The Edna Smith Trio (piano, bass and drums), and finally a trio (piano, bass and drums) called Two Plus One (two females plus one male).

She retired from the music business in the late 1960s, becoming a receptionist and switchboard operator in Washington, D.C. Braddy retired again in 1994 and returned to her family in Brax-ton, Mississippi. She passed away on January 28, 1996. (See her obituary in *The Washington Post,* February 2, 1996, p. D5.)

> HELEN (Pauline) COLE
> drums
> b. May 11, 1926, Texarkana, Texas

"Seems as if I was in Texarkana only long enough to be born. Shortly thereafter, we moved to Denison, Texas. There the family remained," says Helen Cole. She was introduced to the drums in high school. At Prairie View College in Prairie View, Texas, Cole played with an all-woman outfit, the Prairie College Co-Eds. She was accompanied by her classmate, trumpeter Clora Bryant.

The Prairie View College Co-Eds started out performing on weekends in neighboring cities. In the summer of 1944 the group toured the East Coast, making an appearance at the famous Apollo Theater. The group of sixteen young women eventually separated from the school. Cole went on the road with another member of the group, saxophonist Bert Etta "Lady Bird" Davis. This was a six-piece combo that spent time performing in Hous-ton, Detroit, and Peoria, Illinois.

Another woman's combo had Ernestine "Tiny" Davis as its leader. Known as the Hell Divers, the group toured the United States and South America. Cole then fronted the Helen Cole Quartet, which included pianist Maurine Smith, two unknown men on bass and clarinet, and Cole on drums. The Helen Cole Trio had Margaret "Marge" Backstrom on bass and Toby Butler on trumpet. Finally, she and Maurine Smith made up the Helen Cole Duo.

Cole retired from the music business in 1971. Returning home to Denison, she obtained a certificate from a local business school and then accepted a job as an accountant in the banking business. Her message to women who desire to pursue a career in music is, "Education, first priority" (questionnaire and telephone conversation with author, July 13, 1996).

> ELAYNE JONES (Kaufman)
> timpani, percussion
> b. 1928 (?), New York City

Elayne Jones first attracted national attention in 1949, when she joined the New York City Ballet and Opera Company Orchestras. She remained with the former until 1952 and the latter until 1961. Jones began studying piano with her mother at age six. Graduating from Music and Art High School, the Harlem-born and -raised timpanist entered Juilliard on a scholarship sponsored by Edward Kennedy "Duke" Ellington. The summer following graduation (1949) was spent at Tanglewood in Lenox, Massachusetts.

Jones's professional symphonic involvements included also the CBS Symphony, Brooklyn Philharmonic, Caramoor Festival Orchestra, Symphony of the Air, Boston Women's Symphony, New Jersey Symphony, Westchester Symphony and Long Island Philharmonic. She was timpanist with the American Symphony Orchestra from the group's 1962 inception until her departure for San Francisco in 1972. She was timpanist with the Dimitri Mitropoulos Conducting Competition Orchestra from 1961–71. She served as "percussion extra" with the New York Philharmonic (1969–71) and Metropolitan Opera Orchestra (1970–71). Other theatrical/orchestral involvements were the New York City Light Opera Company, American Ballet Theatre, San Francisco Opera Company and Broadway productions that included *On a Clear Day You Can See Forever*, *Purlie*, *Carnival*, *The Conquering Heroes*, and *Greenwillow*. Jones was one of the "select" American blacks (three women) who performed with maestro Arthur Fiedler's World Symphony Orchestra in October 1971.

Teaching assignments have included the Metropolitan Music School (New York City), Bronx Community College, Westchester Conservatory of Music and San Francisco Conservatory. As the 1960 pressures for more black visibility in the performing arts increased, Jones made over three hundred solo appearances as performer and lecturer in schools and resorts throughout New York City, Long Island, New Jersey, and Connecticut. In 1965 National Educational Television prepared a half hour special for national viewing entitled "A Day in the Life of a Musician," featuring timpanist Elayne Jones. The same year, she received the LaGuardia Memorial Award, "in recognition of her outstanding achievement in the field of music."

She was one of the founding members of New York City's Symphony of the New World and served as the ensemble's first president. Jones was a frequent radio and television panelist when the topic was "Integrating American Orchestras." In 1972 she emerged winner of a competition with forty others for the position of timpanist with the San Francisco Symphony Orchestra. She then became the first black (male or female) to hold a principal position in a major American symphony orchestra.

Just prior to this outstanding achievement, renowned maestro Leopold Stokowski wrote the following for the periodical *Music and Artists:*

> Elayne Jones . . . is a very great artist. I know the timpani players in other countries and some of them are very great; but she is equally great. She is one of the greatest in the whole world for her instrument, for technique, but particularly for imagination, because timpani parts on the paper sometimes look very dry. . . . She has to make it sound; she has to make it suggest certain mysterious things or very powerful things and she does that wonderfully ["Leopold Stokowski Speaks," January 1972, p. 12].

The San Francisco press routinely singled out Elayne Jones following San Francisco Symphony concerts (1972–74); "If the world has a finer timpanist, I have not heard one"; "Special note should be given Elayne Jones in her unbeatable reading of the solo tympani part"; "Orchestra as a whole is sounding better than ever"; "Miss Jones the star—brilliantly and subtly rhythmic, and subtly in tune"; "Elayne Jones, sure the best tympanist in the business today"; "Sensational! Absolutely sensational; she is a major addition to the orchestra and community"; "A musician first, a percussion virtuoso second. Clear articulation, fine intonation and technical savvy"; "We have a drummer who can phrase like a Lieder singer." (*San Francisco Chronicle, San Francisco Post,* and *San Francisco Examiner*).

But as reported in the nation's leading newspapers and best capsuled in *Newsweek:*

Jones, the only black, and Nakagawa, the only native Japanese in the orchestra have been fired. In San Francisco, players are hired by open auditions (they play behind screens) for a two-year probation and then come up for tenure before a seven-member players' committee elected by the orchestra. Disapproval by the committee is tantamount to dismissal from the orchestra. In May 1974, six out of eight applicants for tenure, all of them white, were approved by the committee; Jones and Nakagawa were not. Why? ["Votes vs. Notes," June 17, 1974, pp. 109–110].

Lengthy articles appeared in major publications throughout the country, all deploring the action of the players' committee.

Shortly thereafter the following appeared in the *San Francisco Chronicle,*

> Elayne Jones [has] asked the U.S. District Court . . . to order the San Francisco Symphony and Musicians Union Local 6 to grant her tenure as the Symphony's first-chair tympanist . . . Her suit . . . also demanded $50,000 damages for emotional distress and anguish caused by denial of her tenure . . . Miss Jones charged the tenure committee members turned her down for reasons of racism, sexism and jealousy" ["Tympanist Sues for Her Tenure," June 21, 1974, p. 3].

Jones and bassoonist Ryohei Nakagawa were offered (and accepted) employment with the orchestra for the following season. The initial suit was dropped when, in August 1975, she was granted another audition before a new committee—with a court monitor. Again denied tenure, she filed a $1.5-million damage suit in August, 1976.

The "Support Committee for Elayne Jones, Tympanist" included such well-established artists as singers Leontyne Price, Shirley Verrett, George Shirley, and Harry Belafonte; conductors Leopold Stokowski, Leonard DePaur, and Everett Lee; pianists Don Shirley and Billy Taylor; author/actress Maya Angelou; and community leaders Representative Ronald Dellums and publisher Carlton Goodlett.

On April 15, 1977, Elayne Jones wrote the following to her friends and sponsors:

> The first Hearing on the defendants' motion for summary dismissal . . . ended in the judge's denial of the request. . . . I have already

spent ten hours giving depositions . . . There is at least another day
of depositions ahead of me on April 28th.

On December 20, 1977, Jones wrote the following to the same
constituency:

This is probably the most painful letter I have ever had to write. . . .
My endeavor to expose racism has been thwarted.

Summary judgment had been granted; the case was dismissed.

The establishment of a players' committee was the outgrowth
of long-standing disputes in the San Francisco Symphony between the orchestra's musical directors and orchestra personnel.
Throughout the Jones/Nakagawa vs. San Francisco Symphony
dispute Japanese conductor Seiji Ozawa was at the helm. His only
public statement indicated that "both musicians deserved to get
tenure." But following the 1976 reauditioning Ozawa lined up
with the committee and subsequently resigned to take up full-
time leadership of the Boston Symphony. In the words of *New
York Times* music journalist Donal Henahan:

And the cause of orchestral democracy, while still breathing
strongly, has felt the heavy hand of "I'm All Right, Jack" unionism
pressing against its windpipe. Bad show, all around ["About That
Timpanist Who Got Drummed Out," September 7, 1975, p. D25].[4]

Jones remained in San Francisco, continuing to play with the
San Francisco Opera and for a brief period serving on the faculty
of San Francisco Conservatory. She continued to do some private
teaching. Lecture-demonstration concerts were also on her
agenda. Jones's object was to bring people into the world of symphonic music and to make music come alive for those who have
a mistaken perception of what classical music is and who plays
it.

The National Association of Negro Musicians bestowed its Distinguished Service Award on her in 1993. The following year, preparing for a vacation in Barbados, she wrote, "I am not physically
or emotionally ready to retire. So I have taken a one year leave of
absence [from the opera company] to investigate how I can best
use my years of experience to benefit young African-American
people (correspondence with the author, January 9, 1994).

BARBARA J. BURTON (Tuten)
timpani, percussion
b. January 25, 1948, Chicago

Burton's primary motivation is "excellence in pursuit of perfection" (correspondence with the author, March 1979). Such a self-imposed musical standard has always gained for her the highest respect.

Her musical training began at age seven, and under the guidance of black high school band director Walter Dyett (Chicago), she went on to pursue the entire percussion and keyboard families. She studied at the Loop Junior College and Juilliard School of Music. Percussion instructors included Donald Koss and Gordon Peters (timpanist and percussionist, respectively, Chicago Symphony), Saul Goodman (New York Philharmonic), and Elayne Jones (American Symphony/San Francisco Symphony).

Orchestral affiliations for Burton included the Chicago Civic Orchestra, New Jersey and Brooklyn symphonies, Brooklyn Philharmonic, Alvin Ailey Dance Theatre, Dance Theatre of Harlem, Harlem Philharmonic, and Symphony of the New World. Substitute affiliations included the New York Philharmonic, City Center Ballet Orchestra, and Chicago Ballet Company. She has also performed with the Music-Sound Awareness and Juilliard Percussion Ensembles, Afro-American Total Theater, Harlem School of the Arts Theater, and radio station WBAI's Contemporary Music Concerts in New York City.

Burton's professional experience included personal appearances, recordings, and tours with such popular artists as Wayne Shorter, Melvin Van Peebles, Marvin Gaye, Duke Ellington, The Staple Singers, and The Temptations. In 1975 vibraphonist Burton toured Japan and Australia with vocalist/pianist Roberta Flack. She was drummer with the Broadway production *The Wiz* for four years.

DARALYN RAMEY
percussion
b. September 14, 1952, New York City

A graduate of New York City's High School of Music and Art, Daralyn Ramey's primary percussion instruments included drums and vibraphone. A Jazzmobile employee, around Columbia University attendance, Ramey performed with the Jazzmobile Workshop Ensemble, New Muse Community Museum Band, and Jazz Interactions. She was one of the features of New York City's summer '78 "Salute to Women in Jazz" (Casa Blanca 2).

TERRI LYNE CARRINGTON
percussion (composition/vocals)
b. August 4, 1965, West Medford, Massachusetts

Drummer Terri Lyne Carrington, whose career began at age five, was well launched into the jazz world when she "guest appeared" as vocalist and tambourine player with Rahsaan Roland Kirk. She "jammed" with him again at age ten, this time as jazz drummer.

Granddaughter of a professional drummer and daughter of a professional saxophonist (Matt "Sonny" Carrington, President of the Boston Jazz Society), she began studying saxophone under her father's tutelage, after hearing Illinois Jacquet perform. The loss of her baby teeth presented her with "saxophone playing" problems, and rather than wait for the permanent teeth replacement she turned to her deceased grandfather's drums.

Carrington's first drum instructor was again her father. At age eight she enrolled in the Lexington Music Center. At age ten she enrolled at the Berklee College of Music, where she was offered a lifetime scholarship by the school's president. Also at age ten Carrington appeared with trumpeter/flugelhornist Clark Terry at the prestigious Wichita (Kansas) Jazz Festival. Performing on veteran drummer Louis Bellson's instrument, she received three standing ovations. By the tender age of ten Carrington had already enjoyed the distinction of being the youngest endorser for Avedis Zildjian cymbals and Slingerland drums, "two of the world's foremost instrument manufacturers whose endorsers usually answer to such names as Max Roach, Buddy Rich and Jo Jones" ("Oooowee, Man, That Little Girl Can Play!," *Ebony*, April 1977, p. 134).

By the time she was eleven jazz journalist Jack London wrote the following for *Modern Drummer*:

> [N]ot just an average little drummer. She happens to be one of the
> most remarkable new jazz drumming talents on the scene today.

. . . Jazz drummers—look out. Terri Lyne's on the scene, and she's only just begun ["Terri Lyne Carrington: She's Only Just Begun," October 1977, p. 10].

In addition to the persons named above, her list of "orchestral" associations included such jazz luminaries as Buddy Rich, Art Blakey, Oscar Peterson, Dizzy Gillespie, Nat Adderley, Dexter Gordon, Lionel Hampton, Sonny Stitt, Eddie "Lockjaw" Davis, Major Holly, Jackie McLean, and Keter Betts. She provided the strong backbeat and percussive colorations for such vocal giants as Helen Humes, Jimmy Witherspoon, and Betty Carter. For a *Reader's Digest* program of incentives for young people, Carrington prepared (with Roberta Flack) a tape for distribution to school systems. She appeared with Linda Hopkins in the 1977 theater production of *Me and Bessie*. Her earlier television appearances included WGBH's "Zoom" show (with Clark Terry), WCVB's "Good Day" show (with Milt Buckner and Illinois Jacquet), and "To Tell the Truth" (with Buddy Rich).

Following an April 1979 appearance at Washington, D.C.'s Blues Alley ("Stars of the Future" session arranged by bassist Keter Betts) critic W. Royal Stokes wrote:

Terri Lyne Carrington is not yet 14, but if you close your eyes, you can believe you're hearing a drummer of professional stature a decade older . . . With remarkable technique in several extended solos, she delivered fusillades of one- and two-handed rolls across her snare and toms, peppered with rim shots and drenched in showers from the cymbals . . . a fluency far beyond her years ["Terri Carrington," *Washington Post*, April 25, 1979, p. D11].

As *Down Beat* journalist Richard Brown wrote, "She shines most brightly as a soloist. . . . [I]t is her grasp of the formal concept of music that gives her playing real depth" ("Terri Lyne Carrington," March 22, 1979, p. 34).

Teri Lyne Carrington began doing drum clinics with Louis Bellson for Slingerland. By age fourteen she was on her own as a clinician. She verbalized her skills with the know-how of a master pedagogue and as the exposures grew, study and practice increased. For as Terri Lyne Carrington stated, "I want to be a *total* musician, . . . I don't want to be known as just a drummer."

Over the next fifteen years, she came to be known as a com-

poser vocalist, and leader as well. She moved to New York City
in 1983 and to Los Angeles in 1989, to be drummer on the *Arsenio
Hall Show*. Though she remained with the show for only a brief
period, she maintained residence on the West Coast. Carrington
was by now a special feature at leading festivals of the world
and completed several tours abroad under auspices of the United
States Information Agency. The list of persons with whom she
has worked now includes Wayne Shorter, Pharoah Sanders, Al
Jarreau, Grover Washington, Oscar Peterson, David Sanborn, and
Patrice Rushen. Carrington has also appeared in several feature
films: *Beat Street, Harley Davidson and the Marlboro Man*, and *Without You I'm Nothing*.

> CECILIA SMITH
> vibraphone (composition)
> b. Cincinnati, Ohio

Cincinnati-born Smith grew up in Cleveland Heights, Ohio, remaining there through high school graduation. She is the oldest
of five children, including her twin sister. Smith began studying
the piano when she was eight and percussion at eleven. When
the high school band director needed a mallet player, Smith vol-
unteered, thinking it "the perfect meeting ground for her pianistic and drumming skills." She remembers her piano instructor,
Earl Todd, fondly, stating, "He taught me not only how to play
but how to practice."

Smith is a leading vibraphonist of the four-mallet technique,
which she mastered under the tutelage of Ed Saindon and Gary
Burton. She is a graduate of the Berklee College of Music, where
she was a member of the faculty until moving permanently to
New York City. Prior to this, she taught briefly in the Boston public schools. She performs primarily in the quartet format (vibraphone, piano, bass and drums, guitar occasionally replacing the
piano in earlier years).

As early as 1991, the *Cape Cod Times* labeled her "a jazz star on
the rise, . . . [with] extraordinary command of her instrument
[and] first rate musicianship" (Joe Burns, "Cecilia Smith's Cool
Jazz Refreshing," July 21, 1991, p. E7). A few days earlier, she had
told the writer that "my music is pretty inside. I consider myself
a straight-ahead, main-stream jazz artist. I'm also very much in

love with the romantic period, in terms of classical (music), so most of the music I write is very melodic. But it's still jazz and it still swings" (Joe Burns, "Career in Jazz Hits Right Note," *Cape Cod Times*, July 13, 1991, p. C3).

Smith's composition talents are being recognized as she is receiving more and more commissions. She was commissioned to write music based on African-American and Native American idioms for the Cooper Hewitt Museum, Smithsonian Institutes, National Museum of Design and Music for the Boston Museum of Science for the Black Achievers in Science exhibition. Two previously released compact discs (*The Takeoff: Cecilia Smith— Vibraphonist* and *CSQ: Volume II*, both on the Brownstone label) include several of her compositions and arrangements, each attesting to her abilities as a composer. Anxiously awaited is her film score for the feature film *Naked Acts*.

The vibraphonist does not have a booking agent or a publicist. All business matters (including bookings) are handled by Smith personally. Consequently, few compromises are necessary. She paces herself well and is in no hurry to reach stardom. In addition to her quartet collaborators (Frank Wilkins, piano; Steve Kirby, bass; and Ron Savage, drums), she has appeared with Milt Hinton, Alan Dawson, Donald Harrison, Billie Pierce, Mulgrew Miller, Vanessa Rubin, and Cecil Bridgewater, to name a few.

Now based entirely in New York City, she describes her brand of jazz as "hard swinging, inspired by Bobby Hutcherson, Miles Davis, John Coltrane, and McCoy Tyner." She is (or has been) artist in residence at several colleges and universities: Cornell, Williams, Wooster Poly Technical Institute, and Bunker Hill Community College. She appeared on the Good Vibes series at Lincoln Center, along with Milt Jackson and Jay Hoggard. Hers is one of the most popular jazz groups on the New England Foundation for the Arts touring roster.

Notes

1. For more on Irma Young and the Young Family Band, see Sally Placksin, *American Women in Jazz* (New York: Seaview Books, 1982).
2. Though a percussion instrument in the strictest sense, the "celesta"

is played by the orchestra's pianist and is herein treated in Chapter V, "Keyboard Players."

3. One is hired to play a "battery" of percussions, not an isolated instrument.

4. For more on the Jones/Nakagawa firing see Arthur Bloomfield, "Sour Notes to and from the Symphony," *San Francisco Examiner*, May 24, 1974, p. 35; Alexander Fried, "Opera House Cheers for Tenure-Less Pair," *San Francisco Chronicle/Examiner*, May 26, 1974, p. 7; Arthur Bloomfield, "The Other Side's View of Symphony Freeze-Out," *San Francisco Examiner*, May 29, 1974, p. 1; Lacey Fosburgh, "2 Musicians' Jobs Stir Coast Conflict," *New York Times*, June 12, 1974, p. 38; Robert Commanday, "Symphony Buys Time in Players' Dispute," *San Francisco Chronicle*, July 31, 1974, p. 46; Lacey Fosburgh, "Two Musicians Reinstated for a Year in Coast Dispute," *New York Times*, August 2, 1974, p. 12; Robert Commanday, "The Symphony Scandal," *High Fidelity/Musical America*, September 1974, pp. MA28–29; "Elayne Asks New Committee Hearing," *San Francisco Chronicle*, January 18, 1975, p. 9; Paul Ciotti, "The Stuff of Courage," *San Francisco Chronicle*, February 1975, pp. 16, 18; James A. Finefrock, "Fired Black Symphony Tympanist to File $1.5 Million Damage Suit," *San Francisco Examiner*, August 13, 1976, p. 6; Jacob Wortham, "Shoot the Piano Player . . . and the Cellist, the Oboist and the Drummer," *Black Enterprise*, December 1976, p. 86.

V.

Keyboard Players

Though not an orchestral instrument in the strictest sense of the word, the piano has been variously used: to interplay with other instruments of the orchestra, to provide a backdrop for solos taken by other instruments, and to contribute to the common orchestral base. Additionally, the piano has provided its own independent, imaginative, and personal ingredients to the orchestral whole.

Conventional wisdom of the past (and perhaps even of the present) stated that next to the harp the piano was *the* instrument for females to play. Professionally, the possession of piano skills was a lady's best entrée to the business of music. Other keyboard skills were also acceptable. The identification of a keyboard player with a specific instrumental organization and the accompanying keyboard profiles offer proof that black women keyboardists have been active participants in all kinds of instrumental ensembles in America and that their participation is not of recent vintage.

Minstrel/Ragtime/Vaudeville Bands

Contemporary records reveal that several "lady" pianists played in nineteenth-century minstrel bands and ragtime and vaudeville bands of the early twentieth century. For example, Mrs. Henry Hart toured with her husband's Alabama Minstrels during the 1860s and '70s. Mrs. Theodore Finney played in her husband's popular Quadrille Band in Detroit during the 1880s. Lisetta Young, mother of famed tenor saxophonist Lester Young, toured with husband Billy Young's band during the first decade of the twentieth century, playing for small circus companies and tent shows. Another family unit touring in Louisiana at the same time was The Williams Ragtime Band, whose "Mistress of the Keyboard" was Lucy Williams.

In the second decade of the twentieth century ragtime pianist Laura Brown played regularly with The Peerless Orchestra in Newark, New Jersey, and in the third decade Alberta Simmons's name appeared on the roster of various pick-up orchestras in New York City. In 1921 Luella Anderson walked away with the title "Champion Ragtime Piano Player" at a competition that continued for several weeks in St. Louis. To be certain, all of Anderson's piano playing was not solo. Lewis Anderson ("Minstrel Rabbit") recalled that his mother played the accordion in The Muse Family Band during the early decades of this century in Franklin County, Virginia. Its repertory consisted of "country dances, ragtime, blues, traditional jazz and the pre-Depression output of Tin Pan Alley" (Bustard, "Pagliacci of Colt Day: Minstrel Rabbit Muse," *Richmond Times Dispatch*, April 9, 1978, p. k 1).

Pearl Wright traveled on the vaudeville circuit with singer Ethel Waters for several years. With her solid musicianship and piano proficiency, she "whipped in shape" accompanying instrumentalists for the dynamic blues/jazz songstress. Marion Roberts (Borders) filled a similar assignment with actress/singer Mae West, and Isabele Taliaferro Spiller "tickle[d] a mean set of ivories" with The Musical Spillers' vaudeville act ("Musical Spillers," *Chicago Defender*, July 19, 1925, Part 1, p. 7).

Early Theater Orchestras

Early New York bandleader Marie Lucas directed the musical affairs of her many theater orchestras from the keyboard. Mattie Gilmore's name appeared briefly on the roster of Lucas's Lafayette Theatre Orchestra in early 1915 and that of Pearl Gibson on the roster of Lucas's 1917 Ladies Orchestra at the Howard Theatre in Washington, D.C. This is the period when leader/pianist Hallie Anderson was an organist and Maude White was a pianist at New York City's Douglas Theatre.

Mamie Lee was at the keyboard with Richard Jackson's Orchestra at the Pioneer Theatre in Indianapolis, Indiana. According to the *Indianapolis Freeman:*

> Miss Lee is of particularly good ability, reading at sight the more difficult music and executing it with precision. With or without music before her, she is "perfectly" at home on the piano. She assists very materially in the making of a fine orchestra . . . [December 25, 1915, p. 5].

In the early 1920s Laura Miller's responsibilities as musical director at the Lincoln Theatre included accompanying at the keyboard for guest performers. In 1926 she served as director/pianist for the touring company of "Connie's Inn Frolics."

In neighboring Newark, New Jersey, Ruby Mason was a pianist in the pit band at the Orpheum Theatre. Let us note that she also played accordion (and saxophone) with the band. In the late '20s Marie Williams served as substitute with the Hippodrome Theatre Orchestra in Richmond, Virginia. More frequent with the group at a later date was Marion Burroughs.

Other late-1920s female "available theater keyboardists" (as indicated by their listing in *The Official Theatrical World of Colored Artists the World Over*) were Evelyn Bundy, Blanche Jefferson, Shelby Kelly, Edythe Turnham, and Aurelia Wood—Seattle, Washington; Virginia Clarke, Harriett Chinneth, Geneva Gaskins, Myrtle Harrold, Henryetta Makins, Irene C. Morton and Mrs. H. M. Palmer—Omaha, Nebraska; Blanche Smith–Gary, Indiana; Mrs. J. H. Butler, Bessie Marshall, and Emma Smith—Chicago; Mayme G. Artis, Lillian Davenport, and Hattie Edwards—Columbus, Ohio; Martha Banks—Martin's Ferry, Ohio; Josephine Queen—Parkersburg, West Virginia; Charlotte Fletcher and Mamie L. Hope—New Haven, Connecticut; Sarah Coleman—Greenburg, Pennsylvania; Evelyn Burwell, Louise Curtis, Lillian Davenport, Marie Ely, Ella Gilbert, Florence Hirhirt, Mable L. Harsey, A. Naomi Jackson, May Neely, Margaret Rhodes, Inez Smith, and Viola Scudder—New York City. Each remained "on call" for theatrical ensemble assignments.

Early Jazz Ensembles and Big Bands

The list of names of black women pianists who were affiliated with early jazz bands is extensive, particularly in New Orleans and Chicago. Despite prohibitions of the community and parents—many mothers just would not let their daughters join jazz bands—women won local recognition for their skills.

In addition to Dolly Adams, Emma Barrett, Jeanette Kimball, and Olivia Cook in New Orleans, there was Camilla Todd, who played with The Charles Hyppolite Orchestra, and The Maple Leaf Orchestra during the early 1920s.[1] That decade also saw the participation of Margaret Kimball in John Robichaux's Orchestra and Wilhelmina Bart in Joe "King" Oliver's Creole Jazz Band, The Willie Pijeaud Band, and The Amos White Orchestra.

Pianist Edna Mitchell worked with various groups that played at Tom Anderson's popular cabaret, several of which included young trumpeter Louis Armstrong. Lottie Taylor played occasionally with Oliver's band in the early 1920s, and Sadie Goodson was a regular with Buddy Petit and Henry "Kid" Rena's bands well into the 1930s. Mercedes Garman Fields often played with Oscar "Papa" Celestin's Orchestra during the 1930s and '40s.

In Chicago "Lil" Armstrong and Lovie Austin were nationally recognized early jazz band pianists. But there were others. Ethel Minor was pianist with Estella Harris' Ladies Jass Band in 1916. In the 1920s bandleaders Ida Mae Maples, Lottie Hightower, and Garvinia Dickerson all led their groups from the keyboard. In 1924 Diamond Lil Hardaway played with "King" Oliver at Lincoln Gardens and with The Lee Collins Band in 1931 at King Tut's Tomb.

Pianist/leader Irene Armstrong (Wilson/Kitchings), a Marietta, Ohio native was very much a part of the Chicago jazz scene during the late '20s and early '30s, as were Georgia Corham and Dorothy Scott, also leaders of their own groups. During this period the names of Laura Crosby and Dorothy Rogers appeared on the roster of Johnny Long's Roaming Troubadours; Hattie Thomas's name appeared on the roster of Billy Bailey's Rhythm Girls, and Mattie Walker-King's name was on the roster of various pick-up orchestras.

In New York City Mattie Gilmore was at the keyboard in Will Marion Cook's New York Syncopated Orchestra; and she accompanied the group on its tour of Europe. At the same time, Helen Ray worked regularly at the City's Crescent Cafe, joined by a male cornet player and a male drummer. Other names that frequently appeared on the New York Cafe band circuit were Cleo Desmond and Cora Cross.

Lil Armstrong's replacement with Joe "King" Oliver's band on the West Coast in 1921 was Bertha Gonsoulin. When the band returned to Chicago in 1922 to play an engagement at the Royal Garden, Gonsoulin was still on piano. Jazz archivist William Russell recorded:

> [Louis] Armstrong had joined the Oliver band on second cornet. Lil met Louis when Oliver brought him to the Dreamland [where she was working with black violinist/leader May Brady's band] to ask her to rejoin his band. Gonsoulin went back to California and Lil rejoined Oliver at the Royal Garden [interview with Russell/"Lil" Armstrong, July 1, 1959, Chicago].

In 1940 Gonsoulin was cited by the *Chicago Defender* for her work at the Booker T. Washington Community Service Center in San Francisco; she had "the enviable reputation of being one of the finest instructors, composers and trainers of aspiring musicians in the west" ("Trainer of Musicians," February 3, 1930, p. 9).

In and around St. Louis, Margie Creath [Singleton] worked with her brother Charlie's band in the early 1920s. Jazz researcher Frank Driggs placed Marcella Kyle and Jane Himingway with the same organization. Given the times, we conclude that both ladies were black (*Women in Jazz*, p. 12). During the same period Mary Colston and Desdemona Davis were working with The George Morrison Orchestra in Denver, Colorado. These ladies were preceded in the Morrison band by Mary Kirk, wife of bandleader Andy Kirk.

In Washington, D.C., during the late teens and early 1920s Gertie Wells was one of the piano rages, performing solo and with small combos, for several of which she served as leader. It was in 1925 that Ethel Waters's pianist Pearl Wright recorded with Waters's Ebony Four, along with trumpeter Joe Smith and saxophonist Coleman Hawkins. Pianists from the glorious Kansas City 1920s and early '30s who performed with local bands were Roselle Claxton and Edith Williams.

In the late '20s Bobbie Brown was the pianist with Jimmie Lunceford's band for a brief period. In the early '30s Victoria Raymore toured the Middle West with the eleven-unit band of Eli Rice and his Dixie Cotton Pickers, and Marie Williams traveled through the South with The Deluxe Harmony Players.

Orvella Moore was the pianist with Sylvester Rice's Harlem Playgirls, working throughout the South and Midwest in the mid-

'30s. In the late '30s Mary Alice Clarke played with Fess Whatley's Vibra Cathedral Band, working out of Birmingham, Alabama. Other black female pianists whose names appeared on the
Whatley Band roster during the early 1940s were Dolly Brown,
Grace Chambliss (Pinkston), and Leatha Lowe (Bell). During the
same period Judy Dupree was "tickling the keys" with Richard
Baker's New York City dance band, and Georgia's Edith Curry
was out front swinging her band with the accordion.

Johnnie Mae Rice was pianist with the popular International
Sweethearts of Rhythm. In the 1950s she was replaced by Jackie
King. The group's songbird (and trumpet player) Edna Williams
also doubled on accordion. The pianist with The Swinging Rays
of Rhythm (who followed the Sweethearts at Piney Woods Country Life School) was Eleanor Moore, called "the little dynamo of
swing and rhythm." Pianist Rita Thornton covered the Ivy
League colleges and rock 'n' roll circuit with The Thornton Sisters' Combo from the late '50s through the mid-'70s.

Several black women played piano for short periods of time
with name bands. There was, for example, Margaret "Countess"
Johnson, who established quite a reputation in Kansas City dur-
ing the 1930s. She played with the bands of Harlan Leonard and
Andy Kirk, as substitute for Mary Lou Williams with the latter.
We recall the second-piano work of singer Sarah Vaughan with
Earl "Fatha" Hines in 1943. In 1945 pianist Vivian Glasby joined
The Fletcher Henderson Band for an engagement at the Rhum-
boogie in Chicago. Maurita Gordon substituted with Sidney
Bechet's New Orleans Footwarmers for a 1947 appearance in the
nation's capital.

Several black women pianists have been associated with jazz
trios. Camille Howard led her group from the piano. The Howard
Trio played regularly in D.C. and throughout the East Coast during the 1940s. In the mid-'50s bassist Carline Ray covered both
piano and organ with The Edna Smith Trio in New York City.
Two black women organists/pianists who created much excitement in the New York area with jazz trios in the mid- and late
'50s were Dorothy "Dottie" Dudley and Sarah McLawler, whose
career began in the early 1940s in Chicago.

McLawler fronted several small combos, many all-female,
made up of former Darlings of Rhythm and Harlem Playgirls
members. The most popular group was the Syncoettes combo,
working in Chicago and New York City (1948–53). For more than

two decades, she worked as a duo with her husband, violinist Richard Otto (now deceased). During the early 1980s, she was musical director of the Universal Jazz Coalition's Big Apple Jazzwomen in New York City. An early 1982 correspondence from McLawler indicated that she was temporarily in Abu Dhabi, United Arab Emirates, performing at the Centre Hotel. She wrote, "Receiving great publicity from the international press for my one-woman performance on organ and piano together" (correspondence with author, January 20, 1982).

Pianist Bettye Miller (d. 1977, age 49) reigned as "Queen of Kansas City Jazz" for close to three decades. Recognized for her originality and versatility, the Missouri native and Lincoln University graduate (Voice, 1945) performed primarily in solo or in twosome with husband Milt Abel (bass). Not infrequently, the advertisement read Bettye Miller Duo "plus one".

The 1960s and '70s saw much keyboard activity among black women as the Profiles at the end of this chapter will reveal. Others who should be mentioned are pianist/trombonist/composer L. Sharon Freeman; pianist/singer Pamela Watson; pianists/ leaders Daphne Weekes and Lea Richardson; organist/leader Bu Pleasant; organist/bassist Dorothy Harney; and pianists/composers Valerie Simpson, Linda Williams, Cheryl Bridgewater, Dona Summers, and Lisette Wilson. Organist/pianist Ruby Young began her keyboard activities in the late 1940s and was still active in the late '70s.

Since the early 1960s, Bertha Hope has been a strong pianistic force in improvised music. A popular New York City personality, Hope has been visibly and audibly present at the Kool, Newport, and JVC jazz festivals. As a member of the four jazzwomen group Jazzberry Jam, she (and the group) appeared at the 1996 Sung and Unsung Jazz Women symposium and concerts, sponsored by the Smithsonian Institution and Arts Center 651.

Pianist/organist Truty Pitts has been holding her own in Philadelphia for more than forty years. She has performed with numerous jazz greats, for example, John Coltrane, Clark Terry, Lionel Hampton, Rahsaan Roland Kirk, Sonny Stitt, and Grover Washington. She performs primarily solo and with the Mr. C. (her husband) Trio. Pitts has been featured on Marian McPartland's *Piano Jazz*. An alumna of the University of the Arts, she is now a member of the faculty, teaching jazz piano and coaching the jazz ensemble.

"Elite Art" Instrumental Ensembles

Participation in groups that concentrated on the more "serious" orchestral literature began (to our knowledge) in the twentieth century. A number of black women pianists have been symphony orchestra "Guests for a Day"—among them Hazel Harrison (Berlin Philharmonic; Chicago, Minneapolis, and Los Angeles Symphony Orchestras); Florence Price (Chicago Symphony); Margaret Bonds (Chicago Women's, Chicago, and New York City symphony orchestras, and Scranton Philharmonic); Carol Blanton (Diggs) and Jean Coston Malone (New Orleans Philharmonic); Eileen Southern (Louisville Symphony); Natalie Hinderas (Philadelphia, Cleveland, San Francisco, and Pittsburgh symphony orchestras; New York and Los Angeles Philharmonic orchestras; Symphony of the New World); Margaret Harris (Detroit Symphony); and Armenta Adams (Cleveland Symphony and Symphony of the New World). Other black female keyboardists have been affiliated as "Members of the Ensemble."

Pianist with New Orleans's Bloom Philharmonic in the early part of the twentieth century was Ida Rose. Mary Catherine Baker played piano with the Martin-Smith Music School Orchestra in New York City during the second decade. Playing with the same group in the 1930s was Ann Osborne. Pianist Olive Jeter toured the East and Midwest with the Jeter-Weir-Jeter Trio in the early 1920s (on cello, Olive's brother Leonard Jeter; on violin, Felix Weir—both members of the Negro String Quartet). In Chicago, Gladys Bell (Williams) was pianist with the 1920s and early '30s Harrison Ferrell Orchestra. In New Orleans there was Lillian Dunn (Perry), now a retired teacher and music consultant to the New Orleans Public Schools, who played with the William J. Nickerson Young Peoples' Orchestra of the late '20s and early '30s.

Bennie Parks (Easter), a New England Conservatory graduate, returned to her home city of St. Louis in the early 1930s to join the McKinney Symphony Orchestra. The eleven-piece Colonial Park String Ensemble of Baltimore included Mable Johnson and Emma Martin, as pianist and assistant pianist respectively during the mid-1930s. In 1935 a Monarch Symphonic Band Concert in New York had saxophonist Isabele Taliaferro Spiller at the keyboard.

The West Virginia State College Strings, conducted by Harrison Ferrell from 1939 to 1946, included on its roster pianists Katherine May Mickey, Rosamund Juanita Satterwhite, and Marcia Andrea Bohee. Finally, Mabel Billings was the pianist with Gladys Anderson Seals's 1950–65 Symphonette in New York City. Geneva Handy Southall, Gladys Perry Norris, and Hildred Roach were pianists with this writer's chamber group Trio Pro Viva between the years 1955 and 1971. And Sonya Sessoms was pianist with the Petersburg Symphony Orchestra in 1979. The American Symphony Orchestra League's publication *The Participation of Blacks in Professional Orchestras* (1990) included the names Wanda Harris (Dayton Philharmonic) and Patricia Prattis Jennings (Pittsburgh Symphony).

When the Black Music Repertory Ensemble gave its world premiere performance in 1988, the pianist was Toni-Marie Montgomery, then assistant dean of the School of Fine Arts, University of Connecticut. Almost a decade later, the group continues and Montgomery remains the pianist. She holds a similar administrative position at Arizona State University. She earned a doctorate in piano chamber music performance from the University of Michigan and has performed with the Detroit Metropolitan Orchestra and the Landsdowne Pennsylvania Symphony. Montgomery has appeared at such arts centers as the Academy of Music in Philadelphia and the American Conservatory in Fountainebleau, France.

Profiles

CAMILLE NICKERSON
piano, organ (composition)
b. March 30, 1887, New Orleans/ d. April 27, 1982,
   Washington, D.C.

Musicologist Doris E. McGinty's interviews with Camille Nickerson in 1973–74 centered around the artist's three careers: teacher, collector of Creole folksongs, and performer. Excerpts from McGinty's several interviews appeared in the Spring 1979 issue of *The Black Perspective in Music* ("Conversation with . . . Camille

Nickerson, The Louisiana Lady," pp. 81–94). Nickerson mentioned her father William J. Nickerson's Ladies' Orchestra in New
Orleans, but failed to mention that she was for many years the
pianist in this organization. This she indicated in a correspondence to one of this writer's Jackson State University students
(Charlemagne Payne, May 9, 1966) and confirmed in a telephone
conversation with the writer, May 2, 1979. Following is additional
data on the career of this orchestral participant.

Nickerson's membership in the Nickerson Ladies' Orchestra
began around 1900 and continued until she entered Oberlin Conservatory in 1912. Early musical training was provided by her
gifted father. She received the B.Mus. degree from Oberlin and
upon graduation returned to New Orleans to teach with her
father in the Nickerson School of Music. She joined the faculty of
Howard University in 1926, remaining there until 1962, when she
retired with the title Professor Emeritus. In the interim she engaged in further study at Columbia University and received the
M.Mus. degree, also from Oberlin.

With the help of a Rosenwald Fellowship Nickerson did extensive research on the music of Louisiana Creoles, following many
years of interest in discovering, developing, and preserving this
music of her native state. She began performing the songs in Creole costume in the 1930s, adopting the title "The Louisiana
Lady." Her arrangements of *Five Creole Songs* were published by
Boston Music Company, and her 1940s/early-'50s lecture-concerts were popular on college campuses and at concert halls
throughout the country. In 1955 she took these songs and her
interpretations to France. Finally, it should be noted that Camille
Nickerson was President of the National Association of Negro
Musicians, 1935–37.

> LOVIE AUSTIN (Cora Calhoun)
> piano (conducting, composition)
> b. September 19, 1897, Chattanooga, Tennessee/d. July
>   10, 1972, Chicago

Pianist Mary Lou Williams was greatly inspired by Lovie Austin.
She wrote in 1977:

When I was between 8 or 10 years of age, my stepfather and my
brother-in-law, Hugh Floyd, often took me to dances and theatres

to listen to musicians. Well, there was a TOBA theatre in Pittsburgh where all black entertainers came. I remember seeing this great woman sitting in the pit and conducting a group of five or six men, her legs crossed, a cigarette in her mouth, playing the show with her left hand and writing music for the next act with her right. Wow! I never forgot this episode . . . My entire concept was based on the few times I was around Lovie Austin. She was a fabulous woman and a fabulous musician, too. I don't believe there's any woman around now who could compete with her. She was a greater talent than many men of this period [liner notes for the album "Jazz Women: A Feminist Retrospective," Stash, ST-109].

Lovie, like Lil Armstrong, was most popular in Chicago's Golden Age of Jazz, the 1920s. The early years of her career were spent with vaudeville companies. Settling in Chicago during the early 20s, she soon became one of the city's most popular pianists. Her "live" performance associations were mostly with Chicago Theatres, particularly the Monogram, where she was a music director.

She specialized in backgrounds for blues singers, leading a group that was billed as Lovie Austin and Her Blues Serenaders. She and her group backed such singers as Ida Cox, Ma Rainey, Edmonia Henderson, Viola Bartlette, and Ethel Waters. One of her strengths rested in providing strong pianistic support for gifted soloists, both instrumental and vocal. Members of her Blues Serenaders included such masters as Johnny Dodds, Jimmy Noone, and Tommy Ladnier.

During the 1920s she recorded extensively, primarily for Paramount. She recorded again in 1961, accompanying blues singer Alberta Hunter. During World War II Austin did defense work, but returned eventually to theater work and later served as a dancing-school pianist.

> EMMA BARRETT ("Sweet Emma the Bell Gal")
> piano (vocals)
> b. March 25, 1898, New Orleans/d. January 28, 1983

Emma made her Jazz Hall debut in a 1961 concert, when she stood in for pianist Lester Santiago with Louis Cottrell's band. She arrived on the bandstand with what became her standard attire—a red beanie cap [with the inscription "Sweet Emma the

Bell Gal"] and a red dress, below which showed garters with tiny tinkling bells. She was then well on her way to becoming the un-crowned queen of the New Orleans jazz revival.

Barrett's career dates back to Oscar "Papa" Celestin's Band, 1923. In the late '20s she performed with the William "Bebe" Ridgely Original Tuxedo Orchestra (a splinter group of the original Celestine/Ridgely Tuxedo Orchestra), with Sidney Desvigne and the Piron-Gaspard orchestras. Despite her inability to read music she was a regular with the city's top "reading" bands. For more than a quarter of a century Sweet Emma toured with trumpet player/leader Percy Humphrey. She refused to travel by plane, yet she played as far west as California's Disneyland and as far north as New York City's Stork Club.

After her 1961 New Orleans success Barrett formed her own band, including an "all-star" cast of players; trumpeter Percy Humphrey, clarinetist Willie Humphrey, trombonist Jim Robinson, banjoist Narvin Kimball, and drummer Josiah "Cie" Frazier. With this group she also recorded ("New Orleans' Sweet Emma and Her Preservation Hall Jazz Band, Preservation Hall," VPH/VPS-2, 1964; "Sweet Emma the Bell Gal and Her New Orleans Jazz Band at Heritage Hall," Nobility LP-711, 1968). On most recordings Barrett's unique vocals could be heard, a treat she rarely denied her "live" audiences.

Despite a stroke in 1967 (which left her partially incapacitated), Barrett continued to play with various ensembles and to appear regularly at the New Orleans bare-floored, former art gallery know as Preservation Hall. Television appearances were frequent, and few elite Mardi Gras functions failed to include "The Bell Gal" pianist.

AUZIE RUSSELL DIAL
piano
b. July 25, 1900, Greenfield, Tennessee/d. 1983,
    Minneapolis

The late 1970s found Auzie Dial doing clerical work in the office of the State Coordinator for Concerned Seniors for Better Government in Minneapolis; volunteer work for local and national elections; and attending workshops and seminars at area colleges and universities—"all in the interest of benefitting senior citizens."

Retirement was in name only. She enrolled at the Vocational Technical High School in Minneapolis in 1969 and completed a course in general office work. In 1977 she received a certificate in speedwriting from the same school. Since 1976 she has performed only occasionally, primarily for benefits.

Dial had much to look back on. She wrote, "The fact that I grew up in St. Louis, Missouri, where music was an integral part of the lifestyle of every black, seemed to be the answer. Music was clearly my destiny" (correspondence with the author, September 7, 1979). Her career began in St. Louis with a four-piece combo led by Everette White, in 1920. The following year she began playing with Al Jenkins, also in St. Louis.

She began fronting her own combo as early as 1922, playing for club and house parties in St. Louis and Minneapolis, as well as Peoria and Springfield, Illinois. Dial spent nine months in Minneapolis in 1924, playing local dates and broadcasting from the Nicollet Hotel [now Soul's Harbor] over radio station WCCO. She joined Al Wynn's ten-piece Creole Jazz Band in Chicago in 1926 and worked with Al Jenkins's Cottonpickers in 1927 and '28 in Cleveland.

Dial left the Cottonpickers in 1929 and established her own band in Detroit, where she remained until the mid-1930s. The next four or five years found her working as an intermission and show pianist/singer in Cleveland, Pittsburgh, Baltimore, Buffalo, and New York City.

Following a three-month stay at The Three Deuces in Chicago, working with Darnell Howard and Baby Dodds, Dial returned to Minneapolis in 1940 and for the next thirty-six years entertained as a single in lounges at the city's finest hotels and Minnesota's beach resorts. Discriminating party-givers in the Twin Cities and suburbs selected Auzie Dial to provide musical entertainment.

LILLIAN ("Lil") HARDIN ARMSTRONG
piano (vocals)
b. February 3, 1902, Memphis, Tennessee/d. August 27, 1971, Chicago

Piano lessons for Lil began with Miss Violet White, as soon as she entered grade school. She later enrolled in Mrs. Hook's School of Music, "graduating" at the tender age of eleven. She played only the classics, marches, and hymns. She was exposed to jazz gradually by a guitar-playing cousin.

Lil enrolled at Fisk University at age fourteen, but when her mother and stepfather moved from Memphis to Chicago in 1918 she joined them there and never returned to Fisk. Later she studied at the Chicago College of Music and the New York College of Music, earning a teacher's certificate and a post-graduate diploma.

She secured a job in 1918 as a song demonstrator in Jones's Music Store on State Street. The owner (Mrs. Jones) also booked bands and sent Lil to audition for one from New Orleans. She secured the job, thus beginning her long and exciting involvement with many pioneer bands—Joe "King" Oliver, Freddie Keppard, "Sugar" Johnny Smith, Hugh Swift, Ralph Cooper, Red Allen, and Zutty Singleton.

Hardin joined "King" Oliver's legendary Creole Jazz Band in 1921. Oliver sent to New Orleans for Louis Armstrong in 1922. Louis accepted his friend and mentor's offer to play second trumpet, finding in Chicago not only "an ideal school of higher learning," but also a second wife. Lil and Louis married in 1924. (They separated in 1931 and divorced in 1938.)

"Miss Lil," as she liked to be called, was credited (by friends, the press, and Louis himself) with doing much to influence Louis' career. Lessons in music theory were also provided. As jazz journalist John Chilton wrote,

> Lil's place in jazz history will not rest solely on her piano playing, which was sturdy rather than spectacular. Her composing skills and the role that she played in Louis' life during his formative years in Chicago were much more important ["Lil—Louis' Second Lady," *Melody Maker*, September 4, 1971].

Lil spent all of her professional life in Chicago, except for a few years in New York City, where between 1937 and 1940 she worked as "house pianist" for Decca Recording studio. She played at the Windy City's finest clubs and theaters, as well as those in New York City, Canada and Europe.

She led many superb bands, from 1920 onward, often personally adding the vocals. Her recording output (Okeh, Paramount, Gennett, Columbia, Black and White, and Decca) was most extensive. She recorded always in musical association with giants of the business, e.g., Buster Baily, George "Pops" Foster, Kid Ory, Zutty Singleton, J. C. Higginbotham, Johnny and Baby Dodds, Jonah Jones, and husband Louis. A 1927 reissue (featuring Lil, Louis, Kid Ory, Johnny Dodds, and Johnny St. Cyr) appeared on the 1978 Stash Records release entitled "Women in Jazz: Pianists," ST-112. Her compositions, many of which were recorded, numbered over 150.

"Miss Lil" returned to New York City in 1968 to play with a select group of Chicago jazz veterans, sponsored by the Massachusetts and Connecticut Traditional Jazz Clubs. Less than three years later she suffered a fatal heart attack while playing at the Louis Armstrong Memorial Concert in Chicago.

JULIA LEE
piano (vocals)
b. October 31, 1902, Kansas City, Missouri/d. December
    7, 1958, Kansas City, Missouri

According to Kansas City jazz authority Ross Russell,

> There was more music in Kansas City than had been heard in America since the gilt palaces and funky butt dance halls of the Storyville section of New Orleans closed their doors at the beginning of World War I [*Bird Lives! The High Life and Hard Times of Charlie (Yardbird) Parker*, p. 31].

One group in the center of activity was the band led by George E. Lee, and performing with the group for seventeen years was the leader's younger sister, Julia.

Julia played with George's ten- and fourteen-piece bands, as well as the smaller Novelty Singing Orchestra, working beside such future jazz notables as Count Basie, Hot Lips Page, Jo Jones, Chuck Berry, Ben Webster, Bennie Moten, and Lester Young. Her 1958 death followed George's only by a couple of months. Working up to the day of her death, Julia Lee's keyboard and vocal style never changed.

Lee made her singing and playing debut with the father's dance string trio at age three. By age fourteen she was singing and playing at house parties. From 1943 to 1944 she toured as a single artist. Beginning in mid-1940 she recorded regularly for Capitol, always with all-star jazzmen. Her records sold in the thousands.

Recording under the title "Julia Lee and Her Boy Friends," this company included such notables as Red Callender, Red Nichols, Vic Dickenson, Red Norvo, and Benny Carter. As a vocalist she recorded with Jay McShann's Kansas City Stompers (1944).

Others left Kansas City when interest declined in the 1930s, but Julia Lee remained and became a celebrity. In 1949 she performed in the nation's capital for President Harry Truman and White House correspondents. She made her last tour in 1955.

In describing the Kansas City jazz community, Duke Ellington cited Jimmy Rushing as Senator, Joe Turner as Major, Peter Johnson as Majority Leader, and Julia Lee as Corporation Counsel (*Music is My Mistress*, p. 232). Though lasting fame somehow eluded her outside of Kansas City, jazz connoisseurs never forgot.

DOLLY MARIE DOUROUX ADAMS
piano (bass, drums)
b. January 11, 1904, New Orleans/d. November 6, 1979,
    New Orleans

Adams's entire life, professional and otherwise, centered around New Orleans. Both her mother and father were musicians; her mother played piano, violin and trumpet (nonprofessionally), and her father (trumpeter Louis Douroux) was a well-known musician who worked with such groups as the Eureka and Excelsior brass bands. Dolly's uncle was Professor Manuel Manetta (band leader, master of several instruments, and "professor of music" for white and black children in Algiers, Louisiana), from whom she received her first music instruction.

But as Adams pointed out in an interview with jazz archivist William Russell, "I went to him to learn how to read music, not how to play music. This I could already do" (interview with William Russell, April 18, 1962, New Orleans).

She began playing at age seven. By age nine she was playing parties with her brother, a violinist. She joined Manetta's band at age thirteen. With this group Dolly had the experience of playing with such New Orleans luminaries as Kid Ory, Joe "King" Oliver, and Louis Armstrong. Others with whom she worked through the years were Luis "Papa" and Lorenzo (Jr.) Tio, Willie Humphrey, and Alphonse Picou.

At age fifteen she joined Peter Bocage's Creole Serenaders, remaining with the group until she organized her own band in the early 1920s. With this band she worked at the Othello Theatre. The band played for various stage acts, and Adams provided piano music for the silent movies on the screen. She also worked professionally with her brothers.

Dolly Adams represented a third generation of professional musicians. Following her fifteen-year furlough to raise a family, she returned to the performing scene in the late '40s, bringing along her three sons. The Dolly Adams' Band, including her sons (playing drums, bass, and guitar) and several others, provided music for the city's 1966 Creole Spring Fiesta Ball. She, her uncle (Manetta), sons, and several others played for the same event in 1968.

Those who recall her playing through the years always commented on her ability to change with the times—from Dixieland to swing to modern jazz. Adams was still performing in the early '70s, in between periods of failing health.

WILHELMINA ("Billie") GOODSON PIERCE
piano (vocals)
b. June 8, 1907, Marianna, Florida/d. 1974, New Orleans

"Rough and ready" pianist Billie Pierce's name is generally associated with that of her husband, cornetist "De De" Pierce, whom she married in 1935. But Billie was a well-established professional before the two met. According to Billie,

> Most all my days I've been playing music. I started playing the blues. My mother and father you know, were very religious people. Me and my [six] sisters would get around the piano and have a good time playing ragtime and singing the blues. Somebody watched out for daddy and when he'd come, we'd break into, "What a Friend We Have in Jesus." He never knew the difference [liner notes for the album "New Orleans' Billie and De De and Their Preservation Hall Jazz Band," Preservation Hall, VPH/VPS-3, 1966].

Raised in Pensacola, Florida, Billie moved to New Orleans in 1929. With her sister Edna, a pianist, Billie toured with the Mighty Wiggle Carnival. Among the blues singers she accompanied at various times were the celebrated Bessie Smith and Ida Cox. She also wrote songs, such as "Get a Working Man" and "Panama Rag," and sang blues in the classic tradition.

Billie's first piano job in New Orleans was as a substitute for her sister Sadie Goodson with Buddy Petit's Band on the Lake Pontchartrain excursion-steamer *Madison*. At different times she played with Kid Rena, Punch Miller, Alphonse Picou, and Oscar "Papa" French.

Pierce fronted her own four-piece band in the '30s. The clarinetist was George Lewis and the cornetist, De De Pierce. During the '40s and '50s she and De De kept busy, working primarily at the popular weekend club Luthjen's, despite a waning interest in New Orleans jazz.

Pianist Billie and De De were still around in the '60s, during the period often referred to as "the second coming of jazz." They traveled extensively throughout the '60s and reigned as one of the principal attractions of Preservation Hall until Billie's death in 1974, just a few months after that of her husband.

JEANETTE SALVANT KIMBALL
piano (organ)
b. December 18, 1908, Pass Christian, Mississippi

A veteran of The Original Tuxedo Jazz Band, Kimball began her career at an early age: at eleven she was teaching music, and by fourteen she was playing with a band (Boise D. Legges and Mason and Mason shows). She wrote,

> I had a good teacher. Her name was Anna Stewart, a graduate of Boston Conservatory. And I just loved music always and had a natural talent from God, which my deceased mother recognized—God bless her soul [correspondence with the author, January 11, 1978].

Though she performed with various New Orleans groups (including The Herbert Leary Orchestra), her primary association was with The Celestin/Albert "Papa" French Group. When "Papa" French died in 1977 Kimball remained pianist with the group continued by his sons Bob and George. She performed throughout the U.S. and Europe with the band—including a command performance for President Dwight D. Eisenhower in 1953—and made occasional jaunts to the Bahamas.

In addition to her orchestral involvement, she served as pianist for New Orleans's Durden School of Dance and as organist at Holy Ghost Church. As Harlan Wood wrote in 1975, "A lady of great dignity and conviction, she is a superb pianist who commands both the personal and musical respect of all who know and hear her" [liner notes for the album "Albert 'Papa' French at Tradition Hall," Second Line, 0112]. And as Ione Anderson wrote in 1978,

> There is no touch on the piano like that of Jeanette Kimball. Once you have heard it you will not forget it. Her incredible right hand and striding left have [long] been a part of the music scene . . . [liner notes for the album "Traditional New Orleans Jazz," Dulai 800].

CLEO PATRA BROWN
piano (vocals)
b. December 8, 1907, Kemper County, Mississippi/d. April 15, 1995, Denver, Colorado

In a 1935 *Chicago Defender* article that Dan Burley wrote about "pianos and piano players" he focused on the originality of "sensational Art Tatum and the marvelous Cleo Brown." He said of Brown,

> [She] writes a new epoch into jazz music in each piece she plays. I don't believe she could play the same piece twice in exactly the same way ["Backdoor Stuff," August 3, 1935, p. 5].

Pianist Dave Brubeck always listed Brown as one of his greatest influences. He wrote and recorded the composition "Sweet Cleo Brown" as a tribute to her memory. In 1985, Brown was a guest on Marian McPartland's *Piano Jazz* (NPR). Pianist Marian McPartland listed Brown as one of her inspirations to experience "the joy and feeling of freedom in playing jazz . . . [S]he impressed me with her powerful, rambling, swinging attack, colored by full, dark chords" ("You've Come a Long Way Baby," *Esquire's World of Jazz, 1975*, p. 134).

She having disappeared from the scene where the name Cleo Brown reigned supreme, speculation led many to proclaim her "deceased" as early as 1960. But the name surfaced again in the same circles in 1978, when Stash Records issued a rerelease of "Mama Don't Want No Peas an' Rice an' Coconut Oil," featuring Cleo Brown on piano and vocals ("Women in Jazz: Pianists," ST-112). In a totally different circle, 1979 found Cleo, now "C. Patra" Brown, appearing weekly on Denver, Colorado's radio station KQXI, no longer playing her famous interpretation of "Pinetop's Boogie Woogie" (Decca-477) or playing and singing such tunes as "Lookie, Lookie, Here Comes Cookie" or "When a Fat Gal's Blue," but now playing and singing "Show Me a Rainbow and I'll Show You the Lord." In addition, she was serving as pianist for Denver's Park Hill Seventh Day Adventist Church and part-time Literature Evangelist.

During the spring of 1980 Brown said:

> People often ask, "Why don't you make a comeback?" I answer, "I haven't been any place. All I've done is come out—gone into." Once love comes in from the Lord, you don't want nothing to mar that. If I play the boogie beat, I'm just back into something that I came out of [interview with Jennie Rucker, Denver, Colorado, April 9, 1980].

In a telephone conversation with C. Patra Brown on April 3, 1980, the writer requested a taped interview. She kindly consented to record her story in the presence of educator Jennie Rucker, and during the same session verbally and vocally related her story of "spiritual transformation." Entitled "I'm Living in the Afterglow of God's Love," Brown's rendition of this original work indicated clearly that "comeback requests" were out of order. Fingers slowed only slightly by arthritis, the seventy-two-year-old's voice was richer, mellower, and more vibrant than ever. The composition retained chordal brilliance and typical Brown inventiveness. The only difference was a slower-moving beat and a sacred rather than secular text, reflecting the composer/performer's movement "out of" and "into."

Daughter of a baptist minister, Brown began studying piano at the age of eight under the tutelage of Boston Conservatory-trained Nettie Pearl Reese, then teaching at Meridian Baptist Seminary. At age ten she was elected junior pianist for the Baptist Young People's Union (BYPU) Congress. When her father was called to pastor in Chicago she began studying with Alfred Simms of the American Conservatory.

She began playing for her father's church at age fourteen. The gifted young pianist soon became envious of her older pianist brother Everett's $25 weekly earnings (compared with her $6 weekly earnings), as well as his freedom to play dance music. As she recalled,

> I could beat him playing. But my parents forbade me to play the music that I had become attracted to [boogie woogie]. So I ran away and married [1923]. A son was born of that marriage, but my dad had it annulled [*ibid*].

The break from home soon became permanent, first with a traveling orchestra on a tour of Canada. Upon returning to Chicago, Brown began "gigging" with various local bands. In 1933 she played the World's Fair with Texas Guinan. She further recalled that at around this time, she also worked with a group led by "Eddie" something (probably Eddie South).

> I can't remember his last name. He was a violinist. I played all over Chicago—Lake Villa, Frolic Cafe, Three Deuces, etc. I was what they called the musician's musician; I was the woman with the heavy left hand [*ibid*.].

In 1935 Brown left for New York City, replacing Fats Waller on CBS radio. There followed a recording contract with Decca, bookings at the most prestigious clubs and theaters throughout the country and several guest appearances on Bing Crosby's Kraft Music Hall.

In the early '40s illness began to plague the talented jazz pianist. During an interview in 1945 she said:

> I have been plagued by bad breaks and bad health throughout the past few years, but I'm feeling fine now and ready to get back into action [Sharon A. Pease, "Health Better, Cleo Brown Set for Comeback," *Down Beat*, July 1, 1945, p. 12].

While playing an engagement in 1949 at Jim's Steak House in San Francisco Brown experienced what she later called a "conscience breaker."

I began pulling back from the clubs, though they continued to book me. Persons like Gladys Palmer, Rose Murphy and Nellie Lutcher were on the upswing and I guess this had a part in helping me to let go. They booked me in Las Vegas and then Denver, and Pueblo, Colorado. It was in the latter city that I secured a job as a nurse maid. In 1952, I began working as a nurse attendant at Colorado State Hospital and then went to nursing school. I received my nursing license in 1959 and nursed—off and on—until 1973. Baptized in 1953, I have never looked back [*ibid.*].

Though Brown and the writer had been in communication since 1979 (by way of correspondence and telephone), they did not meet formally until 1986, when the writer presented an address before the Colorado Endowment for the Humanities conference entitled "Jazz: An American Idiom" in Denver. Though Brown did not attend the conference, she agreed to make an appearance at the evening social at the Oxford Hotel. Her first comment upon arriving was, "I once worked here as maid." She consented to play (after passing out Bible cards), which was a highlight of the conference. Many newspaper articles followed. Several submitted her name to the National Endowment for the Arts for consideration as an American Jazz Master, which carries a $20,00 award. This she received in 1987.

> MARY LOU WILLIAMS (Mary Elfreida Scruggs-Burley)
> piano (composition/arranging)
> b. May 8, 1910, Atlanta/d. May 28, 1981, Durham, North
>   Carolina

The career of Mary Lou Williams, better known as "The First Lady of Jazz," began at age six, by which time she was already a professional, playing at parties for a dollar an hour. By age twelve she was working occasional jobs with Pittsburgh's union bands; and while still a teenager she toured the Theater Owners Booking Association's vaudeville circuit in "Hits and Bits" with Buzzin Harris. The teen years also found Williams touring on the Gus Sun Circuit and B. F. Keith and Orpheum circuits with Seymour and Jeanette. Following Seymour's death she continued with Jeanette James.

One of the groups with which Williams "sat in" during these early years was Duke Ellington's Washingtonians; another was

The Syncopators (also known as The Synco Jazzers), fronted by her future husband, alto and baritone saxist John Williams. When her husband John went to Oklahoma City to join The Andy Kirk Band in 1929, Mary Lou remained in Memphis for a period of time, continuing as The Syncopators' leader. When she joined her husband she also began a memorable, long-standing group affiliation. Actually, she did not join the Kirk band as a pianist until 1931, since during the first two years she was part-time chauffeur, arranger, and pianist. When the group (now based in Kansas City) secured a Brunswick recording contract, the "part-timer" substituted as recording pianist. Before long, "the substitute" was permanent.

Critics unanimously agreed that Williams's addition to the Kirk band marked the beginning of the group's rise to competitive status. Her billing with Kirk read, "The Lady Who Swings the Band." She remained with Andy Kirk and his Twelve Clouds of Joy until 1941. During this period she took on arranging assignments for Benny Goodman, Louis Armstrong, Cab Calloway, Tommy Dorsey, Glen Gray, Gus Arnheim and Earl Hines.

Following the Andy Kirk years, Williams began fronting her own combo, which included her second husband, Harold "Shorty" Baker, on trumpet and drummer Art Blakey. When Baker joined The Duke Ellington Band, Mary Lou joined as arranger. In the mid-1940s and early '50s she worked as a single or with a trio, mainly in New York City but also on the West Coast and in Europe. In the mid-'50s she embraced Catholicism and began devoting much of her time and energy to religious activities. For brief periods she exited from public performance.

She completed a residency at The Composer in New York City and appeared with The Dizzy Gillespie Orchestra at the Newport Jazz Festival in 1957. Williams then resumed her regular public performances and throughout the 1960s and '70s appeared at many jazz festivals and completed residences at The Embers, Hickory House, Cafe Carlyle, and The Cookery in New York City and other clubs in Washington, D.C.; Rochester, New York; San Francisco; Toronto; and London. Solo, duo, and trio appearances on college campuses were numerous, as were her lecture-concerts at the Smithsonian Institution and Whitney Museum. She initiated and produced the Pittsburgh Jazz Festival in 1964.

While her career as a composer is beyond the scope of this

publication, it should be noted that she will be remembered for her "Froggy Bottom," "Mary's Idea," "In the Land of Oo-Bla-Dee," "Night Life," "Mess-a-Stomp," "Walkin' and Swinging," "Little Joe from Chicago," "What's Your Story Morning Glory," and "Roll Em." No less important are her extended compositions, including "The Zodiac Suite," which she performed with the New York Philharmonic in 1946, the "Black Christ of Andes," and "Mary Lou's Mass." The latter work was given its world premiere in 1971 at City Center, New York. The work was choreographed by Alvin Ailey. *Newsweek* critic Hubert Saal wrote:

> Mary Lou's Mas turns out to be almost an encyclopedia of black music, richly represented from spirituals to bop and rock . . . It reflects the self-effacing style of Mary Lou Williams, both as a musician and as a woman, as well as the persuasions of her spiritual convictions ["The Spirit of Mary Lou," December 20, 1971, p. 67].

Williams returned to Kansas City, where a street had been named in her honor (1973), to be featured performer at the International Premiere Concert of the Women's Jazz Festival in March 1978. But on the subject of Mary Lou Williams and the "woman musician" issue, she wrote:

> As for being a woman, I never thought much about that one way or the other. All I've ever thought about is music. No musician ever refused to play with me. No one ever refused to play my music or my arrangements. I was always accepted [liner notes for the album "Jazz Women: A Feminist Retrospective," Stash ST-109, 1977].

Also in 1978 Mary Lou Williams was featured at President Jimmy Carter's White House Jazz Party.

Williams recorded extensively (from 1930 onward) for such companies as Brunswick, Decca, Columbia, Varsity, Asch, Disc, Victor, Onyx, Avant Garde, Folkways, Pablo, and Mary Records. She served as president of the latter company, the oldest black artist-owned label still in existence (1979). In more recent years television appearances included "Today," "Tonight," "AM America," and "Lamp Unto My Feet." In 1977 and '78 she appeared in CBS's "Christmas Eve Specials," playing and singing with students from Duke University.

Recognition of her contribution to the world of music came in the form of honorary degrees (Fordham, Boston, and Loyola universities and Manhattan, Bates, and Rockhurst colleges); two Guggenheim Fellowships; and an artistic residency at Duke University.

Following are a few of the many observations made about Mary Lou Williams:

Jazz journalist John S. Wilson:

> Because she has lived and played through almost every development that has happened in jazz, Miss Williams is a unique, living repository of jazz history ["Mary Lou Williams," *International Musician*, January 1973, p. 8].

Jazz pianist Marian McPartland:

> Mary Lou is one person who has entirely transcended the label of "woman musician". . . . Mary Lou is respected by everybody because she knows her craft so well and everyone knows she knows. And it is the reason why she achieved such a high place in the jazz hierarchy so early in life and has continued as an innovator ["You've Come a Long Way Baby," *Esquire's World of Jazz, 1975*, p. 138].

Jazz pianist/composer/arranger Duke Ellington:

> Mary Lou Williams is perpetually contemporary. Her writing and performing are and have always been just a little ahead and throughout her career. . . . her music retains—a standard of quality that is timeless. She is like soul on soul [*Music Is My Mistress*, p. 169].

> ROSE ELOISE MURPHY (Matthews)
> piano (vocals)
> b. April 18, 1913, Xenia, Ohio

Playing since age three and before the public since age seven, Rose Murphy was still performing six decades later—consistently attracting a large following, maintaining the respect of her peers and attracting favourable attention of the critics. *New York Times* critic John S. Wilson wrote of her performance in mid-1979:

"fresh and sunny and lightly rhythmic, swinging easily but irresistibly . . ." ("Cabaret: Rose Murphy," July 14, 1979, p. 12).

When asked to label her piano style, she responded: "I play what comes from the heart; there is no label" (telephone conversation with the author, December 26, 1979). One of the features of her piano playing was a simultaneously pounding right foot on a small rectangular board, a practice that began in the late 1930s while she was performing at The Turf in Cleveland. As she explained to John Wilson:

> I played an old upright. . . . It was up on a little platform. I was used to playing with bands, and I like that solid rhythm I got with the band. Playing by myself, my feet started moving, and I realized I played with my feet as well as my hands. I get a tone quality that's a mix of the piano sound and my foot ["Rose Murphy's Back With That Old Chee-Chee," *New York Times*, August 3, 1975, p. C8].

During the late 1940s Murphy's piano playing became a secondary consideration to her distinct, novel, high-pitched vocalizing. Because of her clever use of the words "chee-chee" (which she explains was the result of unknown lyrics to a requested song), she became identified as "the chee-chee girl." But "the chee-chee girl" is here remembered as a pianist and orchestra/band affiliate. While enrolled at Wilberforce University, with intentions of becoming a teacher, she began playing with a dance band. Following her junior year she began playing at Cleveland's Cedar Gardens and later The Turf. A successful career launched, the need for further formal training no longer existed.

Her group associations have primarily been with trios fronted by herself on piano. An international star, she completed several successful tours in England, Germany, Italy, Australia, New Zealand, and Hawaii. Before moving to New York City (1961) she enjoyed extended artistic periods in Los Angeles. Her New York City residencies included Cafe Society, Upstairs at the Downstairs, Bon Soir, The Cookery, and The Syncopation—all centers for the appearances of the most select of the jazz world. She appeared at the Newport Jazz Festival in the mid-1970s. Rose Murphy recorded for Majestic, Victor, Design, and Decca and was included on the Stash recording "Women in Jazz: Pianists," ST-112, 1978.

OLIVIA ("Lady Charlotte") COOK
piano, organ
b. May 11, 1913, New Orleans

"Lady Charlotte" obtained her musical foundation primarily from her grandfather. She also studied privately with Beatrice Stewart Davis and later at New Orleans and Straight Universities (B.S. in Music) and Xavier University.

Cook's natural flair for jazz revealed itself by age seven, to the consternation of her grandmother. She stated:

> I studied the classics so long until I was really interested in being a concert pianist. . . . But after I grew up and found out what was happening at that time, I changed my mind. There wasn't much opportunity for me as a black person to be a concert pianist. Then I really began to go back to jazz [Buerkle and Barker, *Bourbon Street Black,* p. 35].

Her professional career was filled with excitement. At the Olivia Cook studio she taught piano, organ, trumpet, and clarinet. She served as music supervisor in the Jefferson Parish Public Schools and gave lecture-concerts on "Jazz and Its Origin." She served as secretary of predominantly black Local 496, American Federation of Musicians, and was cited on two occasions by the mayor of New Orleans for her accomplishments.

"Lady Charlotte" performed with the William Houston and Herbert Leary orchestras, June Gardner's "Hot Foot Six," her own "Lady Charlotte and Her Men of Rhythm," and Wallace Davenport's Jazz Band, with whom she traveled to Hawaii, France, Holland, Spain, Finland, and Norway.

NELLIE LUTCHER
piano (vocals)
b. October 15, 1915, Lake Charles, Louisiana

Lutcher was known in Los Angeles as a successful businesswoman (real estate) from the 1960s onward. But few who called themselves knowledgeable on the subject of jazz pianists failed to recall the name Nellie Lutcher, always adding, "an excellent pianst and fantastic musician."

Lutcher's career began at age fifteen, when she joined The Clarence Hart Band in Lake Charles. Piano lessons began at age seven. She gave credit to her teacher for encouragement and credit to her bass-playing father for inspiration. Her father (Isaac Lutcher) was a member of the Hart band, as was trumpeter Bunk Johnson. The Hart group played one-nighters throughout Louisiana and Texas, "making the music that made them jump, at $1.50 per night" (Dorsey, "Character-tures," *New York Age*, January 1, 1949, p. 14). Nellie also played with The Southern Rhythm Boys.

In the mid-'30s she departed for the West Coast, where she consistently filled club and theater assignments. She also was a keyboard favorite in New York City. As a song stylist, she was frequently referred to as "the female Nat Cole." Now having added vocals to her act, Lutcher recorded for Okeh, Capitol, and Liberty. Recordings of her own compositions "Hurry on Down" and "He's a Real Gone Guy" were immediate successes. The former was reissued in 1978 on the Stash recording "Women in Jazz: Pianists," ST-112. The "keyboard sorceress," whom many thought had disappeared from the performing scene, returned to New York City's Cookery in 1973.

MARY ALICE CLARKE (Stollenwerck)
piano
b. Birmingham, Alabama

Mary Alice and four brothers all became professional musicians. In fact, an appearance of The Clarke Family Band was for several years one of Birmingham's popular musical attractions. The brothers all established names for themselves in New York; only Mary Alice remained in the Steel City.

She has cited as her strongest influences musical parents and early church opportunities and experiences (correspondence with the author, August 31, 1979). She joined The Fess Whatley Band in the late 1930s, during which time she, director Whatley, and many other band members doubled as educators in the Birmingham Public Schools.

A graduate of Miles College (B.A.), Stollenwerck engaged in further study at the Sherwood Music School and De Paul and Atlanta universities. The late 1970s found her serving as church organist and pianist with The Leo Hines Modern Pioneers, still in her native Birmingham. The interim years were occupied with musical service to her church and community.

HAZEL SCOTT
piano (vocals)
b. June 11, 1920, Port-of-Spain, Trinidad/d. October 2, 1981, New York City

Hazel Scott began studying piano with her mother at age two and made her debut at age three in her native Port-of-Spain. In 1924 the family came to the United States, and at age five Hazel made her American debut at New York's famed Town Hall. Three years later she enrolled at Juilliard on a six-year scholarship.

While still in her early teens Hazel played with her mother's group, Alma Long Scott's All-Woman Orchestra, American Creolians. By 1936 she was being featured on the Mutual Broadcasting System, performing a mixture of classics and jazz, and during that year she made her Broadway debut, playing with The Count Basie Orchestra at the Roseland Dance Hall. She later told journalist Hollie I. West, "It scared me to death. I had three footprints on my back—those of Lester Young, Joe Jones and Basie" ("Hazel Scott Reflects," *Washington Post*, July 4, 1970, p. C2).

In the late '30s Scott began a new career, appearing in the Broadway musical *Singing Out the News* and thereafter in *Priorities of 1942*. Hollywood beckoned, and she performed in *Something to Shout About, I Dood It, The Heat's On* (1943), *Broadway Rhythm* (1944), and *Rhapsody in Blue* (1945).

Scott achieved national recognition from her longtime performing association with New York's Cafe Society Downtown and Uptown (1939–45). She made her recording debut during the first year of her residency (1939), performing with The Sextet of the Rhythm Club of London. This was a mixed band composed of musicians recently returned from Europe and others of British origin; the three involved blacks were all of West Indian descent.

In the late '40s she married the flamboyant preacher/politician Adam Clayton Powell. Following many years of separation the well-publicized marriage ended in divorce. There followed an extended stay in Paris. She returned to America and the West Coast in 1967 and appeared in the television shows "Julia" and "The Bold Ones."

During the '70s, Scott completed residences at Washington, D.C.'s Emersons, Ltd., and New York City's Downbeat and Ali Baba East. She was inducted into the Black Filmmakers Hall of Fame in 1978. The inductees were selected around the theme "The Black Musical Presence in Cinema." There to induct the "gifted, sophisticated, elegant, glamorous, outspoken and uncompromising" Hazel Scott was representative Ronald Dellums.

A woman of great racial pride and dignity, Scott never hesitated to speak out against racial injustices. Even during the 1940s her contract included a clause that required promoters to forfeit if an audience was separated racially. Scott said, "What justification can anyone have who comes to hear me and then objects to sitting next to another Negro" (*ibid.*).

BERYL BOOKER
piano
b. June 7, 1923 (?), Philadelphia/d. 1980

Jazz journalist/encyclopedist Leonard Feather wrote in 1952:

> Beryl Booker deserves national recognition more than any other pianist we've heard . . . [Her] combination of pianistic and vocal charm, combined with what we know about her as a person, inclines us to a prejudiced interest in her success ["Beryl Best Since Mary Lou?," *Down Beat*, April 4, 1952, p. 8].

Feather felt that she might already have attained the deserved recognition were it not for numerous setbacks, such as ill health and bad breaks. Both seemed to have followed her, since by the late 1970s she still had not acquired her predicted place in jazz history.

A self-taught pianist, Booker's group involvements were limited to small ensembles, including Two Dukes and a Duchess, The Toppers, The Slam Stewart Trio, The Cats and a Fiddle, and The Austin Powell Quintet. In 1946 she recorded with guitarist Mary Osborn and bassist June Rotenberg (both white) for Victor's "Girls in Jazz."

In 1953 Booker organized The Beryl Booker Trio, including bassist Bonnie Wetzel and drummer Elaine Leighton (both white). Said an anonymous writer:

While individual women musicians have made notable contributions to the jazz art, it has been only on rare occasions that an all-
female instrumental group has proved itself good enough to hold
its own against the men who dominate the jazz world . . . [J]azz
critics are welcoming the Beryl Booker Trio as one of those rare
instances ["All-Girl Jazz Trio," *Ebony*, November 1953, pp. 81–84].

The trio remained together for approximately one year. But before its demise it toured Europe with the Jazz Club USA Show,
recorded on Disc and Cadence labels, and filled numerous exclusive club assignments.

In 1978 Stash Records reissued a recording that Booker made in
1954 with Norma Carson, trumpet; Mary Osborne, guitar; Bonnie
Wetzel, bass; Terry Pollard, vibes; and Elaine Leighton, drums
("Women in Jazz: All-Women Groups," ST-111). This group was
one assembled specifically for the recording date and, with the
exception of Booker and Pollard, all were white.

DOROTHY DONEGAN
piano
b. April 6, 1924, Chicago/d.   1998

At age seventeen Dorothy Donegan held down a piano spot with
The Bob Tinsley Band in Chicago. At age fifty-four Chicago
Mayor Michael Bilandic proclaimed her birthday "Dorothy Donegan Day in Chicago." The years in between were filled with
pianistic splendor, as she electrified audiences with her ingenu-
ous piano style.

Referred to as "Queen of the Eighty-Eights," Donegan began
studying music at age five. Daughter of a guitar-playing mother,
she went on to study at Chicago Musical College with master
pianist/coach Rudolph Ganz. She engaged in further study at the
University of Southern California in the early '50s, after she was
already a nationally recognized pianist.

Donegan was trained in the classical manner; she had several
years of experience as a church organist. Through the years she
was referred to as "the wild one"; "the triumphantly unfettered";
and "the shoulder-shaking, finger-popping, hip-slapping lioness
of piano rooms." An advertisement for one of her 1959 Capitol
Records releases read, "She jumps, she wiggles, she bounds and

pounds and scowls and growls." But the writers always added, "wild but polished"; "possessor of enormous technical skill"; "one of the great contemporary jazz pianists—she's brilliant, ridiculously talented"; "for all of the arm-flinging antics, Dorothy can really play" ("Wild but Polished," *Time*, November 3, 1958, p. 78).

Donegan appeared in the motion picture *Sensations of 1945* and the Broadway play *Star Time* (1945). She recorded for Continental, Decca, Victor, Jubilee, Roulette, and Capitol. In 1949 she headlined the brilliant cast of the first all-black show appearing at Hollywood's famous Tom Breneman Cafe. In 1956 she broke the house record at New York City's Embers, "An East Side sanctuary for jazz pianists." She was a regular at Chicago's London House and New York City's Jimmy Weston. The Dorothy Donegan Trio (piano, bass, and drums) was a regular on the club-and-steak-house circuit and in 1979 appeared at the Newport Jazz Festival in New York (Carnegie Hall).

Jazz historian Frank Driggs wrote in 1978:

> Dorothy Donegan may have the best pair of hands in the business and can play any style well. She is often frustrating for a hard-core jazz fancier, since she will play some brilliant passages and then upstage that with some very show-biz stuff for the squares in any club . . . [liner notes for the album "Women in Jazz: Pianists," Stash, ST-112].

Indeed, she swings the classics, but she has also played them straight, as she revealed at Tulane University in 1976, when she performed the Grieg Piano Concerto with the New Orleans Philharmonic. She is a master of boogie-woogie and the blues, but she is also a master of contemporary jazz.

Donegan is "a master of the sneak attack." As noted by Nina J. Hodgson,

> When she sits down at the keyboard and cuts loose with a blazing arpeggio run from the Grieg piano concerto and melds it into the opening notes of "My Funny Valentine," you wonder what hit you. . . . Dorothy will test your musical literacy ["The Classical Side," *Jazz Now*, October 1994, p. 9].

This was clearly evident at her April 30, 1996, performance at the Mary Lou Williams Women in Jazz festival, Kennedy Center, Washington, D.C. Her appearance was a festival highlight.

Donegan is a major attraction at jazz festivals throughout the world, including the Kool, JVC, Playboy, Chicago Classic, and New Orleans Festivals. She played on the SS *Norway* during its 1990, 1991, and 1992 jazz cruises and was given the National Association of Negro Musicians' Distinguished Contribution Award. Other citations and awards include American Jazz Masters Award (National Endowment for the Arts, 1992), Honorary Doctor of Fine Arts (University of Maryland, Eastern Shore, 1992), and Distinguished Achievement Award (University of Massachusetts, Amherst, 1993).

JULIE ("Juliette") GARDNER (Archer)
accordion, vocals
b. February 8, 1925, Augusta, Georgia

Most remember Julie Gardner as the girl accordionist who played for a brief perioid with the Earl Hines Band in 1943 (at the same time that Sarah Vaughan was on second piano). Following this affiliation Gardner attracted attention as a "versatile artist," playing and singing favorites at clubs and cafes in Boston and New York City. Other bands with which she worked were those fronted by Sabby Lewis, Charlie Barnet, Lucky Millender, and Louis Jordan. Primarily, however, she appeared with her own group (duo/trio) or in strict solo.

Though best known in the eastern part of America, Gardner's skillful accordion playing (and her voice) carried her on tours throughout the Caribbean, China, Japan, Alaska, and Greenland. Upon hearing her play, critics often commented that it was difficult to distinguish the sound from that of an organ. She was considered a blues singer "through and through" and often hummed in octaves with the accordion.

Julie was one of the racially mixed six-piece ladies' band that appeared at New York City's Jazz Museum in November 1973. For the all-female jam session she brilliantly contributed both her accordion playing and her voice.

CONSUELA LEE MOOREHEAD
piano (composition)
b. November 1, 1926, Tallahassee, Florida

A most unusual "piano/member of the ensemble" relationship was one experienced by pianist/composer Consuela Moorehead. The New York Bass Violin Choir was a team of seven bassists *par excellence*—Richard Davis, Ron Carter, Milt Hinton, Sam Jones, Michael Fleming, Lisle Atkinson, and founder/director Bill Lee, Consuela's brother. The Choir occasionally expanded to include percussion, voice, and piano and took its musical message to nightclubs, outdoor arenas, and reputable concert halls (including New York City's Judson, Alice Tully, and Town halls). The group was very popular on the college circuit and participated in the 1971 Newport Jazz Festival. The expanded New York Bass Choir found Consuela Moorehead at the keyboard. *New York Times* critic John S. Wilson described her playing with the group as "strong, flowingly rhythmic" ("Jazz: Wide Range of Styles Is Shown," *New York Times*, July 5, 1971, p. 23).

Moorehead, the daughter of a school-band-leader father and a concert-pianist mother, spent her formative years in Snow Hill, Alabama. A graduate of Fisk and Northwestern universities (B.A. and M. Mus.), she completed additional study at Eastman and Peabody schools of music. Her teachers included mother Alberta, jazz pianist Alphonso Saville, and master teacher/concert pianist Leon Fleisher.

Additional group affiliations included The Richard Davis Trio and the vocal/instrumental family group "The Descendants of Mike and Phoebe." Popular in the early and mid-1970s, the two boys and two girls took the name from their slave ancestors, Mike and Phoebe. They performed music rooted in jazz, folk, and blues idioms. From her Hampton, Virginia, residence (since 1965), she has managed to keep a busy performance and lecturing schedule. During the academic year 1976–77 Moorehead served as artist-in-residence to the Prince Edward (Virginia) Schools. Following a July 1979 solo appearance at Hampton's Strawberry Banks Lounge reviewer Phil Wilayto wrote:

> From quiet, pensive interpretation of well-known popular songs to more personal musical statements that send flashing sparks from the keyboard, Miss Moorehead's strong and expressive music re-

flects both her own spirit and sensitivity and the influence of the great jazz musicians she has been associated with ["Female Jazz Pianist Draws Hampton Raves," *Norfolk Journal and Guide*, July 28, 1978, p. 15].

In the early 1980s, noted Tidewater pianist and composer Moorehead returned to her past and reopened Snow Hill Institute, a center for learning in Wilcox County, Alabama. She and her siblings grew up on the campus of the school founded in 1893 for black youth by her grandfather William James Edwards. There on 1,465 acres was now the Snow Hill Institute of the Performing Arts, Consuela Moorehead, Director. For the school's centennial celebration, the principal speaker was filmmaker Spike Lee, Edwards's great-grandson and Moorehead's nephew.

PATRICIA ANNE ("Patti") BOWN
piano (composition, vocals, actress)
b. July 26, 1931, Seattle, Washington

There were eight children in the Bown family. The seven girls played piano and the one brother played violin. Their mother was a painter who also played piano "by ear." All studied clasical music, but as Patti wrote, "I am a self-taught jazz musician from two years old."

She performed for the governor of the state of Washington, in the governor's mansion, at the age of two. Bown accompanied Danny Kaye and substituted for Savannah Churchill (with Roy Milton's Band) when she was only eight years of age. She won first place in the Morley-Gearhart piano concerto contest (at age 16) and made a first prize concerto appearance with the Seattle Symphony Orchestra (at age 20). Bown was voted "the most likely to succeed" in her high school class and was the recipient of forty-seven scholarship offers to various colleges and universities in the United States and Europe. She enrolled at Seattle University but graduated from Cornish Conservatory (1955).

In 1956 Bown moved to New York City. Years earlier, she had substituted with Dizzy Gillespie in Seattle. Several of her first jobs in the city were obtained through his contacts. She was a member of the Quincy Jones (also from Seattle) Band that toured Europe in 1959 with the Harold Arlen/Johnny Mercer musical

Free and Easy. She performed with other instrumental ensembles that Jones assembled to play movie scores and played the piano on recordings featuring such artists as Aretha Franklin, James Brown, Nina Simone, Sarah Vaughan, Dinah Washington, Marvin Gaye, Etta James, Billy Eckstine, and Paul Anka. Others with whom she has recorded are Gene Ammons, Zoot Simms, Illinois Jacquet, Sonny Stitt, Thad Jones, Charles Mingus, Duke Ellington, Benny Golson, Oliver Nelson, and George Russell.

Patti Bown Plays Big Piano (Columbia, #1379) was released in 1961 and included four of her own compositions: "G'wan Train," "Nothing but the Truth," "Head Shakin'," and "Waltz de Funk." Other Bown compositions have been recorded by Count Basie, Quincy Jones, Duke Ellington, Jimmy Smith, J. J. Johnson, Kenny Burrell, Melba Liston, and Billy Byers. She was music director for both Dinah Washington and Sarah Vaughan. As an actress, she appeared in the South African play *The Long Journey of Poppi Ngeno* (1982).

The Library of Congress filmed Miss Bown's life story and original music for its permanent archives. A videotape narrative of her life, prepared by New York University, is often seen on cable television. A documentary of her life done for the Hatch-Billops Foundation's Oral History Library is available at the Cohen Library of the City College of New York.

The Bown approach to jazz piano has been shared with hundreds of students at Bennington College, New York University, Rutgers University (New Brunswick campus), as well as in private lessons. Her awards and honors include a National Endowment for the Arts grant (1979), two Meet the Composer grants (1981 and 1984), and the Mary Lou Williams Foundation Award for Excellence in Musicianship (1986). She was a member of the jazz panel of the Arts Endowment in 1988 and 1989 and a member of the U.S. Information Agency's 1988 music panel.

In August 1982 Bown returned to her hometown, and her visit brought many bravuros from the local press. In regard to her appearance at Seattle's Jazz Alley, jazz critic Regina Hackett wrote, "She strode up to the stage like an imposing teacher taking charge of an unruly class. Her mere presence commands attention. During her warm up . . . she got more respectful attention from the Alley crowd than other pianists playing there get during their entire runs" ("Bown Hits Home with Her Bop, Blues and

Funk," *Post Intelligencer*, August 17, 1982). Despite the review's caption, (bop, blues, and funk), Patti Bown is essentially a jazz musician, in the words of *New York Times* jazz critic John Wilson, "one of the most exciting performers in contemporary jazz." *New Yorker's* Whitney Balliett has dubbed her a "mischievous wonder."

Bown's resume offers the following description of her music:

> [She is] a contemporary improvisational musician and composer working in a large variety of modern musical idioms while drawing on a long history and tradition of American and world music. A lyricist who sings, as well as a composer who plays piano. [She] appears internationally. Born in Seattle, Washington, [she is] none-theless a Third World woman who hopes to bring peace to the whole world through her music. [Her] music embodies crosscultural unity while remaining a unique and direct expression of herself.

Bown herself has said, "Having the gift of music continues to teach me and inspire me to the most exquisite ectasy, wherefrom I have learned to heal myself and to help heal others" (author's questionnaire, May 1996).

TERRY POLLARD (Morris)
piano, vibraphone
b. August 15, 1931, Detroit

Basically self taught, pianist Terry Pollard toured with the 1957 Birdland All-Stars (including Sarah Vaughan, Lester Young, Billy Eckstine, and Count Basie); appeared on the *Steve Allen, Ed Sullivan,* and *Today* television shows; and between 1953 and 1957, enjoyed extensive popularity as a duo vibraphonist with Terry Gibbs. Leonard Feather said of her role in the duo engagements, "She seldom emerged outswung" (*The Book of Jazz*, p. 135). *Down Beat* critics concurred and rated Pollard as "new star on vibes" in their 1957 poll. She was vibraphonist with a 1954 six-piece pick-up band—an integrated all-female group, including black pianist Beryl Booker and trumpeter Norma Carson, guitarist Mary Osborne, bassist Bonnie Wetzel, and drummer Elaine Leighton ("Women in Jazz: All-Women Groups," Stash ST-111, 1978).

It is as a pianist, however, that Terry Pollard wished to be remembered, the position for which she was hired as a replacement

with Gibbs's quartet—the only black and only female. Following
the Gibbs experience she enjoyed the luxury of performance "by
personal choice" only. First was her Detroit home, her husband,
and her two children; second was performance. But Pollard's keyboard playing was never second-rate, despite her refusal to practice at home and the home's lack of a piano. She said to Detroit
reporter James Dulceau, "From 2 A.M. to 9 P.M., my name is
Terry Morris. From nine until two, I'm Terry Pollard. I really keep
the two quite separate ("Good Vibes Lady," *Monthly Digest,* April
1978, p. 78). Dulceau added, "A Motor City jazz veteran of thirty
years now, she thinks of herself as a mother while fellow jazz
musicians continue to think of her as a trusty musical mainstay"
(*ibid.,* p. 77).

Pollard's early ambition was to be a nurse, but the accident of
becoming replacement pianist in her high school graduation
dance band made show business seem more attractive. Prior to
the Gibbs affiliation she played with Johnny Hill (1948–49), The
Emmit Slay Trio (1950–52), and Billy Mitchell (1952–53). In February 1978 she appeared with Detroit's Paradise Theater Orchestra. Later in the year she performed at the University of
Pittsburgh with veteran jazzman/jazz professor Nathan Davis.

Though she found the club scene less and less enticing, Pollard's appearances at Baker's Keyboard Lounge in Detroit
spanned three decades. She appeared with such jazz all-stars as
Clark Terry, Dizzy Gillespie, Yusef Lateef, Sonny Stitt, and Zoot
Sims.

SHIRLEY SCOTT
organ, piano
b. March 14, 1934, Philadelphia

Following graduation from Girls' High School, Shirley Scott studied at the Ornstein School of Music. Although acknowledged as
a pianist of outstanding competence, it is as organist that she
made her greatest impact.

According to jazz journalist Stanley Dance:

> Shirley is the only member of her sex to achieve real prominence
> on the instrument. Like Mary Lou Williams on the piano, it is obvi-
> ous that she did bring something special, something feminine, to

the music. It was not so much delicacy, fragility or prettiness, but a quality of neatness that avoided those failings of roughness, rudeness and braggadacio to which the male is prone [liner notes for the album "On a Clear Day," Impulse A-9109].

Others described her playing as "refreshing—like coming out of the subway into a clear, balmy spring day"; a perfect example of "professionalism, creativity and excitement."

Beginning in 1956 the "First Lady of the Organ" worked with The Eddie "Lockjaw" Davis Trio. In the early '60s she formed a cooperative trio with Stanley Turrentine, who later became her husband. Another interesting association was one with The Hi-Tones, a Philadelphia group including John Coltrane on tenor sax and Albert Heath on drums. She was featured on several "definitive" jazz recordings, along with such all-stars as Count Basie, John Coltrane, Duke Ellington, Terry Gibbs, Ben Webster, Charlie Mingus, and Coleman Hawkins.

VALERIE (Gail) CAPERS
piano, composition, arranging, vocals, education
b. May 24, 1935, New York City

"My musical influences have been universal in scope. I find that in every area of music there is creativity and inspiration—something I take from it on a conscious or subliminal level. I have reached out to such varied sources as Wagner, Monk, Ellington and Bach, among others. Their vibrations and challenges have created an excitement for me as a performing artist and composer. The inspiration is everywhere. John Coltrane was a very personal day-to-day mentor, emotionally, sentimentally, and artistically. It goes without saying that as a pianist, my influences have been Art Tatum, Oscar Peterson, Bill Evans, Ahmad Jamal, and Les McCann. They were all influential in my musical development" (author's questionnaire, June 1996).

Classically trained, Capers identifies jazz influences as having been her father, a pianist with close ties to Fats Waller, and her brother, Bobby Capers, who played tenor saxophone and flute in Mongo Santamaria's band. Both are now deceased.

Capers lost her sight to a streptococcal infection when she was six. She subsequently enrolled in the New York Institute for the

Education of the Blind. There she began taking piano lessons, and her talent was obvious. She received the B.S. degree in 1959 from the Juilliard School of Music and the M.S. in 1960. She was Juilliard's first blind graduate, completing the prescribed seven-year program in six years. Her instructors were Elizabeth Thode (NYIEB) and Irwin Freundlich.

As an educator, Capers has taught at the High School of Music and Art, Manhattan School of Music, and Hunter College (all in New York City). She has always done private teaching and coaching. Her career as a jazz composer/arranger was launched by affiliation with Santamaria's Afro-Cuban band. Capers's composition "El Toro" was one of Santamaria's biggest hits. Since then, she has composed continuously. One of her best-known compositions is the jazz cantata *Sing about Love*, presented at Carnegie Hall in 1978 and later in Cleveland and Atlanta. The selection "Out of All (He's Chosen Me)" from the cantata is represented on her current CD *Come on Home* (Columbia, 1995). The result of a National Endowment for the Arts grant was her jazz operatorio (her own classification) *Sojourner*, based on the life of Sojourner Truth. *Sojourner* premiered at St. Peter's Church (New York City) in 1981. In 1985 it was performed and staged by Opera Ebony. The company also presented her *In Praise of Freedom* (based on Martin Luther King Jr.'s "I Have A Dream" speech), videotaped for Charles Kuralt's *Sunday Morning* (CBS).

A few of her other compositions include *Escenas Afro Cubano*, written for the New Music Consort, and *Songs of the Seasons*, a song cycle for soprano, cello, and piano, written expressly for the Smithsonian Institution's Program in Black American Music (1987). *The Washington Post* observed that "[a] highpoint of the afternoon . . . music rooted in the tradition of Debussy, endowed with a lovely feeling for melody and a nice sense of texture. Capers also wrote the poetry" (Joan Reinthaler, "Music of the Black American Composer," *The Washington Post*, May 4, 1987, p. C11). When an excerpt from her operatorio *Sojourner* was performed the following year (also at the Smithsonian Institution), *The Washington Post* commented that "the concert reached its apex with a monologue from *Sojourner* . . . One longed for a complete performance, for the excerpt was riveting" (Norman Middleton, "Black American Composers Series," May 18, 1988, p. D3). Other works of Capers can be heard on the albums *Portrait in Soul* (Atlantic) and *Affirmation* (KMA Arts).

Valerie Capers the vocalist made her abilities apparent at the black American music symposium held at the University of Michigan (August 1985) to those who journeyed to a local club after the evening concert. They are fully realized on the 1995 CD, *Come on Home*. Her journalistic abilities were in evidence in an article that she wrote for the June 18, 1986, *Village Voice* ("John Coltrane: Bringing Verismo to Jazz").

Capers showed leadership skills and administrative know-how during the eight years she chaired the Department of Music and Art at Bronx Community College (1987–95). Currently artist in residence at the college, one of her final accomplishments before retiring from her nine-to-five responsibilities in order to devote more time to performance and composition was to complete the application, secure and administer the grant, and file the final report for a National Endowment for the Arts jazz special project. This jazz series, held at the Bronx Museum for the Arts, brought celebrity jazz artists to borough audiences—a first for the Bronx.

Capers appears throughout the country as lecturer, clinician, and performer on college campuses. She is a regular at New York City's Knickerbocker and performs at other popular club sites. Following a local gig, she may fly to the West Coast and perform a Mozart concerto. One such appearance was at Pepperdine Center for the Arts in Malibu; another, with the Bronx Arts Ensemble Chamber Orchestra on the Fordham University campus; and another, the Malibu Music Festival in Santa Monica. Festival appearances (with her trio) have included Newport, Kool, JVC (USA); Grande Parade International, Nice; and North Sea, The Hague. Jazz artists with whom she has performed reads like a Who's Who: Dizzy Gillespie, Ray Brown, Wynton Marsalis, Mongo Santamaria, Max Roach, Paquito D'Rivera, Donald Byrd, Hubert Laws, Slide Hampton, and Nat Adderley. Capers reached a national audience when she appeared on Marian McPartland's radio series *Piano Jazz*.

Capers has received many honors and awards. She was asked to deliver the commencement address of the New York Institute for the Education of the Blind (1985), and she serves on the President's Committee for the Disabled. She won the Creative Artist Public Service Award, the Certificate of Merit, New York City's Mayor Edward Koch; Outstanding Musical Achievement— Dedicator's Cup, Brooklyn College; and grants from the National

Endowment for the Arts, Meet the Composer, and City University of New York Research Foundation. She was one of the first recipients of *Essence* magazine's Women of Essence Award, along with Oprah Winfrey and Marla Gibbs. In 1995, Susquehanna University bestowed upon her the Honorary Doctor of Fine Arts.

Capers offers the following words of wisdom: "Because the pursuit of music and the arts is so difficult, it is impossible to be eternally optimistic. The aspiring artist *must* remain focused. For me, the key words have been and continue to be, *discipline, determination and resilience*" (author's questionnaire, June 1996).

FRANCES ELAINE COLE
harpsichord, piano, violin (vocals)
b. July 12, 1937, Cleveland; d. January 24, 1983, New York City

Frances Cole came to the harpsichord late in her career by way of the piano and organ, though by the mid-1970s she was one of the few harpsichordists bringing the instrument into the twentieth century and expanding its orchestral/solo horizons. She began studying piano privately with a local choir director and soon thereafter at the Sutphen School of Music on a scholarship from the Phillis Wheatley Association. At ten she began violin studies with Dorothy Smith of the Cleveland Women's Symphony. Later she studied at the Cleveland Institute of Music.

Entrance to Miami (Ohio) University was by way of scholarships in both violin and piano. Cole was concertmistress of the University Orchestra and completed requirements for the undergraduate degree (B. Mus.) in three years. She moved to the "do or die" city of New York in 1957. There she worked as a public school music teacher, a "pop" pianist (under various names), and as a domestic, continuing her piano studies privately with Juilliard's Irving Freundlich. She enrolled at Columbia University's Teachers College and before long earned both the master's and doctoral degrees (1966).

Cole continued her orchestral involvement (on violin) with the city's National Orchestral Association and other local instrumental ensembles, abandoning the idea of becoming a permanent orchestral violinist only in 1966. For her doctoral thesis she analyzed *The Goldberg Variations* of J. S. Bach, the work that "turned her on" to the Baroque era and the harpsichord. She soon began studying with Denise Restout at the Landowska Center in Connecticut. While studying with Restout, she received grants from the Martha Baird Rockefeller and World Arts Foundations.

During the summer of 1967 she filled a residency assignment as harpsichordist with the Gallery Players (primarily winds) at Provincetown, Massachusetts, Art Museum. According to Cole,

> Then something magic happened. I made my first of several appearances on NBC's "Today Show," as a solo harpsichordist. A bit later, I appeared on the children's show "Mr. Roger's Neighborhood." And though the Affiliate Artists Program primarily supports vocalists, I convinced the sponsors that their assistance should include harpsichordist Cole [conversation with the author, March 27, 1979, Petersburg, Virginia].

Between 1969 and 1973 she appeared in more than a hundred concerts and recitals. She made her debut tour of Europe in 1973. The press was most enthusiastic. Wrote the London *Times*: "Miss Cole is a player who uses her strong technique to underline robust rhythms"; the *Suddeutsch Zeitung* (Munich): "Frances Cole has her public in her hands at all times. She played the old masters with color, rhythm and expression."

Also in 1973 she organized the first of three Harpsichord Festivals. The first two were held at Westminster Choir College (where she served on the faculty) and the third on the Westminster campus, at Carnegie Hall, and at Lincoln Center, New York (Ericson, "A 10-Day Festival for Harpsichord," *New York Times*, June 14, 1975, p. L22).

In 1976 *New York Amsterdam News* music journalist Raoul Abdul wrote:

> Frances Cole, the only major Black harpsichordist, is an unusually fine musician. She is also a fine comedienne. [For an outdoor concert on the North Plaza of Lincoln Center] she stepped into the character of "Magdalena." She arrived in what can only be described as the Grand Manner. A startled crowd of nearly a thousand watched intently as a horse driven carriage pulled up to the stage. When its door opened, Miss Cole emerged as Anna Magdalena Bach. . . . It took only a few bars of the Allegro movement of Mozart's Sonata

in C to turn this dramatic moment from the ridiculous to the sublime. Miss Cole played with her customary strong rhythmic drive, scrupulous attention to interpretative detail and real elegance ["Miss Cole as 'Magdalena,' " August 28, 1976, p. D8].

For the event Cole used a jazz bassist and a percussionist, a common happening, since her programs now included music from the Baroque through twentieth-century jazz.

Cole participated in the Bach Festival at Carmel, California, in 1977. Her outreach to college campuses continued to expand. Then, in 1978, Howard Thompson's New York City "Going Out Guide" called attention to a "neat twist" at Oliver's Lounge. He was excited over its pianist/singer "Elaine Francis" (harpsichordist Frances Elaine Cole). Thompson indicated that the Lounge

> hit the jackpot with its newest entertainer and her astonishing cavalcade of show tunes and ballads. Now and then Miss Francis sings in pleasantly husky tones. She also laces her medleys with classics, expertly. The fun . . . was guessing what music would come next. . . . Playing deftly and crisply, . . . Miss Francis was in fine free form, with no sentimental dawdling [*New York Times*, March 23, 1978, p. C17].

Beginning in the spring of 1979 Cole appeared regularly on CBS's nationally aired "Sunday Morning," serving as music reporter, performer, and critic.

ALICE MC LEOD COLTRANE
keyboards (harp, tamboura, percussions, composition)
b. August 27, 1937, Detorit

The successor to Terry Pollard as vibraphonist with The Terry Gibbs Quartet (early '60s) was keyboardist Alice McLeod. Like Pollard she played piano and vibraphone in the early years, but following the death of her husband, John Coltrane (1967), extended herself to include in live and recording sessions the organ, harp, tamboura, and percussion.

Pianist Alice Coltrane replaced McCoy Tyner in the legendary Coltrane outfit in 1966. Jazz journalist Bill Cole wrote the following about the Tyner replacement:

If for no other reason, bringing Alice into the band would have been appropriate at this time, if only because of the need to promote more women players. Unquestionably, there has been tremendous male chauvinism in jazz and too often women have been treated as mere sex objects or exploited as Billie Holiday was by members of the orchestra. But there is certainly more to Alice Coltrane than just her symbolic value in the band [*John Coltrane,* p. 192].

The "beyond symbolic value" of Alice's presence can be heard in the Coltrane recordings made during the final year of John's life.

The Coltranes were together for four years. Musical spiritualism and mysticism occupied both Alice and John. Alice credited her husband with having taught her "to explore . . . to play thoroughly and completely." Continuing in the tradition, she said, "I would like to play music according to ideals set forth by John and continue to let a cosmic principle, or the aspect of spirituality, be the underlying reality behind the music as he did" ("Alice Coltrane Interviewed by Pauline Rivelli," in *Black Genius,* p. 122).

Alice Coltrane led her own groups for club, concert, and recording dates, appearing at such reputable places as the Village Vanguard and Carnegie Hall. Her personnel included such jazz and nonjazz all-stars as saxmen Pharoah Sanders, Ornette Coleman, and Archie Shepp; string players Julien Barber, Alan Shulman, Ronald Lipscomb, and Ron Carter; and percussionists Ben Riley and Elayne Jones. She frequently recorded her own compositions and arrangements, including "Universal Consciousness," "Oh Allah," "Journey in Satchidananda," and "Blue Nile." In 1987 she and her three sons performed in tribute to John Coltrane a concert at New York City's Cathedral of Saint John the Divine.

PATRICIA PRATTIS JENNINGS
piano (organ, harpsichord, celesta)
b. July 16, 1941, Pittsburgh

Symphony orchestras commonly employ one person to play the piano, celesta, and harpsichord. Filling these assignments with the Pittsburgh Symphony is Patricia Jennings. She joined the orchestra in 1964.

Jennings began piano study at age six and at age ten began taking lessons from the Pittsburgh Symphony's pianist, Harry

Franklin. With the exception of a brief postgraduate period at Indiana University, Jennings's postsecondary training was acquired at Carnegie-Mellon University, where she received the B.F.A. and M.F.A. degrees. In addition to Franklin, her instructors were Sidney Foster and black concert pianist/teacher/coach Natalie Hinderas.

An additional preparation for Jennings's professional orchestra involvement was her years as a violinist. Studying violin between the ages of eight and twelve, she was concertmistress of her high school orchestra, with the current Pittsburgh Symphony's other black member, Paul Ross, serving as the associate concertmaster. The violin-playing years provided membership in Pittsburgh's All-City Orchestra and that of Carnegie-Mellon.

Jennings's first piano solo appearance with the Pittsburgh Symphony took place in 1956, at age fourteen. In 1962 she made a solo appearance at the celebrated Marlboro Festival in Vermont. During the final semester of study at Carnegie-Mellon she was informed of the Pittsburgh Symphony pianist's inability to make the orchestra's forthcoming European tour. She had completed a successful audition for the position, and the three-month substitute experience no doubt served as Jennings's audition for the permanent position. When the orchestra's 1964 season began, she was under contract. When maestro Arthur Fiedler sought a pianist for his brief October 1971 World Symphony Orchestra tour, his choice was Patricia Jennings.

In addition to making solo appearances with the Butler, Baltimore, Houston, Pacific, Wheeling, and Pittsburgh Youth symphonies, Jennings appeared as recitalist with flutist Bernard Goldberg (Pittsburgh Symphony), Eliot Chapo (former concertmaster, New York Philharmonic), and Mildred Miller (Metropolitan Opera). She was featured "Artist in Concert" on WQXR radio in New York City and throughout the month of February 1976 was featured artist on WQED-FM's "Music from Pittsburgh."

A good season for Jennings was 1975–76, providing the beginning of broader visibility. In June 1976 she performed George Gershwin's *Concerto in F* with the Baltimore Symphony, with black maestro Darrold Hunt (the orchestra's assistant conductor) on the podium. In December 1976 Jennings performed again with the Baltimore Symphony, sharing the spotlight with clarinetist

Benny Goodman and playing Gershwin's *Rhapsody in Blue*. So outstanding was her performance that Goodman arranged for her to share the spotlight with him again, at New York City's Avery Fisher Hall, May 2, 1977, with Morton Gould conducting an eighteen-piece orchestra. The following month Jennings toured as soloist in the Gershwin work with Goodman and Company, doing programs at Concord, California; Chandler Pavilion in Los Angeles; and Wolf Trap Farm Park in Virginia. The latter event was taped for a 1978 Fall showing on the Public Broadcasting System.

Jennings made her television debut along with that of the Pittsburgh Symphony on February 27, 1977, on PBS. She joined host/commentator/pianist/conductor André Previn at the piano, playing fragments from three of Mozart's early four-hand sonatas. Pittsburgh's 1977–78 season saw the programming of the complete *Two-Piano Concerto in E-flat*, by Mozart, K. 365, featuring André Previn as conductor and second pianist and Jennings as first. Local critic Robert Croan wrote, "flexible, liquid in her phrasing . . . sure . . . underlying rhythmic drive. She imparted the relaxed spirit of chamber music" ("Previn Returns to City, Energy Crisis Dims Hall," *Post Gazette*, February 11, 1978, p. 18). American viewers shared the experience by way of an April 1978 telecast, again on PBS.

Pianist Jennings served as church organist for Pittsburgh's Wesley Center A. M. E. Zion Church, beginning at age twelve. This grass-roots association contributed greatly to the pianist's ability to enjoy and participate in all styles and forms of music. Frequently the choir rendered one of Jennings's gospel compositions, with the composer/organist taking the vocal lead.

Following her participation in a three-day conference at Harriman, New York in 1988, the topic of which was "Toward Greater Participation of Black Americans in Symphony Orchestras," Jennings began publishing the newsletter *Symphonium*. "For and about Professional African-American Symphony Musicians," *Symphonium* existed for five years. She has also contributed articles to the American Symphony Orchestra League's publication *Symphony*.

Also in 1988, the weekly publication *In Pittsburgh* voted Jennings best instrumental performer. In September 1991, she was inducted into the international music fraternal organization

Sigma Alpha Iota as a national honorary member. Jennings serves on several boards: Pittsburgh Literary Council, Steinway Society, and the project String Training and Educational Program—Pittsburgh.

AMINA CLAUDINE MYERS
piano, organ (composition, vocals)
b. March 21, 1942, Blackwell, Arkansas

Though formal piano instruction did not begin until age seven, Amina Myers began playing and singing as early as age four. Throughout high school she served as pianist and organist for both school and church choirs. While enrolled at Philander Smith College she was concert choir pianist and for two years student director. Also while a college enrollee she played (piano/organ) and sang at a local club and spent the summer months doing the same in Lexington, Kentucky.

Following graduation (B.A. in Music Education), Myers taught in the Chicago public schools for six years. The music educator practiced her trade further at the Micheaux School of Music in Chicago and at the College of Old Westbury (SUNY), where she also directed the institution's gospel chorus.

In the mid-'60s Myers began playing organ with The Gerald Donavan Trio. In 1966, already revealing a great deal of talent and interest in composition, she became one of the few female affiliates of the Chicago-based Association for the Advancement of Creative Musicians (AACM), an organization dedicated to serious music and the performance of new, unrecorded compositions.

The affiliation with AACM also established meaningful contacts for Amina Myers. She began touring the country with saxophonist Sonny Stitt in 1970, followed by a two-year musical association with tenor saxophonist Gene Ammon's Quartet. She began appearing with the AACM Big Band, Ajarama Ensemble, Muhal Richard Abrams's piano trio, and in duo with Joseph Harman. Obviously the AACM experience prepared her for the move to New York City.

By 1977 *Down Beat* journalist Scott Albin was able to write:

[Y]oung organist made a lasting impression. She was soulful, fleet and original, . . . great talent, warmth . . . diverse piano stylings . . .

Amina Claudine Myers is a name to remember. Watch for it ["Amina Myers: Environ New York City," October 6, 1977, p. 45].

In *Down Beat's* Twenty-fifth Annual Jazz Critic's Poll (1977) Myers's organ talent was voted as one "deserving wider recognition." There followed a tour of Europe with The Lester Bowie Quintet, a tour of the West Coast and Canada with The Leroy Jenkins Trio, recording dates, radio and television appearances, composition grants from the National Endowment for the Arts, and the position of assistant musical director with the Broadway hit *Ain't Misbehavin'*. Evenings of music composed and performed by Myers occurred frequently. She began doing workshops for the "Artist in the Schools Program," Lincoln Center for the Performing Arts, and making appearances with the legendary Art Blakey and the phenomenal Rahsaan Roland Kirk.

Myers's 1975 musical *I Dream* premiered in Chicago. It was given a second performance in 1978 in New York City, with indications that other bookings would follow. Solo piano recitals at Amherst and Hampshire colleges and Yale and New York universities were a part of her 1978–79 season. She was a member of the " 'Big Apple' Jazz Women" Band of New York City that, according to the press, "broke it up" at the Kansas City Women's Jazz Festival, in 1979. The "Salute to Women in Jazz" served as an adjunct to the 1979 Newport Jazz Festival in New York. Myers's "Improvisational Suite for Chorus and Pipe Organ" was one of the featured works. In late 1970 she organized her own five-piece group (keyboard, reeds, and percussion), Amina and Company.

The 1980s were good years for Myers professionally. Regarded as one of the foremost musicians in contemporary jazz/new music, she drew on the complete spectrum of African-American music. Performing in a solo capacity or with her quartet (plus tenor saxophone, bass, and percussion), pianist/organist/vocalist/composer Myers is always in rare form. She tastefully melds gospel, blues, funk, R&B, and jazz. She has received composition grants from the National Endowment for the Arts and on several occasions has served as a music program panelist.

PATRICE RUSHEN
keyboards (composition, arranging)
b. September 30, 1954, Los Angeles

According to the liner notes on her first album, "Prelusion" (released in 1974), keyboardist Rushen was "following in the footsteps of such giants as Herbie Hancock, Keith Jarrett, McCoy Tyner, Oscar Peterson, Wynton Kelly and Bill Evans" (Wilson, liner notes for the album "Prelusion," Prestige 10089). On this album Rushen played acoustic and electric piano, clavinet, and ARP synthesizers and was represented as both composer and arranger. Two additional albums ("Before the Dawn" and "Shout It Out") featured Lady Rushen on organ as well.

Afro-American journalist Frederick L. Douglass referred to Rushen as "[s]exy, sassy and sultry . . . one of the meanest keyboard players on the contemporary scene . . . tiny fox with the big talent" ("Patrice Rushen . . . Wicked Organist," *Richmond Afro-American*, April 2, 1977, p. 23). Others referred to her as "a musical force to be reckoned with" and "a painter of musical landscapes."

Patrice began studying the piano at age five. She also participated in a preschool program for musically gifted children at the University of Southern California called "Eurythmics."[2] She later began studying flute, becoming a member of her high school's marching and concert bands. She reached the decision to make jazz her life's work while still in high school, during which time she joined the Msingi Workshop Orchestra, led by Reggie Andrews. In an interview with journalist Doris Worsham, Rushen stated:

> I was attracted to the pretty harmonies of jazz. . . . [It] offered me extensions upon some of the things I was playing when I was playing classical music ["Ladies in the Band," *Oakland Tribune,* September 28, 1975].

It was Reggie Andrews who served as a guiding spirit in the development of a potentially outstanding career and he who was the producer of her first album. Studies at USC toward a degree in music education were combined with professional performance, including appearances at the Monterey Jazz Festival and with The Melba Liston-Leslie Drayton Band. Her achievement awards included "Best Soloist," Monterey Junior Festival, and "Outstanding Instrumentalist," Hollywood Bowl Battle of the Bands. Music collaborators in live performance and recordings included such established personalities as Stanley Turrentine, Donald Byrd, Jean-Luc Ponty, and Hubert Laws. She once did a road tour with the popular singing group The Sylvers.

Rushen began touring extensively in the 1980s. In 1982 she was nominated for a Grammy for best R&B vocal performance ("Forget Me Nots") and for best R&B instrumental performance ("Number One"). She was music director for Janet Jackson's world tour. She was the first woman to serve as music director for the Emmy Awards, for the NAACP Image Awards, and for the Peoples' Choice Awards. She has provided scores for HBO's *American Dream* and PBS's *A. Philip Randolph*, as well as *Jack's Place, Brewster Place,* and *The Midnight Hour*.

GERI A. ALLEN
piano
b. June 12, 1957, Detroit

Upon graduation from Howard University's Department of Jazz Studies (B.Mus.) in 1979 pianist Geri Allen was awarded a National Endowment for the Arts Jazz Fellowship Grant for private study with pianist Kenny Barron. During all of her three years of matriculation at Howard University's College of Fine Arts she received the Special Talent Scholarship.

The Detroit native arrived in the nation's capital with a wealth of experience and a superb musical background. A graduate of Cass Technical High School (where she participated in the school's jazz ensemble), Allen studied piano privately at the Detroit Conservatory of the Arts for eleven years and participated in the Interlochen Center for the Arts.

While still in high school Allen sang with Detroit's popular Madrigal Singers and its Harp and Vocal Ensemble. For the latter group she wrote "Feelin' Good!," a staple in the ensemble's repertory. She also composed the theme song for the children's show *Deeterdoor,* aired on Detroit's WXYZ-TV.

During the summer of 1978 pianist/singer/composer Geri Allen served as codirector of Wayne State University's Improvisation Workshop. She served as music director of the Alexander Crummell Center and the D.C. Black Repertory Company's production of *Face of Love,* also in 1978.

Artists with whom Allen performed included Les McCann,

Woody Shaw, Lionel Hampton, Cecil Bridgewater, and Donald Byrd. She performed with the Warren Shad Group on the *A.M. Washington Show*, WJLA-TV, Washington, D.C. When veteran bassist Keter Betts put together his company of "Stars of the Future" in April 1979 for appearances at Baltimore's Famous Ballroom and D.C.'s Blues Alley, he took along pianist Geri Allen. The trio, quartet, and quintet ensembles glittered all the brighter as a result of Allen's affiliation.

Allen delayed study with Kenny Barron while she matriculated at the University of Pittsburgh, receiving a master of arts degree in ethnomusicology. She took up residency in New York City in 1982. It was not long before she was one of the most talked about and sought-after pianists on the New York scene.

Allen was soon affiliated with a group known as M-Base that mixed elements of black American musical traditions and various world musics. Group members were mostly newcomers to New York City. One exciting performance was presented at the Brooklyn Academy of Music's Next Wave festival. (See Suzanne McElfresh, "Try to Play Life: The Music of M-Base," *On the Next Wave*, October 1988, pp. 20–22.) Allen also worked for a brief period with the eclectic Black Rock Coalition Orchestra and spent six months with Mary Wilson (one of the original Supremes) "playing straightahead Motown."

As a tribute to pioneering pianist Lovie Austin (1887–1972), Allen performed two concerts of Austin's compositions at the Smithsonian Institution, National Museum of American History (Washington, D.C.) in March 1987. The concerts were standing room only. *Down Beat* magazine in its critics polls in 1993 and 1994 recognized Geri Allen as the top talent deserving wider recognition. In April 1996 she appeared at Kennedy Center, participating in the Mary Lou Williams Women in Jazz Festival.

To the earlier list of persons with whom Allen has performed must be added the names Dewey Rodman, David Murray, Ron Carter, Oliver Lake, Steve Coleman, Wallace Roney, Julius Hemphill, Lester Bowie, James Newton, Arthur Blythe, Charlie Hayden, Andrew Cyrille, Wayne Shorter, Ornette Coleman, and vocal divas Cassandra Wilson and Betty Carter. Allen is now an international pianist/composer who appears throughout the world. Briefly teaching and coaching at the New England Conservatory of Music, she is currently an assistant professor of music at her alma mater, Howard University.

Notes

1. In later years Todd served as organist and choir director at the First Street United Methodist Church, New Orleans.

2. Expression of the rhythmical aspects of music through improvised bodily movement—for Rushen, an experimental course designed to introduce young children to music.

VI.

Non-Playing Orchestral Affiliates

Players and leaders alone do not an orchestra make. Policies must be established; contracts must be negotiated; funds must be raised and funds must be managed; and personnel must be hired and personnel must sometimes be fired. Orchestral advocacy is a constant necessity. Sales, publicity, and booking are all high on the list of orchestral priorities. These responsibilities have been carried out by numerous black women, and within recent years the numbers have increased. The questions arise: Who are these black women? What has drawn them to orchestras? What are some of the groups with which they have been affiliated?

We are relatively certain that Hallie Anderson handled business matters for her orchestras in New York City at the beginning of the twentieth century. She advertised that she could provide an "orchestra for any occasion." Mrs. B. J. Covington not only served as violinist with Madam Corilla Rochon's Ladies Orchestra in Houston (midway in the second decade of this century), but also served as the group's manager.

The affairs of the Clef Club Orchestras, from 1924 onward, were managed by Lillian Galloway (Elnor). She and her Harlem-based Apex Musical Bureau successfully booked the entire entertainment for affairs held in the ballrooms of many leading white hotels in New York City and its vicinity. New York cellist/bassist Olivia (Porter) Shipp verified that she personally handled all business matters of her 1920s to early-'30s Jazz-Mines and the Negro Women's Orchestral and Civic Association, even when members of the latter group played under the name of Lil Hardin Armstrong.

The affairs of Isabele Taliaferro Spiller's Women's Excelsior Temple Band, which was based in New York City during the

1920s and '30s, were handled by one Mrs. Kimbough. President Laurence C. Jones was the principal administrator of The International Sweethearts of Rhythm at the Piney Woods Country Life School in Mississippi, but Rae Lee Jones was the orchestra's effective manager-chaperone. These responsibilities she carried out while the group was affiliated with the school and after it left (1939 through the mid-'40s). Much of the group's early success can be attributed to her skill in working with its members, booking agents, and the general public. A final example of management in the 1940s is bassist Bell Durham, who served as an agent for Richard Baker's Dance Band in New York City—a well-integrated outfit from the standpoint of gender.

Few names of persons who served American orchestras in managerial positions during the 1950s have come down to us, except for Lucille Dixon, whose management efforts were most prominent in the 1970s. We know, however, that such individuals did exist. We speculate that unless a group was well established, where black women served as band leaders, they also doubled as managers, booking agents, and in all other "group survival" positions.

In the 1960s a unique assignment was carried out in New York City by a unique person. Violinist Marie Hense worked in the enviable position of contractor—the individual who makes available orchestral employment—beginning in the fall of 1961. Hense was the first female contractor (black or white) on Broadway. As she explained,

> I arrived in New York City [1960] absolutely fearless. I accepted no negative vibes (of which there were many), though I was totally unaware that I had any business acumen whatsoever. I started at the Imperial Theater. The show was *Carnival*. I was house contractor. I remained at the Imperial from 1961 to 1966. Then I was transferred to the Broadway Theater as houseman [the always-present instrumentalist, show or no show] [conversation with the author, July 9, 1976, New York City].

Despite Hense's initial lack of business skills she obviously fulfilled her assignment well, since she remained in the business for almost a decade.

In 1972 bassist Lucille Dixon, one of the founding members of the Symphony of the New World, became the orchestra's manager. Dixon's primary duties were administrative, but as she explained:

> with an orchestra such as ours [1975–76 season: six subscription concerts/quarter-of-a-million-dollar budget], the position of manager means doing any and everything—from cleaning the office, to typing, to duplicating, to doing lay-outs, answering the telephone, handling the mail and running errands. If there is something to be done, you do it [Handy, "Conversation with Lucille Dixon: Manager of a Symphony Orchestra," *Black Perspective in Music*, Vol. 3, No. 3, Fall 1975, pp. 302–303].

Dixon had worked on the business end of the orchestra since its inception. Although she had managed her own jazz orchestra for more than a decade, she nevertheless took advantage of the American Symphony Orchestra League's training sessions to sharpen her skills. She remained in the managerial position until 1976, and, in the opinion of many, the orchestra would not have survived as long as it did had it not been for the astuteness of Lucille Dixon.

Also in 1972 Plainfield, New Jersey native Marilyn Knordle was elevated to the position of manager of the New Jersey Symphony Orchestra. According to journalist Phillip Truckenbrod,

> Marilyn Knordle of East Orange is not the first woman to manage a major orchestra, although women in such positions are rare, but she is believed to be the first black woman to serve as manager of a major orchestra in this country ["The Music Woman: Symphony Picks First Black Manager," February 27, 1972, *Sunday Star-Ledger*, Section 1, p. 27].

Knordle's promotion (her orchestral association had begun in 1966) was in recognition of her managerial skill and devotion, having "functioned as a de facto manager of the orchestra while a succession of men . . . officially held the position." She moved from office secretary to private secretary to assistant manager, always with several other responsibilities. For the press she stated,

> In between managers I was always the assistant manager or the acting manager and most of the time there [was] no one else in an administrative position in the office except me [*ibid.*].

By 1978 American symphony orchestras had become more acceptable to the general public; blacks were increasingly in evidence. In 1979 this author sent out a questionnaire (see Appendixes III and IV) to thirty-one major symphony orchestras and twenty-three regional symphony orchestras in the United States, requesting the following information for the 1978–79 season:

1) *Managerial Staff:* a) Total Number, b) Number of Blacks, c) Number of Women, d) Number of Black Women, and 3) Names of Black Women;
2) *Board Members:* a) Total Number, b) Number of Blacks, c) Number of Women, d) Number of Black Women, and e) Names of Black Women;
3) *Women's Committee Members:* a) Total Number, b) Number of Black Women, and c) Names of Black Women.

The managerial staff represents that group of individuals to whom more and more power is being given, as orchestral operations become more and more sophisticated. As viewed by CBS Records' Ernest Fleischmann (currently executive vice president/managing director, Los Angeles Philharmonic) over two and a half decades ago,

> Whether we like it or not, we are in the throes of a managerial revolution in the orchestral world. The orchestra manager is undergoing a metamorphosis. He is emerging from the cocoon in which he was the servant of his board and the amanuensis of his music director, to become the master, on whom depend not only his orchestra's administrative and financial fortunes but also its artistic future. . . . The manager will be the one to determine the orchestra's policy, in conjunction with his board, and if the board is an intelligent one, it will give the manager his head ["Who Runs Our Orchestras and Who Should?," *High Fidelity/Musical America*, May 1969, p. 62].

Board members, generally nonmusicians, represent orchestral control. Of this governing body, Fleishmann wrote,

> With some notable exceptions, conductors pay homage to them, managers spend sleepless nights over them, and managers' wives

run up prohibitively high couturiers' bills because of them [*ibid.,* p. 59].

Thousands of women work incessantly to support America's symphony orchestras. Even before the formation of the American Symphony Orchestra League, women had created the Association of Women's Committees for Symphony Orchestras (1937). As an organized body, they are identified as Women's Guild, League, Association, Auxilliary—all workers

> who have organized committees, sold tickets, raised funds and formed the flames of community enthusiasm. . . [I]t is probably safe to say that America would only have a handful of orchestras, and those in far more precarious condition, if it were not for the energy, dedication and resourcefulness of those women who have worked far more strenuously for local orchestras than did their Victorian counterparts for the poor [Paramenter, "God Bless the Ladies, for They Have Helped Build Orchestras," *New York Times,* August 16, 1959, Section 2, p. 7].

In the cover letter orchestras were assured that the data would be reported by category (Major/Regional) rather than by orchestra name. Fourteen major orchestras (45 percent) and fifteen regional orchestras responded (65 percent), though not all provided answers to all questions. Nevertheless, the respondees provided the information given on the following pages.

MANAGERIAL STAFF
(1978–79 Season)

MAJOR ORCHESTRAS   N = 14

	Total Number	Number of Blacks	Number of Women	Number of Black Women
A.	44	4		2
B.	7		2	
C.	22	2	11	1
D.	23	1		
E.	19	2	13	1
F.	36	4	22	3
G.	26	3	19	2
H.	17	8	11	6
I.	81	1	32	
J.	22		8	
K.	13		8	
L.	25	2	17	2
M.	5		3	
N.	18	1	5	
Totals	358	28 (7.8%)	151 (42.1%)	17 (4.7%)

Note: Black women represented 60.7% of all blacks and 11.2% of all women.

REGIONAL ORCHESTRAS   N = 14

	Total Number	Number of Blacks	Number of Women	Number of Black Women
A.	6		4	
B.	17	5	12	5
C.	8		7	
D.	12		9	
E.	14		10	
F.	8		6	
G.	9		5	
H.	13	1	8	1
I.	5	1	4	1
J.	13		10	
K.	8		7	
L.	6		5	
M.	11	1	9	
N.	10		9	
Totals	140	8 (5.7%)	105 (75%)	7 (5%)

Note: Black women represented 87.5% of all blacks and 6.6% of all women.

BOARD MEMBERS
(1978–79 Season)

MAJOR ORCHESTRAS   N = 13

	Total Number	Number of Blacks	Number of Women	Number of Black Women
A.	39	2	5*	1
B.	77	2	17	
C.	76	7	36	2
D.	73	3	28	2
E.	30		6	
F.	40	2	8	1
G.	56	3	12	2
H.	63	1	20	
I.	90	2	20	
J.	50	1	12	1
K.	33	1	9	1
L.	60	2	27	1
M.	26	1	3	
Totals	713	27 (3.7%)	203 (28.4%)	11 (1.5%)

Note: Black women represented 40.7% of all blacks and 5.4% of all women.

*Exact number not provided; writer's speculation.

REGIONAL ORCHESTRAS   N = 15

	Total Number	Number of Blacks	Number of Women	Number of Black Women
A.	36	1	9	
B.	73	5	27	3
C.	36		10	
D.	41		10	
E.	34			
F.	83	2	24	1
G.	60	1		
H.	65	2	27	2
I.	140	1	45	1
J.	55	2	21	1
K.	52	1	14	
L.	36		14	
M.	22		10	
N.	42	2	9	
O.	45	2	19	1
Totals	820	19 (2.3%)	239 (29.1%)	9 (1%)

Note: Black women represented 47.3% of all blacks and 3.7% of all women.

Women's Committee Members

The exact figures for the number of black women serving on Women's Committees were hard to come by. Most orchestras indicated an inability to provide data on black women's involvement, since their records "carry names only." The data indicate that, as far as major orchestras are concerned, the total membership varies from a low of forty to a high of 5,000. With regard to regional orchestras, the total membership varies from a low of twenty-four to a high of 1,100.

Update

Roughly fifteen years later, a decision was made not to attempt a follow-up survey. Times had changed, and attitudes concerning affirmative action had grown somewhat hostile. Many were convinced that discrimination was nonexistent in the orchestral business (though the evidence revealed otherwise). The zeitgeist was well reflected in the report of the National Task Force for *The American Orchestra: An Initiative for Change* (*Americanizing the American Orchestra*, June 1993) and the subsequent reaction from the field itself. Of seven chapters, the one that provoked the greatest controversy was "Achieving Cultural Diversity" (chap. 2).

As the profiles will indicate, progress has been made in terms of managerial staff, board membership, and women's committee membership. Other committees are known variously. Blacks (male and female) are represented everywhere.

In the early 1980s (until the orchestra's demise in the late 1980s), Evelyn Battiste was a member of the New Orleans Philharmonic's board of directors. In July 1990, DeLisa Ellison was appointed publications and educational manager for the Savannah Symphony. In April 1990, Jean Patterson Boone was appointed to the Baltimore Symphony Orchestra's administrative staff as the orchestra's community affairs manager, offering professional guidance to the orchestra's community outreach committee. The objective pursued by Boone and the committee was to include the black community in all aspects of the orchestra's activities and to offer a black presence at symphony concerts.

They succeeded. With a background in community organization and administration, her accomplishments were significant, and the American Symphony Orchestra League did not hesitate to draw on her skills at the national level, that is, ASOL Conferences and Committees. (See Janet E. Bedell, "Building Bridges: The BSO's Community Outreach Committee," *Overture*, November 2, 1990–January 12, 1991, pp. 38–43.) The Houston Symphony recently announced that Debra J. Garner was the new director of finance and administration.

The eleven-hundred-plus member board of directors of the Atlanta Symphony includes four black women: Mary Frances Early (member-at-large), Azira Hill, Barbara Yarn, and Joyce Wilson (wife of the lone black orchestra member—a trombonist). Two black women, Marva Carter and Mary Frances Early, made two of the twenty-five concert preview presentations during the 1995–96 season. Carter also taught one of six music appreciation courses for the orchestra ("The African-American Roots of Gospel Music").

There existed at the National Endowment for the Arts a thirteen-week program in arts administration. A carefully selected arts administration fellow was assigned to an individual program to provide familiarity with that discipline (from a national perspective) and a broad-based introduction to the political, cultural, and government-oriented organizations in the nation's capital.

During my tenure as assistant director, acting director, and director of the music program of the National Endowment for the Arts (1985–93), three black women with an interest in orchestral management served as arts administration fellows in the agency's music program. They were Lauren Generette (Floyd), Alisa Mayfield (Smallwood), and Jennifer Jackson. Upon completing her tenure with the agency, Generette moved immediately to a position with the Cleveland Orchestra. Mayfield and Jackson moved on to the highly competitive American Symphony Orchestra League's orchestra management fellowship program.

Launched in 1979, the American Symphony Orchestra League's orchestra management fellowship program offers the aspiring orchestra manager a full season that includes a two-week orientation at the league's office in Washington, D.C., three extended residences with professional orchestras of various budget sizes, one week with a small-budget orchestra, and two weeks in New York City learning about publishing, licensing, concert presenting, and artist management.

Profiles

CLARISSA WILHELMINA CUMBO
b. January 15, 1903, Roseau, Dominica, West Indies/d. August 20, 1988, New York City

A student of both the piano and voice, Clarissa Cumbo is better known as the wife of black concert cellist Marion Cumbo and as a patron of the arts. She has been called "head mistress of black involvement in the New York City musical scene." Music journalist Raoul Abdul once referred to her as the woman who "works minor miracles as an impresario" ("The Combos: Living Music History," *New York Amsterdam News*, July 31, 1976, p. D2).

Cumbo's devotion to symphonic music making and the full inclusion of blacks has spanned several decades. She explained her interest and enthusiasm as follows:

> I knew from experience what Marion [her husband] and other musicians of his calibre had gone through. They never had opportunities to play with the major orchestras simply because they were Black [*ibid.*].

Along with others, she organized the short-lived interracial symphony—the State Orchestra (under the direction of David Mendoza) in 1946. She was on the Board of Directors of black conductor Everett Lee's Cosmopolitan Little Symphony, which she assisted in organizing in 1947. She was a member of the Women's Committee of Fifty, which devoted every free minute to fund raising for the orchestra (Mrs. George D. Canon was Chairman of the Board and Women's Committee.)

Her husband Marion was a member of the cello section of the Symphony of the New World (organized in 1965), "the first totally integrated professional Symphony in the United States" ("In Retrospect: The Symphony of the New World," *Black Perspec-*

tive in Music, Vol. 3, No. 3, Fall 1975, pp. 312–330). Clarissa Cumbo assisted in organizing the Friends of the Symphony of the New World and cochaired the Manhattan-Bronx Division. Early in the Symphony of the New World's history, she assumed a more official role, accepting membership on the Board of Directors. Other black women who served on the Board of Directors were Marian Anderson, Leontyne Price, Frances D. Young, Dorothy Hirsch, Evelyn Cunningham, Gayle Dixon, Lucille Dixon, Alberta James, Ruth Ellington, Mrs. F.D. Patterson, and Bess Pruitt.

In 1970, when the Symphony of the New World seemed firmly established, Cumbo (with the help of husband Marion) undertook another project, namely, Triad Presentations. This organization's purpose was "aiding and encouraging black artists by presenting them in community concerts." Twenty years earlier she had organized the Community Friends of Music, committed to the same purpose. But her commitment to the Symphony of the New World remained; she continued to serve on the Board of Directors, and Marion continued to play in the ensemble.

On November 11, 1978, the Eastern Region of the National Association of Negro Musicians honored "the head mistress" with an award. On September 16, 1979, she was presented with the Harold Jackman Memorial Award, "in recognition of her many years of service to musicians and composers." Hundreds of others acknowledged her contributions and expressed their gratitude by continuing the struggle for full musical equality, particularly in America's symphony orchestras.

LOIS TOWLES CAESAR
b. ca. 1913, Texarkana, Arkansas/d. March 18, 1983, San Francisco

Lois Towles was well established as a concert pianist during the 1940s and '50s. She had made her debut at Town Hall in New York and had completed an American and European concert tour. According to *The Negro Yearbook* (1952), she was

> singled out by Arthur Rubinstein as a gifted interpreter and was given [a] fellowship in Master Coaching at his Hollywood studio.

During her four years of residence in Paris she assisted Marcel Ciampi, Professor of Piano at the Paris National Conservatory.

Lois Towles received the B.A. degree from Wiley College and the M.A. and M.F.A. from the University of Iowa and did further study at the Juilliard School of Music, University of California at Berkeley, and Paris National Conservatory. In the late 1940s and early '50s she served as Assistant Professor of Piano at Fisk University and as Artist-in-Residence at Tennessee State University.

Following these experiences (and marriage) Lois Towles Caesar the cultural activist emerged. Settling in San Francisco, she began a career of volunteerism, and at the core of her volunteer work was music. A feature article that appeared in the *San Francisco Examiner and Chronicle* noted that

> [S]he helped establish the Symphony-in-Schools Program, which provided summer and fall workshops for young people with musical interests. In 1958, she co-sponsored the first appearance of Leontyne Price in solo recital at the [San Francisco] Opera House. . . . Through LINKS, a philanthropic organization of black women, Caesar helped develop an art program for youths and a show representing the work of young artists from seven states. She also helped establish an art and scholarship program [Pixa, "Passing on Her Love of Music," March 19, 1978, Scene, p. 2].

And then there were other involvements, including membership on the Mayor's 1) Youth Services Task Force, 2) Criminal Justice Council Executive Committee, and 3) Juvenile Justice Commission (the first female). Wife of a dentist, she once served as president of the Women's Auxiliary of the San Francisco Dental Society. As Lois Caesar once stated, "kids turn me on!" With this concern and outstanding leadership abilities, she was named president of the San Francisco Chapter of WAIF, the international children's organization founded by actress Jane Russell.

Lois Towles Caesar merits recognition here for her many years of service to the San Francisco Symphony. She served as a member of the orchestra's Board of Governors and Symphony Foundation. Elected as director of the Foundation in 1966, she was reelected for a term ending in 1969.

> During her tenure, [she] created an award winner which provided opportunity for families otherwise deprived, to participate in symphony foundation benefits, through her "Start a Symphony Family" plan [*Norfolk Journal and Guide*, September 3, 1966, p. 14].

She was a 1978 recipient of the American Institute of Public Service's Jefferson Award for Community Service. Wrote the *San Francisco Examiner and Chronicle,*

> Lois Towles Caesar has forged a lifetime interest in music with a desire to help disadvantaged youth, and in so doing, has become a strong role model and positive force for community betterment ["The Jefferson Awards," *San Francisco Examiner and Chronicle,* March 19, 1978, Scene, p. 1].

To this let us add that her many years of service to the San Francisco Symphony represented a positive force for symphonic orchestral betterment.

GLADYS RIDDLE HAMPTON
b. 1914 (?), Lehigh, Oklahoma/d. April 29, 1971, New York City

When vibraphonist Lionel Hampton joined Benny Goodman, Teddy Wilson, and Gene Krupa in 1936 to form the small "hot unit" within the larger Benny Goodman Band, he brought along a new wife, Gladys Riddle. She was to be the key to "Mr. Excitement's" financial success. When the two met she was a modiste in Los Angeles, serving such movie stars as Joan Crawford and Rosalind Russell.

According to columnist A. S. "Doc" Young,

> At the end of four years, Hamp left Goodman to form his own jazz band. Gladys Hampton was the manager. And thus, aside from love, was found one of the most unique and profitable marital relationships in the history of show business. Hamp played the music and Gladys managed the money ["Lionel Hampton's Wife Gladys Was Buried in L.A.," *Chicago Defender,* May 15–21, 1971, p. 16].

Gladys was the band's manager and frequently served as its booking agent. She was highly respected for her business acumen. The Lionel Hampton Band ranked at the top of the charts throughout the 1940s and '50s. The combo-sized "Inner Circle," established in 1965, carried on in the Hampton tradition, both from the standpoint of Lionel's musical leadership and Gladys's management.

She died in their New York City office, shortly after returning with the band from a U.S. State Department tour of Spain, Italy, France, Belgium, Germany, Poland and Hungary. Together they had established the Lionel Hampton Enterprises, including Glad Hamp Records, Glad Hamp Music Publishing Co., Swing and Tempo Music Publishing Co., and Lionel Hampton Housing.

A strong civic worker, Gladys was very active in the Lambda Kappa Mu business and professional women's sorority, serving as chair of the group's Music Project Committee. An alumna of Fisk University, she offered assistance to black colleges through the years. Another of her concerns was the Harlem Hospital.

At the time of her death her husband Lionel stated,

> She was the smartest of all the band managers. . . . She knew how to work with the wolves on Broadway. Gladys during the war times and during the '50s, was always good to book $1 million to $2 million a year. She knew how to bargain. She knew how to say "yes" and "no" [*ibid.*].

President Richard Nixon and Governor Nelson Rockefeller sent condolences, and a rosary was conducted by Archbishop Fulton Sheen. At the funeral services Manhattan borough president Percy Sutton represented the City of New York; singers Lou Rawls, and Sarah Vaughan and members of The Lionel Hampton Band performed.

MARJORIE PEEBLES-MEYERS
b. October 5, 1915, New York City

Marjorie Peebles-Meyers, M.D., became a member of the Detroit Symphony Orchestra's Board of Directors in 1973 and, with regret, declined membership on the Board's Executive Committee because of time restraints. She wrote,

> I have been a long-time active member of the Detroit Symphony Orchestra Women's Committee[1] as well. . . . My interest in music (and the arts in general) stems from my exposure in childhood. Born and brought up in one of the world's great cities [New York], I was fortunate to have parents and teachers who exposed me to all a great urban center has to offer. Unfortunately, I am merely an

auditor and not a performer [correspondence with the author, August 17, 1979].

Peebles-Meyers received the B.A. degree from Hunter College and the M.A. degree from Columbia University. Following two years at the Medical School of Howard University she enrolled at the Wayne State University School of Medicine and became the school's first black woman to complete an Internship at the Detroit Receiving Hospital (now Detroit General). She was engaged in private practice in Detroit as an internist for thirty years (1947–77) and in 1977 became Chief Physician for the World Headquarters of the Ford Motor Company.

Peebles-Meyers's professional involvements were extensive, including the National Medical Association, American Medical Association, Wayne County and Michigan State medical societies, Michigan Diabetes Association (now American Diabetes Association—Michigan Affiliate), and the Michigan Heart Association, often filling board and select committee assignments. She was the first woman to serve as a member of the Standing Committee for the Diocese of Michigan of the Episcopal Church and admirably filled her responsibilities as a clergyman's wife (Reverend Canon F. R. Meyers).

Her honors have been numerous, including the Detroit Chamber of Commerce (One of the Top Ten Women Who Work–1968), Michigan Medical Society, and the United Committee on Negro History. She was awarded an Honorary Doctor of Science Degree from Central Michigan University in 1969, Wayne State University School of Medicine's "Distinguished Service Award" in 1971, and was elected to the Hunter College Hall of Fame in 1977.

Civic involvements were always a strong part of Marjorie Peeble-Meyers's daily existence. She rendered service to such organizations as the Detroit YWCA, Urban League, United Community Services, Boys' Republic, Detroit Adventure, United Foundation, Michigan Arts Commission, and the Founders Society of the Detroit Institute of Art, again participating as a board and/or advisory committee member.

MARIETTA (Hall) CEPHAS
b. February 21, 1917, Chicago, Illinois

Cephas joined the music faculty of Virginia State College in 1938 and remained there until 1979. She made her home in the Petersburg/Richmond area following retirement. Known as "Chicago's prodigy," she began the study of piano at a very early age and recalls giving her first public recital at age seven. She was a student of Camilla Lampton, Jesse Merriweather, and the noted black piano composer Florence Price.

Cephas enjoyed the performance of two-piano compositions with Price's famous pianist/composer student Margaret Bonds for a period of "two or three years." She recalls sitting at Price's kitchen table (along with Bonds), "copying parts for the Chicago Symphony Orchestra's performance of Florence Price's symphony." Cephas received her postsecondary training at the University of Illinois, completing the four-year program in three years. At that time, she was performing recitals on radio station WILL three times per week.

During the bicentennial, Cephas was a Virginia representative to the Black Music Colloquim/Competition in Washington, D.C. (Kennedy Center). Since her retirement, Cephas has remained active in the music community. In 1994, she was appointed to the board of directors of the Petersburg (Va.) Symphony Orchestra. The following year (1995), she was appointed to the Petersburg Music Festival's board of directors.

JUANITA WALLACE JACKSON
b. March 7, 1931, Cincinnati, Ohio

Jackson is a born leader with extensive administrative experience. She has held leadership positions in education, the arts, and human services organizations. In late 1995 *Symphony* magazine showed that Jackson had three resumes: one as a teacher/administrator, one as a performing artist, and another as a community volunteer. Educated at the University of Cincinnati and Miami University of Ohio (B.S. and M.Ed. respectively), she was prepared well for the various activities she went on to pursue. Primarily, however, it was the person that made the difference—her interests, capabilities, sensitivities, integrity, and credibility.

Jackson began teaching in 1955. Her specialties were reading and early childhood education, which she shared with students, faculty, and staff from kindergarten through graduate school.

Jackson remains a consultant in early childhood education. Between 1988 and 1990 she served as director of business maintenance organization (BMO) for the State University of New York at Albany. BMO is one of nine centers throughout the state that were established to provide technical assistance and other services to women and minority entrepreneurs. A prolific writer, Jackson has contributed articles to various publications, including American Association of University Women's official publications, American Symphony Orchestra League's official publications, and *Grade Teacher*. She has presented papers for the American Association of University Women, the American Symphony Orchestra League, and various universities and churches.

A contralto, Jackson studied voice with the late Louis John Johnen. She performed primarily as an oratorio singer: soloist in Handel's *Messiah*, Vivaldi's *Gloria*, Haydn's *Mass in Time of War*, and Mozart's *Coronation Mass*. On one occasion she sang the lead role in *Carmen* with a Central State University production. Recitalist throughout the Midwest, she was in summer stock with the Kenley Players in Dayton, Ohio. She has appeared as soloist with the Vienna Choral Society and is a member of the Chautauqua Choir in Chautauqua, New York. She still finds time to study and coach with Mary Ann Stabile Cooper in McLean, Virginia.

Jackson understands the arts and knows their need for continuous support. Her volunteerism began when she worked with a subscription campaign for the Cincinnati Opera Guild and the Women's Committee of the Cincinnati Symphony. While she and her family (an attorney husband and two children) were living in Albany, New York, she was a board member of the St. Cecilia Chamber Orchestra and the Albany Symphony. Before long, she became president of the Albany Symphony Orchestra's Women's Committee, also known as Vanguard.

Under her leadership, which includes a special talent for motivating others, the level of support provided by Vanguard rose from $3,000 to $30,000. She was soon selected to join the American Symphony Orchestra League's Volunteer Council and served for seven years. She successfully fulfilled various assignments: vice president of the Council for Regional Workshops, vice president and chairman for the National Conference, and chairman of the nominating committee. The name Jacqueline Jackson was known at the national level of the symphony orchestra universe.

The Jackson family relocated to the D.C. area in 1990. Before long, she was asked to join the board of the McLean Orchestra and the Women's Committee of the National Symphony Orchestra in the nation's capital. In June 1995 Jackson assumed the presidency of the Women's Committee of the National, for a two-year term. The "1,000-member organization . . . biannually raises more than a million dollars" for the orchestra. She also sits on the orchestra's board of directors and the executive committee. Another responsibility is her membership on the board of visitors, School of Music, University of Maryland, College Park. Her insights contributed to the work of the American Symphony Orchestra League. She participated in the league's national task force issues forum on cultural diversity, 1993 ("The American Orchestra: An Initiative for Change") and the advisory committee of the league's Music Assistance Fund.

Jackson's varied accomplishments have earned awards and honors. The mayor of Albany, New York, declared July 10, 1990, "Juanita Wallace Jackson Day." Jackson has listings in *Who's Who in Women Executives* (1989–90) and *Who's Who in American Education* (1993–94). She has received the Minority Business Council's Extra-Mile Award and the National Academy of School Executives of the American Association of School Administrators' Certificate of Achievement. Most recently, Jackson was initiated into Sigma Alpha Iota as a Friend of the Arts. (See Chester Lane, "Credibility and Support, *Symphony*, November/December 1995, pp. 66–67; additional information from telephone conversation with author, July 3, 1996.)

ANNA DIGGS TAYLOR
b. December 9, 1932, Washington, D.C.

Taylor is a judge in the U.S. District Court, Eastern District of Michigan. She came to her judgeship in 1979. Previous assignments included Supervising Assistant, Corporation Counsel, City of Detroit, Law Department, 1975–79; partner in the law firm of Zwerdling, Maurer, Diggs, and Papp, 1970–75; Assistant U.S. Attorney, 1966; Assistant Wayne County Prosecutor, 1961–62; and attorney for Office of Solicitor, U.S. Department of Labor, Washington, D.C., 1957–60. Between 1972 and 1976, Taylor was on the faculty of the Wayne State University School of Labor and Industrial Relations and the Wayne State law school.

A graduate of the Northfield School for Girls in East Northfield, Massachusetts (1950), she received a bachelor's degree from Barnard College of Columbia University (1954) and a law degree from Yale Law School (1957). Her volunteer activities include serving as a trustee for the Detroit Receiving Hospital, membership on the Metropolitan Detroit Health Council, membership on the Board of Directors, United Foundation, and serving as a trustee for the Detroit Symphony Orchestra Hall. Her background and experience allow her to make a significant contribution to the board.

EILEEN (Tate) CLINE
b. June 25, 1935, Chicago, Illinois

Cline is presently a university fellow in arts policy at the Johns Hopkins University Institute for Policy Studies and immediate past dean of the Conservatory, Peabody Institute, The Johns Hopkins University (1983–95). Prior to that, she served as associate dean of the Peabody Conservatory of Music.

Cline received a liberal arts certificate from the University of Chicago in 1952, the B.Mus. in piano performance and the B.Mus.Ed. in vocal music education from Oberlin Conservatory in 1956. The same year, she was inducted into Pi Kappa Lambda (the national honorary music society). She earned the M.Mus. in piano performance from the University of Colorado in 1960 and the D.Mus.Ed. from Indiana University in 1985. Cline is a student of Geneva C. Robinson, Axel Skjevne, Rudolph Ganz, and Storm Bull. Always seeking growth and development, Cline has pursued postdoctoral involvements, including the Aspen Institute Executive Seminar, Harvard University Institute for Educational Management, and Johns Hopkins University Fellow Program for Organizational Development.

Cline has amassed a wealth of experience. She served as executive director of the Neighborhood Music School in New Haven, Connecticut (1980–82), coordinator of continuing education in piano at the University of Colorado (1960–75), and founder/director of the Boulder Children's Choir (1972–75). Between 1959 and 1975 she operated an independent community piano studio.

The many boards and committees she has served on include the Kenan Institute for the Arts; Harvard University John F. Kennedy School of Government, advisory board; community outreach/music/education committees, Baltimore Symphony; board of directors of the National Guild of Community Schools of the Arts and the Chamber Music Society of Baltimore; and International Advisory Council, Van Cliburn International Piano Competition and Metropolitan Opera Regional Auditions. Between 1981 and 1987 she was on the board of trustees of Oberlin College.

Cline has been a member of several Commissions on Higher Education evaluation teams and a competition judge/clinician for music schools and for regional and state auditions in Colorado, Connecticut, Maryland, Massachusetts, and Wyoming. She was a participant at the National Association of Schools of Music invitational seminar on minority access to music study (1994). She has served on many National Endowment for the Arts panels, as well as those of the New Jersey State Council on the Arts and the Massachusetts Cultural Council. Between 1983 and 1987, she was a member of the college theory test development committee for the Educational Testing Service.

Cline is a popular lecturer. Her keynote presentation at the Chicago Symphony Orchestra symposium, in collaboration with the University of Chicago and the American Symphony Orchestra League in 1991 ("Training Future Orchestra Musicians") was especially memorable, as were her preconcert lectures for the Baltimore Symphony (1994–96). Her scholarly writings have appeared in National Association of Schools of Music and College Music Society publications, *The American Music Teacher,* and the *American Suzuki Journal.* Articles written by her have also appeared in *The Baltimore Sun* and *The Boulder* [Colorado] *Camera.*

In 1989 Eileen Cline became the first "woman of color" to sit on the board of directors of the American Symphony Orchestra League. In 1995, she was elevated to the league's executive committee. She participated in the league's national task force, which addressed the issue "the orchestra as music educator" (*The American Orchestra: An Initiative for Change*) in 1992. She also participated in the New World Symphony Orchestra's invitational conference, "Developing Cultural Diversity in the New World Symphony" in 1994 (Miami, Florida). She was a panelist for the Gateways Festival of Blacks in Classical Music in 1993 (Winston-Salem, North Carolina).

Cline's achievements have been recognized with the Award for Distinguished Service to Music, National Black Music Caucus (1995), the Torchbearer Award for Distinguished Service, Coalition of 100 Black Women (1991), Peabody Student Council Faculty and Administrative Award for Outstanding Contribution to the Peabody Community (1986), and the Outstanding Woman Award, National Executive Club, Washington, D.C. (1984). Her eleven-page resume concludes with recreational activities that she enjoys: backpacking, ski touring, rock climbing, downhill skiing, cycling, tennis, folk dancing, field hockey, and basketball.

MARY FRANCES EARLY
b. June 14, 1936, Atlanta, Georgia

Early's life has been devoted to music education. She taught in the Atlanta public schools between 1957 and 1983. She served as coordinator of music for the Atlanta public schools from 1984 to 1994. Early is currently an adjunct professor at Morehouse and Spelman Colleges and is completing doctoral work in educational administration at Clark Atlanta University. She received the B.A. in music education from Clark College (1957), the M.M.E. in music education from the University of Georgia (1962; she was the first African-American to receive a degree from this institution), and the Ed.S. in music education from the University of Georgia (1967).

Early's many professional experiences and involvements include member-at-large, Georgia Music Education Association's board of directors (1975–91); member of the editorial committee of the national *Music Educators Journal* (1986–90); member of the board of directors of the National Black Music Caucus (1990–95); and black consultant for Macmillan's *Music and You* series (1985–90). Her expertise has been utilized by the National Endowment for the Arts, the Fulton County Arts Council, the Bureau of Cultural Affairs, the South Carolina Arts Commission, and the Governor's Honors Committee (auditioner, 1984–94). Early is a frequent presenter at various national and regional conferences.

Early, as a member of the orchestra's board of directors, is a voice for the black community with the Atlanta Symphony Orchestra. She also serves as chairperson for the orchestra's Action Committee for Development of Black Audiences and lectures for the orchestra's concert series. She is also a member of the Chicago Symphony Orchestra's national advisory council on minority recruiting.

ARMENTA ADAMS HUMMINGS
b. June 27, 1936, Cleveland, Ohio

Armenta Adams-Hummings made her artistic mark as a concert pianist, soloing with l'Orchestre de la Suisse Romande, the Cleveland Symphony Orchestra, North Carolina Symphony Orchestra, The Greensboro Symphony Orchestra, The Raleigh Symphony Orchestra, the Symphony of the New World, and the Pierre Monteux Festival Orchestra. She had a distinguished career as a concert artist that included performances at Town Hall (New York City), West Africa's Independence Ceremony in Sierra Leone, and the World Festival of Negro Arts in Dakar, Senegal (1966). She has also given performances in Australia, India, Pakistan, and various European and African countries. She was cited by the U.S. State Department for her contributions to American foreign relations.

Adams Hummings's parents were church musicians who played violin and piano, and her brother is the internationally acclaimed violinist Elwyn Adams. She has been featured in the *New York Times, Washington Post, Triad Style* (Greensboro, N.C.), *Musical America, Ebony, Jet,* and *Essence.* She (and her project) were recently featured in the black publication *about . . . time* (December 1995) as founder and artistic director of the Gateways Music Festival, based at the Eastman School of Music in Rochester, New York. She serves as distinguished community mentor for the festival, teaching young people from urban Rochester to play classical music. The first two Gateways festivals were held in Winston-Salem, where she resided. Sponsored by the Eastman school, the festival included orchestras of various sizes. The group of seventy-five black artists worked under the batons of Awadagin Pratt (also the concert soloist), Alfred Duckett, and Michael Morgan (also the music coordinator). Said Adams-Hummings, "The budget put the cap on 75, but for every performer who was asked to participate, there is a replacement" (Georgia East, "Gateways Music Festival: Hitting All the Right Notes," *about . . . time,* December 1995, p. 7).

"The idea for the festival sparked when she decided to create a supportive atmosphere and community for her first son, Amadi Hummings" (*ibid.*). Amadi is a gifted violist who now teaches at Old Dominion University in Virginia. Adams-Hummings's mission is "to increase the visibility of African-American classical musicians, to heighten public awareness of their musical contributions, and to specifically encourage young African Americans to study and seek out careers in the field of classical music" (*ibid.*).

She entered the preparatory division of the New England Conservatory of Music at age four, studying with Jeannette Giguere. At age sixteen, she enrolled at the Juilliard School of Music, where she studied with Sascha Gorodnitzki. She earned the B.S. and M.S. degrees from Juilliard.

Adams-Hummings retired from the concert stage in order to rear her family. During this time the gifted and visionary musician gave private lessons. She also taught at the North Carolina School of the Arts and North Carolina A&T University, having previously taught at the Harlem School of the Arts and the Juilliard School of Music's preparatory department. She has returned to the concert stage, and the orchestra world is indeed grateful for her creating the Gateways Music Festival. The festival will continue on a biannual basis, with presentations in various cities.

GWENDOLYN COCHRAN HADDEN
b. April 18, 1943, Atlanta, Georgia

Atlanta-born Hadden currently resides in Gloucester, Massachusetts. She is president and owner of Cochran Hadden Royston Associates, consultant to public and private sector clients on matters of equal opportunity, affirmative action, human rights, cultural diversity, management, and organizational development. Hadden founded the company in 1986, whose list of illustrious clients includes Northeastern University, the Association of Performing Arts Presenters, the Atlanta Symphony, the Alabama Shakespeare Festival, and the Seattle Repertory Theatre.

Hadden received the Bachelor of Arts degree from Morris Brown College in Atlanta, Georgia (1965), majoring in music, and attended Wellesley College as an exchange student. She has completed her course work for a master's degree in psychology from

Goddard College in Vermont. Prior to forming her own company, she was associate director for personnel administration, Greater Boston Legal Services in Boston, Massachusetts (1980–83), and director of civil rights for the Boston Housing Authority (1983–86).

Hadden served on the board of overseers of the Boston Symphony for five years (1991–96) and spent the final year as vice chairperson. She was a member of the board of directors of the American Symphony Orchestra League in Washington, D.C., from 1993 to 1995. She was secretary of the executive committee from 1994 to 1995. In 1995 she joined the Chorus North Shore in Rockport, Massachusetts, becoming a board member at the same time. Hadden also joined the Yale University Graduate School of Drama as a visiting professor in 1995.

HANSONIA (LaVerne) CALDWELL
b. November 22, 1944, Washington, D.C.

Though born in Washington, D.C., Caldwell spent her formative years in Baltimore, Maryland. There she studied piano with the popular black pedagogue Ada Killian Jenkins. Caldwell has been making education inroads at California State University at Dominguez Hills since 1972, when she joined the faculty as an assistant professor of music and taught in the music department, the African-American studies program, and the interdisciplinary humanities external degree program.

Caldwell earned a bachelor's degree in musicology from Boston University, and a master's degree and a doctorate from the University of Southern California. She is the author of *African-American Music, A Chronology: 1619–1995*. A graduate of the Institute for Educational Management at the Harvard University Graduate School of Education, Caldwell was prepared to assume many other responsibilities at Cal State Dominguez Hills: dean of graduate studies and research, executive director of the National Council for Black Studies, interim affirmative action coordinator, and for twelve years, dean of humanities and fine arts.

Caldwell is founding conductor of the Dominguez Hills Jubilee Choir and founding director of the annual Jubilee Creative Arts summer camp. A pianist, she has appeared as soloist with her university's chamber orchestra, the Compton Community Orchestra, and the Carson/Dominguez Symphony Orchestra. She has been a review panelist for the California and Arizona Arts Councils, the city of Los Angeles's cultural affairs department, and the National Endowment for the Arts. Caldwell is also an accreditation evaluator for the Western Association of Schools and Colleges.

Her activities include many significant community connections. She serves on the advancement committee of the Los Angeles Music Center, the board of directors of the Public Corporation for the Arts (the Long Beach Regional Arts Council), and the board of directors of the BEEM Foundation for the Advancement of Music (Black Experiences Expressed through Music). She is a member of the fiftieth anniversary/jubilee planning committee for the Southeast Symphony Association and a guest lecturer/evaluator for young audiences.

Caldwell is a member (and former chairperson) of the Community Advisory Committee of the Los Angeles Philharmonic Association. This committee established the Fellowship for Excellence in Diversity program, "one step in a projected comprehensive program whose purpose will be to identify, nurture and support talented minority instrumentalists and to encourage their interest in pursuing symphonic careers." She is currently vice president of the board of directors of the Los Angeles Philharmonic Association and a member of its educational advisory committee. Caldwell is also a member of LINKS, Inc., a national service organization, and the Alpha Kappa Alpha sorority, where she also conducts the AKA chorus and codirects the annual Alpha Kappa Alpha Martin Luther King commemorative concert.

JACKIE LaMONTE JOHNSON BANKS
b. August 25, 1945, Fort Worth, Texas

To have good black representation at a Fort Worth Symphony Orchestra concert was a source of great satisfaction for Jackie Banks. In less than a year following her affiliation with the orchestra the *Texas Times* wrote,

> Part of that satisfaction comes from the mere fact that there are blacks in the audience and some of it comes from knowing that she

is responsible for putting them there ["Jackie Banks: Working to Bring People and Music Together," April 5, 1979].

Banks began working with the Fort Worth Symphony in June 1978. She progressed from receptionist to office secretary to personal secretary to the general manager. Assigned to special projects, primarily of an orchestra-outreach nature, she soon merited the title of administrative assistant.

The mother of four listed as her duties: 1) writing grant proposals; 2) writing a monthly news article for three black local newspapers, updating the community on blacks in the area of symphonic music; 3) handling the orchestra's Lollipop Series (concerts for children between three and eight years); 4) enhancing group sales; and 5) working with the black community (centers, newspapers, churches, and organizations).

Many exciting things happened in Fort Worth during the 1978–79 season. Under Banks's initiative the Fort Worth Symphony and Jaycees brought over a thousand "black, brown and white disadvantaged children" from the triethnic area of North Side to Fort Worth's Convention Center Theater for a concert featuring the Dallas Cowboys' defensive tackle Jethro Pugh as narrator (February 1979). Providing the orchestra with its first opportunity to go into the black community to play a concert, the ensemble (which had one black member) offered a "Symphony Goes Disco" Concert (May 1979). Black conductor Dingwall Fleary of Washington, D.C., was on the podium, and the Miller Brewing Company and the black-oriented radio station KNOK sponsored the event.

Banks cleverly brought in the predominantly black Mandinkas, an African Bandits Motorcycle Club, to assist local police with crowd control at the May 1979 park event. According to journalist John Zacharias,

> For many years there has been a tendency among major symphony orchestras to broaden their appeal. . . . For a symphony such as the Fort Worth Symphony to attempt to reach, in particular the black population of the city, displays an effort that shows more than just an interest in expanding their appeal. . . . The story behind the story would have to be about one of the Administrative Assistants of the Symphony Association. A young woman named Jackie Banks . . . conceived the idea. . . . Says Ms. Banks, "We want to project to black

kids that there is no limit and if they really like music, there is a place for them" [Ft. Worth Symphony Gets Down with Disco," *Texas Nickelodeon,* June 1979].

In a very short period Jackie Banks, a graduate of Tarrant County Junior College (and a student at the University of Texas) proved to be a tremendous asset to both the Fort Worth Symphony Orchestra and the total community. The future for Jackie Banks in the area of Arts Administration seemed exceptionally promising.

PATRICIA ("Pat") UPSHAW
b. June 24, 1951, Columbus, Georgia

Pat Upshaw assumed her duties as assistant manager of the Atlanta Symphony in December 1978. The position carried with it two subtitles: Manager of Symphony Hall and Manager of the Atlanta Symphony Youth Orchestra. The former meant: 1) bringing in as much income as possible by renting the hall when not being used by the Symphony; 2) handling contract negotiations for hall rentals; 3) hiring all house personnel, 4) controlling the master calendar of all events in the hall; and 5) serving as House Manager for all events sponsored by the Atlanta Symphony Orchestra. As Manager of the Atlanta Symphony Youth Orchestra, Upshaw 1) recruited the membership; 2) coordinated auditions, concerts, rehearsals, and special events; 3) set up and carried out policy and procedures; 4) scheduled all rehearsals and concerts; 5) served as an ex-officio member of the orchestra's Education Committee and Parents Association; and 6) handled all of the orchestra's public relations (correspondence with the author, August 27, 1979). These were heavy responsibilities, but Pat Upshaw admirably met the assignment.

She received the B.A. degree from Albany State College and the M.A. degree from Bowling Green State University. At both institutions Upshaw majored in Speech and Theater Communications. Extracurricular activities included the band, chorus, dramatics club, and cheerleaders (captain). At Bowling Green she served as Director and Coordinator of the Black Theater and was that Institution's first black female to receive the M.A. in theater.

Postgraduate activities included courses in property management, accounting, and marketing and involvements with Richard Hunter's Acting Ensemble, Odyssey Theatrical Productions, and the Miss Black Georgia Pageant (dramatic coach). Prior to joining the Atlanta Symphony Orchestra's management team Upshaw worked as Manager Trainee for Sears Roebuck and Company (Louisville), Area Supervisor for the Georgia State Labor Department (Atlanta), and Property Manager for Management Enterprises (Atlanta).

MYRAN PARKER-BRASS
b. September 20, 1953, East Chicago, Indiana

Parker-Brass joined the staff of the Boston Symphony Orchestra in 1992. She holds the powerful position of director of education. For the last twenty years, she has worked extensively with teachers to develop integrated curricula using music and to develop and provide arts education opportunities at many levels.

As director of education, she develops educational programs for children and adults. These programs include the Youth and Family Concert series, school music education programs, professional development workshops for teachers, adult preconcert discussions and workshops, community concerts and educational programs, and an eight-week residential arts program at Tanglewood (Lenox, Mass.).

Parker-Brass grew up in Chicago, Illinois. She received a Bachelor of Arts degree from the University of Illinois/Chicago Circle (1975) and a Master of Fine Arts degree from Governors State University, University Park, Illinois (1977). Her area of concentration for both degrees was music performance. She continues to work as a professional musician (voice) in classical, jazz, and gospel idioms, giving concerts in the United States and abroad and engaging in recording and commercial adventures.

She has work experience in the area of music education: she taught at St. Thaddeus School, Chicago, Illinois (1976–77); she chaired the vocal music department for the American Youth Music and Arts Program, Chicago, Illinois (1980–85); she taught adult education at the Chicago City Colleges, Chicago, Illinois (1981–82); she was director of curriculum/elementary programs at Chicago Teachers Center—Northeastern Illinois University, Chicago, Illinois (1986–88) and education manager for the Massachusetts Cultural Council, Boston, Massachusetts (1990–92). These experiences richly prepared Parker-Brass for her current position.

She has become a popular panel participant and a presenter at professional meetings: American Symphony Orchestra League ("Building Educational Partnerships"); Rhode Island State Council on the Arts (review panelist, arts education) and panel moderator (Arts Education and Cultural Diversity conference); and University of Massachusetts at Boston, Field Center for Teaching and Learning. Her publications include *Educational Resources and Curriculum Materials Guide* for the Massachusetts Cultural Council, *Marsalis on Music*, five educational music programs for young people, 1994 (Parker-Brass served as adviser for the series, which aired on PBS stations in the United States and abroad), and *A Tribute to Roland Hayes*, a educational video and curriculum materials for classroom teachers, 1995. These materials are currently being used in two hundred Massachusetts schools, the Columbia College Black Music Research Library, and the Georgia Music Hall of Fame.

LAUREN (Marie) GENERETTE (Floyd)
b. March 22, 1955, Cleveland, Ohio

Generette, who is now the wife of an attorney and mother of two young children, has been associated with music most of her life. She studied flute with Joseph Juhos, Harold Jones, Cathy Course, and Norman Brentley.

She received a Bachelor of Music Education degree from Howard University in 1977. She then accepted a teaching position in the Atlanta public school system. In 1986 Generette received an MBA degree from the State University of New York at Binghamton and became an arts management fellow in the music program of the National Endowment for the Arts.

Generette was instantly hired as assistant director of educational activities and manager of the youth orchestra for the Cleveland Orchestra. As assistant director of educational activities, her duties included program development for preschool through adult educational outreach, concert production and design, and development of student and teacher curriculum materials. She held this position from 1986 to 1993.

Her primary position with the Cleveland Orchestra was as manager of the youth orchestra. Founded in 1986, the orchestra was a first for the Cleveland. Lauren Generette was its first manager and held that position for a decade (1986–96). Consisting of youth between the ages of twelve and twenty, the orchestra is regarded as the artistically superior youth orchestra in the northeast Ohio region (perhaps in the nation). Generette's managerial responsibilities included budgeting, purchasing, short- and long-range planning, library management, recruitment, inner institutional coordination and communication, design and development of promotional materials, concert production, and program editing.

Generette's other professional activities have included board member and officer of the American Symphony Orchestra League's youth orchestra division; board member, Cleveland Music School Settlement; member of the national advisory council for diversity of the Chicago Civic Orchestra; and grant panelist, National Endowment for the Arts and the Ohio Arts Council. Her talents and skills have been recognized in *Who's Who among Students in American Colleges and Universities* (1986) and *Outstanding Young Women of America* (1986). Howard University honored her with its Distinguished Alumni Award (1989).

JENNIFER (Camille) JACKSON
b. November 14, 1964, Atlanta, Georgia

Jackson holds three degrees: a Bachelor of Music in vocal performance (1988) from Oberlin Conservatory and a Bachelor of Arts in sociology (1989) from Oberlin College as well as a Master of Arts in arts administration from Indiana University (1993). Her performing medias were violin, piano, and voice. She appeared in various theater and operatic roles in high school, at Oberlin Conservatory, and at Indiana University. During the summer of 1988, she served as a faculty member at the Oberlin Theatre Institute (coteaching a voice class), having previously given private voice lessons to secondary students (1987–89).

While at Indiana University, Jackson held many interesting posts: assistant to the director, office of music development; booking agent/road manager, Afro-American Choral Ensemble; and booking agent for the Afro-American Arts Institute. She spent a semester in Washington, D.C., as an arts administration fellow and researcher in the music program of the National Endowment for the Arts.

Following a strenuous interview, Jackson was selected to participate in the American Symphony Orchestra League's orchestra management program. Her assignment was four months each with the following: Charlotte, Pittsburgh, and Boston Symphony Orchestras. She participated fully in all aspects of their operations. Between this experience and her current assignment, Jackson worked as coordinator of community programs at the 651 Arts Center at the Brooklyn Academy of Music's Majestic Theater in Brooklyn, New York.

Jackson has been director of development with the Floating Hospital in New York City since February 1996. She came to the position with a wealth of experience. Though the performing arts are not a meaningful part of the institution, the position allows her to utilize all past experiences. As director of development, she implements, oversees, and evaluates development activities and special events; prepares development plans and strategies; creates systems and procedures and maintains all record keeping; and engages in extensive research.

CAROL PORTER
b. April 23, 1967, Yazoo City, Mississippi

A preacher's kid, Porter is the oldest of three children. The family's other musician is her sister, who conducts a piano studio in Meridian, Mississippi, and shares teaching at a studio (CAPO) conducted by sister Carol (also in Meridian). Carol Porter's principal job is in Jackson, the state's capital. She is employed as administrative coordinator of the Mississippi Symphony Orchestra.

Porter's undergraduate training (piano performance) was received at the University of Southern Mississippi in Hattiesburg (1989, B.Mus.). While in residence, she received the Mu Phi Epsilon Junior Piano Achievement Award, the Tonya Chaney Memorial Music Scholarship. She won first place in the Mississippi Music Teachers Association's Piano Award. In 1991 she was inducted into Gamma Beta Phi Honor Society. She participated in a musician exchange in 1992.

Porter performs in all styles—classical, jazz, gospel, pop,

boogie woogie, and new age—and she is capable of teaching all styles. While at the University of Southern Mississippi (as a student and beyond), Porter was an accompanist for the university's Opera Theater and worked as accompanying music assistant for the Hattiesburg Civic Light Opera. She received the M.A. degree in arts administration from Columbia University Teachers College in 1993. Through Columbia University she worked with programs for the Community School of Music and Arts in Mountain View, California.

She came to the Mississippi Symphony well prepared. In New York City she engaged in volunteer work for the Association of Performing Arts Presenters (APAP); served as office assistant in the payroll and arts administration departments at Columbia University; and worked as a marketing intern in the marketing and public relations department of the New York Philharmonic (in preparing for the orchestra's 150th anniversary celebration). For a relatively brief period in 1993 Porter worked as a program director, managing state and federal grants for the Mississippi Arts Commission. She also promoted community arts programs at local arts councils throughout the state.

Expanding her horizons, Porter was a contract worker for public radio in Mississippi, reporting local news and announcing statewide events during weekend and morning national programming. She worked briefly for Circum-Arts Foundation, as director of membership services, providing assistance to performing and visual artists. In addition to these activities, she taught adults and children reading music and playing by ear methods at a local music store in Jackson. Even during college breaks, Porter organized and coordinated music and creative arts activities for the Girl Scouts and church youth.

ALISA MAYFIELD-SMALLWOOD
b. September 21, 1968, Buffalo, New York

Currently director of marketing and development with the Peoria (Ill.) Symphony Orchestra, Mayfield-Smallwood has always worked in the orchestral field. Her work with the Peoria Symphony began in 1995. Since her arrival, she has directed a $1 million endowment campaign in celebration of the orchestra's centennial season, has increased single ticket sales by more than

3 percent, and has generated a 40-percent increase in grant moneys from businesses and foundations. Mayfield-Smallwood is also a member of the Grants Distribution Committee of the Women's Fund of the Peoria Area Community Foundation. A review of her resume indicates that her orchestral experiences fall into three broad categories: management and program administration, operational administration, and artistic administration.

Though born in Buffalo, New York, she spent her formative years in Durham, North Carolina. She received her academic training at North Carolina Central University (B.A., music, 1989) and Indiana University (M.Mus., music theory, 1992). Her performing instrument is the violin. As an undergraduate, she interned with the North Carolina Symphony. Prior to completing the master's degree, she was selected to be an arts administration fellow with the music program of the National Endowment for the Arts (Washington, D.C., 1991). While awaiting notification of selection for another exciting program, she worked as assistant to the manager of the Durham Symphony Orchestra.

The word finally came that she had been selected to participate in the American Symphony Orchestra League's orchestra management fellowship program (1992–93). She was assigned to the Atlanta, Long Beach, and Chicago Symphony Orchestras. Her duties with the three orchestras included directing a search for one orchestra's director of choruses, directing another orchestra's search for an associate conductor, handling housing and travel documents for one orchestra's European tour, preparing and executing annual budgets for volunteer ensembles of an orchestra, and revitalizing another's youth orchestra (devising a minority recruitment plan and new audition requirements). The first assignment she found in the real job market was as manager of volunteer ensembles for the Charlotte Symphony Orchestra.

Notes

1. According to Dr. Peebles-Meyers, three black women in particular have been active on the Detroit Symphony Orchestra Women's Committee: Dorothy Hollaway, Mary Agnes Davis, and Inez Wright-King. The author recognized the name of black City Councilwoman Erma Henderson, also a member of the orchestra's Board of Directors.

2. Since September 1998, Early has served as acting head of the department of music at Clark-Atlanta University.

Appendix

Letter to Black Women Orchestra Players and Leaders

For Second Edition

Dear

As the enclosed will indicate, *Black Women in American Bands and Orchestras* was released in 1981 by Scarecrow Press. It was selected as one of the most Outstanding Academic Publications of 1981 by *Choice* (American Library Association). Scarecrow will now release (15 years later) an enlarged, revised edition.

There were several significant omissions; several new faces are on the scene; many profiles are in need of updating. I have also enclosed the original "survey instrument." Will you be kind enough to complete the survey instrument and add anything that will strengthen your profile. A black and white glossy photograph would be appreciated.

Please let me hear from you soon.

Sincerely yours,
D. Antoinette Handy

For Original Publication

20224 Loyal Avenue
Ettrick, Virginia 23803

Dear

By way of introduction, my name is D. Antoinette Handy. I have been a professional flutist for some twenty-odd years. For more details, I refer you to the enclosed.

All criticism of others terminated, I began writing (while continuing to play, of course) several years ago. I am now in the process of completing my most ambitious writing project to date; namely, a documentary of BLACK WOMEN IN AMERICAN OR-

CHESTRAS. "Orchestra" is here defined as "an instrumental ensemble"—nothing more and nothing less. (I tend to oppose artistic dichotomies.)

WON'T YOU PLEASE ASSIST ME BY COMPLETING THE ENCLOSED QUESTIONNAIRE (stamped envelope enclosed), AS SOON AS POSSIBLE? Though many hours have and continue to be spent in the library, much of the data that I desire is not to be found there. It is in your personal files, head, and scrapbooks.

PLEASE FEEL FREE TO "TELL IT ALL." GO EGO-TRIPPING IF YOU SO DESIRE. Knowledge of your contribution to the world of music is essential, if for no other reason than our young women need models.

I would appreciate any and all assistance. I await your response.

Most sincerely yours,
D. Antoinette Handy

P.S. Feel free to enclose brochures, clippings, reviews, etc. *AND* a photograph if available.

Survey Instrument: Black Women Orchestra Players and Leaders

Full Name _____

Professional Name _____

Place of Birth _____

Family Data (parents, children, brothers, sisters—indicating if any others pursued careers in music)

_____

_____ (Continue on reverse side)

Present Address _____

_____ Zip _____

Marital Status _____ Children (?) _____

Telephone Number _____

Date of Birth _____

Instrument (primary) _____

Education (including degrees, certificates, diplomas)

_____

_____ (Continue on reverse side)

Student of (Teachers) _____

_____

Honors/Awards (including publications in which you have been cited). _____

Orchestras (groups) with Which You Have Played (indicate whether on a substitute or permanent basis)

_____ (Continue on reverse side)

Additional Professional Involvements

_____ (Continue on reverse side)

Additional Activities Worth Noting _____

_____

Current Musical Activities _____

_____

_____ (Continue on reverse side)

Musical Influences _____

Any "MESSAGES" You Would Like Gotten Across? Words of Wisdom? Advise?

_____

OTHER BLACK AMERICAN FEMALE INSTRUMENTALISTS THAT HAVE PLAYED OR ARE PLAYING WITH ORCHESTRAS (Groups) THAT I SHOULD KNOW ABOUT: (Please give current address or lead(s) as to how she (they) can be contacted. If deceased, please provide any and all data that you might have and/or a research source.)

Bibliography

Books

Allen, Walter C. *Hendersonia: The Music of Fletcher Henderson and His Musicians.* 2d printing. Highland Park, N.J.: Allen, 1974.

Bekker, Paul. *The Story of the Orchestra.* New York: Norton, 1936.

Blesh, Rudi. *Shining Trumpets: A History of Jazz.* New York: Knopf, 1946.

———, and Janis, Harriet. *They All Played Ragtime.* 4th ed. New York: Oak, 1971.

Bradford, Perry. *Born with the Blues: Perry Bradford's Own Story.* Westport, Conn.: Hyperion, 1973.

Buerkle, Jack V., and Barker, Danny. *Bourbon Street Black.* New York: Oxford University Press, 1973.

Calloway, Cab, and Rollins, Bryant. *Of Minnie the Moocher and Me.* New York: Crowell, 1976.

Carse, Adam. *The Orchestra.* New York: Chanticleer, 1949.

Charters, Samuel Barclay, and Kundstadt. *Jazz: A History of the New York Scene.* New York: Doubleday, 1962.

———. *Jazz: New Orleans, 1885–1963.* Rev. ed. New York: Oak, 1963.

Chilton, John. *Who's Who of Jazz: Storyville to Swing Street.* London: Bloomsbury Book Shop, 1970.

Cole, Bill. *John Coltrane.* New York: Schirmer, 1976.

Cuney-Hare, Maud. *Negro Musicians and Their Music.* Washington, D.C.: The Associated Publishers, 1936.

Dahl, Linda. *Stormy Weather: The Music and Lives of a Century of Jazzwomen.* New York: Pantheon Books, 1984.

Dance, Stanley. *The World of Earl Hines.* New York: Scribner's, 1977.

———. *The World of Swing.* New York: Scribner's, 1974.

Delauney, Charles. *New Hot Discography: The Standard Dictionary of Recorded Jazz.* New York: Criterion, 1963.

De Toledano, Ralph, ed. *Frontiers of Jazz.* 2d ed. New York: Ungar, 1962.

Driggs, Frank. *Women in Jazz: A Survey.* New York: Stash Records, 1977.

Ellington, Edward Kennedy. *Music Is My Mistress.* Garden City, N.Y.: Doubleday, 1973.

Ewen, David. *Music Comes to America.* New York: Crowell, 1942.

Farmer, Henry George. *The Rise and Development of Military Music*. London: Reeves, 1912.

Feather, Leonard G. *The Book of Jazz: A Guide to the Entire Field*. New York: Horizon, 1965.

————, and Gitler, Ira. *The Encyclopedia of Jazz in the Seventies*. New York: Horizon, 1976.

————. *The Encyclopedia of Jazz in the Sixties*. New York: Horizon, 1967.

————. *The New Edition of the Encyclopedia of Jazz*. New York: Horizon, 1960.

Fernett, Gene. *Swing Out: Great Negro Dance Bands*. Midland, Mich.: Pendell, 1970.

Fletcher, Tom. *The Tom Fletcher Story: 100 Years of the Negro in Show Business*. New York: Burdge, 1954.

Gillis, Frank J., and Miner, John W., eds. *Oh, Didn't He Ramble* (The Life Story of Lee Collins as Told to Mary Collins). Urbana: University of Illinois Press, 1974.

Goffin, Robert. *Jazz from the Congo to the Metropolitan*. New York: Doubleday, Doran, 1944.

Goldman, Richard Franko. *The Wind Band*. Boston: Allyn and Bacon, 1961.

Graham, Alberta. *Great Bands of America*. New York: Nelson, 1951.

Guzman, Jessie Parkhurst, ed. *The Negro Yearbook*. New York: Wise, 1952.

Handy, D. Antoinette. *Black Conductors*. Metuchen, N.J.: Scarecrow Press, 1995.

Handy, William Christopher. *Father of the Blues: An Autobiography*. New York: Macmillan, 1941.

Hart, Philip. *Orpheus in the New World* (The Symphony Orchestra as an American Cultural Institution). New York: Norton, 1973.

Howard, John Tasker. *Our American Music*. 3d ed. New York: Crowell, 1946.

Hughes, Langston, and Meltzer, Milton. *Black Magic: A Pictorial History of Black Entertainers in America*. New York: Bonanza, 1967.

Jasen, David A., and Tichenor, Trebor Jay. *Rags and Ragtime*. New York: Seabury, 1978.

Johnson, James Weldon. *Black Manhattan*. 3d printing. New York: Knopf, 1940.

Jones, Laurence C. *The Bottom Rail*. New York: Revell, 1935.

————. *Piney Woods and Its Story*. New York: Revell, 1922.

————. *The Spirit of Piney Woods*. New York: Revell, 1931.

Keepnews, Orrin, and Grauer, Bill, Jr. *A Pictorial History of Jazz: People and Places from New Orleans to Modern Jazz*. New ed. New York: Crown, 1966.

Kinkle, Roger D. *The Complete Encyclopedia of Popular Music and Jazz, 1900–1950*. New Rochelle, N.Y.: Arlington House, 1974.

Kmen, Henry A. *Music in New Orleans: The Formative Years, 1791–1841.* Baton Rouge: Louisiana State University Press, 1966.

Locke, Alain. *The Negro and His Music.* Washington D.C.: The Associated Publishers, 1936. (Reprint, New York: Arno Press and the New York Times, 1969.)

McCarthy, Albert J., et al. *Jazz on Record: A Critical Guide to the First 50 Years, 1917–1967.* London: Hanover, 1968.

Mezzrow, Milton "Mezz," and Wolfe, Bernard. *Really the Blues.* New York: Random House, 1946.

Mitchell, George. *Blow My Blues Away.* Baton Rouge: Louisiana State University Press, 1971.

The Movement for Symphony Orchestras in American Cities (A Report Compiled by the Construction and Civic Development, Chamber of Commerce of the United States of America), mimeo, 1938.

Mueller, John. *The American Symphony Orchestra.* Bloomington: Indiana University Press, 1951.

Murray, Albert. *Stomping the Blues.* New York: McGraw-Hill, 1976.

Mussulman, Joseph A. *Music in the Cultured Generation* (A Social History of Music in America). Evanston, Ill.: Northwestern University Press, 1971.

The Official Theatrical World of Colored Artists (1928 Edition). Vol. 1, No. 1. New York: Theatrical World, April 1928.

Olsson, Bengt. *Memphis Blues and Jug Bands.* London: Studio Vista Limited, 1970.

The Participation of Black, Hispanic, Asian, and Native Americans in American Orchestras (1991–92 Inclusive Survey by the American Symphony Orchestra League). Washington, DC: ASOL, 1992.

Pavlakis, Christopher. *American Music Handbook.* New York: Free Press, 1974.

The Performing Arts: Problems and Prospects (Rockefeller Panel Report). New York: McGraw-Hill, 1965.

The Participation of Blacks in Professional Orchestras: Survey and Study by the American Symphony Orchestra League. Washington, D.C.: ASOL, 1990.

Placksin, Sally. *American Women in Jazz: 1990 to the Present (Their Words, Lives and Music).* New York: Seaview Books, 1982.

Pugh, Douglas. *Job Status of the Negro Professional Musician in the New York Metropolitan Area.* Mimeo. New York: Urban League, 1958.

Rose, Al, and Souchon, Edmond. *New Orleans Jazz: A Family Album.* Baton Rouge: Louisiana State University Press, 1967.

Russell, Charles Edward. *The American Orchestra and Theodore Thomas.* Garden City, N.Y.: Doubleday, Page, 1927.

Russell, Ross. *Bird Lives! The High Life and Hard Times of Charlie (Yardbird) Parker.* New York: Charterhouse, 1973.

————. *Jazz Style in Kansas City and the Southwest*. Berkeley: University of California Press, 1971.

Sablosky, Irving L. *American Music*. Chicago: University of Chicago Press, 1969.

Schuller, Gunther. *Early Jazz: Its Roots and Musical Development*. New York: Oxford University Press, 1968.

Schwartz, H.W. *Bands of America*. Garden City, N.Y.: Doubleday, 1957.

Shapiro, Nat, and Hentoff, Nat, eds. *Hear Me Talkin' to Ya*. New York: Rinehart, 1955.

Simon, George T. *The Big Bands*. Rev. ed. New York: Collier, 1974.

Soblosky, Irving. *American Music*. Chicago: University of Chicago Press, 1969.

Sousa, John Philip. *Marching Along: Recollections of Men, Women and Music*. Boston: Hale, Cushman and Flint, 1941.

Southern, Eileen. *The Music of Black Americans: A History*. New York: Norton, 1971.

Story, Rosalyn M. *And So I Sing*. New York: Warner Books, 1990.

Sverre, O. Braathen. *Circus Bands: Their Rise and Fall*. n.p.

Thornton, Yvonne S. *The Ditchdigger's Daughters*. New York: Carol Publishing Group, 1995.

Trotter, James Monroe. *Music and Some Highly Musical People*. Boston: Lee and Shepard, 1878. (Reprint, New York: Johnson Reprint Corp., 1968.)

Ulanov, Barry. *A History of Jazz in America*. New York: Viking, 1959.

Walton, Ortiz M. *Music: Black, White and Blue*. New York: Morrow, 1972.

Washington Intercollegiate Club of Chicago, Inc. *The Negro in Chicago, 1779 to 1929*. Chicago: Washington Intercollegiate Club of Chicago, 1929.

Wright, Al G., and Newcomb, Stanley. *Bands of the World*. Evanston, Ill.: The Instrumentalist Co., 1970.

Articles and Periodicals

Abdul, Raoul. "The Cumbos: Living Music History." *New York Amsterdam News*, July 31, 1976, p. D2.

————. "Miss Cole As 'Magdalena.'" *New York Amsterdam News*, August 28, 1976, p. D8.

Albin, Scott. "Amina Myers: Environ New York City." *Down Beat*, October 6, 1977, p. 45.

"Alice Coltrane Interviewed by Pauline Rivelli," in *Black Genius*, ed. Pauline Rivelli and Robert Levin and quoted in *John Coltrane*, by Bill Cole, p. 173.

"All Black Orchestra Debuts in Philadelphia." *Norfolk Journal and Guide*, June 2, 1978, p. 12.

Allen, Cleveland G. "Cause of Negro Music Advanced by Year's Activities." *Musical America*, December 30, 1922, p. 26.

Allen, Sanford. "Why Hasn't the Negro Found a Place in the Symphony?" *New York Times*, June 25, 1967, p. D13.

"All-Girl Jazz Trio." *Ebony*, November 1953, pp. 81–84.

"And Now Miss Spivey Leads a Swing Band." *Chicago Defender*, January 27, 1940, p. 20.

"Angel City Symphony Orchestra." *Sepia*, May 1, 1965, pp. 20–23.

"Ann Cooper Plays with Bibb's Band." *Chicago Defender*, February 17, 1940, p. 20.

"Are Girl Musicians Superior?" *Up Beat*, January 1939, pp. 8, 27.

"As Good as Armstrong." *Baltimore Afro-American*, January 21, 1933, p. 12.

Bady, Pauline. "Working World." *Essence*, May 1979, p. 36.

"Begin Rehearsal for New York Girls' Ork." *Chicago Defender*, November 4, 1939, p. 21.

"Bennett College Girls' Orchestra Set for Tour." *Chicago Defender*, March 7, 1942, p. 8.

Bloomfield, Arthur, "The Other Side's View of Symphony Freeze-Out." *San Francisco Examiner*, May 29, 1974, p. 1.

———. "Sour Notes to and from the Symphony." *San Francisco Examiner*, May 24, 1974, p. 35.

Borders, James. "Jazz Singer's Career Started Off Bass." *New Orleans States Item*, April 10, 1976, p. A13.

"Boss Lady," *Our World*, August 1950, pp. 36–37.

"Bronxite Heads Harlem Show." *New York Age*, March 25, 1950, p. 23.

Brown, Richard. "Terri Lyne Carrington." *Down Beat*, March 22, 1979, pp. 32–34.

Burley, Dan. "Backdoor Stuff." *Chicago Defender*, August 3, 1935, p. 5.

Bustard, C. A. "Pagliacci of Colt Day: Minstrel Rabbit Muse." *Richmond Times Dispatch*, April 9, 1978, p. K1.

Calvin, Dolores. "Valaida Returns to Re-Capture 'Great White Way.' " *Chicago Bee*, May 9, 1943.

Campbell, Dick. "Black Musicians in Symphony Orchestras: A Bad Scene." *The Crisis*, January 1975, pp. 12–17.

Campbell, Mary. "A 'Hair' Raising Conductor." *News and Observer*, June 13, 1971, p. 4–V.

"Chicago Suburb Orchestra Moves to Bar Hiring Bias." *New York Times*, August 2, 1963, p. L17.

Chilton, John. "Lil—Louis' Second Lady." *Melody Maker*, September 4, 1971.

Commanday, Robert. "Symphony Buys Time in Players' Dispute." *San Francisco Chronicle*, July 31, 1974, p. 46.

———. "The Symphony Scandal." *High Fidelity/Musical America*, September 1974, pp. MA 18–29.

"Concert Orchestra Rehearses." *Pittsburgh Courier*, January 9, 1932, Section 2, p. 8.

Cooper, Gypsie. "Can Women Swing?" *The Metronome*, September 1936, p. 30.

Cortese, James. "Little Feet Keep On Dancing, Big Voice Keeps On Singing." *The Commercial Appeal*, September 20, 1976.

Croan, Robert. "Previn Returns to City, Energy Crisis Dims Hall." Pittsburgh: *Post Gazette*, February 11, 1978, p. 18.

Cromwell, John W. "Frank Johnson's Military Band." *Southern Workman* 29 (1900): pp. 532–535. (Reprinted in *Black Perspective in Music*, July 1976, pp. 208–212.)

"Crowds in Olympia Park Thrill to 'Hot' Music of Famed Florida Orchestra." *Pittsburgh Courier*, July 7, 1934, Section 2, p. 8.

Curtin-Burlin, Natalie. "Black Singers and Players." *The Musical Quarterly*, October 1919, pp. 499–504.

"Dance Bands That Made History." *International Musician*, October 1950, pp. 20, 22, 35.

Dane, Barbara. "It's Hard to be Mistreated." *Sing Out*, No. 3, 1966, p. 25.

"Darlings of Rhythm Swing in Midwest." *Pittsburgh Courier*, September 15, 1945, p. 13.

"The Daughter of a Famous Father." *The Etude*, May 1939, p. 305.

Davis, Peter G. "Gail Hightower Gives Recital on Bassoon." *New York Times*, December 23, 1979, p. 32.

"Director." *Chicago Defender*, July 9, 1932, p. 7.

Dixon, Lucille. "Is It 'Artistic Judgment' or Is It Discrimination?" *New York Times*, August 1, 1971, pp. 11, 18.

———. "Put Down" [Letter to the Editor]. *New York Times*, May 30, 1971, p. D12.

Dorsey, Bob. "Character-tures." *New York Age*, January 1, 1949, p. 14.

Douglass, Frederick L. "Bobbi Reads the Afro." *Richmond Afro-American*, November 19, 1977, p. 23.

———. "Patrice Rushen . . . Wicked Organist." *Richmond Afro-American*, April 2, 1977, p. 23.

Dulcea, James R. "Good Vibes Lady." *Monthly Digest*, April 1978, pp. 77–78.

Dullea, Georgia. "A Janitor Who Dreamed That His Daughters Would Be Doctors." *New York Times*, June 20, 1977, p. 22.

Duning, Natalie. "Outdoor Concert 'Easy Listening.'" *The Tennessean*, May 31, 1976, p. 20.

"Earl Out to Prove Value of Mixed 'Ork' Personnel." *Pittsburgh Courier,* September 11, 1943, p. 20.

Eaton, Quaintance. "Brooklyn Hears Its Own Orchestra for the First Time." *Musical America,* March 1949, pp. 3–4.

———. "Women Come into Their Own in Our Orchestras." *Musical America,* February 15, 1955, pp. 30, 179.

"Elayne Asks New Committee Hearing." *San Francisco Chronicle,* January 18, 1975, p. 9.

"Ella Fitzgerald to Lead Chick's Band." *Chicago Defender,* July 1, 1939, p. 21.

Ellis, Jack. "The Orchestras." *Chicago Defender,* June 1, 1935, p. 7; July 30, 1935, p. 7; January 25, 1936, p. 8.

Ericson, Raymond. "A 10-Day Festival for Harpsichord." *New York Times,* June 14, 1975, p. L22.

———. "The Fight for the Integrated Orchestra." *New York Times,* October 20, 1974, p. 21.

———. "Two Conductors Plan Offbeat Events." *New York Times,* January 8, 1978, p. D17.

Feather, Leonard. "Beryl Best Since Mary Lou?" *Down Beat,* April 4, 1952, p. 8.

Finch, Anselm J. "Piney Woods Prexy Gives School's Side of Bolt Taken By Sweethearts of Rhythm." *Pittsburgh Courier,* May 3, 1941, p. 21.

Finefrock, James A. "Fired Black Symphony Tympanist to File $1.5 Million Damage Suit." *San Francisco Examiner,* August 13, 1976, p. 6.

Fleishmann, Ernest. "Who Runs Our Orchestras and Who Should?" *High Fidelity/Musical America,* May 1969, p. 62.

Floyd, Samuel A. "Alton Augustus Adams: The First Black Bandmaster in the U.S. Navy." *Black Perspective in Music,* Fall 1977, pp. 173–187.

"Former Pianist for Andy Kirk Is Dead." *Chicago Defender,* August 19, 1939, p. 21.

Fosburgh, Lacey. "2 Musicians' Jobs Stir Coast Conflict." *New York Times,* June 12, 1974, p. 38.

———. "Two Musicians Reinstated for a Year in Coast Dispute." *New York Times,* August 2, 1974, p. 12.

"Four Women Lead Bands in Chicago." *Chicago Defender,* June 12, 1926, Music Section, p. 2.

Freeman, H. Lawrence. "A Review of the Two Leading New York Orchestras—The Lafayette and New Lincoln." *Indianapolis Freeman,* January 20, 1917.

Fridlund, Hans. "The Only Girl in a Big Band." *Expressen,* September 2, 1975.

Fried, Alexander. "Opera House Cheers for Tenure-Less Pair." *San Francisco Chronicle/Examiner,* May 26, 1974, p. 7

Gehrkens, Karl. "Questions and Answers." *The Etude,* March 1943, p. 168.

"A Gifted Harpist." *Indianapolis World,* July 27, 1895, p. 5.

"Girl Band Directors' Troupe Tops." *Chicago Defender,* September 21, 1940, p. 21.

"Girls' Orchestra Scores Successes." *Chicago Defender,* February 14, 1942, p. 9.

Gourse, Leslie. "In the Limelight: Women Who Play Jazz." *American Visions,* April 1989, pp. 32–36.

"Grandma's Ragtime Band." *American Magazine,* May 1950, p. 116.

Grimes, Nikki. "Essence Women." *Essence,* November 1979, pp. 30, 32.

Handy, D. Antoinette. "Conversation with Lucille Dixon." *Black Perspective in Music,* Fall 1975, pp. 299–311.

"Harlem Play Girls Swing in Memphis." *Chicago Defender,* June 24, 1939, p. 20.

"Harlem Play Girls Now on Dixie Tour." *Chicago Defender,* February 3, 1940, p. 21.

"Harlem Rhythm Girls Corps." *Chicago Defender,* January 11, 1941, p. 19.

Harvey, Duston. "What It's Like Being a Black Female Drummer in a Major Orchestra." *Richmond Afro-American,* March 24, 1973, p. 6.

"Heads Coast Band." *Chicago Defender,* September 2, 1939, p. 21.

Henahan, Donal. "About That Timpanist Who Got Drummed Out." *New York Times,* September 7, 1975, p. D25.

———. "An About Face on Black Musicians at the Philharmonic." *New York Times,* June 11, 1972, p. D15.

———. "Only Black in Philharmonic Is Resigning After 15 Years." *New York Times,* August 29, 1977, p. C36.

———. "Philharmonic's Hiring Policy Defended." *New York Times,* July 31, 1969, p. L26.

———. "Philharmonic Plans Workshop, It's First to Train Minorities." *New York Times,* August 27, 1971, p. 17.

"Henry Hart and His Family of Musicians Always in Demand." *Indianapolis News,* April 6, 1901, p. 24.

"Henry Hart, Colored, Is Dead at Age of 75." *Indianapolis News,* December 7, 1915, p. 22.

Hentoff, Nat. "The Strange Case of the Missing Musicians." *The Reporter,* May 28, 1959. (Reprinted by the Urban League of Greater New York.)

Holly, Hal. "Mrs. Cugat Can't See Gals as Tooters; Kills Glamor." *Down Beat,* May 4, 1951, p. 13.

Hopf, Rudolf. "Valaida Snow, Queen of [the] Trumpet." *Jazz Podium,* October 1972, pp. 8–9.

"The Hormel Girls' Caravan." *International Musician,* November 1951, pp. 16, 35.

Hume, Paul. "Urban Philharmonic." *Washington Post,* May 8, 1978, p. B13.

Iadavaia-Cox, Angela. "The Tug Between Conducting and Composing." *Essence,* December 1976, p. 72.

"In Retrospect: The Symphony of the New World." *Black Perspective in Music,* Fall 1975, pp. 312–330.

"Jackie Banks: Working to Bring People and Music Together." *Texas Times,* April 5, 1979.

"Janitor and His Six Daughters Prove 'We Can.' " *Ebony,* September 1977, pp. 33–42.

"Jazz Harpist." *Ebony,* April 1952, pp. 97–99.

"Jean Calloway Going Strong." *Chicago Defender,* June 1, 1935, p. 6.

"Joan Lunceford Is New Band Sensation." *Chicago Defender,* September 13, 1941, p. 20.

Jones, Laurence C. " 'Swinging Rays of Rhythm' is Newest, Hottest Band on Tour." *Chicago Defender,* January 21, 1941, p. 20.

Kaye, Evelyn. "Why Are There So Few Blacks in Symphony Orchestras Today?" *Boston Globe (New England Magazine),* May 15, 1977, pp. 22, 25, 27, 30, 32.

Kimbrough, Mary. "The Great Lakes Experience." *Globe-Democrat (Sunday Magazine),* October 17, 1976, pp. 8–12.

Knight, Celia. "Mary Lou Williams—Embodiment of Jazz History." *Africa Woman,* January/February 1978, p. 24.

Krebs, T. L. "Women as Musicians." *Sewanee Review,* November 1893, pp. 76–87.

Kupferberg, Herbert. "Women of the Baton—The New Music Masters." *Parade,* May 14, 1978, pp. 4–5.

"Lafayette's Strong Bill." *New York Age,* December 3, 1914.

"Lafayette Theatre." *New York Age,* November 26, 1914.

Lee, Cathy. "First Women's Jazz Festival K O's Kaycee." *Sojourner (Jazz Supplement),* May 1978, pp. 11–12.

Lee, Everett. "A Negro Conductor Appeals for a New Kind of Pioneering." *New York Times,* December 26, 1948, p. X7.

London, Jack. "Terry Lyne Carrington: She's Only Just Begun." *Modern Drummer,* October 1977, p. 10.

Lucas-Thompson, Grace. "What Our Women Are Doing." *Indianapolis Freeman,* January 30, 1915, p. 3; February 13, 1915, p. 3.

"Lucille Dixon." *Chicago Defender,* April 23, 1949, p. 25.

McCarthy, Jim. "A Jazz Band Flees." *The Afro-American,* May 3, 1941, p. 13.

McCord, Kimberly. "History of Women in Jazz." *Jazz Educators Journal,* December/January, 1988, pp. 15–19, 65, 79–80.

McGinty, Doris Evans. "Black Women in the Music of Washington, D.C.,

1900–20." In *New Perspectives on Music: Essays in Honor of Eileen Southern,* ed. Josephine Wright with Samuel A. Floyd Jr. Warren, Michigan: Harmonie Park Press, 1992, pp. 409–49.

McGinty, Doris E. "Conversation with Camille Nickerson, the Louisiana Lady." *Black Perspective in Music,* Spring 1979, pp. 81–94.

McLellan, Joseph. "The Making of a Musical Fixture." *Washington Post,* May 7, 1978, pp. L1, 8.

McPartland, Marian. "You've Come a Long Way Baby," in *Esquire's World of Jazz, 1975.* New York: Crowell, 1975.

Mason, Bryant S. "And the Beat Goes On." *Essence,* November 1972, pp. 50, 51, 81, 86.

"Member of All-Women's Band Barred from Hotel." *Chicago Defender,* August 5, 1939, p. 3.

Merritt, Robert. "Harpist Says Her Profession Worth Trouble." *Richmond Times Dispatch,* January 23, 1978, p. B6.

"Miss Myrtle Hart's Success." *Indianapolis World,* December 5, 1896, p. 8.

"Mrs. Nickerson's Death." *Daily Picayune,* December 18, 1908, p. 13.

"Music, A Beginner. His Capabilities." *Negro Music Journal,* Vol. 1, No. 4, December 1902, p. 56.

"Music Power." *Sepia,* April 1968, pp. 38–41.

"Musical Spillers." *Chicago Defender,* July 18, 1925, Part I, p. 7.

Nadel, Norman. Re: Vivian LaVelle Weaver [Brochure]. *Columbus Citizen,* January 31, 1948.

"The Negro's Place in Music." *Opera Magazine,* April 1815, pp. 31–32. (Reprint from *New York Evening Post.*)

"News from Albany, N.Y." *New York Age,* May 3, 1906.

Newton, George. "Hits and Bits." *Chicago Defender,* December 21, 1935, p. 9.

"New York Stage." *Chicago Defender,* September 5, 1942, p. 21.

"Nina Mae's Band Clicks in Dixieland." *Chicago Defender,* November 13, 1940, p. 21.

"Nina Mae's Ork Goes to Gale's Unit." *Chicago Defender,* February 10, 1940, p. 20.

Nurridin, Aquil. "Shanta Nurullah: The Sister with the Sitar." *Bilalian News,* September 2, 1977, p. 29.

Nurullah, Shanta. "The Family Struggles of Sisters Makin' Music." *Black Books Bulletin,* Vol. 6, No. 2, 1978, pp. 20–27.

O'Neal, Jim. "Blues for the Tourists at Blues Alley in Memphis." *Living Blues,* November–December, 1978, pp. 28–29.

O'Neill, Catherine. "Swinger with a Mission." *Books and Arts,* December 7, 1979, pp. 30–31.

"On Tour with Her Own Band." *Chicago Defender,* November 23, 1940, p. 20.

"On Vacation." *Chicago Defender*, July 1, 1939, p. 21.

"Oooowee, Man, That Little Girl Can Play!" *Ebony*, April 1977, pp. 131–134.

"Orchestral Women." *Scientific America*, November 23, 1895, p. 327.

"Orchestra 'Symbol' Resigns." *Richmond Times Dispatch*, August 30, 1977, p. B7.

"Orchestras." *Chicago Defender*, January 3, 1931, p. 5.

Osgood, Marion G. "America's First Ladies Orchestra" [Letter to the Editor]. *The Etude*, October 1940, p. 713.

"Outdoor Concerts." *Boston Guardian*, August 19, 1939, p. 3.

Paige, Raymond. "Why Not Women in Orchestras?" *The Etude*, January 1952, pp. 14–15.

Palmer, Robert. "Women Who Make Jazz." *New York Times*, January 21, 1977, p. C3.

Parmeter, Ross. "God Bless the Ladies, For They Helped Build Orchestras." *New York Times*, August 16, 1959, Section 2, p. 7.

Pease, Sharon A. "Health Better, Cleo Brown Set for Comeback." *Down Beat*, July 1, 1945, p. 12.

Per-Lee, Myra. "Reaching Out to Minority Musicians." *Symphony News*, April 1979, pp. 16–17.

Peyser, Joan. "The Negro in Search of an Orchestra." *New York Times*, November 26, 1967, p. D17.

"P. G. Lowery and His Band Entertained." *Chicago Defender*, June 25, 1921, p. 7

"Phil Spitalny's Orchestra." *International Musician*, April 1951, p. 15.

"Piney Woods to Present School Bands." *Pittsburgh Courier*, April 19, 1941, p. 23.

Pitts, Lucia Mae. "Gertrude Martin, Violinist: An Opinion." *Negro Woman's World*, March 1935, p. 5.

Pixa, Bea. "Passing On Her Love of Music." *San Francisco Examiner and Chronicle*, March 19, 1978, Scene section pp. 1–2.

"Poro College Ladies' Orchestra." *Norfolk Journal and Guide*, May 2, 1925, p. 1.

"Poro Graduates Largest Class in Its History." *Norfolk Journal and Guide*, June 18, 1927, p. 5.

" 'Poro In Pictures' Tells of Remarkable Growth of Big Business Started by Woman." *Norfolk Journal and Guide*, December 18, 1926, p. 9.

Powell, William C. "Letter to the Editor." *New York Times*, January 15, 1978, p. D20.

Purdy, James H., Jr. "Beale Street Band to Play for Postmen." *Chicago Defender*, September 2, 1939, p. 6.

"Race Amateurs Capture Places on Bowes' Hour." *Chicago Defender*, January 11, 1936, p. 9.

Ramsey, Frederic, Jr. "The Singing Horns." *Saturday Review*, June 25, 1955, pp. 31, 32, 41–44.

Reemes, Jackie. "Death of Valaida Snow Leaves Void in Theater." *New York Amsterdam News*, June 9, 1956, p. 34.

Reinthaler, Joan. "Does a Trombone Sound Different if There's a Woman Playing?" *Washington Post*, March 13, 1977, pp. G1, 8.

"Remembering Blanche Calloway." *Richmond Afro-American*, December 30, 1978, p. 19.

Rice, Willa Mae. "Pat Jennings, Baltimore Symphony Guest, Draws Enthusiastic Response." *Pittsburgh Courier*, July 3, 1976, p. 10.

"Richmond Negro Names to Board of Symphony." *New York Times*, June 25, 1971, p. C18.

Rockwell, John. "The Apollo Theatre Reopens with Ralph Mac Donald." *New York Times*, May 7, 1978, p. 70.

"Rose Johnson Tops Female Band MC's." *Chicago Defender*, August 17, 1940, p. 21.

Rowe, Billy. "All Girl Orchestra Is Getting Prepared to Crash the Big Time." *Pittsburgh Courier*, May 31, 1941, p. 20.

Roy, Rob. "Dolly Hutchinson's Band, Chicago's Latest Acclaim." *Chicago Defender*, July 30, 1932, p. 5.

Russcol, Herbert. "Can the Negro Overcome the Classical Music Establishment." *High Fidelity Magazine*, August 1968, pp. 42–46.

Saal, Hubert. "The Spirit of Mary Lou." *Newsweek*, December 20, 1971, p. 67.

Scott, Lillian. "A Woman Violinist Breaks Down Two Barriers." *Chicago Defender*, April 23, 1949, p. 25.

"17-Girl Band Which Quit School at Piney Woods, Rehearses for Big Times." *Pittsburgh Courier*, April 19, 1941, p. 21.

"She'll Head Band." *Chicago Defender*, August 5, 1939, p. 20.

Shonberg, Harold. "The Symphony Has Refused to Die." *New York Times*, May 7, 1978, pp. D19, 27.

Smith, Clay. "The Girl in Bands." *Jacob's Band Monthly*, February, 1930, pp. 9, 38.

Snelson, Floyd G. "Broadway Bound." *Pittsburgh Courier*, January 16, 1932, Section 2, p. 7.

"Soldiers Hear All-Girl's Band." *Chicago Defender*, January 16, 1943, p. 19.

Southern, Eileen. "Black Music in the United States." *National Scene Magazine Supplement*, November–December 1976, p. 5.

———. "Frank Johnson and His Promenade Concerts." *Black Perspective in Music*, Spring 1977, pp. 3–29.

Spitalny, Phil. "The Hour of Charm." *The Etude*, October 1938, pp. 639–640.

"The Stage." *The Freeman*, November 14, 1896.

Stoddard, Hope. "Ladies of the Symphony." *International Musician*, May 1953, pp. 24–25, 35.

Stokes, W. Royal. "Terri Carrington." *Washington Post*, April 25, 1979, p. D11.

Stokowski, Leopold. "Leopold Stokowski Speaks." *Music and Artists*, January 1972, p. 12.

"Sweethearts of Rhythm." *Chicago Defender*, June 22, 1940, p. 20.

"Symphony Foundation Director." *Norfolk Journal and Guide*, September 3, 1966, p. 14.

Taubman, Howard. "An Even Break." *New York Times*, April 22, 1956, p. X9.

————. "Making Friends." *New York Times*, January 22, 1956, p. X9.

"They Make Music in Baltimore." *Our World*, April 1954, pp. 48–53.

Thompson, Howard. "Going Out Guide." *New York Times*, March 23, 1978, p. C17.

Tillis, Wilma. "With Her Help, Students Hit High Note." *Currents*, December 12–13, 1978.

Tompkins, Grace W. "Chicago Retains Place as Center of Nation's Musical Activities." *Chicago Defender*, January 11, 1941, p. 12.

"To Organize Swing Band." *Chicago Defender*, May 24, 1941, p. 9.

"Trainer of Musicians." *Chicago Defender*, February 3, 1930, p. 9.

"A Treat to Beat Your Feet on Connecticut—Av." *Washington Daily News*, January 11, 1947, p. 12.

Truckenbrod, Phillip. "The Music Woman: Symphony Picks First Black Manager." *Sunday Star-Ledger*, February 27, 1972, Section 1, p. 27.

Tyler, Millicent. "35 Richmond Girls Play the Harp." *Richmond Afro-American*, June 29–July 3, 1976, p. 9.

"Valaida Snow, Ex-Blackbirds Star, POW Dies." *New York Amsterdam News*, June 9, 1956, p. 1.

"Votes vs. Notes." *Newsweek*, June 17, 1974, p. 109.

Walton, Lester. "Theatrical Comment." *New York Age*, January 14, 1915, May 20, 1915.

"The Week's Best." *Jet*, January 21, 1971, p. 33.

Wehle, Eleanor. "Music Still Sounds Sour When It Comes to Color." *Standard-Star*, July 10, 1970, p. II-1.

Weinreich, Regina. "Play It Momma." *Village Voice*, July 3, 1978, pp. 64–65.

West, Hollie I. "Hazel Scott Reflects." *Washington Post*, July 4, 1970, p. C2.

"What Happened to Melba Liston?" *Ebony*, June 1977, p. 122.

White, Clarence Cameron. "The Musical Genius of the American Negro." *The Etude*, May 1924, pp. 305–306.

White, Lucien H. "Lafayette Theatre." *New York Age,* November 2, 1916.

Wilayto, Phil. "Female Jazz Pianist Draws Hampton Raves." *Norfolk Journal and Guide,* July 28, 1978, p. 15.

"Wild but Polished." *Time,* November 3, 1958, p. 78.

Willse, Jim. "Up from Louisiana." *Ann Arbor News,* December 5, 1976, p. 18.

Wilson, John S. "Cabaret: Rose Murphy." *New York Times,* July 14, 1979, p. 12.

———. "Jazz: Wide Range of Styles Is Shown." *New York Times,* July 5, 1971, p. 23.

———. "Jazzwomen Prove Strong on Rhythm." *New York Times,* November 9, 1973, p. 30.

———. "Joyce Brown: Conductor of the Broadway Hit 'Purlie.' " *International Musician,* December 1970, p. 8.

———. "Mary Lou Williams." *International Musician,* January 1973, p. 8.

———. "Rose Murphy's Back with That Old Chee-Chee." *New York Times,* August 3, 1979, p. C8.

———. "Six Groups Start Off the Salute to Women in Jazz." *New York Times,* June 28, 1978, p. C19.

———. "Women in Jazz, Past and Present." *New York Times,* June 11, 1978, pp. 25, 38.

"Women in American Symphony Orchestras." *Symphony News,* April 1976, pp. 13–14.

"Women in the Orchestra." *Literary Digest,* February 26, 1916, pp. 504–505.

"Women On Their Own." *Time,* December 16, 1935, pp. 52–53.

"Women's Lib in New York." *Black Perspective in Music,* Spring 1974, p. 197.

Wong, Willie Lee. "Nazis Gone, Germans Rave Over 'Sweethearts of Rhythm' Band." *Chicago Defender,* September 8, 1945, p. 14.

"World Symphony Orchestra Displays Artistic Harmony Among Nations." *International Musician,* November 1971, p. 3.

Worsham, Doris. "Ladies in the Band." *Oakland Tribune,* September 28, 1975.

Wortham, Jacob. "Blacks in the World of Orchestras." *Black Enterprise,* December 1976, pp. 31–32, 86–87.

Yates, Ted. "Nina Mae in Debut." *Chicago Defender,* December 23, 1939, p. 21.

Young, A. S. "Doc." "Lionel Hampton's Wife Gladys Was Buried in L.A." *Chicago Defender,* May 15–21, 1971, p. 16.

Zacharias, John. "Ft. Worth Symphony Gets Down with Disco." *Texas Nickelodeon,* June 1979.

Zeppernick, Werner. "Nashville Symphony Opens Summer Park Concerts." *Nashville Banner,* May 31, 1976, p. 28.

Miscellaneous

Interviews

Russell, William./Lottie and Willie Hightower, June 3, 1958, Chicago
Russell, William./Lillian Hardin Armstrong, July 1, 1959, Chicago
Russell, William./Dolly Adams, April 18, 1962, New Orleans

Liner Notes

Anderson, Ione. "Traditional New Orleans Jazz," Dulai 800
Charters, Sam. "The Great Jug Bands: 1927–1933," Origin Jazz Library OJL4
Clark, A. Grayson. "Sweet Emma the Bell Gal and Her New Orleans Jazz Band at Heritage Hall," Nobility LP711
Dance, Stanley. "On a Clear Day," Impulse A-9109
Driggs, Frank. "Women in Jazz: Pianist," Stash ST-112
Napoleon, Art. "Women in Jazz: All-Women Groups," Stash ST-111
"New Orleans' Billie and De De and Their Preservation Hall Jazz Band," Preservation Hall VPH/VPS-3
Rolontz, Bob. "The Fantastic Jazz Harp of Dorothy Ashby." Atlantic 1447
Russell, William. "New Orleans' Sweet Emma and Her Preservation Hall Jazz Band," Preservation Hall VPH/VPS-2
Segal, Joe. "Charlie Parker Memorial Concert," Cadet 2CA 60002
Williams, Mary Lou. "Jazz Women: A Feminist Retrospective," Stash ST-109
Wilson, Gerald. "Patrice Rushen—Prelusion," Prestige 10089
Wood, Harlan. "Albert 'Papa' French at Tradition Hall," Second Line 0112

Obsequies

Francisco, Maurine Elise Moore. Avery Chapel A. M. E. Church, Oklahoma City, March 25, 1978
Ruffin, Penelope Johnson. Abyssinia Baptist Church, New York City, March 9, 1979
Williams, Pauline Braddy. Taylor Hill M. B. Church, Braxton, Mississippi, February 3, 1996

Papers

Isabele Taliaferro Spiller—Moorland-Spingarn Research Center, Howard University

Public Document

Public Law 87-817, October 15, 1962

Announcement

Symphony of the New World Formation Announcement

Index

About the Author

D. Antoinette Handy (B. Mus., New England Conservatory of Music; M. Mus., Northwestern University; Diploma, Paris National Conservatory) is a native of New Orleans, Louisiana. A flutist, Ms. Handy spent more than twenty years as a symphony musician, both in the United States and abroad. She served as organizer, manager, and flutist with the chamber group Trio Pro Viva (specializing in the music of black composers) for three decades. Her teaching tenures include Florida A & M, Tuskegee, Jackson State, Southern (New Orleans), and Virginia State Universities. In 1971, Ms. Handy was a Ford Foundation Humanities Fellow at North Carolina and Duke Universities. She joined the staff of the National Endowment for the Arts in 1985 as Assistant Director of the Music Program and assumed the duties of Director in 1990. Ms. Handy retired in July 1993. Also in 1993, she received an honorary Doctor of Music degree from the Cleveland Institute of Music and delivered the commencement address. Handy received the Honorary Doctor of Humane Letters from Whittier College in 1977. She is a frequent lecturer, has published articles and book reviews in numerous professional journals, and has published *The International Sweethearts of Rhythm*, second edition (1998), and *Black Conductors* (1995), both published by Scarecrow Press.